Mercer Commentary on the Bible

Volume 1
Pentateuch/Torah

Mercer University Press

Mercer Dictionary of the Bible
July 1990; 5th and corrected printing August 1997

Mercer Dictionary of the Bible Course Syllabi
July 1990

Mercer Commentary on the Bible
November 1994

Cover illustration: *Coburg Pentateuch* (Coburg, 1395) by Simhah ben Samuel Halevi. A rabbi reading from the Torah. Reproduced by permission of the British Library (British Library Reproductions), London.

Mercer Commentary on the Bible

Volume 1
Pentateuch/Torah

GENERAL EDITORS
Watson E. Mills, Richard F. Wilson

ASSOCIATE EDITORS
Roger A. Bullard, Walter Harrelson, Edgar V. McKnight

MERCER UNIVERSITY PRESS EDITOR
Edmon L. Rowell, Jr.

WITH MEMBERS OF THE
National Association of Baptist Professors of Religion

MERCER UNIVERSITY PRESS
March 1998

ISBN 0-86554-506-5   MUP/P133

Mercer Commentary on the Bible: Pentateuch/Torah
Volume 1 of an 8-volume perfect-bound reissue of
the *Mercer Commentary on the Bible* (©1995).
Copyright ©1998
Mercer University Press, Macon GA 31210-3960
All rights reserved; but see cover-illustration acknowledgment on p. ii, above
Printed in the United States of America
First printing, March 1998

The paper used in this publication meets the minimum requirements
of the American National Standard for Information Sciences—
Permanence of Paper for Printed Library Materials, ANSI Z39.48-1984.

Library of Congress Cataloging-in-Publication Data

Mercer commentary on the Bible.
Volume 1. Pentateuch/Torah /
general editors, Watson E. Mills and Richard F. Wilson;
associate editors, Walter Harrelson . . . [et al.].
lviii+228pp. 6x9" (15x23cm.).
1. Bible—commentaries. I. Mills, Watson Early. II. Mercer University Press.
III. National Association of Baptist Professors of Religion.

CIP data available from the Library of Congress.

Contents

Preface vii

Introduction (articles from the *Mercer Dictionary of the Bible*)

    Cosmology .... *(Douglas A. Knight)* ix
    Covenant .... *(John H. Hayes)* xiii
    Covenant with Noah .... *(Jack Weir)* xxii
    Creation .... *(V. Steven Parrish)* xxiii
    Exodus .... *(Russell I. Gregory)* xxvii
    Law in the O.T. ...... *(Bruce T. Dahlberg)* xxxiii
    Moses .... *(Russell I. Gregory)* xlii
    Religion of Israel ... *(Frank E. Eakin, Jr.)* 1
    Ten Commandments ... *(Walter Harrelson)* lii
    Torah .... *(Bruch T. Dahlberg)* lvii

Commentaries (from the *Mercer Commentary on the Bible*)

    Genesis .... *(Bruce T. Dahlberg)* 1-66
    Exodus .... *(John I Durham)* 67-113
    Leviticus .... *(James W. Watts)* 115-44
    Numbers .... *(Jack G. Partain)* 145-84
    Deuteronomy .... *(John H. Tullock)* 185-226

Preface

This volume comprises commentaries on the books of the Pentateuch/Torah (Old Textament/Hebrew Bible: Genesis–Deuteronomy) from the *Mercer Commentary on the Bible* (MCB) with certain appropriate articles from the *Mercer Dictionary of the Bible* (MDB). This portion is for use in the classroom and for any other setting where study focuses on the Pentateuch/Torah and where a convenient introduction text is desired. This is number 1 in this series of MCB/MDB portions or volumes.

1. **Pentateuch/Torah (Genesis–Deuteronomy)**   Isbn 0-86554-506-5 P133
2. History of Israel (Joshua–Esther)   Isbn 0-86554-507-3 P134
3. (Wisdom) Writings (Job–Song of Songs)   Isbn 0-86554-508-1 P135
4. Prophets (Isaiah–Malachi)   Isbn 0-86554-509-X P136
5. Deuterocanonicals/Apocrypha   Isbn 0-86554-510-3 P137
6. Gospels (Matthew–John)   Isbn 0-86554-511-1 P138
7. Acts and Pauline Writings (Acts–Philemon)   Isbn 0-86554-512-X P139
8. Epistles and Revelation (Hebrews–Revelation) Isbn 0-86554-513-8 P140

That these divisions—and their titles—are arbitrary is obvious. These divisions originate in the classroom as convenient and provisionally appropriate blocks of text for focused study during a semester- or quarter-long course of study. Other divisions are possible, perhaps even desirable (combining Acts with the Gospels, for example, rather than with Paul), but the present divisions seem appropriate for most users.

Regarding the use of this and other MCB/MDB portions, please note the following.

A bracketed, flush-right entry at the head of each MDB article and MCB commentary indicates the page number(s) in the original: for example, "Cosmology [MDB 175-76]" and "Exodus [MCB 127-55]." The text of both MDB and MCB is essentially that of the original, for the most part differing only in format, that is, it is redesigned to fit a 6x9-inch page (MDB and MCB are 7x10 inches). (Some minor corrections—of typographical and other errors—have been made.)

References to other MDB articles are indicated by small caps: for example, PLAGUES at the head of the fifth paragraph and RED SEA and KADESH-BARNEA in the sixth paragraph of the MDB article on the "Exodus" refer to the articles on "Plagues," "Red Sea/Reed Sea," and "Kadesh-Barnea" in MDB; CANAAN in the first paragraph of the MCB commentary on Genesis refers to the MDB article on "Canaan." In addition, the *See also* sections at the end of the MDB articles indicate other articles that are appropriate for further study.

(Notice, however, that small caps are used also for B.C.E. and C.E., for certain texts and versions [LXX, KJV, NRSV], for the tetragrammaton YHWH, and for LORD when citing certain English translations.)

In addition to the *Mercer Dictionary of the Bible* and the *Mercer Commentary on the Bible*, there is available a booklet of sample course syllabi that includes actual outlines of courses in which a Bible version and MDB are the required texts. (Regarding this booklet, please contact the Mercer University Press marketing department.)

For abbreviations, see the lists in either MDB or MCB. Regarding the editors and contributors, please see both MDB and MCB. The *Course Syllabi* handbook has a complete listing of MDB articles alphabetically arranged (pp. 73-80); MDB includes a complete listing of articles arranged by contributor (pp. 989-93).

We intend that these texts be available, appropriate, and helpful for Bible students both in and out of the classroom and indeed for anyone seeking guidance in uncovering the abundant wealth of the Scriptures. Your critical response to these and other texts from Mercer University Press is most welcome and encouraged.

March 1998
Macon, Georgia USA

Edmon L. Rowell, Jr.
Mercer University Press

Introduction

Torah and Environs

Cosmology [MDB 175-76]

•**Cosmology.** A comprehensive view of all reality, attending both to the nature of the whole and also to the place of all parts within the whole. The origin, order, meaning, and destiny of all that exists are key issues in a cosmological system, as is also the question of what this "reality" in fact embraces.

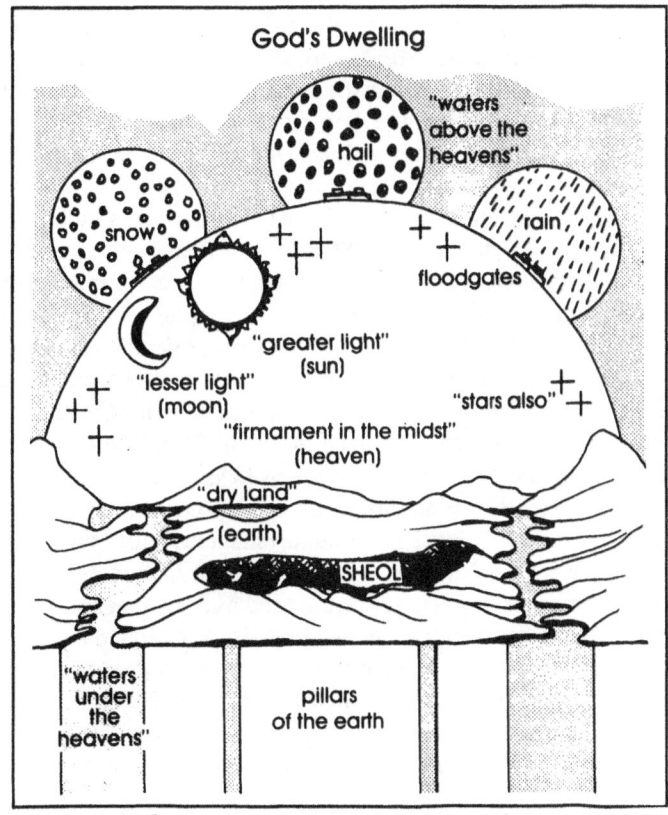

Ancient Hebrew conception of cosmos (cf. Gen 1:1-19)
[MDB 175]

The Bible does not develop a cosmology in the sense of a speculative philosophy, as in ancient Greece, or a scientific system, as in the modern world. Nonetheless, all-encompassing perspectives are present in both the Hebrew Bible and the NT, and from these and from ways in which the various components of reality are described it is possible to extrapolate a cosmology, or rather cosmologies, from the biblical literature.

Hebrew has no single word equivalent to cosmos, universe, or reality. Instead, various phrases are employed to express all-inclusiveness: "the heavens and the earth" (Gen 1:1; 2:4; more than seventy-five times in the Psalms), "the heavens and earth and sea" (Exod 20:11; Pss 69:34; 146:6—often with an addition such as "and all that is within them"), or "heaven above, earth beneath, and the waters under the earth" (Deut 5:8). The common word "all" or "everything" (*kōl*, sometimes with the definite article, "the entirety") can also occur in an attempt to embrace the whole of existence (Isa 44:24; Jer 10:16; Ps 103:19; Eccl 3:1; Sir 36:1).

The ancient Israelites' view of the physical world can be reconstructed from such texts as Gen 1 and 7–8; Pss 33, 74, 104, 148; Job 38–41; and elsewhere. The universe, for them, is largely a closed entity consisting of three stories or levels. The earth is a flat disk surrounded by mountains or sea. Above is the firmament, a solid dome covering the entire world and resting on the mountains at the edges of the earth. Down in the heart of the earth is Sheol, the abode of the dead. The waters above and the waters below envelop the universe. The firmament overhead is transparent, allowing the blue color of the celestial water to be visible, and it has "windows" or sluices to let down water in the form of rain. The heavens, including the sun, moon, and stars, are under this vast canopy. The earth is supported from below by pillars sunk into the watery abyss. A variation of this conception is evident in Job 26:7, according to which the earth is hung over the void (see also Job 38:12-13). God, humans, and the dead each have their respective abode in the cosmos (Ps 115:16-17). However, God, who cannot be contained by the heavens (1 Kgs 8:27), is present on the earth and even in Sheol (Ps 139:8) as well.

This conception of the physical cosmos seems to have been widely held among the Israelites of the Hebrew Bible, although there were differences on certain specific details. Other ancient Near Eastern cultures shared similar perspectives also, as is evident from the creation myth of old Babylonia, the *Enuma Elish*, dating back to the first part of the second millennium B.C.E., and its Sumerian antecedent of one thousand years earlier. Cosmological parallels are also to be found in Ugaritic texts shortly before the advent of Israel's history. The Hebrew words used for the earth's surface (*tēbēl*), the waters of the abyss (*tĕhôm*), and the underworld (*šĕ'ôl*) usually occur in the Hebrew Bible without a definite article—almost as if they were proper names—and this is thought by many to indicate a mythic background of the Israelite conceptions.

Of particular importance in understanding the biblical cosmology is the language used to express it, especially in poetic contexts. Without employing philosophical or scientific categories, the ancient Hebrews drew on images and concepts from their everyday life to articulate the nature and interrelationships among all that existed.

The awesome otherness of the world is often expressed through images of enormous features in nature: the mountains, a prominent place of God's revelation (Exod 19), can quake and smoke; the sea is fathomless and threatening; the sun, moon, and stars "rule over" the day and night (Gen 1:14-18) and seem to have some influence over humans (Judg 5:20; Ps 121:6; Job 38:33). Remarkable characteristics of animal life—bird migration, the undulating movement of a snake, the work of ants, the arrogant stride of lion and goat (e.g., Prov 30:18-19, 24-31; Jer 8:7)—underscore the mystery of all creation.

A series of human images also occurs cosmologically. The navel of the earth is Jerusalem (Ezek 38:12; referred to as the "center" of the earth in Ezek 5:5 and Ps 74:12). Breath is related to the wind and God's spirit. The underworld has a mouth and a ravenous appetite (Isa 5:14). Emotions are evident in nature: the heavens and mountains sing, the depths of the earth shout, nature groans in pain. Birth and death occur in consonance with the world (Ps 139:15; Gen 1:12, 20, 24; Job 1:21; 5:26; 14:7-19; Eccl 3:19-21). Domestic images—the father as provider, protector, and redeemer, and the mother as caretaker, seamstress, and source of compassion—are used especially of God's relation to life in this world. Familiar architectural features are projected to the structure of the cosmos: the firmament as a tent, windows in the sky, doors holding back the seas, beams supporting the upper level, the foundation and cornerstone of the earth, gates to the underworld, storehouses for the snow, hail, and wind.

From the political sphere come images of justice and order suggestive of the cooperative social structure of tribal life. Hierarchical notions of dominion and power in the cosmos parallel the people's experiences with the monarchy, just as also a vision of destructive cosmic oppositions (especially in apocalyptic thought) draws on military images. The religious categories of clean and unclean indicate a sense that there are anomalies and dangers in the world—among certain animal species, in human sexuality, and in sickness and death (Lev 11–15; Deut 14:3-21).

The universe, described with such images stemming from the familiar spheres of life in Israel, is evaluated in three main ways within the Hebrew Bible. Most broadly it is held to be ordered, rational, and reliable, functioning well according to the divinely ordained principles of justice and harmony, and deleterious consequences fall to those who subvert this order. Also widespread, especially in the wisdom literature, is the view that the cosmos is precarious and unpredictable, holding no guarantees that moral and faithful living will always bring blessings and prosperity. The third cosmological evaluation, minimally evident in the Hebrew Bible but much more prominent in early Jewish and Christian apocalyptic movements, considers the world to be divided within itself between the forces of good and the forces of evil, an antagonism which can only be overcome through radical intervention by God.

New Testament cosmology, drawing on these traditions as well as ancient Greek thought, views the world both as alienated from God yet also as the object of God's salvific plan. All-embracing terms are *kosmos* ("cosmos," the totality of all that exists) and *aiōn* ("aeon," temporally designating this world in contrast to the world to come).

Viewed negatively, the world is characterized fundamentally by the sinfulness of humanity, is severely judged by Jesus (John 16:8-11), is transient and should not be loved (1 John 2:15-17), and is incapable itself of attaining knowledge of God (1 Cor 1:20-25). Since it will soon pass away, Christians must "put off the old nature" (Eph 4:22) and "not be conformed to this world" (Rom 12:2).

More of a positive or hopeful conception is evident in the offer of God's salvation to the world, which was indeed divinely created (Acts 17:24) and continues to be sustained through God's providence (Matt 6:25-34). Paul gives a picture of "the whole creation groaning in travail together until now," awaiting the revelation of God (Rom 8:19-23). Jesus inaugurates the "kingdom of God" (or "of heaven," Matt 4:17 and elsewhere) on earth, bringing to fruition God's rule over all that exists. The world, the new creation, is thus reconciled to God through Christ (2 Cor 5:17-19), and his followers are charged with a mission to carry this message throughout the earth (Matt 28:18-20; Acts 1:8).

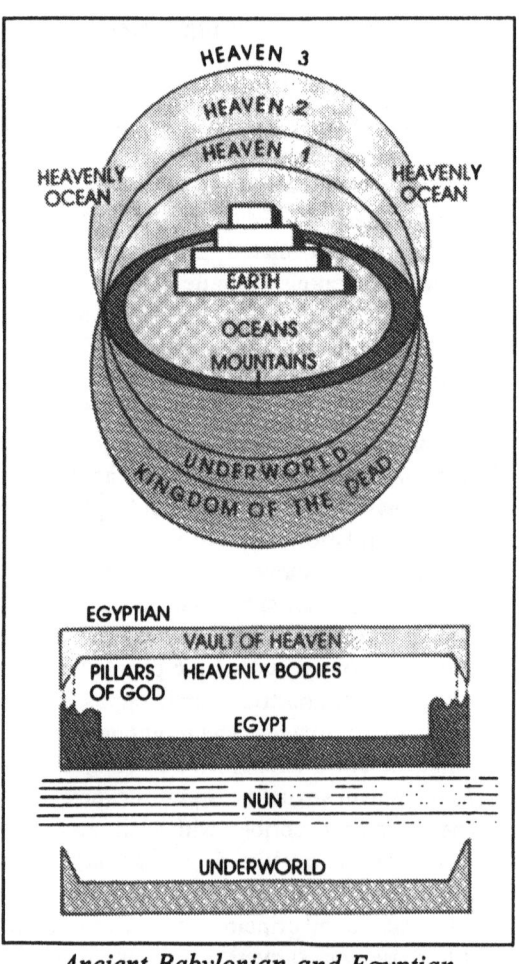

Ancient Babylonian and Egyptian conceptions of the cosmos [MDB 177]

Biblical cosmology exists in neither the Hebrew Bible nor the NT as a doctrine or teaching in itself. To find it one must look to the many ways in which tangible and intangible realities are described. Theologically, these views of the universe are linked to beliefs in God as creator, lord, judge, and redeemer, and humans are consequently expected to act in moral harmony with God's intention for the world.

See also FIRMAMENT; HEAVEN; HELL; SHEOL; SKY.

Bibliography. H. D. Betz, "Cosmogony and Ethics in the Sermon on the Mount," in *Cosmogony and Ethical Order*; H. and H. A. Frankfort, J. A. Wilson, T. Jacobsen, and W. A. Irwin, *The Intellectual Adventure of Ancient Man*; W. Harrelson, "The Significance of Cosmology in the Ancient Near East," *Translating and Understanding the Old Testament*, ed. H. T. Frank and W. L. Reed; D. A. Knight, "Cosmogony and Order in the Hebrew Tradition," *Cosmogony and Ethical Order: New Studies in Comparative Ethics*, ed. R. W. Lovin and F. E. Reynolds.
—DOUGLAS A. KNIGHT

Covenant [MDB 177-81]

•**Covenant.** The Hebrew term בְּרִית (*bĕrît*), often, and traditionally the only term, translated as "covenant" in the OT, has a wide semantic usage signifying in different contexts what could be and sometimes is rendered in English as "promise, pledge, obligation, agreement, contract, pact, or treaty." Although the OT speaks of many different covenants, the plural form of *bĕrît* never occurs.

In spite of various proposals and their defenses, the etymology of the word remains uncertain. The most widely advocated suggestions are: (1) from the verb *brh* "to eat, feed"; (2) from the verb *brh* "to see, decide"; (3) from a preposition *birit*, unattested in Hebrew but found in Akkadian, meaning "between"; and (4) from a noun parallel to the Akkadian and Talmudic *biritu/byrnt* "clasp, fetter."

The most likely OT synonyms for *bĕrît* are *'amānâ* (from *'mn* "to be firm, steadfast") in Neh 10:1; 11:23 *ḥōzeh/ḥāzût* (from *ḥzh* "to see"?) in Isa 28:15, 18; *šĕbû'â/'ālâ* ("oath") in some texts (see Gen 26:3); and *'ēd/'ēdût/'ēdôt* (from *'dh* "to witness"?) in Gen 31:44-52; Josh 24:27; Isa 32:14 (reading *bĕ'ad* as *kĕ'ēd*), and in expressions like the Ark of the *'ēdût*. The latter would parallel the terms *adū/adê* in Akkadian and *'dn/'dy* in Aramaic. Such synonyms occur very infrequently in the OT. Terms such as "peace" (*šālôm*), "good, friendship" (*ṭôb*), "law" (*tôrâ*), and "oath" (*'ālâ*), which may occur in covenantal contexts, are not to be viewed as interchangeable synonyms for *bĕrît* nor does their appearance in a text always presuppose that reference to a covenant stands as background to the text. Some terms, such as "peace," "friendship," and "brotherhood," were used however to refer to the conditions produced by covenant relationships.

In the OT, the term "covenant" (*bĕrît*) is employed with reference to three types of obligatory conditions. (1) In some cases, such as the covenant between God and NOAH and the Israelite patriarchs, the obligation is self-imposed by the deity. (2) In other contexts, the obligation is imposed by the divine or the superior party on an inferior or another party (cf. Jer 34 and Hos 2:18-23). (3) Elsewhere, as in the SINAI covenant, both parties are committed to reciprocal obligations (see Exod 34:10, 27).

The term "covenant" (*bĕrît*) could thus be used to refer to a variety of solemn, binding obligations or agreements involving two or more parties in a relationship. (1) The obligation might be self-assumed by the primary party for the benefit of the secondary party. In this case, the covenant was more like a pledge or a promise. The expected attitude of the primary party to the obligation was one of fidelity and the attitude of the secondary party was one of acceptance and trust. (2) When the obligation was imposed on the secondary party, it represented a demand or condition placed upon the obligated party and required obedience. Generally such a covenant relationship was assumed to benefit the party imposing the obligation although obedience to the obligation might be seen as beneficial to the obligated party as well. (3) Conditions and commitments accepted by both or all parties produced a situation of mutual obligation intended to benefit all parties concerned. In all three cases, the gravity and solemnity of the parties' commitment could be enhanced by verbal declaration, swearing, or the taking of an oath.

Diverse terminology is used with regard to making, maintaining, and fulfilling a covenant: cut, give, establish, enter, observe, break, transgress, remember, forget, and so on. This suggests a lack of any limited, specific vocabulary employed to speak about the operations and attitudes toward covenant conditions.

Ancient Near Eastern Evidence. As in the OT, the ancient Near Eastern evidence for covenants or treaties is diverse and reflects various conditions and relationships. Documentary evidence is known from the third through the first millennium (for a selection, cf. *ANET* 199-206, 531-41, 659-61). Although the majority of known texts are preserved in Akkadian cuneiform, Hittite, Aramaic, and Greek examples also exist.

In Akkadian documents, especially during the first millennium, treaties and their stipulations are referred to as *adě* (*'dn/'dy* in Aramaic), a term which, unlike *bĕrît*, always occurs in the plural. The most common use of *adê* is to refer to conditions in which a subordinate party is bound through loyalty oath to a superior party at the initiative of the latter. The inferior party may be either a foreign vassal or a domestic group. Several Assyrian texts bind the entire nation, including members of the royal family, the aristocracy, and the general populace, to observe particular conditions, in regard to succession to the throne and loyalty to the king. However, *adê* is also used to refer to divine promises made by a god to a ruler, to agreements between gods, to treaties between rulers of equal status, and to agreements sought by an inferior party.

The general structural pattern underlying ancient Near Eastern treaties can be seen in Hittite texts from the fourteenth and thirteenth centuries, although it should be noted that these and subsequent treaties vary in very significant ways, no two treaties are identical, and elements in the pattern may be omitted or expanded. The six main elements of the treaty pattern are: (1) a preamble identifying the parties,

(2) a historical prologue noting past relationships between the parties (generally not present in first millennium texts), (3) the stipulations imposed on the inferior party or shared by the parties involved, (4) provisions for safely depositing and consultation/reading of the treaty document, (5) a list of gods and other witnesses to the treaty, and (6) curses and blessings. Many of the texts allude to various rites that accompanied the concluding of the treaty, in particular, actions used to illustrate the calamities and curses that would befall the disloyal and disobedient party for failure to live up to the imposed stipulations. Oaths of loyalty, undergirded with the threat of divine sanction and supervision, were sworn by the inferior party on whom the stipulations were imposed. Failure to live up to the stipulated arrangements and conditions was considered rebellion/sin against both the superior party and the deities called upon to sanction the treaty.

The parties to the treaty are referred to in various ways in the texts. The superior party might be referred to in the third person and the inferior party in the second person, both parties in the third person, or the superior party in the second or third person and the inferior party in the first person. In some texts, the parties are described in the third person and the stipulations imposed to insure the loyalty of the inferior party utilize second person address.

Covenants in Genesis–2 Kings. Numerous covenants/treaties are referred to in the OT and the term *bĕrît* occurs 286 times.

(1) Covenants between God and individuals: Although earlier commentators assumed that ADAM lived under a covenant (of works), the first reference to covenant and the first use of the word *bĕrît* appear in the Noah materials. Here the covenant seems to refer to the divine pledge made to Noah, to all creatures, and even to the earth as a whole (Gen 6:18; 9:9-16). In later interpretation the Noachic covenant was understood as involving the conditions and stipulations imposed on Noah (Gen 9:1-7) and thus all humankind (cf. Isa 24:5) and these stipulations were broadened to include a number of conditions not directly stated in the text (cf. Acts 15:19-21, 28-29; *GenR* 34.8).

The covenant with ABRAHAM, noted in Gen 15:18-19, appears to have been understood as a promise or pledge by the divine to give the land (of Canaan) to Abraham's offspring. Only the divine here is placed under any obligation and presumably the "smoking fire pot and flaming torch" (in v. 17) symbolize the deity and the divine commitment to the promise. This promise—to give the land to the patriarchs and their descendants—is spoken of throughout Genesis–Judges, sometimes using the word covenant (Exod 2:24; 6:4, 5; Lev 26:42-45; cf. 2 Kgs 13:23) and at other times merely referring to the sworn oath/promise to give the land (Gen 26:3; 50:24; Exod 13:5, 11; 32:13; 33:1; Num 11:12; 14:23; 32:11; Deut 1:8, 35; 6:10; 11:9, 21; 19:8; 26:3, 15; 28:11; 30:20; 31:7, 20-23; 34:4; Josh 1:6; 5:6; 21:43; Judg 2:1).

The covenant with Abraham described in Gen 17:1-14 is one of reciprocal obligations. Divine pledges include not only the promise of the land but also other commitments by the deity as well as the obligation of CIRCUMCISION imposed upon

Abraham and his descendants. Circumcision is presented as both an obligation and a sign of the covenant (17:11; cf. 9:13).

Num 18:8-19 speaks of Yahweh's covenant with AARON, called a "covenant of salt" (v. 18; cf. Lev 2:13; 2 Chr 13:5), which grants the Aaronites the priestly perquisites (see Neh 13:29 [cf. Num 18:21-24]; cf. Deut 33:9; Jer 33:21-22; Mal 2:1-9). Although the covenant statement only refers to God's gift of the holy offerings to the Aaronites (v. 19), the preceding passage describing these in vv. 8-18 refers to incidental priestly obligations, in the form of cultic directives (vv. 10, 17b) and might be understood as priestly obligations.

A covenant/promise of perpetual priesthood is given to PHINEHAS in Num 25:10-13 as a reward for his zealous and atoning work on behalf of Yahweh and the community (see 25:6-9; cf. Gen 26:5).

A further example of a divine covenant with an individual (and his descendants) is the covenant with DAVID (2 Sam 23:5; Ps 89:3, 19-37; 132:11-18; cf. 2 Sam 7). Probably the earliest expression of the divine covenant with David was conceived as a promissory pledge made by Yahweh to the Davidic house authenticating and justifying the family's right to rule (cf. 2 Sam 23:5-7). The covenant could also be and was later understood as placing obligations on the rulers of the Davidic line (cf. Ps 89:30-34; 132:12).

(2) Covenants between human parties: Gen 14:13 refers to a covenant of Abraham apparently between the patriarch and his allies (called "*bĕʿālîm* of the covenant") in the war against northern invaders. Abraham and ABIMELECH made a covenant at Beersheba (Gen 21:22-34) as did ISAAC and Abimelech (Gen 26:23-33). LABAN and JACOB made a covenant in Transjordan (Gen 31:43-54) and set up a cairn called Galed (;eq "cairn of witness" or "covenant" if *ʿēd* = Akkadian *adê*, followed by a shared meal, a sign of mutual cooperation. The invading Hebrews made a covenant with inhabitants of the land, the Gibeonites (Josh 9:3-21), a practice discouraged in various passages in the Pentateuch (Exod 23:32; 34:11-16; Deut 7:2; see Judg 2:2). JOSHUA and the Israelites at SHECHEM covenanted to worship Yahweh (Josh 24:25). The people of JABESH-GILEAD sought to negotiate a covenant with Nahash the Ammonite (1 Sam 11:1). David and JONATHAN covenant together on more than one occasion with the covenants declared to be "of Yahweh" or "before Yahweh" (1 Sam 18:3; 20:8; 23:18). David entered a covenant with ABNER (2 Sam 3:12-13) and subsequently, "before Yahweh," with the elders of Israel (2 Sam 3:21; 5:3). SOLOMON and Hiram of Tyre concluded a covenant (1 Kgs 5:12) and both Kings Baasha of Israel and Asa of Judah did so with King BEN-HADAD I of Aram (1 Kgs 15:21) as did a later Israelite king with Ben-hadad II (1 Kgs 20:34). The priest JEHOIADA made a covenant with the military captains, which involved an oath in the temple precincts (2 Kgs 11:5), concerning a conspiracy against Queen Athaliah and later presided over a covenant ceremony, involving the people, the new king, and Yahweh, to be Yahweh's people (2 Kgs 11:17; the reference at the end of the verse "and between the king and the people" is probably a scribal error).

After the finding of the book of the law in the Temple (2 Kgs 22:8), King JOSIAH and the people covenanted "before Yahweh" to obey the stipulations of the book but nothing is said about with whom the covenant was made (2 Kgs 23:3). Jer 34:8-22 tells of a covenant made between King ZEDEKIAH and the owners of Hebrew slaves in Jerusalem (see v. 8). The covenant was made before Yahweh (v. 15) and could be spoken of as "Yahweh's covenant" (v. 18). Since breaking the covenant involved profaning the name of Yahweh (v. 16), an oath of loyalty to the covenant was probably sworn in the name of Yahweh. A particular feature of this account is the reference to passing through the severed parts of a calf (v. 18; cf. Gen 15:9-11, 17) probably as an act of self-imprecation.

Although the term "covenant" is not used with regard to Israel's and Judah's relationships to ASSYRIA and Babylonia in 2 Kings, it can be assumed that such covenants existed since such international relations with Mesopotamian powers, especially with vassal states, were based on treaties. The closest terminology to concluding a covenant appears in 2 Kgs 17:3 which speaks of King HOSHEA becoming a servant to SHALMANESER V (726–722). That such covenants/treaties were concluded with Israelite and Judean kings is not only suggested by non-biblical evidence and international policy but also by Ezek 17:11-21 (cf. 16:59) which comments on the treaty between NEBUCHADREZZAR and Zedekiah. In speaking of this treaty, Ezekiel can describe the treaty and the associated loyalty oath as both Nebuchadrezzar's and Yahweh's treaty and oath (vv. 16 and 19). This indicates that such treaties were concluded and sworn in the name of Yahweh (cf. 2 Chr 36:13), thus making the Israelite deity a party to the arrangement. Thus disloyalty to the treaty was not only a sin against the sovereign overlord but also against Yahweh. Such treaties probably existed between Assyria and Israel from the time of JEHU's submission to Assyria in 841 (cf. *ANET* 281).

Treaties/covenants between human parties, national states, and a ruler with his people, if sworn in the name of God, created what might be called a triangular relationship. The basic bond was between the covenanting parties but, through the oath, the deity became involved as a tertiary participant, as custodian and guarantor of a party's or the parties' fidelity. Breaking the treaty meant breaking an oath, a pledge to the deity.

(3) The covenant between God and Israel: Without doubt, the most prominent portrayal of covenant in the OT is that between Yahweh and the Israelite people as a whole, which differs from the covenants with Noah, the patriarchs, Phinehas, and David. In the latter, the covenant was concluded with an individual although on behalf of subsequent descendants. It also differs from personal or national bilateral treaties in that the deity is a primary partner in the relationship.

Three sections of texts speak of the making of a covenant between Yahweh and Israel—Exod 19–24, 34 and Deut 28–31—but none of these is presented as the renewal of an already existing covenant (however, cf. Exod 34:1; Deut 29:1). The first of these is made after the arrival of the Hebrews at Sinai, the second after the golden calf episode, and the third in the plains of Moab. All three blocks of material presume and reflect elements of a covenant based on reciprocal obligations and refer to a collection of divine commandments to be obeyed by the people (Exod 20–23; 34:17-26; Deut 12–26), the writing down of these divine words (Exod 24:7, 12; 34:1, 27-28; Deut 31:9), the promise of blessings and the threat of curses (Exod 23:20-33; 34:10-16; Deut 28; cf. Lev 26), and the people's acceptance and pledge of obedience (Exod 19:8; 24:7; 34:31-32; Deut 26:17). Although the features reflected in these texts parallel elements in ancient Near Eastern treaty documents, it should be noted that such comparative features are drawn from both narratives and words of Yahweh or Moses, i.e., from both descriptions about the covenant making itself as well as the presumed contents of a covenant document.

Covenant Thought in the Prophets. The eighth-century prophets—HOSEA, AMOS, ISAIAH, and MICAH—were certainly acquainted with and their preaching was informed by covenant/treaty perspectives. Their preaching, however, does not reflect the idea or the existence of a covenant between Israel and Yahweh sealed by loyalty oaths but rather of covenants between two parties in which Yahweh was the guardian of the covenant, having become a party through oaths sworn in the divine name. From the time of David and Solomon, the Israelite monarchs had entered into treaty relationships with other rulers, as was noted above, and these, especially vassal treaties with Assyria, would have been concluded with loyalty oaths in the name of Yahweh. Breaking these treaties constituted sin and brought down upon the offender the wrath of both Assyria and Yahweh and profaned the name of Yahweh, requiring the offending party to offer restitution or suffer punishment. It is possible that the practice of swearing officers and troops to a covenant of loyalty may also have been a part of Israelite life at the time (cf. 2 Kgs 11:4).

The prophets certainly assumed that Yahweh was Israel's God and Israel was Yahweh's people (cf. Exod 6:7; Lev 26:12) but this is simply an expression of the nation-god relationship, not a relationship understood in the categories of covenant thought. While the two ideas are related, they are not identical and should not be confused.

Hosea uses the term covenant five times, in 2:18; 6:7; 8:1; 10:4; and 12:1. In 2:18, Yahweh presides over or imposes the making of a covenant between a female (probably Samaria since Israel as a people is always a male in the eighth-century prophets) and the beasts and birds and so forth. Here Yahweh imposes a covenant on two other parties. Agreements made either among the Israelites themselves or, less likely, with foreign states are referred to in 10:4. The other three references probably allude to Israel's covenant with Assyria. In 8:1, this treaty is referred to as Yahweh's treaty just as is the treaty between Nebuchadrezzar and Zedekiah in Ezek 17:19. "My law" or "my torah" would be a use of synonymous parallelism in which "my law" is equivalent to "my covenant." Whether the covenant referred to in 6:7 is Israel's covenant with Assyria or a loyalty covenant sworn by Pekah and broken when he rebelled against and attacked the Israelite monarch (cf. 2 Kgs

15:25) remains uncertain. Amos was certainly acquainted with the theological and legal considerations undergirding and embodied in international treaty thought and can refer to Tyre's failure to live up to treaty conditions (1:9). Behind much of Isaiah's and Micah's preaching lies the specter of the Assyrian treaty arrangements but their concern is somewhat different from that of Hosea since Isaiah and Micah preached in Judah where the covenant with Assyria remained generally intact. Only with the death of SARGON II in 705 and thus after the termination of a Judean-Assyrian treaty did Isaiah support rebellion against Assyria (Isa 24–27).

If the covenant perspectives of the eighth-century prophets were based on conceptions associated with international political treaties, the matter is radically different for the seventh-century prophets, Jeremiah and Ezekiel. Both prophets speak of a covenant between Yahweh and the people (cf. Jer 11:1-10; 14:21; 22:9; Ezek 16:8, 60-63). Ezekiel still utilized the perspective of international treaty conceptions as well. His allegory of the eagles in chap. 17 provides the clearest insight into the triangular treaty arrangement in the scriptures, especially in 17:11-21 in which the Nebuchadrezzar-Zedekiah treaty and oath are described as Yahweh's treaty and oath. It was the breaking of this treaty, not the Israel-Yahweh treaty, that the prophet proclaimed would bring judgment on Zedekiah (17:20-21).

The differences between the covenant preaching in the eighth-century prophets and the seventh-century prophets is to be explained as follows. In the three-quarters of a century separating the end of Isaiah's preaching (in 701–700) and the beginning (629–628) or early years of Jeremiah's preaching, Judean circles had given expression to the Israel-God relationship in terms of an Israel-God covenant. These circles are to be associated with what is called the deuteronomic-deuteronomistic movement which eventually gave final shape to the book of Deuteronomy and a major history of Israel extending, probably, from Genesis through 2 Kings. The parallels between the covenant material in Deuteronomy (especially in chaps. 1–11 and 28–31) and the treaties of ESARHADDON, especially his so-called vassal treaties dating from 672 to 671 (cf. *ANET* 534-41), suggest a connection between these two documents. Both Esarhaddon and his mother Zakutu swore their own people to fidelity and obedience. The form of this type of treaty, between sovereign and subjects, closely resembles that between Yahweh and Israel. In addition, Deut 28:68, with its reference to going to Egypt in ships, probably reflects ASHURBANIPAL's invasion of Egypt in 664–663 during which Judean troops, if not King MANASSEH himself, accompanied him, some being carried in ships (see *ANET* 294). The OT's particular theology of a covenant between Yahweh and Israel was thus probably formulated in the mid-seventh century.

Marriage as Covenant. Two OT texts, other indirect biblical evidence, and ancient Near Eastern materials suggest that MARRIAGE was understood in ancient Israel along the lines of a triangular covenantal arrangement in which the spouses were the primary partners and God was the custodian and guardian of the marriage relationship. Prov 2:17 describes the woman who forsakes the companion of her youth (her husband) as one who forgets the covenant (*běrît*) of her God, implying both that marriage was a covenant and that the covenant was under the sanction of God. Mal 3:14 speaks of God as witness to a marriage arrangement and the wife is referred to as the covenant woman. That marriage was so understood is also indicated by the fact that throughout the Near East, adultery was considered the "great" sin. Lev 19:20-22 also implies this triangular relation in marriage, here even in betrothal. An outside male who sexually interfered in a man-woman relationship was required to offer a reparation (guilt) offering (an *'āšām*) which was demanded when one transgressed against God by profaning the divine name or desecrating something holy to the deity. This would suggest that an oath in the name of Yahweh was sworn (or assumed to be implied) in marriage-betrothal arrangements. Unfortunately we possess no full descriptions of Israelite marriages nor marriage documents in the Bible, so it is uncertain whether or not marriage loyalty-oaths were made in the name of the deity.

The New Covenant. The prophets speak of a future covenant that God will make with the people (Isa 61:8; Jer 31:31-33; 32:40; Ezek 34:25; 37:26). Only Jeremiah uses the adjective "new" in speaking of this future covenant (31:31). Otherwise this future covenant is simply denoted as being "everlasting" (Isa 61:8; Jer 32:40) or "a covenant of peace" (or "friendship," Ezek 34:25; 37:26). The contexts of all these passages indicate that the prophets were addressing the issue of what conditions would need to prevail for the Israel of the future to be obedient to the divine will. The new or renewed covenant is to be part of a great transformation of both the people and the land. According to Jer 31:31-33, the new covenant will be inscribed upon the hearts of the house of Israel so that each person will instinctively and by nature know and heed the divine torah.

Conclusions. A number of conclusions are in order regarding the nature and role of covenant in the OT. (1) The broad semantic range of the term *běrît* would indicate that "covenant" is not always the best translation of the term especially where "pledge/promise" or "obligation" better fits the context. The term *běrît* functioned in a broader fashion than is implied in the term "covenant." (2) There is a diversity of covenants in the OT and a single structural pattern does not encompass this diversity. (3) The OT contains no full covenant document per se. Hypothetical reconstructions of such are produced by combining narrative and "legal" material. (4) Comparisons between OT texts and Near Eastern treaty texts, for example the Hittite vassal treaties (first done by Karge), are informative but OT materials should not be pressed into a hypothetical stereotyped Near Eastern treaty pattern. (5) The role of treaty agreements between nation-states, with the theology and ethics implied by these, should not be overlooked. These treaties and their interpretation seem to have formed the basic background of the covenant theology of the eighth-century prophets. (6) The idea of a covenant between Israel and Yahweh was probably a literary/theological phenomenon rather than a sociological or institutional reality. There is no evidence in Joshua–2 Kings of a covenant festival or a covenant renewal celebration in which a covenant between Yahweh and the people was regularly reenacted. (7) The present canonical form of the Hexateuch is patterned around a series of covenants (Noah, Abraham, Sinai, after the golden calf episode, in the plains of Moab, and at Shechem). The canonical form of the text should be interpreted in light of this fact.

Covenant in the New Testament. The NT writers inherited from the Greek of the OT the use of the term *diathēkē* as a translation for *bĕrît* although the Greek term tended to denote a last will or testament (cf. Gal 3:15, 17; Heb 9:15-17). This terminology is the source of the designations "Old" and "New" Testaments.

The early church saw its relationship to God in terms of a new covenant, which it closely associated with the death of Jesus and the observance of the Lord's Supper (or Eucharist). Covenant terminology and its association with the blood (death) (cf. Exod 24:8; Zech 9:11) of JESUS are anchored in both the Gospels (Matt 26:28; Mark 14:24; Luke 22:20 [absent from many ancient MSS]; see John 6:52-58) and Epistles (1 Cor 11:23-32). Early Christians used the idea of the "new" covenant (Heb 8:6-10; Luke 22:20) inaugurated by Christ, contrasting it with the "old" covenant. The "old" covenant is sometimes associated with the law or the Pentateuch (2 Cor 3:6, 14; Gal 4:24) or what might be called non-Christian Jewish religion. Elsewhere, the "new" covenant is related positively to the Abrahamic covenant (Acts 3:25; cf. Gal 3:78; but see Acts 7:8). PAUL refers to the covenants of the Israelites (Rom 9:4) and associates the Christians with the divine promise to Abraham and God's fidelity to that promise (Rom 9:6-9; Gal 4:28-31). A central concern of the BOOK OF HEBREWS is to demonstrate the superiority of the Christian covenant (7:22; 8:7-13). The new covenant could also be spoken of in terms of the "spirit" as a "spiritual bond" (2 Cor 3:1-6).

See also TESTIMONY; THEOLOGY OF THE NEW TESTAMENT; THEOLOGY OF THE OLD TESTAMENT.

Bibliography. K. Baltzer, *The Covenant Formulary* (1971); J. Barr, "Some Semantic Notes on the Covenant," *Beiträge zur Alttestamentlichen Theologie: Festschrift für Walther Zimmerli*, ed. H. Donner et al.; R. T. Beckwith, "The Unity and Diversity of God's Covenants," *TynBul* 38 (1987): 93-118; R. Frankena, "The Vassal-Treaties of Esarhaddon and the Dating of Deuteronomy," *OTS* 14 (1965): 123-54; A. K. Grayson, "Akkadian Treaties of the Seventh Century B.C.," *JCS* 39 (1987): 127-60; E. Gerstenberger, "Covenant and Commandment," *JBL* 84 (1965): 38-51; D. R. Hillers, *Covenant: The History of a Biblical Idea*; P. Karge, *Geschichte des Bundesgedankens im Alten Testament*; D. J. McCarthy, *Treaty and Covenant*; G. E. Mendenhall, *Law and Covenant in Israel and the Ancient Near East*; E. W. Nicholson, *God and His People: Covenant and Theology in the O.T.*; R. A. Oden, Jr., "The Place of Covenant in the Religion of Israel," *Ancient Israelite Religion: Essays in Honor of Frank Moore Cross*, ed. P. D. Miller et al.; S. Parpola, "Neo-Assyrian Treaties from the Royal Archives of Nineveh," *JCS* 39 (1987): 161-89; S. Parpola and K. Watanabe, *Neo-Assyrian Treaties and Loyalty Oaths*; L. Perlitt, *Bundestheologie im Alten Testament*; H. Tadmor, "Treaty and Oath in the Ancient Near East: A Historian's Approach," *Humanizing America's Iconic Book*, ed. G. M.

Tucker and D. A. Knight; M. Tsevat, "The Neo-Assyrian and Neo-Babylonian Vassal Oaths and the Prophet Ezekiel," *JBL* 78 (1959): 199-204; M. Weber, *Ancient Judaism*; M. Weinfeld, "בְּרִית," *TDOT*; Z. Zevit, "A Phoenician Inscription and Biblical Covenant Theology," *IEJ* 27 (1977): 116-18.   —JOHN H. HAYES

Covenant with Noah   [MDB 181-82]

•**Covenant with Noah.** The first of three covenants emphasized in the Pentateuchal priestly materials, the other two being the Abrahamic covenant (Gen 17) and the Mosaic covenant (Exod 19–24, 31). The Noah Covenant (Gen 9:1-17) climaxes the primeval themes of GENESIS—creation, rebellion, judgment (the tower of Babel and the flood), and COVENANT. The FLOOD marks the end of the old epoch, and God's word to the new era in the NOAH covenant is one of hope and blessing.

The word "covenant" (Heb. בְּרִית) in its simplest sense means "relationship." It is a metaphorical or figurative term describing a relationship with God by analogy to some type of formal relationship among persons. Pacts and covenants were used extensively throughout the ancient world, ranging from international treaties and business contracts to marriage rules and religious practices. Scholars continue to debate the precise formal traditions behind the various OT covenants.

The Noah Covenant was a universal covenant since it included Noah, all Noah's descendants (not merely the Semites and Israelites), and all living creatures. It also was an everlasting covenant (Heb בְּרִית עוֹלָם)—an unconditional covenant—in which God promised never again to punish the earth by returning it to the primeval watery chaos. Because the covenant was unconditional, some scholars think it was fashioned after ancient suzerainty treaties in which a king made unilateral declarations that were not dependent upon the subject's responses.

The Noah Covenant included a new privilege: meat could now be eaten provided the animals were slaughtered in such a way that the blood was not consumed. Earlier in Genesis, diets were to be vegetarian; humanity's dominion over animals had not included meat-eating (Gen 1:28-30; 3:17-19). The principle of "reverence for life" (Gen 9:4) undergirds the stringent prohibition against the BLOOD: the life is the blood. Life (and hence the blood) was mysteriously and mystically sacred (cf. Gen 4:10-11). Strictly forbidden was the needless, wanton shedding of the lifeblood of any creature, but especially of human persons, for they were created in the image of God.

With the new promise and new privilege came a new sign. The universal covenant was signified by a symbol visible to all creatures, the RAINBOW. God and all creatures could now see and bear witness to the Almighty's promise and sovereignty. The rainbow was a particularly fitting symbol to the ancients, who imagined it as the divine weapon (bow) from which God shot lightning-arrows (Ps 7:12-13; Hab 3:9-11). By hanging up the bow, God showed that the divine wrath had indeed subsided.

Covenant is one of the dominant themes of the OT—indeed, of the entire Bible. After the time of the Mosaic Covenant, Israel both nationally and religiously understood itself as the people who had entered into covenant with Yahweh. David established a royal covenant with Yahweh, and the prophets charged in their "lawsuit" oracles that Israel had broken its covenant with God. Moreover, Jeremiah expressed the hope for the future in terms of renewing the covenant, and in the NT Jesus Christ was understood as the beginning of the new and final covenant.

See also COVENANT; NOAH; NOACHIC LAWS; RAINBOW.

Bibliography. G. E. Mendenhall, "Covenant," *IDB*; P. A. Riemann, "Mosaic Covenant," *IDBSupp*. —JACK WEIR

Creation [MDB 182-84]

•**Creation.** The activity of God that results in the emergence of an ordered cosmos. Especially obvious in the Bible's opening chapters, creation motifs and themes are also found throughout the Bible (e.g., Exod 15:4-10; Job 38–41; Pss 8, 19, 24, 65, 74, 104; Prov 8:22-31; Isa 40–55; Jer 4:23-26; Amos 4:13; 5:8-9; 9:5-6; Sir 24; John 1:1-18; Col 1:15-20). Further, reflections on creation are not limited to biblical literature but are attested by a wide array of ancient Near Eastern texts. A review of the various texts reveals both shared and divergent ideas about creation.

Creation and Chaos. Fundamental to Babylonia, Egypt, and Canaan was the belief that chaos, a force hostile to existence, had been overcome by a victorious god. The Babylonian *Enuma eliš* opens with an account of the origin of the gods, or theogony. From primordial Apsu, the fresh underground waters, and the marine waters, Ti'amat, springs the society of the gods. Conflict within the divine society throws Ti'amat, who personifies chaos, into mortal combat with Marduk. Marduk is victorious and from the slain body of Ti'amat he establishes the heavens and the earth. Subsequently humans are created from the blood of the rebellious god Kingu, and a temple is constructed for Marduk in Babylon.

Egyptian creation accounts speak of a watery chaos called Nun. In one version of creation by the god Atum, a primal hill ascends from Nun. From there Atum creates the other gods in the divine society, the Ennead, by calling their names. The Egyptian cult center is understood to be located at the point where the hill arose from Nun. Another creation story affirms that Ptah is the creator. In "The Theology of Memphis," Ptah first intellectually conceives the thing to be fashioned and then speaks it into existence. The creation of humanity does not figure prominently in most Egyptian creation texts, although one of them tells that humanity is created from the tears of Re's angry eye. However, "The Instructions for King Meri-Ka-Re," a wisdom text, maintains that humans are created in the "images" of god and given plants and animals for food and rulers for leadership.

The Baal texts at Ugarit tell how BAAL becomes ruler by engaging in combat and defeating Yam, the sea. The creator god at Ugarit is El, but Baal is the deity who brings order to creation. Baal's palace is then built on Mount Zaphon with the aid of his wife and sister, Anat. The palace signals Baal's authority. Finally, Baal is challenged by El's son Mot (death). Baal descends into the underworld where he remains until Anat seizes Mot and effectively destroys him. Baal is then revived and reinstated as prince.

Texts from Babylonia, Egypt and Ugarit reveal the shared understanding that chaos is overcome by a victorious god who creates and/or establishes order. The battle with chaos (*Chaoskampf*) is most dramatic in Babylonia and Ugarit. Creation is not *ex nihilo*, from nothing, but results from an ordering of material that already exists. All three civilizations conceive of a plurality of gods who relate within the bounds of a society. Theogony is explicit in the Babylonian and Egyptian stories, implicit in the Ugaritic texts. Finally, creation has as much to do with establishing social and cosmic order as it does in accounting for origins, especially at Ugarit.

The Bible reveals shared and distinctive concerns. Like their neighbors, the Hebrews often speak of a watery chaos (Gen 1:2; Ps 104:6; however, Gen 2 envisions chaos as an arid wasteland). Because chaos is the material from which God creates, it is unlikely that the ancient Hebrews held any notion of *creatio ex nihilo*. The first clear expression of creation from nothing is found in 2 Macc 7:28 from the late second century B.C.E. Still, God's power over the deep is never questioned and is frequently expressed as a victory over surging waves and monstrous sea creatures: dragons, LEVIATHAN, RAHAB, or a SERPENT (Pss 74:13-14; 89:10; Job 26:12-13; Isa 51:9). Unlike other creation stories, however, the biblical accounts do not depict God in mortal combat with the forces of chaos. The raging waters and fearsome beasts that are so threatening in the *Enuma eliš* and in the Baal stories merely yield to the majestic power of God. It is most significant that the creation accounts in the Hebrew Bible know of no theogony. To be sure, certain texts give rise to speculation about a society of the gods (e.g., Gen 1:26; 3:22; 6:2; 11:7; Isa 6:8). However, such thoughts remain undeveloped and there is never any attempt to account for the origin of God.

Creation and Salvation History. The precise relationship between creation and salvation history is currently a matter of debate. Gerhard von Rad's opinion that the creation accounts in Gen 1–2 are merely the prologue to God's redemptive acts in history has been quite influential. In texts like Ps 136, Isa 42:5-9, and Isa 51:9-10 where creation and salvation are spoken of together, creation is ancillary, while the accent falls upon God's saving deeds. In von Rad's opinion, creation does not achieve the status of an independent theme. When one reads "But thus says the Lord, he who created you, O Jacob, he who formed you, O Israel: `Fear not, for I have redeemed you; I have called you by name, you are mine' " (Isa 43:1), one sees that the prophet quickly leaves creation to talk about salvation. For von Rad and those persuaded by him, creation is merely the first of God's historical acts that paves the way for redemption.

Current scholarship is concerned to hear what the many biblical creation texts have to say without imposing von Rad's salvation-historical schema upon them. This, along with consideration of extrabiblical creation texts, has led many scholars to understand that creation says as much about *order* as origins. The priestly creation story in Gen 1 is clearly concerned with order. The waters above are separated from those below; light and darkness, seas and earth are distinguished from one another. One plant is distinct from another plant, and one animal unlike another animal. All boundaries are crisp and sharp. Within this divinely established order humans have their place. When humans act righteously and uphold the order of the cosmos, the world is at peace. When humans display unrighteousness, the order is usurped and, in Hosea's words, "the land mourns, and all who dwell in it languish . . . " (Hos 4:3). As the prophets see so clearly, cosmic and social order are intricately connected. The observation that a divinely established order inheres in the cosmos cautions against subordinating creation to salvation history and calls for a balanced estimation of their relationship.

Creation and the Cosmos. Numerous passages within the Bible reveal that the Hebrews, like their Near Eastern neighbors, conceive the world to be a three-storied structure. The Hebrew Bible presents a picture of the waters above the heavens (Gen 1:6-7; 7:11), the earth supported by pillars (1 Sam 2:8), and the waters below the earth (Gen 7:11; 49:25; Exod 20:4; Prov 8:28). The Bible affirms that it is God who has established this cosmos (Ps 24:1-2). Yet it also confesses that the world is dynamic and depends upon God for its continued existence. The flood story indicates that God, no longer able to endure human sin, opens the windows of the heavens and the fountains of the deep to inundate the earth (Gen 7:11). The account underscores both the total dependence of the earth upon God and the complete power of God who uses the chaotic waters for divine purposes. The appearance of God in 2 Sam 22:8-16 (cf. Ps 18:7-15) causes the earth to shake and tremble. Likewise, Ps 104:31-32 shows that the stability of the earth depends upon God's continued pleasure in the creation.

The role of humans within this cosmos is significantly different from that in the *Enuma eliš*. There humans are fashioned to serve the gods and deliver them from work. In Gen 1, humans share in the rule exercised by God. As God's creatures humans rule over other creatures and the earth. Given the precise care God pays to creation in Gen 1, it is inconceivable that human rule be anything other than careful and contributive to world order. There is no room for exploitation in God's cosmos. Gen 2 also assigns humans a significant role within the creation when God shares the divine prerogative and allows the first human to name the earth's creatures. Ps 8 sings of the special role of humans who exercise dominion over God's world and Ps 104:14-15 affirms God's desire that humans have the means to more than a miserable existence. Far more than mere servants of the gods as in the *Enuma eliš*, human beings are an important part of God's good creation, according to the Hebrew tradition.

God's care does not stop with humanity. Ps 104:16-26 proclaims that God has made the stately cedars of Lebanon solely for the storks' home. Mountain peaks exist for the goats to climb and rocky cliffs shelter the badgers. Day exists for human work, and night for lions that seek food under the cover of darkness. Even the sea, so fearsome in the *Enuma eliš* and the story of Baal and Yam, is a home for numberless creatures, including Leviathan, which sports in the waves. All of these creatures are constantly dependent upon God for their existence. Should God remove the divine presence, they are reduced to the dust whence they came.

The cosmos, then, is a dynamic world that stands constantly dependent upon its creator.

Creation, Wisdom, and Torah. Israel's WISDOM LITERATURE (Job, Proverbs, Ecclesiastes [Qoheleth], Wisdom of Solomon, Sirach) presupposes a divinely ordered creation. The sages assert confidence in the human intellect to observe the world and draw the appropriate conclusions by which to order human life. For example, the teacher urges the student: "Go to the ant, O sluggard; consider her ways, and be wise" (Prov 6:6). To be sure, the sages know that there are limits to human reason and so they counsel: "A man's mind plans his way, but the Lord directs his steps" (Prov 16:9; cf. 14:12; 19:21; 20:24). Nonetheless, the person guided by wisdom and careful scrutiny of the created world gains insights for life. Even the vehement protests of Job, which question the reliability of appearances, and the skepticism of Qoheleth that questions whether or not wisdom is sufficient to discern the order of God's world, presuppose that there is a rational principle behind the world of experience. However, for Job and Qoheleth, human wisdom is simply too limited to be able to discern God's grand design in the world.

That such a design exists is affirmed in Prov 8:22-31. There personified Wisdom claims to be the first of God's creatures. Present from the beginning, Wisdom assumes the role of master builder while God establishes the heavens, restricts the chaotic waters, and shapes the mountains and fields. By the first century C.E. the Wisdom of Solomon extols Wisdom as "the fashioner of all things" (7:22), an emanation of God's glory that penetrates all things (7:24-25), an associate in God's works (8:4), present from the moment when God made the world (9:9).

Two centuries prior to the Wisdom of Solomon, Sirach (Ben Sira, Ecclesiasticus) achieved a remarkable synthesis of creation, wisdom and TORAH. As the creative mist that waters the face of the earth in Gen 2:6, wisdom covers the earth in search of a home (Sirach 24). At God's command wisdom takes up residence in Jerusalem. There she offers instruction on righteous living and finally reveals herself to be the "book of the covenant of the Most High God, the law which Moses commanded . . . " (Sir 24:23). Wisdom is effectively subsumed under Torah, which is now affirmed to have been present at the beginning of creation.

Creation and the Word. While the Jewish traditions came to equate Torah with personified Wisdom present with God from beginning, Christian traditions made parallel claims about Jesus. The author of Colossians affirms that Jesus "is the image of the invisible God, the first-born of all creation; for in him all things were created . . . " (1:15-16). The Fourth Gospel proclaims: "In the beginning was the WORD and the Word was with God, and the Word was God. He was in the beginning with God; all things were made through him, and without him was not anything made that was made" (John 1:1-3). No longer is Wisdom or Torah the preexistent agent of creation, but rather Jesus the Word. The christological claim made by this equation is that Jesus is the means by which to understand God's activity to bring order out of chaos. Just as God spoke the word that separated light from darkness in primeval moments, through the Word made flesh God the creator once again speaks to bring light from darkness.

See also COSMOLOGY; THEOLOGY OF THE OLD TESTAMENT; WORSHIP IN THE OLD TESTAMENT.

Bibliography. W. Harrelson, "The Significance of Cosmology in the Ancient Near East," *Translating and Understanding the Old Testament*, ed. H. Frank and W. Reed; D. A. Knight, "Cosmogony and Order in the Hebrew Tradition," *Cosmogony and Ethical Order*, ed. R. Lovin and F. Reynolds; J. B. Pritchard, *ANET*; H. H. Schmid, "Creation, Righteousness, and Salvation," *Creation in the Old Testament*, ed. B. W. Anderson; G. von Rad, *The Problem of the Hexateuch*.
—V. STEVEN PARRISH

Exodus [MDB 276-79]

•**Exodus.** [ek'suh-duhs] The Exodus from Egypt, climaxed by Yahweh's marvelous victory at the sea, is a watershed in the actual history of Israel and the recording of that history. The narrative that depicts the Exodus includes the horrible oppression and the marvelous liberation of the people who inherited the promises made long before to Abraham.

The biblical account of the Exodus is both a reflection and a transformation of the actual historical event. The biblical story recollects certain events that took place, but these events have been eclipsed by the merging accounts, i.e., the major traditions of the Pentateuch, and the combined effect of these theological perspectives. The transformation arises in the creation of a narrative manifesting the redemptive power of God in what surely would have been viewed as a minor event in the ancient world in which renegades or slaves regularly escaped with no notice. Over time, with the contribution of the distinctive perspectives of several groups, the story developed into the testimony of the whole group bound by covenant to this awesome, powerful, and attentive god, Yahweh.

Historical Roots. Though the story effectively veils the history of this event, scholars are able to date and to reconstitute the chronology and itinerary of the Exodus. Many historians agree that certain biblical texts, e.g., 1 Kgs 6:1, suggest a date for the Exodus. If one accepts the rendering in 1 Kgs 6:1, which claims that 480 years separate the Exodus from the fourth year of Solomon's reign, the date of the Exodus would be ca. 1440 B.C.E. Judg 11:26 echoes this dating when it claims

Israel entered into Canaan 300 years before the judge, Jephthah. This date corresponds with the experience of certain Canaanite cities with the unsettling *'apiru*, or *Habiru* as documented in the AMARNA letters; however, the historical reflections of the Exodus and the eventual conquest of Canaan do not parallel the experience of these Canaanite cities. This date is based on numbers that carry symbolic meaning rather than historical reminiscence. Other texts, such as Exod 12:40-41, which says that 430 years separate the descent of Jacob and his sons from the Exodus, or Gen 15:13-16, which claims Israel will be enslaved 400 years to another nation before it returns in the fourth generation, contradict one another and provide historians with more puzzles to solve rather than data to assimilate.

Many scholars agree, however, that Exod 1:11, which pictures the construction of the "store-cities, Pithom and Ramses," for the Pharaoh, suggests the best possibilities both for the pharaoh of the Exodus and the date of that event. These cities have been identified as Per-Atum and Per-Ramses, which were built during the reign of RAMSES II (1290–1224). His father, Seti I, had begun establishing and erecting fortified cities to protect his territory and to supply provisions to the necessary forces. Ramses II continued this and other building projects. If Exod 2:23 correctly recollects a shift in pharaohs, the Exodus would occur either in the reign of Ramses II (ca. 1250 B.C.E.) or his successor, his son Merneptah (ca. 1220 B.C.E.). However, the "Hymn of Victory of Mer-ne-ptah" (the "Israel Stela") places a group of people known as Israel in Canaan and suggests the Exodus should be dated earlier. On this basis, the pharaoh of the oppression would be Seti I and the pharaoh of the Exodus would be Ramses II, though this conclusion remains unsatisfactory. One could not expect to gain corroboration of the Exodus from Egyptian texts, though there are reports of tribal movements and small groups of escaped slaves, for the event would be too inconsequential or too embarrassing.

The PLAGUES, even though the present arrangement depends on a theological and literary agenda, are rooted in certain features of Egyptian life. Indeed, all these plagues could have natural explanations; certain scholars have prepared schemes whereby the order in the biblical account might actually chronicle an extraordinary collocation of events. Though such a series of events remains a possibility, biblical scholarship largely interprets this attempt to prove the historical accuracy of the biblical account as misdirected. The present narrative primarily presents a composite interpretation of an experience buried in the past but kept alive in the present. These plagues, rooted in history, for the people who leave Egypt, are the signature of their God.

The final event in the series of redemptive actions is the deliverance at the Sea of Reeds (*yam sûp*—wrongly understood as the RED SEA in the LXX). Depending upon whether one maintains that the Israelites started north from Goshen across the marshy section of Lake Sirbonis but later turned south toward KADESH-BARNEA to miss the fortifications along "the way of the land of the Philistines," or east through the marshy segment of the Bitter Lakes at the northern end of the Gulf of Suez toward Kadesh-Barnea, or south over the marshy end of the Gulf of Suez toward Jebel Musa, a traditional site for Mount SINAI, the Israelite experience recorded a miraculous escape that left the Egyptians crippled and unable to subdue the fugitives (PLATE 9). Again, the possibility of a natural event, e.g., the flow of the tides or the effect of the wind, which allowed these fleeing people to escape the pursuing chariots, remains entirely possible. Yet this story, like that of the plagues, points to an affirmation of Yahweh's power and not the coincidental arrangement of natural forces. One must neither explain away these signs by focusing on their natural character, nor accept the story as an eyewitness account, for both of these procedures overlook the difficulty of knowing what actually happened and the clear possibility of interpreting this narrative even if one does not know what happened several centuries earlier.

From a literary point of view, historical speculation and reformulation sometimes obscures the literary power of the account. For example, the omission of the Pharaoh's name creates difficulty for the historian. Yet, this occurs again and again in narratives and is quite natural in the literature of a people who thrived on oral stories that could be applied to their predicament. These people knew that the Pharaohs had names, but an unnamed ruler became any ruler who acted arbitrarily and coarsely, while Israel was a very particular group that lived through several hardships. So, in Deut 5:3 when the phrase is heard: "It was not our fathers who . . . , " or in Deut 6:21 when the phrase is heard: "We were Pharaoh's slaves . . . , " the Exodus reveals its timeless nature.

The same would be true in regard to the ten plagues and their ordering. In Pss 78 and 105, the order, the number, and the types of plagues have been altered, surely reflecting different traditions, and also underscoring the literary characteristics of poetic material and the particular contexts in which the material is placed. In Exod 10, the external darkness, which is the ninth plague, prepares the reader for Yahweh's last dramatic deed: the spread of an internal darkness of grief throughout Egypt in the wake of the nocturnal visit of the angel of death and compels the Pharaoh to release the Israelites. In Ps 105, the darkness begins the series of plagues in order to spread the symbolic nature of darkness over the whole account.

The Exodus Account. In a captivating drama a change of fortune must occur to place the protagonist(s) in a troubled situation. Such is the news that a new ruler, unacquainted with Israel's history and threatened by the numbers and success of the Hebrews, ascends to power. He immediately presses them into forced labor by which he plans to decrease their numbers while they build supply cities for his eastern flanks. Pharaoh's plan fails where he most wants it to succeed; the Israelites seem to become more numerous and more vigorous. Thereupon Pharaoh first charges the midwives to kill the male children born to the Hebrews, and later instructs his subjects to do the same.

In the midst of this danger and oppression, a son is born to a couple, both of whom are descended from the house of Levi. The events in the life of the son, who will be named MOSES by Pharaoh's daughter, prefigure many of the episodes in the Exodus that he will manage for Yahweh. His own rescue from the river points to the miraculous rescue later at the Sea of Reeds. His intervention that leads to the death of an Egyptian who was beating a Hebrew and his subsequent flight from Egypt foreshadow his intervention that leads to the freedom of the Israelites. His assistance to the daughters of Jethro (Reuel), the priest of Midian, ironically anticipates the time when a shepherd will deliver the Israelites out of the hand of the Egyptians (in Exod 2:19, they said: "An Egyptian delivered us out of the hand of the shepherds. . . . "). In addition, the birth incident reminds us that water is an important symbol in this story. For Moses, water signals life and providence; for the Egyptians, water stands for death and defeat.

The accession of a new king in Egypt fails to temper the bondage of the Israelites, and their cries for help reach Yahweh. Yahweh then reveals himself to Moses and instructs Moses to serve as his agent in rescuing the people. Moses' response accords with the typical call narrative in the Hebrew Bible; he resists. After Yahweh's first approach, which states that Moses must get the people out of Egypt, Moses responds with two questions: Who am I? (3:11) and Who are you (3:13b)? The second approach provides more information and a plan by which the people may deceive the Pharaoh in order to leave Egypt. Moses again counters with two hesitations: What if they (the Hebrews) do not believe me? and What about my speech difficulties? Yahweh resolves these difficulties and Moses prepares to return to Egypt. On his departure Yahweh further informs Moses that Pharaoh will be stubborn as a means of glorifying the power of Yahweh. These final instructions, along with the curious story of Zipporah's circumcision of her eldest son, anticipate the climactic final plague—the death of the first-born, the act that will break the will of Pharaoh—and the directions concerning the PASSOVER and the law of the first-born.

After Moses and AARON join, they first go to the elders of Israel who are relieved to know that deliverance is near. Moses and Aaron subsequently meet with Pharaoh who alters an earlier question of Moses and defiantly asks: "Who is Yahweh that I should heed his voice and let Israel go? I do not know Yahweh, and moreover I will not let Israel go." Pharaoh not only refuses their request to go to worship for three days in the wilderness; he increases their burdens. This punishment demoralizes the Israelites and strains their relationship with Moses. There follows a lengthy reassurance and recommissioning of Moses (Exod 6:1ff.) and the story moves toward the protracted struggle between the power of Yahweh and the will of Pharaoh.

On the instructions of Yahweh, Moses and Aaron begin to pressure and to threaten Pharaoh so that he will let the people go. The first step, turning Aaron's rod into a serpent, is duplicated by the Egyptian magicians. The magicians' success evaporates as their serpents are swallowed by Aaron's. Yet, as with other signs to come, Pharaoh becomes more intransigent.

With the struggle fully engaged, Yahweh unleashes a series of plagues through Moses, meant to manifest the overwhelming power of Yahweh and intended to force Pharaoh to release the Israelites. The Nile turns to blood, a feat matched by Egyptian magicians; Pharaoh is unmoved. The magicians match the second plague, hordes of frogs. Pharaoh, in order to end this scourge of frogs, promises that the people may go and sacrifice in the wilderness. As soon as the scourge disappears, however, Pharaoh changes his mind, as he will again and again. The magicians fail to replicate the third plague, clouds of gnats, and call this sign the "finger of God" but Pharaoh remains unaffected. The fourth plague, swarms of flies, which do not affect the land of Goshen, prompts Pharaoh to agree initially to the Israelites' demands but only within the land of Egypt. Immediately, Moses reminds Pharaoh that their sacrifices might offend the people of Egypt. Initially Pharaoh agrees to let them go, but ultimately reverts to his original stance. The fifth and sixth plagues, a plague on livestock and boils on humans and animals, misses the Israelites but leaves the Pharaoh unmoved. The seventh plague, hail and lightning, convinces those Egyptians who fear Yahweh to put their livestock under roof and persuades the Pharaoh to let the Israelites go. When Pharaoh refuses to let the Israelites go, an eighth plague, locusts, occurs. When Pharaoh appears to soften, Moses entreats Yahweh who drives the locusts into the Red Sea. The ninth plague, an intensely thick darkness that does not reach the Israelites, presses Pharaoh to allow the people, without their herds, to go to sacrifice. Moses refuses this offer and Pharaoh, overcome with rage, sends Moses away for the last time. Moses announces the last plague, the death of the first-born, then prepares the Israelites for the weathering of this scourge and the exiting from Egypt. The angel of death fills the land of Egypt with sorrow, and the Pharaoh finally allows the Israelites to go.

Combined with this dramatic account of the last plague are regulations concerning the Passover ceremony and the law of the first-born. These rituals, originally separate and rooted in the life of the semi-nomads, represent rites that protected them from the mysterious forces that disrupted their lives. Both ceremonies, and the festival of unleavened bread as well, have been tied to this Exodus event, and thereby their practice and intent have been forever changed.

Characteristically, Pharaoh changes his mind and sends an army to retrieve the Israelites who are caught between the Egyptian army and the Sea of Reeds. The Israelites lose all composure and faith, and, overcome with fear, begin to complain bitterly to Moses and to recall all their misgivings. After the people are quieted, Yahweh directs Moses to raise his staff and then sends a wind to divide the waters. The Israelites hurry across and the Egyptians pursue them. However, the waters rush back and destroy the army so that the Israelites are delivered and Yahweh is glorified. In a victory song (Exod 15:1-18), or, the Song of the Sea, which has been subsequently revised so that this battle and victory take on cosmic significance, Israel celebrates their deliverance and Yahweh's power. Then, the people head toward the mountain where Moses had met this awesome God and where they will bind themselves forever to this God.

Although the narrative traces their trip to Sinai, and the first commandment ties the Exodus to the covenant, the Israelites never quite internalize either the significance of the Exodus or the sense of the covenant. Before Moses can exhibit the tablets of the Law, the people are worshiping a golden calf that they say are the gods that brought them out of Egypt.

Yet other voices keep alive the marvel and consequence of this event of salvation history. BALAAM cannot bring himself to curse a people who has such a God on their side (Num 23:22). Early in his address to Israel, Moses, the eloquent preacher of Deuteronomy, counters the claim that the Exodus was merely a means to place Israel in the hands of its enemies. Moses maintains that the Exodus was redemptive and led to a covenant that brought life to Israel. Therefore, children should be taught that the Exodus established the basis for the way Israel relates to Yahweh and to others and provides fundamental ceremonies, like Passover, which define the life of the people.

The prophets, as they pondered the historical and metaphorical power of the Exodus, certainly perceived the Exodus experience as basic for Israel, just as they saw the Covenant as the standard for their national life. Amos, a prophet of reversals, affirmed that Yahweh redemptively brought the Israelites out of Egypt but their present unrighteousness prepared them for vigorous punishment. The same love that redeems, also punishes. In addition, Amos claimed that the destiny of all nations rested in the providence of Yahweh; he had even brought the Philistines from Caphtor and the Arameans from Kir. Hosea, who saw his relationship with his wife die as she forgot the covenant of marriage, recalled the mighty acts of Yahweh at the Exodus, which the people had effectively forgotten. Ezekiel castigated his people for their rebellion against Yahweh; he claimed that their harlotry had begun before they left Egypt. Yet, in a more hopeful sense, the words of Jeremiah and Deutero-Isaiah envision another exodus, after the people have weathered the humiliation of exile.

The Exodus also finds its way into the literature of Israel's worship; the Psalms exhibit this event in hymns of praise and this motif in pleas for help. Ps 77 recalls the terrors of Yahweh's redemptive action and asks for that same attention in the present. Ps 80 pictures a vine brought from Egypt, planted in Canaan, but jeopardized now by enemies who will succeed unless Yahweh saves it.

Psalms such as 78, 105, 135, and 136 resound with praise for the God who has redeemed and protected them throughout their history. Primarily, the Psalms capture the fundamental emotion of the Exodus, the ecstasy of release, the celebration of redemption, and the recognition of the worth of the forgotten. The praise arising from the Exodus becomes the praise for all times, just as the Exodus remains the event and the paradigm that both energizes and calls to account the people of Israel.

See also EXODUS, BOOK OF; MOSES; PLAGUES; RED SEA/REED SEA.

Bibliography. B. S. Childs, *The Book of Exodus*, OTL; J. P. Hyatt, *Exodus*; M. Noth, *Exodus, A Commentary*, OTL.   —RUSSELL I. GREGORY

Law in the Old Testament   [MDB 503-507]

•**Law in the Old Testament.** The distinctive character of OT law becomes clearer after first recognizing three components of law shared in common by almost every law tradition, including that of the OT. One of these components is of course a body of particular laws or statutes—a society's specification of whatever obligations and practices it requires of its members as necessary to their life in community. The articles of the United States Constitution are an example. In the OT, the collections of law in its first five books (the Pentateuch) are an example of a special kind.

A second component is the shaping effect had on its law by the particular historical and cultural experiences of a society, including its religious beliefs. This may include founding events, lived history, ethos—all that forms a society's distinctive self-understanding. The historical record and statements of principle contained in the Declaration of Independence exemplify this second component of law. In the OT Pentateuch, it is represented by the epic narrative in which the law collections are embedded, and from which many of the individual laws explicitly take their rationale (e.g., Exod 20:2-3; 22:21;ob20;cb; 23:9; Lev 19:33-36; Deut 26:5-11).

A third component is the formal, informal, and sometimes ad hoc judicial procedures by which law is interpreted and by which, even before formal law exists, disputes and complaints are adjudicated, creating precedents that become a source of law. These may be carried out by persons of recognized authority or simply by consensus in an assembly of the people. In this way is built cumulatively a society's tradition of what is lawful and susceptible to legislation. An example in American history is the impromptu shipboard assembly that drew up the Mayflower Compact of 1620. Illustrations of this role in the OT are many and varied, e.g., Deborah (Judg 4:5), or David (1 Sam 30:24-25).

What distinguishes OT law first of all is the striking way these three elements are now combined and their interrelation made explicit in a single work. This is the Pentateuch (traditionally, "the Five Books of Moses"), forming the first of Judaism's three main divisions of the Hebrew scriptures and entitled, from its content, *tôrâ* (hereinafter, TORAH). Classically this term has been translated as "law" (Gk., *nomos*; Latin, *lex*). It is often held that law is a poor translation of *torah* since the latter's meaning extends so far beyond the subject of laws and legalism. This however describes a relatively recent and reductionist view of law that misrepresents torah because it misrepresents the true dimensions of law.

The Vocabulary of Law in the Old Testament. Derived from the verb *yôrâ* (hiphil form), "teach," perhaps related originally to a root homonym meaning "shoot" or "throw," and associated therefore with the casting of lots to determine divine judgment and direction (Josh 18:6), the noun torah acquired early the inclusive meaning of "authoritative teaching," "direction," "instruction," or even "tradition," whether human (Prov 1:8) or divine (Deut 33:10). During the postexilic period Torah came to signify the Pentateuch itself and its content, comprehending the whole of God's revelation through Moses at Sinai—not only the laws but also the epic story of Israel as a people of God, as well as traditions about the creation of the cosmos and the beginnings of the human race. Torah is indeed a comprehensive term, though in more than a few of its occurrences it refers simply to particular laws or legal decisions (Gen 26:5; Lev 26:46; Ezek 44:5).

Of the dozen or so Hebrew words in the OT vocabulary of law none carries so many connotations as torah. Each of the others signifies respectively some distinct type or element of law; on occasion, even something like natural law. These terms and their most typical translations (RSV) are as follows: *'ēdût* and cognates *'ēdâ* and *tĕ'ûdâ*, "testimony" (Exod 31:18); *piqqûd*, "precept," (Ps 119:15); *miṣwâ*, "commandment" (Deut 8:1, 2); *'imrâ*, "word" (Ps 119:11); *mišpāṭ*, "ordinance" (Exod 21:1) *ḥōq* and *ḥuqqâ*, "custom" (Judg 11:39), "due [of priest]" (Lev 10:13), "statute" (Exod 18:16; Lev 3:17), "fixed order [of nature]" (Jer 31:36), ";obritual;cb ordinance" (Exod 13:10; Ezek 44:5); *dābār*, "word" (Exod 24:3; Amos 3:1), "commandment" (Deut 10:4); *mišmeret*, "charge [assigned duty]" (Deut 11:1); and *dāt* (Persian loan-word in postexilic Hebrew and Aramaic), "law [of the king or of God]" (Ezra 7:26).

A concept basic to OT law, "covenant" (*bĕrît*), receives a separate discussion elsewhere (cf. COVENANT). Israel took over the concept to describe the relationship between itself and God, as well as the resultant obligations, i.e., its law (Exod 19:4-6; 24:3-8).

The Individual Laws. Following Albrecht Alt, biblical scholarship has generally recognized at least two major law types in the Pentateuch: casuistic (or case) law, and *apodictic* law. The distinction is based more on form than on content.

Case law typically takes the form, "If such and such occurs or is done, the one responsible shall be dealt with in such and such a way." Case law considers the circumstances and degrees of responsibility involved in an offense—e.g., the difference between premeditated and unpremeditated murder (Exod 21:12-14), or between an owner who knows and one who does not know that an ox gores (Exod 21:28-32).

Apodictic ("undisputed") law typically takes the form of a categorical directive or prohibition, "You shall . . . " or "You shall not . . . " as in the TEN COMMANDMENTS (Exod 20:2-17). Apodictic law is thought to be distinctive though possibly not unique to Israel in the ancient Near East—whether true analogies occur in certain Hittite treaty texts is debated.

Alt also included among the apodictic laws those that begin with a "whoever" clause, as illustrated by Exod 21:15 ("Whoever strikes his father") or 21:16 ("Whoever kidnaps anyone" [author's translation]), followed by the prescribed penalty. The first two words in English represent a single participial verb form in Hebrew, such laws therefore being categorized as the "participial" type. It has been suggested that this form is in fact closer to case law, since it considers the possible case of violation and prescribes sanctions—unlike laws in the apodictic mode, which simply direct or prohibit and only rarely hint at sanctions (cf. Exod 20:7; 23:7).

The significance of this typological distinction in OT law is disputed. One suggestion is that apodictic law states policy while case law applies it. It is not always clear, however, what apodictic law, if any, might be the particular "policy" behind particular case laws, and certain apodictic examples—e.g., the prohibition against boiling a kid in its mother's milk (Exod 23:19b)—would seem originally to have derived from policy rather than to have articulated any. Another suggestion is that the apodictic form predominates in ritual or cultic law and the casuistic in civil law, but numerous exceptions occur (Exod 22:21; 23:6, 10-11). The distinctiveness of apodictic law may rather lie in its relative simplicity and lack of reference to sanctions—the implication being that, at least in their original cultural milieu, such laws appeared axiomatic and their validity self-evident; to anticipate violations by stipulating punishment would diminish the law's apodictic force. Case law, anticipating cases, demands exercise of discernment and discrimination to determine motive and the degree of guilt (Deut 17:8). Conceivably, then, the two types find some analogy in the modern distinction between "situation ethics" and "ethics of principle." At any rate, the biblical law codes do not appear to rank one type over the other in terms of claim on the hearer or reader.

Another type of law is the ritual malediction or curse (Deut 27:15-26). That a curse replaces more prosaic penalties or punishments implies circumstances in which other means of enforcement are unavailable or violators might avoid detection. A curse was expected to have its effect whether a violator was detected or not.

Law Elsewhere in the Ancient Near East. Archaeological discoveries in the nineteenth and twentieth centuries include a number of legal texts from Near Eastern kingdoms that flourished at various times before and during the period of the Hebrew patriarchs and the rise of Israel. Laws in the Pentateuch and in these recovered texts show some striking points of comparison. The most representative of these law texts, along with other contemporary literature, are brought together in English translation in a now standard anthology edited by James Pritchard. The laws are thought not to have functioned as statutory law for their respective lands or governments but appear rather to be illustrative law, "case studies," to suggest how cases might be handled, not necessarily how they must be.

Resemblances between the ancient Near Eastern laws and OT case law are often close, as in the following examples among many from the great law code of the Old Babylonian King HAMMURABI (1792–1750 B.C.E.): laws on theft (Hammurabi 6-13; Exod 22:1-4); on care of an orchard (Hammurabi 60; Lev 19:23-25); on the goring ox (Hammurabi 250-51; Exod 21:28-32); and on retaliation (Hammurabi 196-201; Exod 21:24).

In view of their shared features the differences between Israel's and its neighbors' law traditions are the more striking. The rarity if not absence of the apodictic form in the extra-biblical texts has been noted. In addition, the variety and diversity of subject matter ranging across the Pentateuchal collections, and the sweep of historical and religious development implied there plainly exceed anything comparable to be found in the extant Near Eastern legal material. The Near Eastern parallels, in their respective prologues—where these survive—invariably portray the king as promulgator and sponsor of the law and its mediator between heaven and the royal realm. The Pentateuch in its present form represents its law with rich symbolism as having been received outside of Israel's land and well before the rise of the kingdom in Israel. After Moses, the priest and not the king remains mediator of the law (Deut 33:10; Mal 2:4-7). The rich component of cultic legislation in Pentateuchal law and the artless way in which narrative and law interact throughout the Pentateuch, resulting in a truly singular literary form, are quite unlike anything in the comparative material cited above. Nevertheless, the similarities between Israel's case law and that of its neighbors indicate the existence of a certain amount of widely shared legal tradition in the Near East upon which Israel drew materially though selectively in the development of its own law.

The Law Collections of the Pentateuch. The laws of the Pentateuch form no monolithic or homogeneous system but are gathered into a number of shorter and longer series or codes, each reflecting its own distinctive cultural and historical context and background ("code" is a somewhat inaccurate designation, but the usage is conventional and retained here for convenience).

(1) "The Decalogue" or "Ten Commandments" (Exod 20:1-17; Deut 5:6-21). "Decalogue," from the Gk., translates literally the Heb. "ten words [*debārîm*]," as in Deut 4:13; 10:4. Its apodictic gravity, simplicity and brevity suggest this law series is the oldest in the Pentateuch, quite possibly going back to Moses.

(2) "The ritual decalogue" (Exod 34:11-26). These are ten apodictic cultic laws (taking vv. 11-16 as prologue), described as the Ten Commandments (Heb. "ten words") written after Moses had destroyed the first tables of stone (Exod 34:1, 27-28 with 32:15-19). Reflecting a settled agricultural background, a relatively well organized cult order, and a monarchic ideology (34:24), these laws may derive from ninth or eighth century Judah.

(3) "Litany of twelve curses" (Deut 27:15–26). Twelve maledictions upon any violator of eleven laws (the twelfth curse recapitulates the whole). An early ceremony associated with ancient Shechem, between Mount Gerizim and Mount Ebal (vv. 12-13), forty-one mi. north of Jerusalem.

(4) "The Covenant Code" (Exod 21:1–23:33; possibly including also 20:22-26). So named from association with the covenant ceremony of Exod 24:3-6 (the titles used for this and the following "codes," respectively, are modern conventions). It is a mixture of cultic and civil law, and of both apodictic and case law, reflecting a background possibly that of the early monarchy. The "angel" (*mal'āk*), literally "messenger," of Exod 23:21, 23, appears to be responsible for enforcement of this

law and may be a priestly figure; cf. the priestly messenger (*mal'āk*) and his instruction (*tôrâ*) in Mal 2:7.

(5) "The Deuteronomic Code" (Deut 12–26). Many of its laws are found in the Covenant Code or elsewhere in the Pentateuch, but much of its content is new. The constraints placed on the king (17:14-20) imply the monarchic period. Other features, including the emphasis on sacrifice only at one central temple (not identified in the code), suggest this as the "book (scroll) of the law" (*sēper hattôrâ*, 2 Kgs 22:8, 11) on which JOSIAH based his religious reform not long before Jerusalem's fall to Babylon (2 Kgs 22:3–23:25). Not part of the Deuteronomic Code itself but preserved in the sermonic introduction to it is the apodictic SHEMA (from the opening Hebrew word, "Hear . . . "), a confession of faith central to Jewish worship down to the present (Deut 6:4-9; cf. Mark 12:29-30).

(6) "The Holiness Code" (Lev 17–26). So named today from its emphasis on holiness as motivation for observing the law (19:2; 20:26), though that is scarcely peculiar to this code (Exod 19:6; Num 16:3; Deut 7:6). On the meaning, in this context, of holiness—a much misunderstood term—cf. the discussion of Lev 11 under "The Priestly Code," below. The laws of this code are grouped together more or less according to subject matter—sacrifice; prohibited sexual practices; what defiles a priest—including physical conditions perceived to disqualify a priest (chap. 21); the liturgical year; and much else.

The proscription in Lev 18 of certain kinds of sexual relations is explained there by ascribing such customs to the non-Israelite peoples among whom Israel once lived or will live (Lev 18:1-2), who are said to defile the land by these practices (Lev 18:24-30), though this begs the question of why they were considered defiling. The stress on holiness in this context (Lev 19:2) gives the most likely clue to the logic at work, analogous to that for the distinction between clean and unclean animals (cf. discussion of Lev 11, below).

For the most part, Lev 19 is concerned with social bonds and with ethics, echoing the Exodus Decalogue tradition (Lev 19:11) and focusing on love for one's neighbor (v. 18) and for the resident alien (v. 33). Even ecology is a concern (vv. 23-25). The Holiness Code is now incorporated into the longer Priestly Code.

(7) "The Priestly Code." Believed to be the work of the latest editors or redactors of what was becoming the Pentateuch in the postexilic community in Babylon, the so-called Priestly Code is scattered in shorter and longer segments through the Pentateuch, though its consistent interest in rite and ritual ("priestly" matters), coupled with a distinctive rhetorical style (fastidious repetition of the same terminology for a given object or idea each time it is mentioned, avoiding synonyms) makes it easy to recognize. Its law sequences belong to a long strand of legal and narrative material (called today the priestly source, or P) traceable intermittently through the first four books of the Pentateuch, beginning with the creation story (Gen 1:1–2:4a) and ending with Num 36.

The laws of the Priestly Code deal with the sanctity of blood as the seat of life, commanded in God's covenant with Noah (Gen 9:1-7; cf. Lev 17:10-11; 19;26); the ritual law of circumcision, commanded in God's covenant with Abraham (Gen 17:1-14); institution of the feasts of PASSOVER and UNLEAVENED BREAD (Exod 12:1-20, 24-27a); cultic instructions concerning the Tabernacle and its furnishings, priestly vestments, the consecration of priests, and related matters (Exod 25–31); and finally, in Exodus, an account of how the preceding cultic instructions, with some elaboration, were carried out (Exod 35–40). Much of this has to be seen as P's idealization of the worship in the wilderness period as a prefiguration of the much later Jerusalem Temple and its liturgy. The law and covenant traditions placed in Genesis likewise must be seen as constructs of the priestly theology rather than as objective history; earlier contributors to what is now Genesis (whatever is not from P) appear to know nothing of them.

The largest sequence of priestly law, including the Holiness Code, occupies all of Leviticus. It is a stately compendium of ritual order dealing with sacrifices, priestly ordination, animals permissible for food, clean and unclean conditions of the body and of human dwellings, and much else. Chap. 16 prescribes Israel's annual DAY OF ATONEMENT (Yom Kippur).

Some law sequences in their present form in Leviticus appear intended less for the instruction of priests than for contemplation by readers, to persuade them of the beauty and drama of the liturgical order and to show that holiness has its liturgical expression. The SACRIFICES in chaps. 1–7, for example, are described in a measured language that lends itself to visualization and contemplation of what takes place. The repetition of certain rubrics at regular intervals is aesthetically satisfying (1:9b with vv. 13b and 17b, or 4:2 with vv. 13, 22, and 27).

The rationale behind the Priestly Code is suggested by the seemingly arcane dietary rules of Lev 11 (cf. Deut 14:3-20) that distinguish between clean and unclean animals (cf. CLEAN AND UNCLEAN). The rules have been explained as early notions of hygiene, as allegories, or simply as preferences of taste; however, their key plausibly is the one stated with the rules themselves: they are for keeping Israel holy (Lev 11:44-45). Clean is associated with the holy, which in turn describes separateness, not in the negative sense of arrogance or hostility but in the positive sense of being distinct, having one's own irreducible identity. Among the animals of Lev 11, the unclean are those of mixed or confused identity: if for example birds typically fly and quadrupeds walk, a quadruped that flies—the bat (v. 19)—is perceived as having a confused identity; it is unclean. The birds listed as unclean (vv. 13-19) swim or dive or in some other way do not behave like birds. The choice of which physical or behavioral details establish identity in a given example may today seem subjective or quaint, but the principle is clear: the animal perceived as "ordered" has its holiness and is clean; the animal having a blurred identity is contaminating and to be avoided (the interpretation follows that of Mary Douglas: cf. bibliography). The ordered character of creation and its creatures is a distinguishing theme in the priestly source, beginning with its highly ritualized account of creation (Gen1:1–2:4a) and ending with its last tradition in the Pentateuch—the ordinance against mixing the tribal inheritances (Num 36:7).

Divine Law in the Old Testament. Ezra's law book—the Pentateuch or a substantial part of it—brought from Babylon to Jerusalem early in the fourth century B.C.E. (Ezra 7:1-6), is described as "the book of the law (*tôrâ*) of Moses which the Lord had given to Israel" (Neh 8:1). It is presented as an object of reverence among the returned exiles in Jerusalem (Neh 8:5-6). Moreover, Artaxerxes, king of Persia, commands and empowers Ezra to "appoint magistrates and judges" and to enforce "the law (*dāt*) of your God and the law (*dāt*) of the king" (Ezra 7:25-26).

The king's equation of divine law and royal law was not in itself unusual; throughout the ancient Near East law was understood to originate with deity. In this general respect the laws of the Pentateuch are not unique; the law "written with the finger of God" (Exod 31:18; Deut 9:10) is an arresting image, but theologically not radical in its time. However, for the Jews as a distinct people, led to reject the polytheisms around them, the relation between their law and that of their immediate neighbors, and between their law and that of the imperial powers to which they were subject, was a perennially pressing problem. This explains the passion for holy separation from the neighboring nations that is behind Ezra's shorter prayer of confession (Ezra 9:10-15), and behind the complaint with which his "great confession" ends (Neh 9:36-37). Fidelity to the law remained a critical issue for Jewish survival in Palestine during the Hellenistic period, a century before the advent of Roman rule (Dan 1–12, esp. chap. 11; 1 Macc 1–4; 2 Macc 3–7).

Therefore, that Israel's law is understood as divine law is taken more or less for granted and is scarcely an issue in the OT. What does matter there deeply is the practical meaning of the Law in terms of Israel's faith and life. How had the Law become known? How could it be known now? Who had access to it? Where was it rightly practiced? Answers to these questions run a gamut in the OT from the symbolic to the literal and from the intimately personal to the forensic and confrontational. For some of its exponents the Law was wholly supernatural; for. others it was present to the human mind and accessible to the understanding.

Early traditions in Exodus, for example, relate how the Law was given to Moses by God, written on two tables of stone. They emphasize the mystery and portent of the encounter but show no great concern for consistency of detail (compare Exod 24:12; 31:18; 32:15-16; 34:1; 34:17-28: the contradictions are apparent). The more literal-minded Deuteronomist presents a thoroughly harmonized and self-consistent narrative, declaring that both sets of tables contained the same Decalogue (Deut 5:6-21; cf. Exod 20:1-17); both were written by God, and the surviving second set is in the ARK of God (Deut 4:13; 5:22; 9:9-10, 17; 10:1-5). The contrast between the impressionism of Exodus and the didacticism of Deuteronomy is evident.

A completely contrasting notion of divine law involves use of the sacred lot to anticipate the outcome of some fateful event (Num 27:21; 1 Sam 14:37; 23:2), or to discover culpability or guilt (Exod 28:30; 1 Sam 14:41). The lot (*gôrāl*; Lev 16:8-10), of which URIM AND THUMMIM (Exod 28:30) was a particular form, presupposed a wholly supernatural and transcendent divine will, discoverable only through circumvention of human and other creaturely factors by casting lots. "The lot (*gôrāl*) is cast into the lap, but the decision (*mišpāt*) is wholly from the Lord" (Prov 16:33). This is the logic behind the Book of Esther, where, though God is never mentioned in the book, Haman's attempt to insure the success of his evil plot against the Jews is foredoomed by his reliance on the lot (Esth 3:7; 9:24). The sacred lot (Gk. *klēros*) appears also in the NT (Acts 1:24-26).

The prophetic literature focuses less on law and laws than on the immediate "word" (*dābār*) of God as the apodictic command for the time and place in which the prophet speaks. Isaiah's "Bind up the testimony (*tĕ'ûdâ*), seal the teaching (*tôrâ*) among my disciples" (Isa 8:16) refers presumably to his own teaching. The prophets can allude to the objective law entrusted to the priests (Hos 4:1-2; Jer 2:8; Malachi, passim) but usually their appeal targets an interior law (*tôrâ*) "written on the heart" (Jer 31:33; Isa 51:7; cf. Mic 6:8). For Elijah, the divine word is described as "a still small voice" (1 Kgs 19:12), though a literal translation is truer to the mystery: "a voice of thin silence" (*qôl dĕmāmâ daqqâ*). For Jeremiah, the prophet is no passive conduit of someone else's words but one from whom is required a discriminating choice of words by which to articulate the divine word: "If you utter what is precious, and not what is worthless, you shall be as my mouth" (Jer 15:19b). Ezekiel suggests the possibility of having to judge the validity even of laws ascribed to God, declaring as the word of God that "I gave them statutes (*ḥuqqîm*) that were not good and ordinances *mišpāṭîm*) by which they could not have life" (Ezek 20:25). Ezekiel's own visionary "ordinances (*ḥuqqôt*) of the temple of the Lord and all its laws (*tôrâ*)" (Ezek 44:5; cf. 40–48), whatever their purpose, never became binding as law.

The OT WISDOM LITERATURE refers often to law (e.g., Prov 28:4) but not explicitly to the Law of Moses. Law appears to belong naturally to the social order (Prov 13:14; Eccl 12:11). Knowledge of it begins in reverence and humility (Prov 1:7). The man Job, a non-Israelite, measures himself by a very high ethic without reference to a particular law tradition (Job 31:1-40). The magisterial Ps 119, meditating on the law of the Lord, does not refer specifically to the Law of Moses nor does it refer necessarily to any written law code; the psalm often suggests a notion of law closer to the wisdom tradition (e.g., vv. 18-19, 27, 64, 89, etc.; cf. bibliography for a relevant study by Jon Levenson). An explicit identification between WISDOM (*ḥokmâ*) and Pentateuchal law (*tôrâ*) is not clearly seen until the deuterocanonical (OT Apocrypha) wisdom literature (Prologue to Sirach; Sir 24:23; Bar 3:9–4:1). The development was anticipated, however, by the Deuteronomist, for whom the Law of Moses replaced the wisdom of the nations (Deut 4:5-8).

Little is said directly in the OT about any role for the king as mediator or promulgator of law, though the Deuteronomic Code is explicit about responsibilities of the king *under* the law (Deut 17:14-20). An editorial theme in Judges, on the other hand, implies that the monarch in Israel was the only reliable guarantor of order (Judg 17:6; 18:1; 19:1; 21:25), and certain prophetic oracles associate the king positively with the law (Isa 9:7; Jer 23:5; Ezek 37:24). A postexilic governor of Judah—Zerubbabel, a descendant of David—seems to have been the focus of such sentiment (Hag 2:23), but he unexplainedly disappears from the scene. 1 Sam 8:11-17 describes as a warning the "ways of the king" (*mišpaṭ hammelek*), that is, the king's prerogatives, reflecting probably the nation's experience under Solomon. The opposition between monarchy and theocracy posited by 1 Sam 8:7 is of course the theological view of a priesthood; such views may account in part for the paucity of connections between king and law in the Pentateuchal tradition, in which priestly editors had the final hand.

Significant references to the law process appear in the Pentateuch and elsewhere in the OT that are not explicitly associated with the Sinai revelation or with deity at all. Examples include Moses as judge and legislator, prior to Sinai (Exod 18:13-27); Joshua as lawgiver (Josh 24:25-26); legal rulings by priests and judges (Deut 17:8-23); Deborah as judge (Judg 4:4-5); the rite (*ḥōq*) remembering Jephthah's daughter (Judg 11:39c-40); and David's booty law (1 Sam 30:24-25). The Pentateuchal stories themselves often turn tacitly on points of law familiar to the culture in which the stories are told: Hagar's surrogate motherhood (Gen 16:2) reflects family-law attested in the Mesopotamian Nuzi tablets (fifteenth century B.C.E.; cf. bibliography). Joseph's brothers deceive Jacob with Joseph's bloodstained coat as evidence both of his death and of their innocence (Gen 37:31-33), following by analogy the prescription of Exod 22:13 [12] (cf. Hammurabi Code, 266).

Taken together, the highly diverse sources and understandings of law in the OT suggest that it be appreciated for the paradox of faith and history that it is. The Law revealed through Moses and the body of law that Israel itself developed over the course of its history are presented in the OT finally not as two realities but one. The Law is described with the language of revelation—the fire, the cloud, the thick darkness, the voice (Deut 5:22)—yet it is preserved and displayed in the OT in such diversity of form and context as to show unmistakably its genesis and long growth in Israel's society. It should be apparent that this carries implications for OT law as a resource for ethics. Because it is historically conditioned, no law or interpretation of law can be considered privileged simply by its being attributed to divine origin. The corollary is that because it is given out of Israel's historic faith, the law can truly function as torah—teaching—an empowering resource instead of an overpowering dictate.

See also COMMANDMENT; LAW IN THE NEW TESTAMENT; LOT/LOTS (CASTING OF) IN THE BIBLE; TEN COMMANDMENTS; TESTIMONY.

Bibliography. A. Alt, "The Origins of Israelite Law," *Essays on Old Testament History and Religion*, trans. R. A. Wilson; H. J. Berman, *Law and Revolution*;

D. Daube, *Studies in Biblical Law*; M. Douglas, "The Abominations of Leviticus," *Purity and Danger*; W. J. Harrelson, "Law in the Old Testament," *IDB*; H. Kleinknecht and W. Gutbrod, "νόμος," *TDNT*; J. D. Levenson, *Sinai and Zion* and "The Sources of Torah: Psalm 119 and the Modes of Revelation in Second Temple Jerusalem," *Ancient Israelite Religion*, ed. P. D. Miller, Jr. et al.; H. P. Nasuti, "Identity, Identification, and Imitation: The Narrative Hermeneutics of Biblical Law," *JLR* 4/1 (1986): 9-23; M. Noth, "The Laws in the Pentateuch: Their Assumption and Meaning," *The Laws in the Pentateuch and Other Studies*, trans. D. R. Ap-Thomas; D. Patrick, *Old Testament Law*; J. J. Petuchowski, "Not By Bread Alone," *Heirs of the Pharisees*, repr. in *Understanding Jewish Theology*, ed. J. Neusner; J. B. Pritchard, ed., *ANET*; G. von Rad, *Old Testament Theology* 1, trans. D. M. G. Stalker; J. A. Sanders, *Torah and Canon*; E. A. Speiser, "New Kirkuk Documents Relating to Family Laws," *AASOR* 10 (1930): 31-33 and *Genesis*, AncB; P. Ricoeur, "Toward a Hermeneutic of the Idea of Revelation," trans. D. Pellauer, *Essays on Biblical Interpretation*. —BRUCE T. DAHLBERG

Moses [MDB 584-87]

•**Moses.** [moh'zis] Moses (Moshe), to whom the Pentateuch is credited, dominates the bulk of the first five books of the Hebrew Bible. His name reflects, like the story of JOSEPH, a genuine but surface knowledge of Egypt for it mirrors names like Thutmose, which means "The god Thut is born". That his name appears to leave out the name of the god born, from an Egyptian perspective, fits the story of this man who seems oblivious of his heritage until he encounters a vibrant god in the barrenness of the wilderness. From the time he meets Yahweh at Sinai in the wilderness, he directs for Yahweh the major events that create and identify the people of Israel. Yet, this central position in Israelite history and tradition does not mean that the historical Moses is near. The advent of modern biblical scholarship—which has recognized that the biblical material is not strictly history, biography or autobiography, but an inspired, creative, and interpretative combination of traditions—has spawned the quests for the people who figured prominently in the biblical story. As a result, the historical Moses proves as elusive as the historical Jesus. Some scholars, e.g., Martin Noth, have argued that Moses was linked to every tradition but rooted in none of them so that Moses seemed a creation, or, at least a later addition. Many, and not conservatives alone, have answered this perspective with skepticism. They agree that Moses has attracted certain traditions and that his role has magnified with time, but there had to be some person who burst into the history of Israel and contributed a surge of creative energy that still excites believers in Judaism, Christianity, and Islam. Moses is witnessed through the thick, opaque glass of the Hebrew Bible; he may never be seen clearly, but his reflection or his outline is there. Many great persons, including Moses and Muhammed, the founder of Islam, assume a great many roles and perform a great many tasks, some in part, some fairly completely, and lay the groundwork for a great many other responsibilities. The result is that, as the endeavor continues, more and more is attributed to them. Just as a seed gives way to the growing and maturing plant, the historical person recedes as that person's significance for an institution develops.

Outline of Moses' Life. According to the biblical narrative, a boy was born among the Hebrew slaves at a time when the Pharaoh wanted every male offspring in that prolific community killed. Moses' family succeeded in hiding him for some time, but circumstances forced them to take a dramatic risk. In a way somewhat reminiscent of the story of Sargon (*ANET*, 119), his mother placed him in a basket calked with pitch and floated him down the Nile near the bathing place of Pharaoh's daughter. The royal lady discovered the child, pitied him, and made arrangements for his care, which included, at the suggestion of Moses' watchful sister, her hiring Moses' mother as the wet nurse. Subsequently, Moses grew up in the house of Pharaoh and enjoyed the privileges there.

One day during an inspection, Moses spotted an Egyptian guard beating one of the slaves. Moses killed the guard. Later, when he realized from the taunt of one of two Hebrew slaves, whom he stopped from fighting, that his murder was public knowledge, he fled to the desert much like Sinuhe, an Egyptian official (*ANET*, 18ff.). Soon, he rescued a group of women victimized by shepherds at a well and subsequently married one of them. He welcomed the opportunity to serve her father, JETHRO (also known as Reuel or Hobab in other traditions), as a shepherd. This second phase of Moses' life moved smoothly until he experienced a THEOPHANY that introduced him to Yahweh. At this meeting, Yahweh convinced a reticent, doubtful Moses to return to Egypt in order to liberate the Hebrew people.

Moses' fear realized itself immediately on his return. The Pharaoh, vehemently opposed to the depletion of his labor force, complicated Moses' task by increasing the work of the slaves. This additional hardship damaged Moses' fragile credibility with his people who complained to him again and again, even later during the wilderness sojourn, when the way proved difficult. Moses therefore attempted to reject his commission. Yahweh comforted and encouraged Moses so that he reaffirmed his commitment. Eventually, after a series of PLAGUES, which exhibited the power of Yahweh but also were met by the intransigence of Pharaoh, and a tenth plague, the death of the first-born of Egypt, Pharaoh freed the Hebrews. Moses led them triumphantly out of Egypt, even though at the last moment Pharaoh tried to reverse his decision. In fact, the decisive act of the exodus occurred at the Reed Sea (RED SEA in many translations) where the Israelites crossed on dry land but the Egyptians perished in the returning waters.

With an urgency that sprang both from his eagerness to weld this people to the God who proved himself so mightily during the Exodus and also from the constant irritation of this demanding and impatient people, Moses quickly brought the Israelites to SINAI (Horeb, PLATES 9, 44). There Moses received the covenant, which would bind this people and this god together forever. Like a magnifying glass, the sojourn at Sinai and the COVENANT concluded there focused the history of Israel into one special moment or one fundamental event that fulfilled some of the history and determined the rest of history for this people; here the Israelites, the descendants of Abraham, and Moses, and Yahweh were moving toward the realization of the ancestral promises and beyond. However, before the covenant was completed but not before the people had endorsed it, they committed apostasy. They claimed that they believed Moses, who had been gone so long atop the mountain, might be dead; accordingly, they constructed a GOLDEN CALF to act as their god. Yahweh almost destroyed the people, but Moses interceded and convinced Yahweh to forgive them.

When the covenant was finally complete, Moses led the people by stages toward the promised land. Moses' administrative skills and his mediating capacities were tested at every point. Several people, e.g., KORAH, and also his brother AARON and his sister MIRIAM, challenged his authority. Ultimately, when the people reached the border of Canaan, the promised land, they decided on the basis of a spy report that the land of Canaan was too difficult to conquer. Moses condemned their faithlessness and instructed them that a whole generation, with the exception of a few faithful persons, must die so that the land of Canaan would be overtaken by persons faithful to Yahweh. Reacting to that news, they made an unsuccessful raid on the Amalekites and the Canaanites. Even Moses could not cross into the promised land, for earlier, at Meribah, he acted contrary to Yahweh's instruction. Indeed, the people could not conquer this land alone, but with Yahweh nothing could stop them.

The BOOK OF DEUTERONOMY relays the last portrait of Moses actively leading the people. The faithless generation lie in their wilderness graves; their children stand on the threshold of the new land. Moses delivers a series of hortatory addresses, reviewing their history, repeating the Law given at Sinai (though there are new sections that complement and extend the legal traditions found in Exodus, Leviticus, and Numbers), and renewing the constant message of Moses—"Choose Yahweh and one chooses life." With these messages, a song of praise, and a blessing, Moses climbs to the top of Mount Pisgah, views Canaan, and dies.

Moses as Deliverer. Though Moses is inextricably linked both to the Exodus from Egypt and the covenant at Sinai, Moses is associated first with the Exodus. He was a party to that oppression and his rescue while a baby from the cruelty of Pharaoh prefigured his role in delivering the Hebrews. Later, as a young man, he would save an Israelite from certain death at the hands of an Egyptian guard and also the daughters of Jethro, the priest of Midian, from the brutality of some shepherds. But the Exodus was the deliverance for which his upbringing in Egypt and his experience in the wilderness had prepared him. His feeling of obligation, his sense of justice, and his relationship with this persuasive and zealous god, Yahweh, spurred him back to the challenges he would find in Egypt. Even though the story of Moses retains his reservations about his qualifications, his story clearly depicts him as a person who was born for such a task, for such a time.

Moses as Wonderworker. Moses was no magician for he lacked the ability to manipulate his surroundings, but he initiated miracles and performed signs that revealed the presence of a powerful God, Yahweh. Before he returned to Egypt, he expressed hesitancy about his credibility before the Israelites. Yahweh fitted him with three wonders—turning his rod into a serpent, altering his hand to one beset by leprosy, and changing some water from the Nile into blood—to testify to Moses' authenticity. When the Egyptian ruler proved obdurate, Yahweh authorized Moses to introduce a series of plagues in order to break Pharaoh's will. The eventual helplessness of the Egyptian magicians, the relentless pressure of the first nine plagues, and the overwhelming sorrow caused by the last plague, broke the Pharaoh's resolve to retain these Hebrew slaves. Yet Moses managed one final miracle, the crossing of the Reed Sea, as he raised his hands to cause the sea to recede so the deliverance "by Yahweh's uplifted hand" could be consummated. On another occasion, Moses would watch another army defeated as he held his arms aloft with the help of Aaron and Hur (Exod 17). Throughout the wilderness sojourn, Moses performed necessary wonders to assure the continued well-being of the people. Yet, all these miracles, with Moses as the agent of their occurrence, pointed to the power and beneficence of Yahweh, the God who claimed that he would be with his people and watch over them.

Moses as Lawgiver. The connection between Moses and the Law (TORAH) recorded in the Hebrew Bible derives from the role of Moses played in forging a covenant between the God of the Exodus and the liberated people. Moses, attentive to the fear and the sense of unworthiness felt by the people, climbed to the top of Sinai, received the stipulations of the covenant between Yahweh and Israel, and delivered them to the people. This law he received, which became known as the written Law of Moses, continued to grow in the traditions so that several bodies of law exist in the confines of the Hebrew Bible. Eventually, a new corpus was accepted as binding as well—the oral Law of Moses included in the Talmud. Just as the miracles were not actually the miracles of Moses, the Law was the Law revealed by Yahweh the Lawgiver. But Moses stands forever in the Hebrew Bible and in sculpted visions as the person holding the ten words (commandments). Covenants that bind two persons together are known by the privileges and responsibilities required of the two parties. Moses, the person who could safely go up to the top of Sinai, received the stipulations of the covenant between Yahweh and Israel and delivered them to the people.

Moses as Intercessor/Mediator. Moses did not possess a natural talent for this task; he slowly developed his skills. His first attempt to mediate between a harsh Egyptian guard and a helpless slave failed. Shortly afterward, his effort to reconcile one Hebrew with another led ultimately to Moses' flight from Egypt, not to a resolution of the argument. Perhaps in the desert he learned to listen, to observe, and to reflect, so that at the burning bush he began to understand how to balance commitment with personal gifts. Up to this point, his story greatly parallels that of Joseph, who lived a privileged life as a youth. His brothers became so jealous that they almost killed him and eventually, sold him into slavery. During that time of forced exile from his family, Joseph learned from his struggles. So Moses, too, learned during his exile from home the skills for mediation.

Though he tried to reason with the Pharaoh upon his return to Egypt in order to secure the freedom of the Hebrew slaves, Moses' arbitration was doomed from the beginning. The awesome power of Yahweh served as the point of that episode and not the insightful intercession of Moses. The supreme example of Moses' mediation surfaces in Exod 32–34. While Moses was receiving the Law on MOUNT SINAI, the people built a golden calf. Yahweh immediately reacted and informed Moses, in a manner reminiscent of the time of Noah, that his stubborn, faithless people would be destroyed and Moses would be the beginning of a new nation. Moses dissuaded Yahweh by musing on the possible reaction of the Egyptians to this act and by referring to the covenant with Abraham, Isaac, and Jacob (here called Israel). Yet, even when Yahweh changed his intention, i.e., repented of the evil, he informed Moses that an angel would be leading them. Moses realized that there must be consequences for this idolatrous act. In a manner resembling the practices associated with holy warfare and the punishment meted out to Achan at Jericho (Josh 7), he commissioned the LEVITES to go through the camp to punish the camp. In addition, a plague affected the rest of the people.

Moses was still troubled by Yahweh's distancing himself from the people. He continued to argue with God; Moses did not want to be the start of a new people and he did not want to go any farther if Yahweh was not in their midst, or totally committed to them. Moses' argument convinced Yahweh and he pledged his presence. Subsequently, Moses asked to see Yahweh's face, but Yahweh declined; he hid Moses in the cleft of the rock to protect his life and allowed Moses to see his back.

The mediation continued as Moses climbed back up to the top of Sinai; the broken treaty had to be restored. When he returned, his face, absolutely radiant from the communion with Yahweh, had to be veiled in the presence of the people. Moses reported the stipulations, including the instructions for the implementation of the wilderness cult, to the people and they began to enforce them. Unfortunately, along with the reprieve of the people, this mediation marked the loss of an originally privileged relationship that was forever lost; the covenant had been breached but repaired by means of a fervent and fearless mediator. Furthermore, a paradigm of atonement lay in this lengthy account.

Moses continued this role throughout his tenure as leader. Whenever the people became disgruntled, they would long for Egypt. Yahweh's natural response would be disgust, e.g., when Yahweh sent fiery serpents to afflict the people (Num 21:4ff.). Moses stood always in the middle, working on a solution that allowed for justice and mercy. On another occasion following the report of the spies sent to view Canaan, the people were overcome with doubt and fear (Num 14). They wished to return to Egypt; Yahweh wished to destroy them there. Moses interceded for the people. Yahweh did not destroy them, but he promised that a new generation would conquer the land. Moreover, when the people did try to conquer the land, Yahweh absented himself from the battle, so that they met defeat. According to one tradition, during one of these incidents Moses' anger overcame him. He struck a rock to bring water to the people, but this act contradicted Yahweh's instructions (Num 20:10ff.). For that unnecessary act, Yahweh barred Moses from the promised land. Even Yahweh's mediator had to stay within certain bounds. However, a tradition reflected in Deut 3:26 interpreted Moses' exclusion as the supreme selfless act of a mediator; Moses stayed behind so that the people who tried Yahweh at every step of the way could enter the land.

Moses' ability to supplicate his God and to mete out the necessary punishment secured his reputation as a mediator. Later generations of storytellers would allude to his skill and commitment. The story of ELIJAH casts a negative judgment on the prophet as a mediator; he travels to Horeb not to argue for his people, sinful though they be, but to impress Yahweh with his own righteousness (I Kgs 19:14). Yahweh exposes Elijah's arrogance and strips him of his responsibility. JEREMIAH, in order to underscore the absolute depravity of his audience, declares that not even Moses could convince Yahweh to forgive them (Jer 15:1).

Moses as Administrator. When Moses was not overseeing the extraordinary events of the Exodus, receiving the covenant, or meeting the persistent demands of the people, he was managing their everyday existence. In particular, with a group this large, he had to administer justice, e.g., the case of the daughters of Zelophehad (Num 27:1ff.) and periodically assess the people by means of a census (Num 1:1ff.). However, the true mark of his administrative skill lay in his ability to take advice and to implement it. Soon after the Exodus, Jethro, Moses' father-in-law, witnessed the enormity of Moses' task (Exod 18:13ff.). He suggested that Moses appoint persons to assist him. Moses accepted this suggestion and delegated his authority so that the people relied on a hierarchy of leaders, with Moses' attention directed only to the most pressing issues. Later, Moses appointed seventy elders who received a portion of the spirit that rested upon Moses (Num 11). They relieved Moses of a part of the responsibility and bother of the Hebrew people.

As administrator, Moses was not spared the constant complaints of the people. Neither was he spared the sporadic challenges to his authority. He confronted his brother Aaron and his sister Miriam when they spoke against him (Num 12). He subsequently interceded on Miriam's behalf when she was afflicted with leprosy as a punishment. Moses swiftly handled the untoward cultic behavior of Nadab and Abihu (Lev 10), just as he would later manage the insolence of Korah, Dathan and Abiram (Num 16). However, Moses correctly praised the behavior of Eldad and Medad; their acts exhibited the spirit of Yahweh, not arrogance. Though on many occasions Moses would have given up his responsibility readily, obligated by the divine commission, he continued with his task as an able administrator who dealt speedily with matters that warranted dispatch and more slowly with matters of concern; he also delegated authority when necessary, so that all matters received due consideration.

Moses as Military commander. Moses never distinguished himself as a military leader like JOSHUA; his work remained preliminary to the CONQUEST OF CANAAN. Yet, he did preside over the battles before the Hebrews entered into the promised land. While Joshua fought Amalek with the warriors of Israel, Moses stood on the top of the hill (Exod 17:8ff.). If his hands were lifted, symbolic of the uplifted hand of Yahweh who delivered his people, the people prevailed; if his hands dropped, the enemies prevailed. With the help of Aaron and Hur, Moses kept his hands raised until Joshua secured the victory. Furthermore, Moses led the people in their battles against Sihon, the king of the Amorites, and against the Midianites. The only skirmish that Moses did not oversee was the ill-fated clash with the Canaanites that the people mounted after Moses berated them for their lack of faith (Num 14:40ff.).

Moses as Priest. Similarly, Moses was not a priest but he received the instructions about the priesthood in his stint upon Sinai. His brother Aaron was the first priest and the beginning of the priestly succession. For as long as Moses led the people, he assisted the priesthood by securing all the materials for the construction of their mobile cult and completing the instructions given to him. Without the law from Sinai and Moses' regimented implementation, the cult would have foundered from the first.

Moses as Prophet. Though prophecy was linked closely with the period and the institution of monarchy, Moses was considered the archetype of the PROPHET. His call narrative contained the elements of divine commission and human hesitation. After his acceptance of his task, he acted courageously and relied almost completely upon Yahweh. He certainly performed signs and wonders, which accomplished his task and testified to the redemptive presence of Yahweh. However, tradition elevated Moses more than any other prophet, for his role was pivotal in the formation of Israel. This perspective was reflected particularly in the narrative concerning the rebellion of Aaron and Miriam. Prophets receive their messages in dreams and visions, but Moses spoke with Yahweh face to face. In another text, Moses' special position lent weight to the criteria for true and false prophecy. Moses was regarded as the standard for prophecy even though he lived long before the line of prophets remembered in the Hebrew Bible; he set up the standard for prophecy by the life he lived for Yahweh and by means of the covenant law he received from Yahweh (cf. Deut 18:15-16; 34:10-12).

Moses as Preacher. The Book of Deuteronomy contains the work of a group that creatively exhorted the people. They picked up the sense of Moses and renewed his message to their contemporaries. They placed Moses at the threshold of a land he would never enter, with the children of the people he had led from slavery to freedom, from insecurity to covenant. There, on that boundary, Moses reviewed their history, restated the covenant stipulations, and recalled the people to their covenant obligations. The hortatory style is unmistakable; the message is clear.

Moses urged the people to choose obedience to Yahweh, even in the face of supreme danger, and thereby to choose life. He did not hesitate to picture the other alternative, rebellion, or disobedience, and its consequence, death, but his definite call addressed a people who could choose to obey and to make a difference in their personal and national life.

Moses as Author. Tradition claims that Moses wrote the entire Pentateuch. Though historical-critical work indicated the impossibility of that feat, Moses' role in the eventual creation of the Pentateuch remains undisputed. His life and work served as fertile soil in which traditions could grow and multiply. His historic place and vision allowed his authority to be borrowed again and again. The Book of Deuteronomy contains more than his sermons; Deuteronomy contains a song and a blessing, creating other contexts from which Moses, through other inspired authors, continued to speak.

Moses' continuing high place in the biblical tradition is reflected in later writings. Among these are the oral law of Moses, which in contained in the Talmud; the pseudepigraphical writing *The Testament of Moses*, which recounts the events of the end of time; the Gospel of Matthew, which grants a Mosaic cast to the life of Jesus in order to underscore the authority of Jesus' teachings leading to the fulfillment of the law of Moses; Paul's use of the Torah and the imagery surrounding Moses to address the issue of the Jews' place in God's plan (Rom 10:5ff.) or to argue for the preeminence of Christian truth (2 Cor 3:12ff.); the Book of Hebrews, which lists Moses among the truly faithful; and the Islamic belief that Moses prophesied the coming of Muhammed, who was to be another great man of faith like Moses.

Moses as Servant of Yahweh. This role includes all the rest and best describes Moses (Exod 14:31). Whether Moses was releasing the plagues of Egypt, receiving the Law upon Sinai, interceding for the people before an angry deity, delivering the judgment for the sins of the people, dealing with the newest complaint of the assembled people, or addressing the people who stood on the border of their new land, Moses performed for Yahweh. What he did, he did for the greater glory of Yahweh so that the promises to Abraham, Isaac, and Jacob could finally be realized. What he accomplished, he accomplished at the request of Yahweh, for Yahweh. This resolve—to point to God rather than the accomplishments of humans—was reflected in the tradition that recorded the poignant final episode of Moses' life. Yahweh buried Moses in an unspecified place (Deut 34:5ff.); his grave could never become a place of pilgrimage. Moses served his God so that Yahweh's will could be done and Yahweh's deeds could be praised. That accomplishment remains the true legacy of this servant; through his life the splendor of Yahweh, his overlord, is revealed.

See also EXODUS, BOOK OF; PLAGUES; REDSEA/REED SEA.

Bibliography. M. Buber, *Moses*; B. S. Childs, *The Book of Exodus*, OTL; W. Harrelson, *The Ten Commandments and Human Rights*; J. P. Hyatt, *Exodus*; M. Noth, *Exodus, A Commentary*, OTL; J. B. Pritchard, ed., *ANET*; G. von Rad, *Moses*; M. Walzer, *Exodus and Revolution*. —RUSSEL I. GREGORY

Religion of Israel [MDB 742-44]

•**Religion of Israel.** ISRAEL referred initially to the people covenantally bound to Yahweh at Sinai. Later, during the period of kingship, it designated a political as well as a religious entity. When the nation split, the North retained the name while the South chose to be called by the name of its principal tribe, Judah. The writers of the biblical materials, however, continued to use "Israel" to denote all of the people of God.

Some modern scholars use the term "Yahwism" to refer to the religion of Israel prior to the time of the Exile. It was characterized by monolatry (the worship of only one god while not denying the existence of other gods, cf. henotheism); a prophetic movement that articulated and criticized the people's faith and their religious practices; and a priesthood that was available throughout the country. Judaism, as distinct from "Yahwism," valued the TORAH, rejected human kingship, allocated greater authority to the priests, and believed in the existence of only one god—MONOTHEISM. A sense of universalism also characterized Judaism.

The Sinai Covenant (ca. 1290 B.C.E.) bound the Hebrew people via a suzerainty covenant to Yahweh, a deity perhaps earliest understood as a god of war who was manifested in fire and storm, but who became known supremely through divine activity in historical events. On the basis of deeds done for Israel (Exod 20:2), Yahweh offered the Hebrews COVENANT. Hearing the stipulations, in the form of absolute demands, they embraced the covenant (Exod 24) and obligated themselves to this god. Although those stipulations are now lost to us, they may have included the Decalogue (as in Exod 20; Deut 5), the Covenant Code (Exod 20:22–23:33), and the Holiness Code (Lev 17–26). From this point on Israel's leaders, particularly the prophets, understood Israel's history to be shaped by God (Yahweh) who revealed himself through the covenant.

The patriarchs (Gen 12–50) embody Israel's prehistory, a period that could not have been precisely known at the time of the literary formulation of the text because within the material are views of God's covenant and of history and justice that reflect later developments of thought. Archaeologists confirm the milieu but not the individuals. The narrative, therefore, records a precursor to historical reality that nonetheless cannot be summarily dismissed.

Similarly, the primeval history (Gen 1–11) does not record historical data; rather, it conveys faith's perception of Yahweh's relationship to the beginnings of both cosmos and humankind. Embedded are understandings about God, human beings, and the mutual responsibility of each. Both the primeval history and the patriarchal narratives are important because they introduce Yahweh's relationship to Israel.

The preexilic era (1290–598/7 B.C.E.) begins with Israel's entrance into CANAAN and the tribal confederacy, an autonomous collection of tribes loosely bound around the Tabernacle, the Ark of the Covenant, and Yahweh's kingship. Judges were empowered by Yahweh with the Spirit of God. Holy war was practiced by Israel, as it was by the surrounding nations.

HOLY WAR ceased with the first fully established monarchy, i.e., with David. Following David's kingdom building, SOLOMON erected the Jerusalem Temple. This structure, serviced by the threefold lineage priesthoods of AARON, LEVI, and ZADOK, increasingly dominated Israel's cultic life. Inevitably the emphasis moved from the earlier covenantal obligations to national allegiance.

During the divided monarchy (922–722/1 B.C.E. in Israel; 922–587/6 in Judah), the prophets, foreshadowed especially by NATHAN during David's reign, addressed a myriad of national and cultic issues. ELIJAH (ninth century) focused upon the separation of Yahwism and Baalism. The classical eighth-century prophets, AMOS and HOSEA in Israel emphasized social justice and covenant fidelity, respectively, while in Judah ISAIAH stressed faith in the holiness of Yahweh. MICAH, no less a proclaimer of judgment than his contemporaries, summarized and emphasized the teachings of his three prophetic peers (Mic 6:1- 8).

JEREMIAH (seventh century) stressed covenantal obligation and proper motivation (Jer 31:31-34). Jeremiah's prophetic ministry was juxtaposed with the political-religious activity of King JOSIAH (640–609 B.C.E.). These were preceded by an aborted reform movement by HEZEKIAH (715–687 B.C.E.) and the deuteronomic reformation (initiated in 621 B.C.E.), which emphasized a recovery of Mosaic covenantal thought and centralizing sacrificial worship in the Temple.

In the preexilic period, a struggle ensued between zealous Yahwists and Baalists. This religious and cultural struggle significantly influenced Yahwism-Judaism, especially in terms of how God was to be understood and worshiped, and even with regard to Yahwism-Judaism's aniconic concerns.

Tragedy befell Judah in 598/7 B.C.E. when Babylonia conquered Jerusalem, initiating the Babylonian EXILE (598/7–539 B.C.E.). During this period EZEKIEL and Deutero-Isaiah (Isa 40–55) spoke, with the latter responsible for the first explicit literary statement of monotheism (cf. Isa 44:6) and the haunting servant poems (Isa 42:1-4; 49:1-6; 50:4-11; 52:13-53:12) as the explanation of the way Yahweh would triumph over evil through his servant, Israel (Isa 49:3). During the Exile the SYNAGOGUE emerged and literature flourished; most of the Torah, the Deuteronomic history, and presumably the words of the preexilic prophets were recorded. The Torah's development permits the affirmation that the seed of Judaism had emerged.

Persia's conquest of Babylon (539 B.C.E.) concluded the Exile, and some captives returned to Judah, albeit under Persian rule. Under Persian domination HAGGAI and ZECHARIAH supervised the rebuilding of the Temple (520–515 B.C.E.), and NEHEMIAH was appointed governor of Judah. Under Nehemiah's leadership the walls of Jerusalem were repaired. Around 400 B.C.E. (or perhaps some decades earlier) the scribe EZRA came to Jerusalem and attempted to focus all of life around the Torah.

The domination of ALEXANDER the Great (d. 323 B.C.E.) and his successors was terminated with the Maccabean Revolt (Temple purification, 165 B.C.E.). Judaism's development was marked by diversity. The Psalter was formulated alongside the WISDOM LITERATURE. Often conflicting thought patterns emerged, such as the struggle between particularism (ESTHER) and universalism (RUTH and JONAH) and the inherent conflict between angelology and demonology. Ultimately apocalypticism emerged, remaining a viable movement until roughly 200 C.E. Apocalypticism gave hope to a persecuted community through cryptic symbolism and imagery and precipitated renewed emphasis upon a messianism no longer restricted to a person but including the renewal of nature, the rejuvenation of humanity, the resurrection of the faithful, and the restoration of elements traditionally at enmity into peaceful coexistence.

What it meant to be a Jew became increasingly important as the people scattered. God's universal concern was accepted, and the gift of Torah was acknowledged as ubiquitous for all people.

Israel was scarcely a millennium removed from its Sinaitic experience as the canonical period closed, but light years removed in terms of its relationship to God, humankind, and the world. Israel's religion is truly a rich tapestry, the beginning of which we can hardly discern, the conclusion of which continually pulls us onward.

See also FAITH AND FAITHLESSNESS; GOD; THEOLOGY OF THE OLD TESTAMENT.

Bibliography. F. Eakin, Jr., *The Religion and Culture of Israel*; G. Fohrer, *History of Israelite Religion*, trans. D. Green; W. Harrelson, *From Fertility Cult to Worship*; Y. Kaufmann, *The Religion of Israel*, trans. and abridged M. Greenberg; H.-J. Kraus, *Worship in Israel*; G. E. Mendenhall, *Law and Covenant in Israel and the Ancient Near East*; J. Muilenburg, "The History of the Religion of Israel," *IB*; J. Pedersen, *Israel: Its Life and Culture*; H. Ringgren, *Israelite Religion*; H. H. Rowley, *Worship in Ancient Israel*; Th. Vriezen, *The Religion of Ancient Israel*.

—FRANK E. EAKIN, JR.

Ten Commandments [MDB 883-85]

•**Ten Commandments.** The religious and moral guidelines received by MOSES atop Mount Sinai, recorded in slightly differing forms in their two listings in the Hebrew Bible (Exod 20:2-17; Deut 5:6-21). This short, pithy list of prohibitions and positive commandments sums up many of the requirements of Israelite faith in God. The text is quoted in part in the NT (Matt 19:16-22; Mark 10:17-22; Luke 18:18-30) and in a few places in the OT (Hos 4:2; Ps 81:9 [Heb: 81:10]). The commandments are not LAW in the full sense of the term, for they are not a criminal code or a collection of precedents to guide the conduct of judges and elders, as are many of the legal collections found elsewhere in the OT (Exod 21-23; Deut 12-26, etc.). They are rather the background and foundation of Israelite law.

Origin. The commandments are said to have been received directly from God by Moses. Their contents are not unique to Israel, although two of the commandments lack any clear parallel in the ancient world (the commandment against image making and the commandment to observe the SABBATH). But there is nothing closely akin to this collection as a collection, presented as absolute demand from the deity, and requiring unswerving obedience by every individual Israelite as well as by the community as a whole.

Nothing in the original short form of the commandments, which can be recovered with fair confidence, requires a date later than the time of Moses. But most scholars hold that the earliest likely date is the time of the organizing of the life of the tribes in Canaan under JOSHUA or his successors (1200–1100 B.C.E.). Many prefer a date at the time of the kingship over North Israel and Judah (tenth or ninth century B.C.E.).

Form. The commandments, without the opening prologue, "I am the Lord your God who brought you out of the land of Egypt, out of the house of slavery," have the form of an opening prohibition followed by a verb and concluding with an object: "You shall not have any other Gods besides me"; "you shall not bear false witness." Some of the commandments are expanded at a later time, giving explanations of just what the commandment in question means. Others are shortened so as to consist of the negation plus a single verb, but no object: "You shall not kill." "You shall not commit adultery." "You shall not steal." This process of addition and contraction probably extended over many years. In the process, a different explanation was offered in Deut 5:12-15 for the observance of the Sabbath than is found in Exod 20:8-11. DEUTERONOMY stresses the need that human beings and animals have for rest, physical rest from labors, while Exodus puts the emphasis upon God's having observed the Sabbath rest at the time of creation (Gen 2:1-3).

Whether the Ten Commandments were shaped through use in the home and in the larger family units or were developed for regular recitation at the centers of religious life in early Israel remains a debated question. In all likelihood, both the public use of the commandments in connection with acts of worship and their local and family use contributed to their shape and to the changes that occurred over time.

Numbering. There is great diversity in the numbering of the commandments. The diversity arises largely as a result of different ways of numbering the commandment to worship no other god or gods and the commandment to make no carved IMAGES. The Jewish, Roman Catholic, and Lutheran traditions make a single commandment of these, while Orthodox and Reformed traditions number them as two. The commandment against coveting is sometimes divided into two commandments in order to retain the number ten. Jewish tradition has numbered as the first commandment the assertion, "I am the Lord your God [or "I the Lord am your God"] who brought you out of the land of Egypt, out of the house of slavery" (or "bondage"), and does not divide the commandment against coveting.

Contents. The numbering used here follows Orthodox and Reformed tradition. The commandments may be divided into four groups: God's absolute demands (commandments 1, 2, 3, against the worship of other gods, against IDOLATRY, and against the misuse of the divine name); God's basic institutions (commandments 4 and 5, against the misuse of the Sabbath and the mistreatment of parents); fundamental personal demands (commandments 6 and 7, against killing and adultery); and fundamental social demands (commandments 8, 9, and 10, against stealing, bearing false witness, and coveting). A few comments follow on each of these groupings.

God's Absolute Demands. Ancient Near Eastern religious communities were familiar with the notion of a highest deity, the god who had the dominant place in the pantheon. The powers of the lesser gods were claimed by this highest god, according to texts that have survived, showing that while there was not MONOTHEISM in most of these societies, there was clearly a recognition that not all gods had the same claim on the life of the worshiping community or the individual. But in Israel the claim was an exclusive one: the deity Yahweh, Israel's God, was not to have any rivals at all.

This demand for the worship of one unique God no doubt allowed for the fact that there were other deities worshiped in the land, deities whose powers seemed real enough. But Israel was to demonstrate loyalty to the one God, the deity who brought the people from the land of Egypt, led them through the wilderness, and eventually brought them into possession of the land that God was giving them.

Most striking in this commandment is the insistence that there is a unitary divine being; deity is not divided. There is God, and there are the creations of God—and there are no other kinds of entity to be found in the whole of the creation. In time, this form of monotheism developed in Israel and challenged the prevailing notion of dark powers that threatened the creation and all its creatures, including the human community. No demons or devils existed apart from such powers as God the Creator had called into being. Such powers might not be doing God's bidding, but they were still creatures of God, not some divine or demonic beings outside the range of God's control.

The commandment against idolatry probably stems from the recognition that nothing in the creation was able adequately to represent the deity, the unique creator of all that had being. Only the human being, created in the divine image, could be a kind of representation of God, sharing responsibility with God for the creation, seeing to its needs, serving as God's agent. The Israelites must surely have known that representations of the gods were not necessarily understood as identical with those deities. Even so, such representations were capable of creating the illusion in the community of Israel that Yahweh could be manipulated for the community's or the individual's good, and that was an unacceptable view for Israel's theological thought.

The third commandment is also striking. It rules out using God's name with the intention of forcing God's hand. Ancient Israel recognized that the power to pronounce God's name, for blessing or for cursing, was a weighty power. The use of God's name to do violence to others or to further one's own personal ends was ruled out by this commandment. It is clear that such a commandment is always of great value in any time or place. This is a central understanding of Judaism and of Christianity.

God's Basic Institutions. The commandment to observe the Sabbath is unique in Israel. The origin of the Sabbath remains obscure. It was not a day of ill omen but a day of rest and rejoicing in the Lord; thus, it cannot be derived directly from days of ill omen known from Babylonia. It did not fall on the phases of the moon, and thus cannot be related to the moon month in any direct way. It seems not to have had any connection with market days in the ancient world, for there is no evidence that these occurred with this seven-day regularity. The number seven is prominent in the festival life of ancient Near Eastern peoples; thus it may be that seven-day festivities and seven-week intervals between festivities played some part in the development of the Sabbath.

Striking indeed is the demand that every seventh day the community of Israel is to cease from its labors and rest. No positive requirements are set for the Sabbath; the only demand is that one stop doing what one normally does and rest. Rest is as much a demand of God as is work; alternation between work and rest gives meaning and depth to both.

The commandment to honor one's parents has in view primarily one's aged parents. The commandment makes clear again that human life consists of more than productive labor. When parents are too old to be productive members of the community, the meaning of their life has not ceased. They are to be honored and respected. Ancient Israel knew the conflicts that develop between the generations, the struggle that the young have in claiming a place among the adults and the struggle that the elderly have in making way for the adults who come behind them. This commandment underscores the requirement that the life of parents be respected at all levels of their existence.

God's Fundamental Personal Demands. Human beings are not to take human life, for life belongs to God. Gen 9:6 underscores the point, even if that text knows no other way to assure that human life be respected than to say that if a human being sheds the blood of another, the killer's own life is forfeited. The verb used in the sixth commandment, $r\d{s}h$, does not mean "murder" in the strict sense, but it does point to acts of homicide outside the context of accidental killing or the taking of human life allowed in ancient Israelite law.

This commandment against willful homicide is of enormous importance for the moral life, for it flatly rules out the "right" of any person to take the life of another human being. Life belongs to God, and God will see to the preservation of life and to its enhancement. Human beings are charged to do the same.

The commandment against ADULTERY can best be understood as a prohibition of sexual violence—whether it be violence of the sort called rape or violence against the institution of the family. In ancient Israel there was a double standard in sexual matters; married men committed adultery when they had sexual relations with the wife of another man, while a married woman was guilty of adultery if she had relations with anyone other than her husband. The young woman was to refrain from sexual relations until the time of her betrothal and/or marriage. More sexual license was tolerated among young men, it seems, although the wisdom literature is full of warnings against their consorting with loose women.

Jesus reminds his hearers that behind the act of adultery is lust in the heart. The act of adultery harms more persons, but the individual is already caught up in the damage that adultery brings when lust begins to take over and threatens to lead to unfaithfulness. And the apostle Paul flatly declares that relations with a prostitute, like any other sexual union, creates a unity of one flesh (1 Cor 6:15-20). Thus there is no such thing as casual sex for Paul. The double standard disappears with such an assertion as that.

God's Fundamental Social Demands. The last three commandments are concerned with the life of the community. The commandment against stealing had a special poignancy in a time when most of the population had very few goods. The loss of a knife in ancient Israel would have been a very severe loss, for with the large knife made of iron one would chop and shape wood, butcher farm animals, do other household tasks, and also wage war—using the knife as one's sword. Life extended into the goods of the family. This commandment is not talking about the poor person's taking some morsel of food from the crop of the wealthy; the poor were to be permitted to gather up a bit of food to stay their hunger. But for ancient Israel, the protection of life required also that property be protected; no social order was possible otherwise.

Similarly, bearing false witness against one's neighbor meant primarily giving false testimony before a judge or before the elders acting as judges. It was not an invitation to people to do harm by spreading even true derogatory tidbits about a neighbor. The community's stability and health demanded that the courts not be corrupted by the telling of lies or the use of bribes to get witnesses to perjure themselves.

Finally, the commandment against coveting seeks to get at the will, the disposition of persons, as well as at their deeds. The word translated "to covet," *hāmad*, sometimes means not only to have an inordinate desire for something but to take steps to get the desired thing. But not always does the word have that active a meaning. It can also simply refer to the hankering for the life or the goods of someone else. In Deut 5:21 a parallel word is also used, "to desire" (Heb. *'āwâ*), showing that it is basically a commandment against being eaten up with the desire for what one does not have. In contemporary affluent societies the commandment would perhaps best refer to that insatiable longing for more and more—beyond any human need.

Influence. The Ten Commandments have had an enormous influence on Western societies, and indeed on virtually the whole of civilization. Other societies have equivalent summary codes of conduct, but this concise drawing together of commandments that tie together God's exclusive claim upon the community and its individuals with God's insistence that certain forms of conduct are ruled out in principle, not to be done under any circumstances, has a distinctive character. The commandments were surely developed for the life of the people of Israel, but there is nothing in them that restricts them to Israel alone.

The commandments also demand that the community define just what these prohibitions mean and aim at. What is justifiable homicide? When has the Sabbath been violated? When have aged parents been mistreated? The whole system of positive law and of the administration of justice has to be developed. But certain absolute demands are laid upon the community and not open to challenge. Not everything is permitted to human beings. Human freedom is defined for ancient Israel and for early Christianity in part at least in relation to these prohibitions given by God.

See also ETHICS IN THE OLD TESTAMENT; IDOLATRY; LAW IN THE OLD TESTAMENT; SABBATH; TORAH.

Bibliography. A. Alt, *Essays on Old Testament History and Religion*; B. F. Childs, *Exodus. A Commentary*; W. Harrelson, *The Ten Commandments and Human Rights*; E. Nielsen, *The Ten Commandments in New Perspective*.

—WALTER HARRELSON

Torah [MDB 926-27]

•**Torah.** [toh'ruh] Heb. *tôrâ*, "teaching," "instruction," "revelation." God's instruction or revelation to Israel through MOSES at SINAI, comprising the Pentateuch or "Five Books of Moses" (first five books of the OT). "Torah" distinguishes this first division of the Hebrew scriptures from the other two, titled in Hebrew, respectively, Nevi'im (*nebî'îm*, Prophets) and Kethuvim (*kêtûbîm*, Writings). From the first letters of these three Heb. words the rabbis derived the acronym *TaNaK* (*Tanakh*) to represent the entire Hebrew canon. The following comments concern Torah as revelation. On the etymology of *tôrâ*, its multiple meanings, and the particular translation of it as "law" (though in a broader sense than "laws").

Early in postbiblical Judaism the revelation to Moses came to be thought of as having included within it, at the time it was first given, "everything that will ever be legitimately offered to interpret its meaning" (G. Scholem). In this conception, the Torah was given in two forms, the written Torah and the oral Torah. The former is the text of the Pentateuch; the latter includes the Mishnah, Talmud, Midrash compilations and related texts that record originally oral rabbinical commentary on the written Torah. As interpretation, oral torah is still evolving. Rabbinical doctrine holds that such commentary was handed down by memory from Moses through a succession of authorities to the earliest rabbis (*'Abot* 1:1). Practically, the notion of a dual Torah recognizes that no text is meaningful or effective without authoritative, i.e., knowledgeable, interpretation.

It is usually said that interpretation began to grow in importance when EZRA brought the written Pentateuch, or a substantial part of it, from Babylon to postexilic Jerusalem (Neh 8:1-8), inaugurating a new chapter in Judaism in which the sacred text became a focus of worship. This view holds that the farther the living and changing community became distanced in time and culture from the fixing of the revelation in writing, the more necessary and complex became the task of interpretation. However, recent studies of the postexilic biblical literature, especially of such Psalms as 19 and 119, suggest that celebration of the Law (*tôrâ*) in these works does not necessarily have in view either a written law or the revelation through Moses, but a divine Law more immediately present and generally accessible in the worshiping community. The notion of oral Torah is seen thus to have antecedents historically in Israel that developed alongside of and even earlier than the developing written Torah. The Pentateuch, of course, contains within itself relatively late traditions that can be seen to comment on or interpret earlier traditions also preserved there.

The rabbinical tradition that all of the Pentateuch was revealed to Moses on Mount Sinai, and that he wrote all of it down (hence, the "Five Books of Moses"), is usually said to be a claim not made in the Pentateuch itself. However, if one should hold a historically pre-Enlightenment view that the Pentateuch is of a piece, and if one reads back into the Pentateuch a later generation's usage equating Torah with the Pentateuch, then Deut 31:9, "Moses wrote this Law [*tôrâ*]," might understandably be construed as just such a claim (cf. Exod 24:4). There is of course abundant empirical evidence in the Pentateuch itself for concluding that it is a composite work, the greatest part of which must be later than Moses.

See also LAW IN THE OT.

Bibliography. J. D. Levenson, "The Sources of Torah: Psalm 119 and the Modes of Revelation in Second Temple Jerusalem," *Ancient Israelite Religion*, ed. P. D. Miller, Jr. et al.; J. Neusner, *The Oral Torah*; G. G. Scholem, "Tradition and Commentary as Religious Categories in Judaism," *Jud* 15/1 (1966): 23-39.

—BRUCE T. DAHLBERG

Genesis

Bruce T. Dahlberg

Introduction

Falling topically into two main parts of unequal length, the Book of Genesis begins with an account of some of Israel's central beliefs about God's creation of the heavens and the earth and about the earliest history of the human race (1:1–11:32). It then relates in its longer part—beginning with traditions about Abraham and Sarah—the legendary deeds of those patriarchs and matriarchs of Israel who lived in CANAAN until, with Joseph and his generation, they moved to Egypt (12:1–50:26).

Israel's origins, moreover, are presented in Genesis not only as directed toward Israel's destiny in history, but as intimately connected with and auspicious for world history generally (e.g., Gen 12:1-3 passim), while Israel's life, anticipated and symbolized by the primordial SABBATH, is seen to derive from the very order of creation itself (2:2-3).

Genesis tells an epic story, anonymously composed from a great variety of oral and written traditions from the ancient Near East and especially from ancient Israel and earliest JUDAISM.

Genesis in the Old Testament

Jewish and Christian tradition refer to the first five books of the OT, including Genesis, as the Law—a somewhat misleading translation of the Hebrew תּוֹרָה *tôrâ* (TORAH). Torah is rendered in English better by "teaching," "instruction," or, in some cases, "revelation," although "law" in the narrower sense of ritual or civil regulation describes significant parts of the Torah.

In its written form the Torah is also referred to as the Pentateuch (Gk. πεντάτευχος "five scrolls/books," probably from ἡ πεντάτευχος βίβλος "the five-fold book") and traditionally, although unhistorically, as the Five Books of Moses.

Because some important threads of the story line begun in Genesis seem not to reach their conclusion until the Book of Joshua (see, e.g., commentary at Gen 12:4-9), many modern biblical interpreters refer to the first six OT books (Genesis–Joshua) together as a broad literary unit called the Hexateuch (Gk., "six scrolls").

Genesis in Early Jewish and Christian Religious Texts

Besides the relatively well-known citations and interpretations of Genesis found in the NT, the Christian patristic writers, the Talmud, and other rabbinical literature, there are other instances of Genesis receiving attention. For example, revisionist expansions and retellings of certain portions of Genesis appear among Jewish and Christian religious writings of the last two centuries B.C.E. and the first two or three centuries C.E. at Qumran, NAG HAMMADI and elsewhere.

Among surviving examples of such texts are the Jewish *Book of Jubilees* (treated as canonical in some OT mss.; see Wintermute 1985; Trafton 1990b) and *The Genesis Apocryphon* (from Qumran; cf. Vermes 1987, 252–59; Trafton 1990a). There are also the Gnostic-Christian *Hypostasis of the Archons* (Layton 1988; Bullard 1990a) and *On the Origin of the World* (Bethge et al. 1988; Bullard 1990b). Of inherent interest in themselves and for the history of Judaism and Christianity, these apocryphal works exhibit the variety and fluidity that obtained in the interpretation of Genesis in the early period of synagogue and church.

Title

The Hebrew title of Genesis is the book's first word, בְּרֵאשִׁית *berêsît*, usually translated as *in the beginning* (Gen 1:1). To name a writing by its opening word or phrase was common in ancient times and is often the practice today with hymns and other poetry.

The English title, Genesis, reproduces the title of the ancient Greek translation of the book. The word has several related meanings, including "origin," "beginning," "generation," and "descendant." The third-century B.C.E. Greek version of the Hebrew Scriptures, the SEPTUAGINT (LXX), chose "Genesis" as the title apparently because in the LXX the word introduces major sections of the book (e.g., 2:4a; 5:1; 10:1; etc.).

Authorship and Date

The ancient but mistaken ascription of the Pentateuch to the authorship of Moses may have been due to a misunderstanding of Deut 31:9 ("Then Moses wrote down this law [*torah*]") as a reference to everything in the five books now called the Torah.

It has long been recognized that Genesis, along with the rest of the Pentateuch, cannot have been written by one author but is, instead, the end result of a process of oral and literary development over at least half a millennium, in which many individuals and groups had a share.

The earliest traditions. Although in its present form Genesis is one continuous narrative, examination of the successive narrative episodes gives clear indication of their having been drawn from quite diverse traditions, many of them originally independent of each other and belonging to diverse literary genres—legends, songs, proverbial sayings, blessings, curses, folk genealogies, ritual laws, etiologies of sacred sites and customs, and other types of shorter or longer literary units. Such units may have been written or originally oral (see Gunkel 1901; Coates 1983; Knight 1990b).

Further, some of the component traditions clearly are drawn from the wider Near Eastern society and culture older than or contemporary with Israel, reworked in Genesis to express Israel's own distinctive beliefs (see, e.g., commentary at Gen 1:1–2:4 and 6:5–8:22).

Narrative compilations prior to Genesis. Before Genesis—and the rest of the Pentateuch—would receive its final form there was an intermediate stage of development in which these diverse and variegated traditions were placed in ordered arrangement in the form of narrative histories. Those predecessor recensions or editions were reworked and incorporated into the final redaction (edition) that is the present Book of Genesis.

Arising from separate geographical regions and time periods, these predecessor documents (or relatively fixed oral cycles of stories) were conflated. Earlier traditions were reworked and expanded by later developments, eventually constituting the present work.

The particular literary and theological features that distinguish each collection or "source" from the others have not been obliterated in the final text. They were editorially harmonized with each other only to a limited extent. As a consequence, although now interwoven, their presence can still be traced as narrative strands or threads distinguishable not only in Genesis but throughout much of the Pentateuch.

The Yahwist source or "J". The earliest such narrative strand begins with the Eden story (Gen 2–3) and as it now proceeds through Genesis it is interwoven with later strands. In Genesis this anonymous source tends to favor the name "Yahweh," which is Israel's particular name for the covenant God (see Humphreys 1990). The name is rendered in most modern English translations as "the LORD." Nineteenth-century German scholars named the source "J" for "Jahveh," the German spelling of "Yahweh." The anonymous final author of this source is thus conventionally referred to now as the YAHWIST. One identifying mark of this strand or source is its typically anthropomorphic representations of the deity, who walks in the garden (Gen 3:8) or dines at table with Abraham (18:1-8).

The J material is supposed by many scholars to be the earliest strand, composed in JUDAH soon after the secession of ISRAEL (i.e., the Northern Kingdom) in the late tenth century B.C.E. (see 1 Kgs 12 and commentary at Gen 13:1-18). The question of date remains open, however. More recently a date as late as the exilic period (sixth-century B.C.E.) has been proposed (Van Seters 1992).

The Elohist source or "E". Interspersed in the text along with J is a second strand of tradition which interpreters have designated as the E or ELOHIST source (derived from Heb. *elohim*, "God," the name this strand favors for the deity). Typically E represents God "calling from heaven" (21:17; 22:11) or speaking through dreams (15:12-16; 20:1-18). The "source" is believed to have been composed in the Northern Kingdom some time after the split with Judah. Where J and E are not clearly distinguishable from each other, as is frequently the case, reference is made simply to JE. It is possible that E is the earlier source of the two, from which J has extracted and reworked certain portions.

The Priestly source or "P". The third and latest major narrative strand is thought to be the end product of the work of a particular community or "school" of tradition. Modern scholarship calls it the "Priestly" source (P) because of its evident interest in the divine origin and validation of particular Jewish religious observances and rituals. Attention to the Sabbath (Gen 2:2-3), dietary laws (9:3-4), and the rite of CIRCUMCISION (17:9-14) are particular examples in Genesis.

Like the E source, P also favors the generic name "God" (Heb. *elohim*) for the deity; both sources apparently hold that the name Yahweh was not known until revealed to Moses; cf. Exod 3:15 (E), and 6:2-3 (P). On the other hand, the J narrator seems to believe God was known as Yahweh from earliest times (Gen 4:26).

The P source appears not only to have been composed after J but, as pointed out in the commentary, certain passages in P seem to be directed at J as a kind of commentary. Although P preserves some very old traditions, it reflects religious rituals and beliefs associated elsewhere in the OT especially with the Jewish late-exilic or early postexilic community in Babylon (late sixth or early fifth centuries B.C.E.), so its final written form is most plausibly dated within that period.

The writers or compilers of P also are thought to have been the final redactors who brought to completion the Book of Genesis, as well as the rest of the Pentateuch. At the latest, this work must have been accomplished by the time EZRA brought the "law of Moses"—believed to be the Pentateuch—from Babylon to Jerusalem (see Ezra 7:1-10; Neh 8:1-12).

The "Documentary Hypothesis." The foregoing treatment is a condensed account of what has been known to several generations of biblical scholars as the "Documentary Hypothesis." Although the work of many scholars contributed to the formulation of the hypothesis, it was most notably set forth by the nineteenth-century German scholar Julius Wellhausen (Wellhausen 1885; see Gregory 1990 and Gottwald 1985, 150–78, 325–34, 469–82).

While the Documentary Hypothesis has undergone considerable criticism and rethinking over the last century, it remains a watershed in the history of Genesis and Pentateuchal studies, and is still very much a critical point of departure for scholarship in that field. The commentary that follows will indicate sources when appropriate by including a J, E, or P after citations.

A diachronic reading of Genesis. To recognize the process of compilation and editing that led to the present narrative work of Genesis is to realize that it, with the rest of the Pentateuch, has preserved side by side different understandings in tension with each other. The tensions exist between earlier and later generations, and between different regional groups concerning particular matters of public issue in Israel's life and faith.

On these terms Genesis can be read with attention to—and appreciation for—its chronologically different layers of tradition and their respective differing emphases as these developed across many generations. Reading Genesis in light of different eras is what scholars identify as a diachronic (i.e., "through time") approach to the text. It is in many ways comparable to reading the NT in terms of the gospel "according to Matthew" or "according to Luke," and so on. Although in Genesis the demarcation between traditional sources is less neat, it is no less legitimate, and illuminating, to speak of Israel's faith "according to J" or "according to P."

A diachronic reading does not at all require drawing invidious comparisons between earlier and later traditions in either chronological direction—that is, from either a Hegelian notion of historical progress from "lower" to "higher" ideas, or (the reverse notion) a romantic idealization of an earlier period's understanding over one that develops later (cf. Rosenberg and Bloom 1990, 9–55). In this respect the method itself is value neutral. Von Rad suggests that:

> source analysis is not the final conclusion of wisdom; but once we know about the differences in the sources we can no longer have the whole without knowing the exact nature of its parts (1972, 11).

A synchronic reading of Genesis. Genesis as a whole also has been given the form of a single epic story. Even though the separate sources behind the present narrative are still delineable, they have been shaped in certain ways and brought together by a final redactor into a mostly-unified literary and theological work possessed of its own interior logic. Genesis can, therefore, also be read synchronically (i.e., as a total statement and a finished work of art, struck off as it were at one telling by a single anonymous narrator). Robert Alter gives voice to such a reading:

> The very mode of narration conveys a double sense of a total coherent knowledge available to God (and by implication, to His surrogate, the anonymous authoritative narrator) and the necessary incompleteness of human knowledge, for which much about character, motive, and moral status will remain shrouded in ambiguity (1981, 184).

Narrative Structure and Major Themes

Episodic arrangement of the narrative. The divisions adopted here for an outline of Genesis are intentionally broad, and overlap to some extent.

The topical and typological variety and complexity of the many traditions, and the way they have been brought together in the book, make tentative and somewhat arbitrary every scheme for outlining Genesis, whether based on subject matter, story-cycles clustering around a particular character, or virtually any other criterion.

The difficulty arises due largely to the fact that in Genesis the different traditions often stand in stark juxtaposition to each other with only the slightest transitional statement or word (if any) to indicate their logical connection.

The logical literary unit often appears freestanding in relation to what precedes or follows—it is not anticipated by anything said beforehand nor is it alluded to in the narrative afterward. The narratives of CAIN AND ABEL (Gen 4:1-16), the binding of ISAAC (22:1-19), JUDAH and TAMAR (38:1-30) are examples of such episodic arrangement.

Israel's destiny in human history. The Book of Genesis falls into two distinct parts that stand in dramatic tension with each other. The stories of the patriarchs and matriarchs (chaps. 12–50), beginning with Abraham's obedience to the divine command to migrate to Canaan (12:1-3), reverse the pattern of recurrent usurpation and violation, alienation, expulsion and scattering abroad—away from God's presence and from each other—that is humanity's typical behavior and experience as described in chaps. 1–11 (see, e.g., 3:1-24; 4:1-16; 6:1-7; 9:20-27; 11:1-9).

God's ELECTION of the patriarchs, and thus of Israel, to be the object of divine promise in history is at the same time represented as restorative for the whole troubled human race: *I will bless you, and make your name great . . . and in you all the families of the earth shall be blessed* (Gen 12:2-3; cf. 18:18; 22:18; 26:3-5; 28:14). The ancestral history is thus understood to have particular meaning not only to Israel, but through Israel for all humanity.

The genealogical framework. The final redactors of the Genesis sources and their diverse traditions have integrated the whole by superimposing a framework of folk genealogies, tables of nations, king lists and the like (principally Gen 5:1-31; 10:1-32; 11:10-32; 25:12-18; 36:1-43). Each such list marks a transition in subject matter at that point in the narrative, from one generation's adventures and deeds to those of another.

A great number of the personal NAMES in these lists are most likely eponymous (i.e., names of peoples, nations, cities, clans or families personified as individuals [see Redditt 1990]). On the related and problematic matter of the artificial or symbolic chronologies cited within Genesis (5:1-32; 15:13, etc.) see Barrois 1952, 142–45 and Christensen 1990, 147–48.

Life under covenant. The most comprehensive term used in Genesis to express Israel's formal understanding of the divine-human relation is COVENANT. The primeval history (Gen 1–11) represents God as entering into covenant with NOAH and his descendants—that is, with all humankind (9:1-17 [P]).

The ancestral history (chaps. 12–50) twice represents God as entering into covenant with Abraham and his descendants (15:17-21 [E somewhat reworked by J] and 17:1-27 [P]).

The analogy or model for the theological concept of a divine-human covenant is the social institution of covenant-making between human parties, widely attested in the ancient Near East, including examples in Genesis (cf. 25:31-32; 26:26-33; 31:43-54).

Covenants are "a variety of solemn, binding obligations or agreements involving two or more parties in a relationship" (Hayes 1990). A covenant relationship—even more than a pact or treaty—is intentional and existential, based on an explicitly declared promises and on the good faith of the parties to it. It is only secondarily a legal arrangement. Primarily covenant is a moral commitment arising out of an occasion of encounter or resolution of conflict. It is well suited, therefore, to express Israel's belief that its God acts in history and can be encountered there.

Promise and judgment. Together, the stories in Genesis present the history of Israel and the human race as a mixed experience of judgment and grace. There is tension between the divine promises to Israel and their postponed fulfillment. Possession of the land of Canaan, promised to Abraham and his descendants (Gen 13:14-17 passim), is delayed by the sojourn in Egypt and the wilderness experience (15:13-16). The promised posterity that Israel will become a great nation is thrown into doubt by the rivalry between Jacob and Esau (27:41-45; chaps. 32–33) and by the strife between Joseph and his brothers (chaps. 37–50).

Blessing and curse. An analogous structure underlies the primeval history of humankind in chaps. 1–11. The goodness of creation, epitomized by the divine image in humankind (1:27, 31) appears compromised by a perplexing human distrust of God (3:1-7), and acts of pride and self-will (4:1-16 passim). Distrust and pride bring upon human history a curse that overshadows the intended blessing (1:28; 3:14-19; 5:29). The blessing and curse dialectic also runs through the ancestral history (12:3; 27:29).

Reversal of the expected. Paradoxically, however, events in Genesis take on the character of epiphanies in which divine purposes are seen as being accomplished in spite of the intentions and expectations of the human actors. A motif typical of the J source, for example, is the recurrent override or reversal, from one generation to the next, of the right of primogeniture—in antiquity, the traditional right of the first-born son to inherit the father's estate.

Contrary to such expectation, the patriarchal inheritance—essentially, God's promise of the land and a famous posterity—passes from Abraham to the younger son Isaac instead of the first-born Ishmael 17:20-21); from Isaac to Jacob instead of the elder Esau (27:36); from Jacob to Joseph's younger son Ephraim instead of the older brother, Manasseh (48:17-20).

In another way the story of Joseph, which concludes Genesis, testifies explicitly to "reversal of the expected" as the mode of divine action in history: "You meant evil against me, but God meant it for good . . . that many people should be kept alive, as they are today" (50:20 RSV).

The deliverance *from* Egypt, the central theme of the Book of Exodus, is preceded by this concluding tale in Genesis of deliverance *in* Egypt. The Joseph story itself would appear to have been composed intentionally to instil such "hope of reversal" in its initial readers, who in all likelihood were Jews exiled from their land into Babylonia in the sixth century B.C.E.

For Further Study

In the *Mercer Dictionary of the Bible*: ANTHROPOMORPHISM; BABEL, TOWER OF; CREATION; ELOHIST; ETIOLOGY; FLOOD; GENESIS; HERMENEUTICS; PATRIARCHS; PRIESTLY WRITERS; SOURCES OF THE PENTATEUCH; YAHWIST.

In other sources: R. Alter, *The Art of Biblical Narrative*; D. Rosenberg and H. Bloom, *The Book of J*; U. Cassuto, *A Commentary on the Book of Genesis*; G. W. Coats, *Genesis: With an Introduction to Narrative Literature*; E. Fox, "Can Genesis Be Read as a Book?" *Semeia* 46:31–40; H. Gunkel, *The Legends of Genesis*; R. S. Hendel, *The Epic of the Patriarch: The Jacob Cycle and the Narrative Traditions of Canaan and Israel*; D. A. Knight, ed., *Julius Wellhausen and His "Prolegomena to the History of Israel," Semeia* 25; J. S. Kselman, "The Book of Genesis: A Decade of Scholarly Research," *Int* 45:380–92; S. Niditch, *Chaos to Cosmos*; G. von Rad, *Genesis*; N. M. Sarna, *Genesis*; D. Steinmetz, *From Father to Son: Kinship, Conflict, and Continuity in Genesis*; E. A. Speiser, *Genesis*, AncB; J. Van Seters, *Prologue to History: The Yahwist as Historian in Genesis*; J. Wellhausen, *Prolegomena to the History of Ancient Israel*.

Commentary

An Outline

I. The Primeval History, 1:1–11:32
   A. Creation of the World, 1:1–2:4a
   B. The Beginning of Human Life, 2:4b–3:24
   C. From Adam to Noah, 4:1–9:29
   D. From Noah to Abraham, 10:1–11:32
II. The Ancestral History of Israel, 12:1–50:26
   A. Abraham, Sarah, and Hagar, 12:1–23:20
   B. Isaac and Rebekah, 24:1–26:35
   C. Jacob, Rachel, and Leah, 27:1–36:36
   D. Joseph and His Brothers, 37:1–50:26

The Primeval History, 1:1–11:32

Creation of the World, 1:1–2:4a

Genesis 1:1–2:4a belongs chronologically to the latest of the Genesis sources—the sixth-century B.C.E. Priestly source. It functions in some ways as an "editor's foreword" to the rest of Genesis and the Pentateuch and thus to the whole OT. Not as science, but as a narrative theology of creation, these chapters set the tone for all the story and history that is to follow.

Somewhat incongruously chap. 1 now ends before what seems clearly to be the actual end of the creation account at 2:4a. Chapter and verse numbers were not added to the text until some time in the Middle Ages, when perception of the limits of a logical literary unit in a text differed in some cases from what might be perceived today.

Of the several different scenarios proposed in the OT for God's creation of the world, the one with which Genesis opens is the best known. It is instructive, however, to compare it with the others—principally Gen 2:4b-25; Job 38:4-33; Ps 104; Prov 8:22-31 and Isa 48:7. Although alike in their degree of profundity and their agreement that creation brings order out of chaos (see Niditch 1985), these portrayals differ considerably from each another in concept, imagery and descriptive detail.

This wide variation suggests that the biblical writers were not concerned primarily with gaining an objective understanding of how the physical world originally came about or how it unfolded in space and time. That would become a primary objective of investigators working in the natural sciences elsewhere and at a later time.

To take the Genesis account of creation as a substitute for (or an option to) today's scientific reconstructions of nature's origin and evolution is anachronistic and reflects a basic misunderstanding of the biblical creation story's purpose and meaning. The biblical accounts are "not a theory but a credo" (Speiser 1964, 8).

To the extent that the world-picture reflected in Gen 1:1–2:4a is scientific, it is heavily indebted to ancient Near Eastern science and myth, in particular to the Babylonian *Epic of Creation* (see Heidel 1951, 82–140; Speiser 1964, 9–11; cf. Gottwald 1985, 476; Knight 1990a, 175–76).

Compared to the approximately 923 lines of the Babylonian text, however, the thirty-five-verse length of the Genesis account signals major substantive differences between the two. The P redactors have radically reinterpreted or "remythologized" the Babylonian mythic elements, and in Genesis the latter have become "broken" myths (Childs 1960, 30–42).

Creation in the Babylonian text, moreover, is an extravagantly portrayed polytheistic warfare among divine powers in nature. The PRIESTLY WRITERS, on the other hand, with laconic and austere understatement, portray the grandeur and also the simplicity of a created order established by one transcendent God.

1:1-2. In the beginning. The traditional rendition of Gen 1:1 as an independent clause, "In the beginning God created the heavens and the earth" (KJV; RSV; cf. John 1:1), although not to be ruled out absolutely, is problematic by the rules of classical Hebrew syntax and grammar (Speiser 1964, 12–13; Sarna 1989, 5).

The NRSV alternative reading has much in its favor: "When God began to create" (mg.) *the heavens and the earth* (v. 1). Not only is it a grammatically sounder option in terms of the Hebrew, but it rhetorically anticipates—and is thus more consistent with—the concluding statement in 2:2, *God finished the work that he had done*. That is, "God began" and "God finished," in 1:1 and 2:2 respectively, form an INCLUSIO to the overall account of creation.

Why the translation of Gen 1:1 has mattered to Jewish and Christian interpreters is its perceived troublesomeness for a theology of creation. If 1:1 is read in the traditional way—as an independent declarative sentence—then, in Gen 1:2, the earth as *a formless void* and *the deep* covered by darkness would appear to be the initial result—the first stage—of God's work, consistent with a theology of creation *ex nihilo* ("out of nothing").

Alternative translations, on the other hand—including the one opted for above—seem to represent the chaotic earth and the deep of 1:2 as existing before creation and alongside of God—a formless "stuff" out of which God formed the world—implying a dualistic view of eternity. Creation out of an unexplained, preexistent and uncreated "something" poses a coeternal "something" alongside of God.

It is unwise, however, to make too much of the philosophical and theological issues that came only later to be associated with translating Gen 1:1-2. It is not clear that the Hebrew writer of 1:1-2 had these particular questions in mind. In these opening lines the writer is using a necessarily mythic mode of expression: "The 'beginning' refers to the period before creation and is a designation, more qualitative than temporal, of the sphere of God" (Brown 1978, 4).

In any case the Hebrew syntax of Gen 1:1-2 and the description of a demythologized CREATION that follows do not preclude that God's creation be understood finally as *ex nihilo*. A monotheistic theology would seem to require such a perspective. The earliest explicit documentation of this understanding known so far occurs in 2 Macc 7:28.

1:2a. Before God spoke. The earth is described as תֹהוּ וָבֹהוּ *tohû wa-bohû*—*formless void*—a devastated wasteland. The same distinctive Hebrew expression is used by Jeremiah, not long before the Babylonian destruction of Jerusalem, to describe the approaching devastation of Judah as the very reversal of creation (Jer 4:23-26).

Jeremiah frames that entire vision in words so clearly reminiscent of Gen 1:1-31 that many have supposed him to be quoting but reversing the latter—foreseeing that the creation described in Genesis will be undone for Judah so that it reverts to wasteland. If, however, the Priestly writers composed the opening chapter of Genesis during or shortly after the EXILE (which would be later than Jeremiah's utterances) the possibility must be considered that the Genesis text is remembering and recasting the words of Jeremiah. The *tohû wa-bohû* that Israel's land and people have at the hands of Babylon actually experienced—not merely imagined or speculated about—will give way to God's work of creation. In the words of a possible contemporary or near contemporary of the Priestly writers, creation is "now, not long ago" (Isa 48:7).

1:2b. Darkness covered the face of the deep. This phrase is further contemplative imaging of the scene prevailing before creation. Hebrew תְהוֹם *tehôm* (*the* [watery] *deep*) is a term cognate to Babylonian TIAMAT, the name of the hostile chaos-goddess according to the Babylonian *Epic of Creation*. In Genesis, by contrast, *the deep* is desacralized. With it divine underpinnings removed it is a "broken" myth.

Although the *darkness* will later be called *night* and will be separated from the created *light* (1:4), the *darkness* of v. 2 is more than "the opposite of light" since light has not yet been created. The *darkness*

> is a figure for invisibility. . . . It is out of the darkness of v. 2 that God's voice comes, uttering the first word in v. 3: "Let there be light!" whose climactic nature is due precisely to its surprising implication that the light proceeds from the darkness (Wyatt 1993, 548; cf. Deut 5:23).

1:2c. A wind from God. Alternatively the phrase may be rendered "the spirit of God" (NRSV mg.) or "a mighty wind." The word for "spirit" (רוּחַ *rûah*) can also be translated as "wind" or "breath"; in concept these are not sharply distinguishable in Hebrew usage. Whether "wind" or "spirit," *rûah* can be God's "messenger" (Ps 104:4), and it can be God's agent of creation and itself an aspect of God (Ps 104:30). Here, it sweeps ("hovers" is better; cf. the same verb at Deut 32:11) *over the face of the waters.*

1:3-31. The six days of creation. Among the many striking features of these lines is the repeated use of the same set of formulaic phrases to frame each successive description of a stage or day of creation: *And God said, "Let . . .; And it was so . . .; And God saw that it was good . . .; And there was evening and there was morning . . .* (cf. Gottwald 1985, 475).

The litany-like pattern suggests an originally ritual setting for the narrative, composed to be used in worship, possibly at the new year. Such would be consistent with celebrations throughout most of the ancient Near East, including Babylon, associating the new year with creation by the gods (cf. Heidel 1951, 16–17; Dalley 1989, 231–32; Bjornard 1990).

For the Jewish exilic or early postexilic community in Babylon, however, the narrative would have done double duty—expressing praise of the creator God, and at the same time putting forward a liturgical answer to the polytheistic rituals of their alien rulers. It thus becomes a manifesto of faith challenging the religious and, implicitly, also the political assumptions of the Babylonian host-culture.

The picture of the world in vv. 3-31 is architectonic, stressing the different and distinct identities that differentiate the respective elements of creation making up the whole. Every creature or created entity is given its unique place and function in what is perceived as an elegant order of creation. Reinforcing this perception are the precisely repeated sequences of particular words or phrases describing the work of creation in terms of "separating" one thing from another (vv. 4, 6, 7, 14, 18); "gathering together" (vv. 9, 10); distinguishing *every kind* of creature (vv. 11, 12, 21, 24, 25). Quite special terms—the *image* and *likeness* of God—set human beings apart from all other creatures (vv. 26-27).

The belief is asserted emphatically—seven times— that everything created is *good* in the eyes of the creator (vv. 4, 10b, 12b, 18b, 21b, 25b, 31a). Nature is seen as not opposed to spirit but as the work of spirit (cf. 1:2). In particular, a high view is taken of human nature as having an original goodness (vv. 26-27, 31).

In light of the attention given to sin and evil in the J account of creation to follow (2:4b–3:24), P's emphasis on an original human goodness perhaps can be seen as an intentional commentary on J, prefaced by P to the chronologically earlier source. J's dark psychology of human character is not denied so much as fundamentally qualified by P's affirmative theology of creation and human nature.

1:5b. Evening and morning. As in Jewish observance still, the day is measured from sundown to sundown. *Evening* and *morning* are more than merely "before bedtime" and "before noon" respectively; here they are more broadly the equivalent of "nighttime" and "daytime."

1:6-8. Separating the waters. *Dome* is a more graphic translation than the older "firmament" (e.g., KJV, RSV). God names *the dome Sky* (v. 8a), behind which is the same Hebrew word that is rendered in 1:1 (with the definite article) by *the heavens*. On the dividing of the waters above and below the sky, and the conception of the world presupposed by such imagery, see Heidel 1951, 114–15; Gottwald 1985, 476 (esp. fig. 1); Knight 1990a, 175–76.

1:14-19. Heavenly bodies. The *lights in the dome of the sky* are created *for signs and for seasons and for days and years*—they are time dividers and sources of light. The COSMOLOGY is geocentric and thus prescientific by modern measure, but the Priestly writers have a distinct theological agenda. Tablet V of the Babylonian *Epic of Creation* mentions the stars first ahead of the moon and sun, and gives them considerable descriptive attention, connecting them to gods—attesting to the Babylonian interest in ASTROLOGY (Heidel 1951, 44; 116–17; Dalley 1989, 255). Perhaps because of that connection the Priestly writers barely mention the stars, and put them last in order (v. 16).

There is, on the other hand, a provocative parallelism between what God does and what the celestial luminaries do: both they and God *separate the light from the darkness* (v. 18; cf. 1:4) and *the day from the night* (v. 14; cf. 1:5). God creates light and darkness, however—and day and night—on the first day, while the sources of light *in the dome of the sky* are not made until the fourth day. In the Babylonian parallel, again, the celestial lights are gods, light being their attribute. The Genesis account, however, "puts them in their place" as creatures and views the ultimate source of light as independent of them.

1:26-31. Humankind in the image and likeness of God. *Humankind* translates Hebrew *adam*, literally "a human"; here it is not a personal name. The Hebrew word is for P grammatically but not semantically gender-specific. Its meaning clearly embraces both *female* and *male*; P states this here and even more explicitly later, in Gen 5:2. Translation of the Hebrew term by *humankind* is intended to preserve the inclusive meaning.

In our image, according to our likeness (v. 26) is an example of hendiadys—two words used to express a single notion. For P *image* and *likeness* are not two separate or distinguishable qualities but are seen as interchangeable (cf. v. 27 with 5:1). On the one hand humankind is related to the animal world—created on the same day (1:24-25) or sharing the same blessing of life (1:22, 28)—on the other hand, humans are set above the other creatures (vv. 26-28) and likened to the creator. In the human being nature and spirit intersect.

The assertion of humanity's *dominion* over all other living creatures has been misunderstood by some as human arrogance on the part of the Genesis writers and as having provided in later times a justification for humanity's increasingly destructive behavior toward the earth's ecology. The assertion that *dominion* over the creatures has been delegated to humankind is simply descriptive of humanity's actual and obvious situation in the world. It is scarcely a claim to privilege; rather, it is a sober statement of human responsibility for the world and its life, to be ignored only with peril to the world and humankind alike. Inherent to this perspective is human freedom seen as a responsible instrument for the stewardship of life rather than a license for its exploitation.

The particular placement of *male and female* in apposition with *the image of God* (v. 27) suggests that relationships between the sexes are not only a metaphor but also a particular testing ground for the "godlikeness" at the heart of human existence in the world (cf. Trible 1978, 12–23).

Like all language about God, this language is metaphorical. While it points toward God, it does not warrant the conclusion that God contains male and female elements any more than would metaphors for deity elsewhere in the OT warrant the notion that God is part faunal and floral (e.g., Hos 13:8; 14:8).

What v. 27c does suggest is that humans are relational beings, not merely a race of individuals. The *imago dei* (image of God) applies not to humanity in the abstract but to actual sexual persons, political persons, family persons, artistic persons, craftpersons, good citizens, outlaws, and everyone. Human sin and error do not remove this image but are judged by it.

It cannot be merely coincidental that here (elsewhere in the OT only rarely; cf. Gen 3:22; Isa 6:8) God is represented as speaking in the first person plural: *Let us make . . . in our image, according to our likeness.* The language and imagery is that of a divine council in heaven (Ps 82:1; cf. 1 Kgs 22:19-22; Job 1:6; 2:1; 38:7).

Thus the relational or societal notion of the image of God in human beings is paralleled by another relational metaphor—the deity conceived of in terms of a "celestial society." The Christian metaphor of the Trinity—"one God in three persons"—is not promulgated in Gen 1:26, but neither is it inconsistent with it.

2:1-3. The seventh day. That in v. 2 God is said both to have *finished* work and to have *rested* (or ceased) from work on the seventh day might seem a contradiction. Verse 1, however, represents creation of the heavens and the earth (which in 1:2 was a *formless void*) as completed in six days.

The noun form of the twice-repeated Hebrew verb "rest" is שַׁבָּת *shabbat*, SABBATH. Although not specifically named, the sabbath is clearly alluded to and represented here as modeled in heaven.

Each of the six days was a time of work; the seventh is marked by cessation from work and is *blessed*, given the power of life, *and hallowed* or declared holy. Holy literally means to separate or to set aside.

The Priestly writers' implication seems to be that in the celestial sabbath—God's cessation or rest from work—God separates himself from work, that is, God declares his transcendence of the created world. God pronounces the world and its creatures *good*, but the created order is not considered divine, as it was thought to be by Israel's neighbors and by many in Israel, as the OT prophets attest.

Analogously, in the sabbath on earth, humans separate themselves from their work. What they have done or made is not to be considered divine. Works of human creation, however good, are not to be worshipped (a prohibition against IDOLATRY). Sabbath observance both celebrates creation and distances the sabbath observer from idol worship.

The Beginning of Human Life, 2:4b–3:24

Introduced at this point in Genesis is a second account of creation unmistakably and significantly different from what has preceded. The name used to speak of the deity suddenly changes. In the P narrative it was "God" (Heb. *elohim*). Here (2:4b–3:24) it is *the LORD God* (*Yahweh elohim*), and scholars accordingly attribute this second account to the J or YAHWIST writer or "source."

How the work of creation is conceived, and the sequence of events in it, are both markedly different from the previous account. Here, for example, a human being is formed before any other creature (2:7); in the P account humans are formed last (1:26-27).

The portrayals of God also are radically different: for P God is a disembodied voice from heaven. In the J, God's voice and actions are described as having a kind of anthropomorphic physicality (e.g., 2:7; 3:8). God engages in dialogue with the human actors (3:9-13) and also seems troubled and taken by surprise at the precocity and godlikeness of the human creature (3:22). In the P account such qualities of humankind were by God's intent and design (1:26-27).

Where P's account of creation showed a contemplative priestly concern and awe for cosmic order (e.g., light and darkness; sea and dry land; sun, moon and stars; the variety of living creatures; human beings overseeing it all, etc.), J focuses on the psychology of the human heart becoming self-aware and estranged both from the creator and other creatures.

Here and elsewhere in the primeval history (chaps. 1–11), a recurrent motif for P is God's blessing of nature and humankind (1:28; cf. 5:2; 9:1). For J, it is Yahweh's curse of the ground (3:17; cf. 4:11; 5:29; 8:21).

The mythic mode of this story means that the *man* (v. 7) and the *woman* (v. 22) are understood by the J writer as "Everyman"—every human being. Their experience, from hearing the voice of the serpent (3:1-5) and the voice of God (3:8-22) to their expulsion from the garden (3:23-24), is understood as experience of the universal human situation.

The mystery of what it means to be *a living being* (2:7) is thus thematic to J's story of creation. Beginning with the earth unwatered and lifeless (2:5), the J narrative concludes with particular reference to Eve as *the mother of all living* (3:20); to God's discovery that the human being has become like God (*like one of us*; 3:22; cf. 1:26-27) and to God's consequent (and troubling) measures to keep human beings from *the tree of life* lest they *live forever* (3:22, 24; cf. 6:3). Finally, humanity is thrust out by *the LORD God* from an ideal, timeless *garden of Eden* into life in history, that is, life in real time (3:23-24).

2:4b-7. The first man. Like P, the J writer draws on pottery-making imagery and well-known ideas from ancient Near Eastern culture and shapes them for a particular purpose. The notion of a human being formed by a god or goddess, as by a potter, from moistened dust or clay is attested in the *Epic of Gilgamesh*, a Mesopotamian legend going well back into the second millennium B.C.E. (see Speiser 1969, 74; Dalley 1989, 52).

2:7. Humanity shaped from the ground. There is an obvious pun between the Hebrew words אָדָם *adam*, *man*, and אֲדָמָה *adamâ*, *ground*; the terms are appropriately rendered as "earth creature" or "earthling" and "earth" (Trible 1978, 80, 140). The J writer exploits the connection in various ways throughout the story.

The generic *adam* is not properly the personal name "Adam" until it appears without the definite article, as in MT and in the NRSV alternative translation at 3:17. The KJV mistakenly uses the personal name first at 2:19 (cf. LXX, 2:16).

The man became a *living being* when God *breathed* (lit. "blew") *into his nostrils the breath of life.*

2:8-11. Eden. The LXX translates *garden* as παράδεισος *parádeisos*, "paradise." *Eden* is a Hebrew term meaning "delight"; thus the garden contains trees that are *pleasant to the sight and good for food, the tree of life also in the midst of the garden* (v. 9). There are precious stones and gold nearby (v. 12).

Elsewhere in the OT, exilic or postexilic prophets cite Eden to draw contrast with the wasteland resulting from the military destruction of nations in their own time (Ezek 28:11-19; 31:8-9; Isa 51:3; Joel 2:3).

A potential threat to the felicity of life in the garden is latent at this point. With typical subtle artfulness the J narrator appends an enumeration of trees, almost as an afterthought—"[Oh yes,] *and the tree of the knowledge of good and evil*" (v. 9).

J gives Eden a geographical location, however vague, *in the east* (v. 8), but consistent with J's terrestriality. The four rivers that branch out from the *river that flows out of Eden*, and the geographical regions in or around which they flow (vv. 10-14) are also consistent with J's world-picture.

Given the inherent fluidity of mythic imagery, it is possible the J writer believes Eden to have included the geographical regions he names. Since the river of v. 10 *flows out of Eden to water the garden*, the lands surrounded by the *four branches* of the river could be thought of as embracing the garden (vv. 11-13).

Havilah (v. 11) is Hebrew for *Haulan*, an ancient tribal group in the region of Yemen. *Cush* (v. 13) is not Ethiopia (as in 2 Kgs 19:9) but is connected with early Babylon (Gen 10:8-10) and is also the eponymous father of Havilah (Gen 10:7). *Assyria* (v. 14) is the region of Mesopotamia north of Babylon. These lands, like Eden, are *in the east* (v. 8), and possibly thought of by the J author as part of Eden. Mythic Eden would be understood then not as a chronologically and anciently sequestered place on earth, but as the primeval paradise that is any earthly place before being drawn into historical time. The distinction between Eden and elsewhere is finally qualitative, not spatial.

2:15-17. Life in the garden. Analogous to P's view of humans as having *dominion* over the creatures (1:26, 28), J represents the first human being as caretaker of the garden, *to till it and keep it* (v. 15). He is *freely* to enjoy the fruit of *every tree of the garden* (v. 16) except one, *the tree of the knowledge of good and evil*, to eat of which God warns will mean having to die (v. 17). Since at this point in the story neither the crime nor the punishment are yet part of the human's experience, the warning is enigmatic. Nonetheless, it suggests a dark side to Eden. Narrative ground is being prepared for the confrontation to ensue later over disobedience of the prohibition (cf. 3:1-19).

2:18-22. Woman. The J narrator writes as if privy to God's innermost thought: It is not good that the man should be alone (v. 18). To find for the man *a helper as his partner* (lit. "a helper corresponding to him"), God resorts to experiment. Animals and birds, like the man, are formed *out of the ground* and brought to the man, who gives them their names (vv. 19-20), but none makes a suitable partner for the man (v. 20b). Then, from *one of [the man's] ribs*, taken after the creature is first put into *a deep sleep* (v. 21; cf. the same expression in Gen 15:12, regarding Abraham), God forms the first woman (v. 21; cf. Rosenberg and Bloom 1990, 178–80).

Animals as initial companions of man before he found the companionship of woman is another example of a motif appropriated from ancient Near Eastern tradition but given a considerably different nuance by the J writer (cf. the character Enkidu in the Epic of Gilgamesh [Dalley 1989, 53–6; Speiser 1969, 74–5]). In the latter story, however, the motif depicts relations with the woman as merely preparing Enkidu for comradeship with the hero Gilgamesh. J, on the other hand, presents companionship between the sexes as good for its own sake.

2:22b-25. Man and woman brought together. J utilizes a proverbial folk etymology for the words *Woman* and *Man* (v. 23). The man's exclamatory *This at last* . . . (v. 23) indicates an Edenic delight with the woman as his opposite, centering on their mutually happy and innocent discovery of their sexuality—as explained in J's appended comments (vv. 24-5); they *were both naked, and were not ashamed* (v. 25). The implication that erotic attraction between the sexes reflects their longing to return to an original unity (vv. 23-24) is a greatly attenuated version of an elaborate and archetypal myth to that effect cited also by Plato (*Symp* 189d–193d; cf. Gunkel 1901, 94, and Gunkel 1997, liii and 13).

3:1-24. Godlikeness as the knowledge of good and evil. Whatever is finally to be comprehended by the expression, *knowing good and evil* (v. 5), according to J, it is recognized by both the serpent and God as tantamount to becoming *like God* (v. 5, cf. v. 22). As might be expected, God and the serpent in this particular story hold divergent views of such an outcome. The J writer does not moralize but, rather, presents both views with cool detachment.

In classical Hebrew, to "know good and evil" is a generic idiom for human knowledge in general—both objective and experiential knowledge. Depending on context it can have any one of several related meanings or nuances such as knowledge of right and wrong (Isa 5:20), the distinction between political competence and incompetence (1 Kgs 3:9), the ability to discern human character and motive (2 Sam 14:17), or, in a more general sense, to grow up, mature, or come of age (Isa 7:15).

Here, in view of what is to follow in chaps. 4–11 concerning the emergence of human civilization, culture and a necessary worldly wisdom, the knowledge of good and evil must be read as "the entirety of knowledge" (NOAB v. 5n.) or "the totality of all possible experience," well described (though judged as futility) by a later OT writer coming out of the Wisdom tradition (cf. Eccl 1:12–2:10).

Thus the knowledge of good and evil is here not a particular body of knowledge among others, but a particular way of knowing. It implies control of one's world, and to be complete it requires foreknowledge, or control of the future—for human creaturehood a goal doomed to failure however much it may attract and mesmerize. Moreover, the attempt to possess such an ultimate and independent control, according to the J writer, must by definition be in God's eyes hubris, the inclination to play God (3:22).

Such an understanding lies behind Ezekiel's rhetorical use of the Eden tradition. His "lamentation over the king of Tyre" (Ezek 28:11-19, esp. v. 13) paints an elaborate picture of "Eden, the garden of God" from which the king, like Adam, has been driven because of a self-aggrandizement such as in Genesis is symbolized by eating from the forbidden tree.

3:1-5. The serpent's interpretation. Under the serpent's tutelage, however, the strictures placed on humanity by God's wisdom are weighed by the woman and man against the possibilities held out for them by their vision and imagination. God will denounce the serpent (3:14), but there is no sign of the narrator doing so. J is matter-of-fact and nonjudgmental toward the actors in the Eden story. In matters of the divine-human relation J does not take sides.

The serpent is described in Hebrew as *arum*, translated by NRSV somewhat pejoratively as *crafty*. "Subtle" (KJV, RSV) or "perceptive" (author trans.) are better alternatives in the context. The Hebrew word is clearly a play on the description in 2:25 of the man and woman as both *arom* ("naked"; *erom* in 3:7, 10, 11). The wordplay, and the serpent's possession of human speech (one of two occasions in the OT in which an animal speaks; cf. Numb 22:28-30 and commentary at 3:14-19) associate the serpent with the voice of human imagination and possibility.

As such, the serpent's role in the story is ambiguous. The J writer sees it, to be sure, as leading the humans into provoking divine judgment (3:11, 22). Perhaps less obviously, what will follow in Gen 4–11 suggests that J sees it also as leading the man and woman from the passive obedience of Eden out into the world of taking life's risks of initiative and responsibility— ingredients basic to a life of faith. It could be said that what God sees as hubris the serpent sees as initiative.

The chronologically later P account of creation will hold that such initiative and responsibility was God's true intent for humankind in the first place and will expand J's problematic expression, *like God*, into the more positive *image and likeness* of God (1:26-28).

Identification of the serpent as the devil or Satan does not appear until the first century B.C.E. (Wis 2:24; cf. Rev 12:9; 20:2). In some second-century C.E. Gnostic or Gnostic-Christian circles the serpent was portrayed in a positive light as "the instructor" of humankind (Layton 1988, 164–65; Bethge et al. 1988, 184–85).

That the serpent's counsel leads to the denial of immortality for humankind (3:4, 22-24) is reminiscent of the snake's role in the *Epic of Gilgamesh* (Tablet XI; cf. Dalley 1989, 119; Speiser 1969, 96)—stealing from Gilgamesh the plant that would give immortality or at least rejuvenation.

3:6-7. The fall. As an event, eating from the forbidden tree would be designated by later Christian interpretation as the "fall from God's grace" of the first humans, and the character of the act as "original sin." Literal interpretations view this episode as a particular act of disobedience at the beginning of temporal history, through which all the descendants of Adam and Eve have genetically inherited the taint of sin and for which all humanity is now held responsible.

More mystical or mythic interpretations see "the Fall" as happening "before" historical time—in effect, before every human action at any time. Thus it amounts to a state or condition of humankind universally (see Niebuhr 1941, 241–64).

In the OT, nowhere is human sin or guilt referred to events narrated in Gen 3:1-6. Related to the more mystical understanding of "original sin," however, is the notion of the "evil inclination" in all humankind (Gen 6:5; 8:21; see Jacobs 1901, 601–602, and commentary at 6:5).

The Hebrew verb translated to know (3:5, 7) is sometimes in classical Hebrew an idiom for sexual intercourse (see Gen 4:1, 25). In the Eden narrative the various connotations of the term are obviously played off each other.

Contrary to some later interpretations, the sin of the man and woman is not represented in Genesis as sexual. This could scarcely be the case given the high view of human sexuality expressed in 2:23-25. That sexual relationships, like all of human life, can become estranged or distorted because of antecedent or attendant human sin and guilt (3:16) is a different matter (cf. Price 1990).

3:8-13. God searches out the man. With irony typical of the J writer, it is precisely in the context of knowledge presumed to be Godlike that J represents God's knowledge as something other than simple foreknowledge or omniscience.

Some ancient rabbinical and Christian patristic interpretations notwithstanding, this and subsequent questions asked by God (vv. 11, 13; cf. 4:9; 18:21) are not rhetorical formalities for the sake of opening a dialogue. The Genesis writers present the human creature as God's experimental "project" by which God can be genuinely surprised either in satisfaction or dismay (cf. 2:18 with v. 20b; 3:22; 6:5-6; 11:5-7; 18:26; 19:21; 22:12).

3:14-19. Judgment. The poetic and proverbial tenor of the three punishment-pronouncements mark them as sayings probably ancient and time-honored well before the J writer adapted them. The writer uses them selectively, but realistically, to describe the hard life in nature and society in contrast to the lost good of Eden.

That the fall of humankind is prelude to the forging of a deeper relationship between humans and God in history—thematic for Genesis as a whole—remains at this point in the story still to be discovered.

The serpent is *cursed . . . among all animals* (v. 14), and expelled from the society of animals and humans known in Eden. A tradition in the second-century B.C.E. *Book of Jubilees* holds that the animals in Eden "used to speak with one another with one speech and one language," and seems to imply that the language was Hebrew (*Jub* 3:28; 12:26; cf. Wintermute 1985, 60, 82).

Concerning what is said to the woman, erotic interaction between humans is not itself condemned. Rather, this human relationship, as every other, is now distorted and corrupted because of the human desire to know *good and evil* (3:5) in such a way as to possess and have control over the other—to play god. Eros, an intended good, has "disintegrated" (Trible 1978, 128; cf. 72-143; see also commentary at 3:20).

3:17-19. The curse of the ground. God's pronouncement on Adam brings the whole Eden narrative full cycle. *The ground* (Heb. *adama*) from which God made the man (cf. 2:7, *adam*) is now *cursed*—its power of life and fertility is weakened and diminished. Nature and the earth thus also suffer in the fall, human stewardship of them (2:15; cf. 1:26-28) compromised by their being exploited by the steward's pursuit of *the knowledge of good and evil* (cf. Hos 4:1-3). The life of human beings and the life-supporting ground from which they are taken are yoked (v. 19).

Relief from the curse of the ground becomes a leitmotif for the rest of the primeval history (Gen 4:2, 11-12; 5:29; 8:21; 9:20, 25; see commentary at 4:1-16).

3:20. Eve. The explanation of the woman's name is a folk etymology—in Hebrew the name "Eve" resembles the word for "living." Of more interest is the import of this particular etymological folk tradition, which sees the woman as *the mother of all living* that is, of "all living creatures" (cf. the same expression at Gen 8:21c). Whether the J writer takes this to mean only human beings or is recalling traditions of a divine woman is not clear.

According to Gen 2:7 and 2:19, both man and animal are formed from the ground; according to 3:20, Eve is their common mother. It may be that J intends with this alternative tradition of woman's status to correct or mitigate the misogynic implications of 3:16. In the midst of a portrait of Yahweh as creator and judge this citation concerning Eve is remarkable.

It should not be overlooked that in the J narratives in Genesis it is women who more often than not drive the action of the story (3:2, 6; 16:1-15; 19:30-38; 21:6-21; 27:5-17, 42-46; 31:19, 33-35; 38:1-30).

3:21. Life under judgment and grace. Being held divinely accountable for whatever they have done is experienced by the man and woman as punishment for hubris or presumption, but they also experience God's compassion. That God makes garments and clothes them may at first thought seem a merely quaint image and a minimal gesture of grace. The *garments of skins*, however, are symmetrical in the story to the futile fig leaves by which the pair sought to hide their nakedness and vulnerability from themselves and from God (3:7, 10). Clothing concretely provides, and in a more general sense symbolizes, protection against the physical rigors and psychological anxieties of human existence, illustrated but not exhausted by the punishment pronouncements of 3:14-19.

3:22-24. The expulsion from Eden. The couple is driven out of the garden of Eden lest they *take also from the tree of life, and eat, and live forever*. It must be understood that "living forever" does not mean "life after death" but living forever in this world.

The OT does not speak of a life in heaven after death. Even the very late notion of resurrection (Dan 12:2) seems to expect a restoration to life in this world, except that there it is understood to be brought about by God, not achieved by humans.

The J writer thus suggests that to live *forever* (Heb. *olam*, i.e., for all time), would transform a knowledge of good and evil like God's to total knowledge that is God's. The expulsion from Eden is a cautionary tale against the inevitable disillusionment for human beings attracted to any idea of knowledge as the way to forestalling death forever.

A similar observation is made by Qoholeth who may have meditated on the Genesis narrative, if indeed he was not a contributor to it: "[God] has put eternity ['all time'] into man's mind, yet so that he cannot find out what God has done from the beginning to the end" (Eccl 3:11 RSV).

Cherubim and *a sword flaming and turning* (v. 24) cut off the way back into Eden. Cherubim are mythic winged beasts. Carved figures of cherubim guard the inner sanctuary of the temple (1 Kgs 6:23-28); elsewhere Yahweh is represented as enthroned on the cherubim (e.g., 1 Sam 4:4). The picture of cherubim as angelic infants or children is a medieval image, not found in the OT.

The whirling sword is not held by one of the cherubim; it is present in addition to them. The iconography of Eden is paralleled and much elaborated in Ezekiel's "lamentation over the king of Tyre" (Ezek 28:11-19; cf. esp. vv. 14-16), but a sword is not mentioned there.

Possibly the image is related to that of the drawn sword in the hand of the mysterious figure guarding the way into the "holy ground" of Canaan (Josh 5:13-15; cf. Judg 7:20; Jer 47:6).

From Adam to Noah, 4:1–9:29

4:1-22. Cain and Abel. Reference to an established and developed system of sacrifice (vv. 3-4), a generally populated world (vv. 14-15), a wife for Cain (v. 17) and cultural developments apparently uninterrupted to the present (vv. 20-22) indicate that at one time the story of CAIN AND ABEL must have been a freestanding tradition independent of both the preceding Eden narrative, to which it is now attached, as well as the flood tradition that follows in chaps. 6–8.

That the narrative opens with a folk etymology of the name *Cain* but not *Abel* suggests that Abel is mostly a foil to the main actor in the story, who is Cain. (*Abel* renders a Heb. word meaning "vanity," in the sense of being feckless or useless; cf. Eccl 1:2).

The present story seems actually to combine two earlier and quite different traditions—that of Cain the farmer (vv. 2-16) and Cain as metalworker (vv. 17-22).

The folk-explanation—which the narrator attributes to Eve—for the name "Cain" (*"I have produced a man with the help of the LORD"* [v. 1]) relates the name to the Hebrew word for "produced." It need not be taken to imply divine parentage for Cain, as some have suggested. The simplest understanding is that it expresses a common view of childbirth in the OT as well as in many other cultures, that the human parents' biological role is necessary to, but not of itself sufficient for conception in the womb, which ultimately happens only with divine assistance or intervention (cf. e.g., Gen 17:7; 18:10; 30:2; 1 Sam 1:19-20; Ps 139:13).

The original purpose of vv. 1-16 may have been etiological—to account for the traditional rivalry between shepherds and farmers for the land, but in the story as now deployed the J writer's interest lies elsewhere. Considering the outcome of events in Eden (chap. 3), the significant connection for J would seem to be the detail that Cain is *a tiller of the ground* (v. 2) which is now cursed (3:17). This is surely the logic behind Yahweh's otherwise gratuitous rejection of Cain's *offering of the fruit of the ground* (v. 3).

That Cain is warned to restrain his anger and dismay over the situation (v. 7) is another example of the paradox of having to take responsibility for conditions not altogether of one's own making, paralleling the description of human existence in the Eden story. The tenor of Yahweh's inquiries put to Cain after the murder of Abel (vv. 9-15) are reminiscent of the exchange between Yahweh and the first man and woman earlier (3:9-19).

Cain's answer to God's inquiry about Abel—*"I do not know"* (v. 9) is of course a lie, and his question, *"Am I my brother's keeper?"* is rhetorically dissembling and disingenuous, if not insolent. In the context, contrary to some popular interpretations, it is scarcely meant to launch a discussion of ethics.

Cain is *cursed from the ground* (v. 11) because he shed the blood of his brother Abel, and, like his parents, he is driven "away from the ground" (v. 14a RSV) and from God's presence. The curse in these several stories early in Genesis is thus portrayed as a universal sickness passing back and forth between the ground and the humans who come from the ground (3:19).

To protect him from any avenger of Abel's death and thus to relieve Cain from having to become *a fugitive and a wanderer on the earth* (v. 14b), God *put a mark on Cain* (v. 15). The nature of the mark is not clear, but in this story it extends the pattern of divine judgment tempered by grace that started with Yahweh's sewing of protective garments for Adam and Eve (see commentary at 3:21).

That Cain *settled in the land of Nod* (v. 16) seems an oxymoron—*Nod* means "wandering"—contradicting the statement that Cain *settled* there. This may be an example of J's proclivity for irony, or it may be another indication that the original tradition had an meaning different from what J gives it. Perhaps J introduces the detail about God's protection of Cain, which appears to obviate Cain's having to become *a fugitive and a wanderer on the earth*. (In place of *Nod*, LXX has "Naid," which has no recognizable meaning.)

Where Cain could obtain a wife (v. 17) in a world empty except for his parents becomes a question only if the story's original independence of the preceding Eden narrative is not recognized. Some ancient Jewish and Christian interpretations thus took recourse to an expansion of the Cain story in which he marries two of his sisters (*Jub* 4:9-12), whose existence seemed allowed for by the reference in Gen 5:4 to Adam's *other sons and daughters*.

In distinction to the popular explanation of the name in v. 1, "Cain" is actually derived linguistically from the Hebrew gentilic term "Kenite," meaning "smith" (i.e., metalworker). Kenites as a people are represented as enemies of Israel in Gen 15:19 and Num 24:21-22; elsewhere they seem to be viewed favorably (Judg 1:16; 4:11; cf. Matthews 1990).

The connection of his name with metallurgy seems in any case consistent with the description of Cain as builder of a city (v. 17), perhaps implicitly a swordsman (vv. 23-24), and progenitor of *Tubal-cain*, who shares his ancestor's name and is a metalsmith (v. 22). J's anachronistic reference to *iron tools* appearing in so ancient a time is one of many details that distinguish this source's archaic knowledge of history from that of modern archaeologists and historians.

The informal genealogy is interrupted here and there to note selected features of emergent civilization (vv. 21-22) in both urban and nomadic culture (vv. 17, 20). Some names in this list of J's plus *Seth* and *Enosh* (vv. 25-26) will be repeated, some only approximated, and others omitted in the Priestly writers' longer list of Adam's descendants through Seth in chap. 5.

4:23-24. The Song of Lamech. The story of Cain ends with an ancient boasting or battle song that recalls his murderous deed (vv. 8-16). From the J writer's ironic perspective, *Lamech* perversely celebrates Cain's violence and mocks Yahweh's words of compassion to Cain by turning them to his own self-glorification (cf. vv. 24, 15a). The song illustrates and dramatizes the worsening condition of human society after Eden and before the Flood.

4:25. Birth of Seth. Seth is the third son of Adam according to this genealogy. Seth's name is chosen by his mother because, as she declares, *"God has appointed for me another child instead of Abel."* In P's variant list of Adam's descendants to follow (5:1-28, 30-32), neither Abel nor Cain are mentioned; there the line of Seth supplants them altogether.

4:26. Enosh and the worship of Yahweh. The meaning of the name *Enosh* is synonymous with *Adam*—"human being"—although it lacks the "earthling" connotations of the latter (see 2:7). Here the name is used in a kind of theological double-entendre: to say that the worship (invocation of the name) of Yahweh (*the* LORD) began with Enosh is also a way of saying that it began with the birth of humankind (see discussion of P's different view in remarks on the Priestly source, under "Authorship and Date," above). For J, Yahweh has always been known.

5:1-32. Adam's descendants through Seth. The rhetorical shape and vocabulary of 5:1 (cf. 1:26-28) and the repetitious form of citation that follows identify the genealogy of chap. 5 as belonging to the P source, with the exception of v. 29, in which the style and subject matter suggests P has drawn from J (see commentary at 3:14-19).

In contrast to J's lineage of Adam (chap. 4), this variant tradition goes through Seth, represented as Adam's firstborn. P either is unfamiliar with the traditions about Cain or—more likely—ignores or suppresses them. The name *Kenan* (5:12-14), except for the final *-an*, is spelled in Hebrew the same as "Cain" and could be a hypocoristic form of the latter, but Kenan is not the firstborn of Adam.

The ancient Near Eastern tradition that human ancestors in earliest times were extraordinarily long-lived was not an invention of the biblical writers. The prebiblical *Sumerian King List*, a text dating from ca. 2000 B.C.E., lists Mesopotamian kings of legend said to have lived "[before] the Flood swept over the earth," each of whose ages is reckoned in tens of thousands of years (Oppenheim 1969, 265–66).

The names on the two lists are different, although their respective repetitious and formulaic styles are similar. The relevance of the comparison, however, is that the Priestly writers in Gen 5 appear not first of all concerned to make the point that humans once lived to fabulous ages. That tradition would in P's time seem to have been taken more or less for granted. Conceivably, the P writers may even have considered that aspect of the tradition archaic and open to question, while they exploit it for their own purposes.

What is added to the citation of each name in Gen 5 is a notation not present in the Sumerian list, namely, that each long-lived ancestor died (vv. 5, 8, etc.). That these "obituary notices" do not occur in the later continuation of this genealogy through the line of Shem (11:10-32)—a list which otherwise has the same formulaic structure as here—suggests that there is a particular purpose for them here.

The P writers seem concerned to make the point that longevity was not to be confused with immortality. Specifically they may be seeking in this connection to forestall misunderstandings concerning the intimation of immortality for humans implied in the J tradition preserved in Gen 6:1-4.

That such is their main concern at this point is supported by the case of *Enoch* (vv. 21-24)—whom P cites as an exception to the others in Adam's line in that Enoch did not die; rather, he *walked with God; then he was no more, because God took him* (v. 24). The Hebrew language here is precise, and describes not Enoch's death or dying but his bodily translation into the presence of God. The only other such exception in the OT tradition is the prophet Elijah (2 Kgs 2:11). In general the OT lacks any doctrine of resurrection until its very latest writing, from the late postexilic period (e.g., Dan 12:1-3).

To "walk with God" is idiomatic in biblical Hebrew for living righteously and in keeping faith with God and one's fellow humans (e.g., Mic 6:8; Gen 6:9; Deut 26:17). Thus the lineage given in Gen 5 serves not only a genealogical interest but also theological, in which the P writers correlate righteousness with life (and by implication, sin with death) in a curious but striking way: on the one hand Enoch, remembered as righteous, has the shortest life on earth among those listed but is granted immortality. Having *walked with God*, Enoch lives forever (vv. 23-24). On the other hand, this righteous but relatively short-lived figure is father to *Methuselah* who, of all Adam's descendants, enjoys the longest life on earth but does not live forever (v. 27).

That the years of Enoch's lifespan number 365 may also be intended by P as significant, since that is the number of days in a solar year. The sun is a widespread symbol for deity in the ancient Near East, including in the OT (Deut 33:2; Judg 5:31; Hab 3:3-4; Mal 4:2 [MT 3:20]).

Possibly P's particular treatment of the Enoch tradition has the purpose of qualifying the theology of J concerning the denial of immortality to humankind (3:22-23). That P has J thus in mind is supported by the use of J's explanation for the name *Noah*, with its hope that Noah will bring relief from the curse of the ground, to conclude P's lineage of Adam (v. 29).

<u>6:1-4. Divine beings cohabit with women.</u> An unusual fragment of mythic tradition now returns the narrative to its theme of humankind overreaching itself—the affront to Yahweh that provoked the expulsion from Eden (3:22-24) and now will provoke a universal flood (6:5–7:24).

That the world's depravity somehow has roots in heaven (referring to the *sons of God*; vv. 1, 4) is but one puzzling aspect of this particular tradition. On the other hand, J seems to represent Yahweh as distancing himself from these *sons of God*.

The identity of the *Nephilim* (v. 4) is unclear; translated in some English versions as "giants" (KJV), the term also can be translated "fallen ones." Possibly the association of this race of semi-divine beings with *the heroes that were of old* (v.

4) is intended to recall the long-lived ancestors cited in Gen. 5, with the particular stress there on their mortal nature.

The final meaning of this somewhat lurid fragment seems in any case to be that the moral situation in human society on earth has become intolerable and must be brought to an end. (On Gen 6:1-4 in relation to its analogues in ancient Near Eastern mythology, cf. Speiser 1964, 45–46.)

6:5–8:21. The flood. As has been known for well over a century, the flood story in Genesis is unmistakably indebted in considerable detail to older versions of the tradition of a worldwide catastrophic flood, copies of which are extant due to archaeological recovery of them in the nineteenth century. The best preserved of these is found in *The Epic of Gilgamesh* (tablet XI; cf. Speiser 1969, 93–5; Dalley 1989, 109–16). This extrabiblical version explains the legendary disaster as brought about by mere caprice owing to rivalries among the gods, with humans as merely pawns.

By contrast, the biblical version sees the flood from a moral perspective. The narrative in Genesis is bracketed with explicit reference at its beginning and end to the perennial "evil inclination" of the human heart (6:5; 8:21-22) which provoked both the flood and the curse of the ground. God's lifting of the curse is seen as happening in spite of the continued presence of the "evil inclination" and because of the offerings sacrificed to God by Noah (8:20-22; cf. 6:9).

References in 6:5 and 8:21 to a chronic "evil inclination" (*yeser hara*) in the human heart gave rise later to the Jewish rabbinical doctrine of "the evil inclination" (or "evil imagination"), more or less a counterpart to the Christian doctrine of "original sin" (cf. Jacobs 1901, 601–602).

The flood narrative is a composite of the J and P sources which are here for the most part intertwined rather than presented in parallel blocks as with the creation narratives (1:1–2:4a and 2:4b–3:24) or the line of Adam's descendants (4:17-26 and 5:1-32).

According to J, rain falls *for forty days and forty nights* (7:4, 12, 17; 8:6). In P's account, *the waters swelled on the earth for one hundred fifty days* (7:24; 8:3); for P, the flood is not only a matter of heavy rain, but *the fountains of the great deep burst forth and the windows of heavens were opened* (7:11). P thinks of the deluge as a reversal of the dividing of the waters at creation; the world returns to the watery chaos out of which it first came (cf. 1:6-7).

P's version has two of every creature enter the ark (6:19-20); J's has fourteen (seven pairs) of *all clean animals*, two (a pair) of the *animals that are not clean* and *seven pairs of the birds of the air* (7:2-3). For a detailed tabulation of the editorial deployment of the J and P sources in the flood narrative, see Gottwald 1985, 326, 470.

The *ark*, or "chest-like boat" built by Noah is not to be confused with the later ark or chest that Moses made, in which the tablets of the Law were kept (Exod 25:10; Deut 10:5). The word "ark" derives from Latin *arca*, "chest," or "cellroom."

In Hebrew, the words for the two objects are different. The Hebrew term for Noah's ark (*teba*) is the same as that for the basket or chest in which the infant Moses' mother kept him hidden and afloat among the reeds of the Nile (Exod 2:3, 5). It is one of a number of motifs shared in common between the Genesis flood narrative and the first fifteen chapters of Exodus.

As the flood waters recede, the ark comes *to rest on the mountains of Ararat* (8:4). Exactly where the ark was believed to have grounded is thus not clear in the story; a region is indicated, not a particular mountain slope (extrabiblical versions of the flood give other geographical locations).

Like the location of Eden (2:8), the location of the grounded ark is finally a place in mythic vision, as is the flood on which it floated that submerged even the highest mountains (7:19). The biblical narrative relegates the universal flood to the realm of myth when God is portrayed as excluding it from the range of what will happen in the world of nature and history (8:21-22; 9:8-17).

The occasional searches for physical remains of Noah's ark undertaken in modern times only demonstrate someone's basic misunderstanding of the mythic character of the ark in sacred symbol and story. Such efforts are not viewed as serious archaeology by most biblical scholars and archaeologists today (cf. Bailey 1989, 28–115, 203–206).

9:1-17. God's covenant with Noah. The distinctive writing style and vocabulary throughout this section are those of the Priestly source (esp. vv. 1-2, 6-7; cf. 1:28-30; 5:1-2).

Life on earth is seen not as merely starting over with the emergence of Noah and his family from the ark, but as entering a qualitatively different history under a COVENANT relationship established by God with the human race and the world of nature (vv. 8-17).

As God undertakes that *never again shall all flesh be cut off by the waters of a flood* (v. 11), so likewise, under this covenant, obligations are laid upon Noah and his descendants, that is, the whole human race, concerning the slaughter of animals and the shedding of human blood (vv. 4-6). Blood is understood as the residence of life.

Therefore living flesh shall not be eaten, which is defined as *flesh with its life, that is, its blood* (v. 4). In Jewish tradition this principle is the basis for the ritual slaughter of animals by draining the blood from the body, so that the meat will be "kosher," "ritually proper," or "correct." Coupled with this injunction is the prohibition against human bloodshed (vv. 5-6).

Since all Noah's descendants fall under this covenant (v. 9), there arose in later Judaism a tradition of the Noachian laws (sometimes, NOACHIC LAWS or "Noahide laws"), obligating not only Israel but all humankind. In its final form the tradition included some but not all of the divine injunctions to humankind in Genesis and added some others. According to the later rabbis, there are seven: prohibitions against idolatry, blasphemy, bloodshed, sexual sins, theft, and eating from a living animal; and the injunction to establish a legal system (Schwarzschild 1972, 1189).

The perpetual sign of this covenant is the *bow in the clouds* appearing after rain (vv. 12-17). The RAINBOW is understood as an archer's bow, representing God's weapon put aside or "hung up" in the rain clouds, unneeded since the battle of the flood is permanently over (v. 15).

9:18-29. Drunkenness of Noah and the curse upon Canaan. The language and style now become that of the J writer. Noah becomes the first vintner (v. 20). The description in English of Noah as *a man of the soil* loses a nuance of MT, where "soil" is the same word translated as "ground" (Heb. *adama*) earlier (cf. 3:17; 5:29; 8:21).

Once again the J writer has fitted out his narrative episode with an artful closure; here it has a sardonic cast. Noah, first introduced as one who *out of the ground that the LORD has cursed . . . shall bring us relief from our work and from the toil of our hands* (5:29), is found at the end of the story as a *man of the soil* (lit., "of the ground") bringing relief from work to the descendants of Shem and Japheth by placing upon Canaan the curse of being their slave (vv. 25-27). A further twist is the association of the curse with Noah's nakedness, covered by a blanket instead of fig leaves or a garment of skins (vv. 22-23; cf. 3:7, 21).

At some point in the development of the tradition the curse upon Canaan and the contrasting blessing on Shem (v. 26) would seem to reflect later history, when the descendants of Shem (Israel) subdued the Canaanites—this being read back into the primeval period as a state of affairs destined from the beginning, as told in this tale.

As used now by the J writer, however, the story of Noah's drunkenness and his cursing of Canaan appears to be saying that the "evil inclination" of the human heart remains alive and well after the flood (cf. 8:21), and the human disorder attendant on it will still have to be dealt with.

From Noah to Abraham, 10:1–11:32

10:1-32. Nations descended from Noah. The descendants of Noah's three sons populate the earth, and the three lines are organized here into a "table of nations." It is a mixed list of political states and ethnic or language groups, some named as such directly; others are "eponyms," that is names of peoples, nations, cities, clans, personified as individuals (cf. Redditt 1990).

The various groupings conform to the understanding of what was seen as already "ancient history" in the time of the J and P writers, whose work is once again intermingled. By the research standards of modern historical study the table is of course precritical and cannot by itself provide a reliable record. As an example of historical understanding in ancient times, however, it is of interest to modern biblical and historical study (cf. Speiser 1964, 71-3).

That *Nimrod . . . a mighty hunter before the LORD* (v. 9) should be the sole individual among the descendants of Noah singled out for extended comment may have something to do with an inference that Nimrod's hunting prowess (presumably with a bow) threatened rebellion against the covenant between God and Noah, the sign of which was God's own hunting bow (cf. Dahlberg 1990).

Consistent with this interpretation is that as legendary founder of the great city-states in Babylonia (*the land of Shinar*) and *Assyria* (vv. 10-12), Nimrod points ahead to the next and last episode in the troubled primeval history, the tower of Babel.

11:1-9. The tower of Babel. The tower is generally understood to mean a ziggurat, or "temple tower"—a pyramid-shaped mound of considerable height with steps ascending to a temple at the summit. The present narrative associates the name *Babel* (v. 9) with the Hebrew word for "confusion." The actual meaning is "gate of God," which the narrator may have known very well—in which case he is simply mocking the name with a derisive etymology.

In contrast to the account in chap. 10 of the orderly spread of populations across the earth, the story of the tower of Babel explains the world's profusion of languages and scattering of peoples (vv. 7-9) as a confusion imposed by Yahweh intentionally, to stem a rising tide of human technological ambition and achievement viewed as an assault upon heaven (vv. 4, 6).

The notion that prior to the building of the tower *the whole earth had one language and the same words* (v. 1) contradicts the picture of linguistic diversity presupposed earlier in the narrative (10:5). The inconsistency, however, only points to the original independence of the present story from the overall narrative in which it is now stands.

Within the primeval history according to the J version, the tower of Babel story provides an ironic conclusion for the "history of religion" up to this point, which had begun with J's assertion that the name of Yahweh was invoked in worship from the beginning of history (4:2-3, 26). Religion itself is shown to have become infected by troublemaking human pride, represented by its attempt to build the ultimate sacred edifice.

For the Priestly editors of the final work, however, the tower of Babel story provides closure to the overall primeval history in a way not unrelated to but nevertheless different from the purposes of the J writer.

It was suggested earlier that P's account of creation (1:1–2:4a), besides being a celebration of God's creation through worship, provided a liturgical challenge to the religious assumptions of the Babylonian culture under which P's exilic Jewish community lived This story of a world thrown back into chaos because of Babylonian religion and culture, must therefore have seemed for P an ultimately fitting conclusion to the primeval history and a confirmation of the priestly theology that informs it.

11:10-26, 32. Genealogy from Shem to Abraham. The repetitive and formulaic format marks this genealogy as a continuation, through Noah's son Shem, of P's earlier list of long-lived ancestors of the human race (5:1-28, 30-32). Noticeably absent are the explicit reminders of mortality appended to each citation in the earlier list (5:5, 8, 11, etc.), probably because the reminder was not thought to be needed in the new context. In spite of the 120-year limit Yahweh placed on human life according to the J narrative (6:3), the persons in Shem's line according to P continue to enjoy very long lifetimes, although considerably shorter than the antediluvian heroes named in chap. 5.

P's genealogical table concludes at the names of *Terah* and his three sons, *Abram, Nahor, and Haran* (v. 26). For the sake of convenience, and because it does not significantly affect interpretation, the present commentary everywhere (except in direct quotation of the NRSV text) renders the names Abram and Sarai by their respective dialectical variants, Abraham and Sarah, even though the latter forms are not introduced until Gen 17:5.

11:27-31. The sons of Terah. The non-formulaic, more discursive style of this section suggests the J source. Abraham is the chief human protagonist in the first chapters of the ancestral history (Gen 12–23), from which position he is remembered today, although in different ways, by three world religions as historically and spiritually their first ancestor—by Judaism through Abraham's son Isaac by Sarah (chaps. 17–18); by Christianity through its Jewish heritage (Gal 3:7), and by Islam through Abraham's son Ishmael by Hagar (Gen 17:20; 21:13).

Sarah's ancestry is omitted, which is curious, since that of Nahor's wife is given (v. 29; cf. 20:12). Sarah's barrenness (v. 30) will prove to stand in dramatic tension with God's promise of a great posterity to Abraham (15:5-6).

Haran is an eponym and does double duty in the story as the name both of Abraham's brother and of the city or region in central MESOPOTAMIA to which Terah brings his family (v. 31) and from which Abraham will migrate to Canaan (12:4-5).

Nahor is apparently likewise an eponym, the name of Abraham's brother and also of a city in which the brother lives, near Haran (cf. Gen 24:10). His granddaughter Rebekah later becomes the wife of Abraham's son Isaac (chap. 24).

Lot, Haran's son and Abraham's nephew, presumably comes under Abraham's protection following Haran's death (v. 28) and therefore will go with Abraham to Canaan (12:4) where he will play a supporting role in that unfolding drama.

The city of *Ur* in southern Mesopotamia did not become associated with *the Chaldeans* (a late synonym for "Babylonians") until some time in the first millennium B.C.E., later than the supposed time of Abraham. It was already a metropolis, however, before 2000 B.C.E., well before Abraham. The tradition of Terah and his family in relation to *Ur of the Chaldeans* has seemed to some scholars as therefore an anachronism, or else as a reference to another place with the same name (Sarna 1989, 87). The tradition appears again at Gen 15:7, however, without reference at all to Haran. Anachronistic reference to a region or its population by a name associated with it only much later than the period being referred is not unusual (cf. references to PHILISTINES at 21:32-34 and in chap. 26).

There may be literary and theological reasons for P's insertion from J of the *Ur of the Chaldeans* tradition just at this point—it is consistent with the scattering of peoples as recounted in the tower of Babel story (11:8-9). "It is a common feature of such ancestors to achieve their final destination in stages" (Van Seters 1992, 202–203; cf. Gen 12:6-9; 13:3; Deut 26:3, 5). That Abraham puts Babylonian religion and culture behind him also fits well with P's critical stance toward things Babylonian (see commentary at 1:3-31 and 11:1-9).

The Ancestral History of Israel, 12:1–50:26

The legendary aspects of the Genesis patriarchal-matriarchal traditions leave us without clear synchronisms with historical events or characters known from extrabiblical sources. Chapter 14 may contain such a synchronism, but the particular events it may connect with are not identifiable. This means that proposals for historically dating the ancestral period (as distinguished from dating the Genesis sources which now tell about it—see "Authorship and Date," above) must be considered tentative. For various reasons, chronological details within the ancestral history itself (e.g., 15:13; 35:28) cannot be relied on for this purpose (Andrews 1990, 653–54; Christensen 1990, 148; Barrois 1952, 143–45).

Most scholars, nevertheless, locate the ancestral period somewhere in the Middle Bronze Age (between 2000 and 1500 C.E.) since certain features of the ancestral history strongly support even if they do not absolutely compel such a conclusion. To begin with, passing comments made here and there by the anonymous narrators about the story being told indicate their own awareness that events in the ancestral history belong to an age much earlier than theirs (see e.g., Gen 12:6; 13:7; 32:32; 35:20).

Additionally, a number of customs and social institutions appearing in the narrative have parallels attested in ancient Near Eastern law codes of the early and middle second millenium (see Daube 1969, 1–73). Further, the personal names of the patriarchs and matriarchs and their families in Genesis are all pre-Yahwistic—containing no theophorous element derived from the name Yahweh (in English transliteration, names beginning with *Jo-* or *Jeho-*, or ending with *-iah* or *-jah*).

Finally, a date in early antiquity for the period in question is suggested by the fact that even though the patriarchal traditions have been revised in the light of the later Mosaic tradition, distinctive non-Yahwistic names for God remain embedded in many of the Genesis patriarchal traditions—especially in those connected with particular sacred sites. Examples include *El Elyon* (*God Most High*, 14:18); *El-roi* ("God of Seeing," 16:13 [mg.]); *El Shaddai* (*God Almighty* or "Mountain God," 17:1; 28:3 [mg.]); *El Olam* (*Everlasting God*, 21:33 [mg.]); and *El Bethel* (*God of Bethel*, 31:13). Collectively these ancient names and understandings of the divine seem to be connected retrospectively in Exod 3:14 to Yahweh, by Yahweh's self-disclosure to Moses as "the God of your ancestors" (cf. Humphreys 1990; Alt 1966, 10–11).

Abraham, Sarah, and Hagar, 12:1–23:20

12:1-4. Abraham's call. Yahweh's summons to Abraham to *go . . . to the land that I will show you* (v. 1), with its attendant promise of becoming *a great nation*, and the promise of blessing to fall upon Abraham and *all the families of the earth* (vv. 2-3) marks a pivotal point for the entire narrative in Genesis. The call to Abraham and his response (v. 4) reverses the pattern of recurrent expulsion, alienation and scattering abroad that characterizes the human experience portrayed in the first eleven chapters. The promise of CANAAN replaces the loss of Eden.

Without idealizing the human actors—indeed, it portrays them at their human worst and best—the ancestral history, culminating in the story of Joseph (chaps. 37–50), sketches a particular historical option to the conditions of human history recounted in the narrative up to this point.

To bless is to bestow life and empowerment; to curse is to invoke or impose misfortune and evil. The blessing and curse formula used here occurs also in Isaac's blessing of Jacob (27:29) and in the prophet BALAAM's oracle concerning Israel (Num 24:9). It echoes a similar pronouncement made to Noah concerning the shedding of human blood (Gen 9:6; cf. 2 Sam 22:26-27).

The genre or form of the pronouncement thus appears to be a proverbial one in the tradition. The use of the CURSE AND BLESSING motif here expresses the seriousness and gravity with which Israel as Abraham's posterity views its vocation. Put in the form of a pronouncement by God, it functions as a confession of faith in God's providence. Like comparable confessional sayings elsewhere in the OT and NT (and in all religions) it runs the risk of being co-opted by ideological self-interest of one type or another, as warrant for privileged status in society or history.

12:5-9. Abraham's entry into Canaan. The boundaries of the land of Canaan are not precisely or consistently defined in the OT. Those given in Gen 15:18 are not geographical but political, designating the claimed boundaries of the empire of David and Solomon (2 Sam 8:3; 1 Kgs 4:21). The Genesis narratives make clear that Canaan was thought of by later generations as having long been occupied by a variety of indigenous and migrant ethnic groups, among whom Abraham, Sarah, and their nephew Lot arrived as strangers, perhaps during the first half of the second millennium B.C.E. (cf. 15:19-20).

Canaan as a geographical region is generally construed as the territory west of the Jordan River to the Mediterranean Coast, bounded on the south by Egypt and on the north by Lebanon, roughly what was referred to in Roman times as PALESTINE.

Abraham's first stop in Canaan is SHECHEM, in the HILL COUNTRY of Samaria below the slopes of Mount Gerizim, about thirty-six miles north of Jerusalem. Shechem was a major Canaanite city and sacred site before Israel's appearance in the land, and it came to play a religious and political role in Israel throughout its history (see, e.g., Judg 9:1-57; 1 Kgs 12:1, 25; John 4:20-24).

In the Hexateuch (Genesis–Joshua) Shechem in Gen 12 marks the beginning of a narrative itinerary that will conclude with Israel's return to Shechem under Joshua for the great covenant ceremony (Josh 24) that concludes Israel's conquest of Canaan.

Lying about twelve miles north of Jerusalem, BETHEL was an ancient city and temple site in what became Israel's Northern Kingdom after its secession from rule by the Davidic house of Judah (cf. Gen 28:17-18; 1 Kgs 12:28). That Abraham *built . . . an altar to the* LORD at these principal holy places (vv. 7, 8; cf. 13:8) implies his laying hold of the promise of the land.

12:10-20. Abraham and Sarah in Egypt. Abraham's brief sojourn in Egypt because of famine in Canaan seems to be a rehearsal for the enlargement of this motif in the eventual movement of Jacob's (Israel's) descents into Egypt because of worldwide famine in the time of Joseph (chaps. 37–50). The Egyptian connection threads through the entire ancestral history in Genesis, requiring the narrator to explain why, unlike his father Abraham and his son Jacob, Isaac does not go down into Egypt in a time of famine (26:2).

The account of Abraham and Sarah in Egypt is dominated by the story of Abraham attempting to pass off Sarah as his sister. The rationale behind this tradition from J and its parallels (20:1-18 [E] and 26:6-11 [J], regarding Isaac) remains enigmatic. It is possible that the narrators themselves passed on a tradition they did not fully understand but used for their own purposes (see Speiser 1964, 91-4).

The J and E writers seem to take the wife-as-sister tradition to illustrate a precariousness in Abraham's and Sarah's situation (or Isaac's and Rebekah's in 26:6-11) from which God delivers them. The detail that deliverance included Pharaoh's bestowal of wealth on Abraham (v. 16) is the first appearance of a tradition associated with the EXODUS, that Israel plundered ("despoiled," RSV) the Egyptians (Gen 15:14; Exod 3:21-22; 11:2; 12:35-36). This tradition may in fact be the real clue to understanding the "wife as sister" tradition (see commentary at 20:1-18).

13:1-18. The promised land; Abraham and Lot separate. The agreement between Abraham and Lot to separate and to divide the region between them is made presumably at Bethel (v. 3), from whose height much of the Jordan Valley is visible (vv. 13-16). The tradition serves an etiological purpose in explaining the eventual political divisions along the Jordan Rift between Israel on the western side and the nations of Ammon and Moab, whose common ancestor was Lot (19:30-38), on the east.

The story nevertheless betrays a bias in favor of the later Davidic and Solomonic Israelite hegemony over the area in that God's promise of the land to Abraham and his posterity (vv. 14-17) appears to include all of the region presumably divided between Abraham and Lot (vv. 8-12).

That in this context Abraham finally settles *at Hebron* (v. 18), which will one day become King David's capital in the territory of Judah (2 Sam 2:1-4) before he moves it to Jerusalem, reinforces the impression of hegemonic bias. It will be reinforced further by the immediately following account of Abraham's military rescue of Lot from his capture by invaders from the east (14:1-16).

Consistent with the favorable Israelite and Judahite slant, the Ammonites and Moabites seem implicitly derogated in the narrative. Their ancestor Lot is shown for the most part as a foil to Abraham, who is always the central character in the stories concerning them both. Lot is little more than a cipher. Where he shares the narrative stage with Abraham, he never speaks. He comes to life only in the story of the destruction of Sodom (chap. 19), in which his character is portrayed as weak and ineffectual.

14:1-24. Abraham's rescue of Lot. This chapter is unique in the sense that it clearly belongs to none of the literary sources traceable in the book (principally J, E, or P). It, therefore, must be considered an independent source.

For example, it portrays Abraham as military commander and warrior, a role he plays nowhere else in Genesis. Further, its name for the Deity is Canaanite—*God Most High* (Heb. *El Elyon*; vv. 18, 20, 22). The priest is *King Melchizedek* whose sanctuary is at *Salem* (v. 18), identified by later tradition—whether correctly or not—as Jerusalem (or "Zion"; cf. Ps 76:2 [MT 76:3]), which was a Canaanite (Jebusite) city in the ancestral period.

Such features of the account would seem to imply that chap. 14 is a very old source. Its association with Jerusalem (v. 18) suggests that the tradition was preserved there. The particular event that it originally referred to, however, and the warring kings that are named, are not now identifiable (see Speiser 1964, 105–109).

The present purpose of the tradition in Genesis, however, seems designed further to contrast invidiously the character of Lot, the progenitor of Ammon and Moab—here associated with Sodom and Gomorrah (vv. 11-12)—with Abraham, the progenitor of Israel and Judah. Lot and his neighbors are portrayed as dependent on Abraham for recovery of their wealth (v. 16); on the other hand, Abraham is portrayed as proudly and virtuously refusing to be made wealthy by anything associated with Sodom (vv. 21-24).

The name *Melchizedek* means "righteous (or rightful) king" (Noth 1928, 161–62; cf. Sarna 1989, 380). Perhaps because of the uniqueness of the tradition in which he appears, and because he predates Israel and is the first priest to be mentioned in the OT, early Jewish and Christian tradition cast the mysterious priest-king MELCHIZEDEK in a messianic role (Ps 110:4; Heb 7:1-17). In Genesis, however, Melchizedek's actions and his association with ancient pre-Davidic Jerusalem are no doubt meant as validation for Davidic Jerusalem's claim to Abraham as ancestor.

15:1-21. God's covenant with Abraham (J). The ceremonial and mythic elements in this passage (vv. 9-12, 17, which interweave the J and E sources) give it the impression of great antiquity (Alt 1966, 84–5). In its present position in Genesis it appears to have been intentionally juxtaposed alongside what is now chap. 14, to counterbalance or even correct the military representation of Abraham given there. In chap. 15, not prowess on the battlefield (14:14-16) but Yahweh is Abraham's *shield* (v. 1; cf. Zech 4:6). Here, Abraham's *reward shall be very great*, not as the booty of war (14:16, 24) but as fulfilment of the promises now to be made.

Perhaps the most significant contrast with the Abraham of chap. 14 is drawn by the twice repeated statement that *the word of the* LORD *came to Abram* (vv. 1, 4). The expression *word of the* LORD, which occurs only here in Genesis (and only seven times elsewhere in the Pentateuch), is a specific technical term in the OT for divine REVELATION through a PROPHET (e.g., 1 Kgs 17:2; Hos 1:1; Jer 1:2). Its occurrence here anticipates the explicit assertion later in Genesis that Abraham *is a prophet* (20:7 [E]). The designation of Abraham as a prophet is the first reference to that vocation in the Bible.

Metaphorically speaking, the authentic prophet in the classical OT tradition has, by definition, access to the divine council (Jer 23:18, 22). As the messenger of God, the prophet's words and the actions associated with them are considered by the prophet and his or her disciples to be not the prophet's but God's.

Assigning the office of prophet to Abraham at this point in the narrative is the tradition's way of saying that the three promises—a posterity as many in number as the stars (v. 5), the predicted release from Egyptian bondage (vv. 13-14), and the promise of the land (vv. 18-19) are truly promises of God and not— the inventions of Abraham.

It is worth noting also that the *vision* (v. 1) is associated simply with Abraham himself—the person. The VISION is not associated with a particular place as are theophanies elsewhere in the Genesis ancestral history.

The name (if it is a personal name and not a title) *Eliezer of Damascus* (v. 3) is already obscure in the MT and its translation is conjectural. The possible connection with Abraham's pursuit of the coalition of armies to a location *north of Damascus* (14:15) makes the NRSV translation at least plausible. *Eliezer* would then be a servant or aide of some kind, or possibly—at least potentially—an adopted son. This associate of Abraham is not elsewhere mentioned in the OT.

In contrast to the righteousness of a royalty or priesthood—a meaning embedded in the name Melchizedek (14:18, above)—Abraham's righteousness (or "rightful reputation") rests on his trust in Yahweh: *he believed the* LORD; *and the* LORD *reckoned it to him as righteousness* (v. 6; cf. Rom 4:3; Gal 3:6).

Jewish rabbinical tradition refers to the central event in this chapter as "the covenant between the pieces" (Sarna 1989, 111–12). The ceremony is quite strange. Verses 7-12, 17-21 appear to be J, while vv. 13-16, appear to be E. The carefully specified and divided animal bodies (vv. 9-11), and the *smoking fire pot* and *flaming torch* that *passed between these pieces* (v. 17) while *a deep sleep* and *a deep and terrifying darkness* descend upon Abraham (v. 12; the Heb. word for the supernatural "deep sleep" is also used regarding Adam in Gen 2:21) effectively portray a trance-like episode. The *flaming torch* and *smoking fire pot*—literally "oven" (perhaps in this case a smoking censor used by a priest, if this ceremony is actually performed) represent the holy presence of God. Fire and smoke are typical representations of the divine presence (cf. Exod 3:2, 4; 19:18).

The logic of the ceremony seems to be that the flame and smoke symbolize Yahweh's presence and his acknowledgement of Abraham's offering, and that if Abraham or his posterity fail to keep covenant trust (v. 6), they will become like these divided pieces. An analogous ceremony is so interpreted in Jer 34:18. There also may be a more gruesome symbolism in the implicitly covenental context of the dividing of the body of the Levite's concubine (Judg 19:27-30; see Trible 1984, 79–82 for a further link between this brutal story and the Abraham traditions).

In form though not in substance, the Christian symbol of the New Covenant sacrifice—bread broken as the "body broken for you" (1 Cor 11:24 KJV; NRSV mg.)—seems related to the type of covenant ceremony in Gen 15.

The Amorites were a people indigenous to the land of Canaan; Genesis uses "Amorite" (lit. "Westerner") as more or less synonymous with "Canaanite." That their *iniquity . . . is not yet complete* (v. 16; i.e., not fully exposed) reflects one of a number of theological explanations in the Pentateuch for God's promise of the land to Israel. In this case, the view is that it is not because of Israel's righteousness but because of the "wickedness of these nations" (Deut. 9:4-5) that Israel will be blessed with the land. On the boundaries of Canaan (v. 18), see commentary at 12:5-9. On the clans and peoples named in vv. 19-21 as occupying the land before Israel, see Laughlin 1990.

16:1-6. Birth of Ishmael to Hagar. Sarah's barrenness introduces a recurrent motif regarding the ancestral matriarchs (cf. REBEKAH, 25:21; RACHEL, 29:31). Reference to infertility here creates dramatic tension regarding how and whether the promise made to Abraham of a great posterity (15:5-6) will be fulfilled. It underlines the belief expressed often in the OT, not that the divine role displaces the role of human parents in the conception of life in the womb, but it is what finally makes the human role fruitful (Gen 17:7; 18:10; 30:2; 1 Sam 1:19-20; cf. Ps 139:13).

Sarah's recourse to providing her *Egyptian slave-girl . . . Hagar* to Abraham as Sarah's surrogate (v. 2), so that he will have posterity, may reflect social custom and family law attested in the fifteenth-century B.C.E. tablets from NUZI (Speiser 1964, 120–21). It appears that in the story Sarah offers Hagar to Abraham out duty rather than with any joy.

Hagar's pride in her pregnancy (v. 4) prompts jealousy and harsh treatment from Sarah; when Abraham indulges Sarah's inclinations Hagar runs away (v. 6).

Although his form is not described, *the angel of the LORD* (vv. 7, 9, 10, 11) is a figure more terrestrial than celestial in most of the OT—a human or humanlike representation of God's presence. The word translated "angel" literally merans "messenger," which is also the meaning of the Greek *angelos*, from which "angel" is derived.

In contrast to the several patriarchs in Genesis who receive the promise of innumerable offpring (15:5; 26:4; 28:14; 48:19), Hagar, who will become a single parent (21:14) is the only matriarch to receive that promise.

Form and appearance aside, as a messenger represents the message-sender, so in an even more close association, the angel ("messenger") of the LORD (or of God) stands for God's presence. And often where the angel of God has been speaking, suddenly at the next point in the narrative it is God (or Yahweh) who has been speaking (cf. vv. 13 and 16:1; 18:2 with 18:18; Exod 3:2 with 3:4). The distinction between Yahweh and an angel or messenger is fluid—God and angel flow into and out of each other in human perception.

Hagar, accordingly, marvels that she has *really seen God and remained alive after seeing him* (v. 13). The reality is that the otherness, and therefore strangeness, of God is by its very nature a threat to anyone who encounters it whether rashly or by inadvertence (cf. Gen 32:30; Exod 19:18, 21; Judg 6:22-23; 13:22). An analogy is with the danger of being careless with fire: it is a question of fire's nature, not its evil intent.

The name *Ishmael* (vv. 11, 15) means "God (El) hears." His descendants are the peoples listed in 25:12-18 (cf. 17:20), and they are mostly from the Syrian and Transjordanian desert regions, and from the Arabian peninsula. In the Islamic tradition, Abraham is the first ancestor of the Muslims through Ishmael, as in the Jewish tradition he is of Israel through Isaac.

17:1-27. God's covenant with Abraham (P). The interest in rite and ritual as divinely ordained—in this case, circumcision (17:10ff.)—and the distinctive rhetorical style, make this chapter easy to recognize as belonging to the P source. P's style is characterized by a fastidious concern for exact and correct form— achieved in part by near-verbatim repetition of the same words and phrases for a given object or idea each time it is mentioned. P typically shows a statistical bent also (1:1a; 24-25; cf. chap. 5). The style and content of this chapter contrast strongly with J's account of the Abrahamic covenant given in 15:7-21.

Insofar as this section deals, as well, with God's promise that Sarah in her old age will bear a son (vv. 15-22), it forms a doublet with the account of the same subject in 18:1-15, which is recognizeably J.

Parenthetically, it might be supposed the occurrence of the name *the* LORD in v. 1 is anomalous in a passage assigned on other grounds to P, but in fact it supports the assignment. P never supposes Yahweh was not the ancestors' God, only that before Moses the ancestors knew Yahweh by other names. Here, Yahweh himself asserts that he is *El Shaddai*—"God Almighty." It is consistent with a statement elsewhere attributed by P to Yahweh, that he disclosed himself to the ancestors as "God Almighty," but he did not make himself known to them as "the LORD" (Exod 6:3).

Meaning literally "to cut around," CIRCUMCISION is the removal by careful cutting away of the foreskin, or loose fold of skin, that covers the end of the penis. Circumcision was in ancient times (and continues today) a religious rite of initiation of the male into the group or community. It was practiced in the ancient Near East before it was introduced to the Hebrews (by Abraham, according to the present tradition), and is practiced still today by Jews and Muslims, and other peoples in the world. It is also viewed and used by some as a merely sanitary measure, carrying no particular religious connotation.

Like other religious rites favored in Genesis by the P source—sabbath observance (Gen 2:3) and dietary regulations (9:4)—circumcision is a practice that can be observed in any place; it does not require presence in the temple or any other particular place. This may well be relevant to the fact that the P source is concerned for the religious identity of a people in EXILE.

Sarai and *Sarah* (v. 15) are linguistic variants of each other; the name means "princess." *Abraham* may also be simply a linguistic variant of *Abram* (v. 5), which means "exalted father," although here *Abraham* is taken by the writer to mean father *of a multitude*. The P narrator cites these as changes of name associated with a significant change in status—in this case, entering into covenant with God. The change of Jacob's name to "Israel" is analogous (Gen 32:27-28).

J's account of the covenant with Abraham (15:7-21) did not mention a change in name. That all three sources (J, E, P) together use the "old" forms Sarai and Abram until v. 5 (the P source), and then the "new" forms thereafter, is an interesting example of P's redactional shaping of J and E.

That Abraham *laughed* on being told Sarah would bear a son (v. 17) makes a wordplay on the name of *Isaac* (v. 19), which means "he laughs." There is immediately another wordplay on the name Ishmael, when God says *"As for Ishmael, I have heard you"* (v. 20; "Ishmael" means "God hears").

18:1-15. Yahweh's promise of a son to Abraham and Sarah (J). The self-disclosure of Yahweh to Abraham (v. 1) in this tradition is a showcase example of the J writer's sophisticated way of representing God. On the one hand Yahweh is Abraham's guest at dinner (v. 8). The portrayal is on the other hand subtle and nuanced: for all that Yahweh is understood to be present, his appearance is not described. There is a calculated ambiguity of identity between Yahweh and his representative. *The Lord* appears, but Abraham sees *three men* (v. 2). Later it is implied that one of the three is the LORD and the other two men are angels (18:22; 19:1), but nowhere is this made explicit, least of all while Abraham plays host to God in vv. 1-8 (NRSV smoothes over the ambiguity of identity in vv. 9-10; cf. KJV or RSV, which are closer to the MT).

This scene of promise takes place *by the oaks of Mamre* (v. 1). Earlier Abraham built an altar at MAMRE (13:18); later he will purchase a burial plot for Sarah in the same area (23:19).

Excluded from the presence of male guests, Sarah is *listening at the tent entrance* (v. 12). Hearing the declaration that she would bear a child at her age, she laughs (cf. 17:17 and Abraham's laughter). The ensuing byplay of challenge and denial about her having laughed stresses the laughter theme—Isaac's name means "he laughs." The extended wordplay over Sarah's laughter (vv. 12-15; contrast 17:17) conveys the narrator's sober suggestion that Isaac's birth—the birth of the people destined to be Israel—is an improbable, unlikely happening, in the sense of being of miraculous origin, a singular work of God.

18:16-33. Problems in Sodom. Whether or not God should disclose to Abraham the fate of Sodom is decided in Abraham's favor (vv. 17-19) on the grounds that it will serve as a cautionary tale to his children *to keep the way of the* LORD . . . *so that the* LORD *may bring about for Abraham what he has promised him* (v. 19). The divine promise is conditioned on Abraham's and his children's fidelity to *righteousness and justice.*

Yahweh's decision to make Abraham privy to the approaching destruction of Sodom suddenly casts Abraham in a priestly role, and he intercedes earnestly for the city. The concept that righteousness of the few can be redemptive for sins of the many emerges clearly in this portrayal of Yahweh being persuaded to spare Sodom if even ten righteous people are found there.

Although the historical connection cannot now be traced, this episode may be the source (or an early example of) the Jewish tradition that ten persons constitute a *minyan*, the number of adults necessary for public worship to take place in the synagogue.

19:1-14. Depravity of Sodom. The beginning of J's account of events in Sodom, where Lot is hosting two of the men—now referred to as *angels* (v. 1; cf. 16:7-14)—at dinner in his house, counterpoints the adjacent account of their recent enjoyment of Abraham's hospitality at his tent (18:1-8). The contrast between nomadic tent and urban house is probably intentional. Rightly or wrongly, cities tend to be viewed from the rustic perspective as centers of evil.

It seems clear enough that the attempted assault on Lot's guests threatens homosexual violation of them. The full meaning of the episode may be less obvious, however. References to Sodom and Gomorrah elsewhere in the OT use the cities either as a simile for total destruction (e.g., Jer 50:39-40; Deut 29:22-23; Isa 1:9; 13:19), or as a standard of comparison regarding false worship, social injustice, or general lawlessness (Isa 1:10-17; Ezek 16:48-50). None of the references cite homosexuality as defining the wickedness of Sodom (see Lance 1989, 141–43).

Three central features of the episode outside the door of Lot's house can be stated simply. First, the evil portrayed is not homosexuality per se, but an attempt at gang rape. Second, Lot's offer of his daughters to the mob, in place of his guests, seems outrageous from any perspective. It also suggests there is a social pattern working at some level that subordinates women to the perceived interest of men. In this connection, it must be pointed out that Abraham, and later Isaac, are willing to put their wives at risk for the sake of their own welfare (Gen 12:12-13; 20:11; 26:7).

The third noteworthy feature of the assault on Lot's guests is no mere stereotype of lust run amok, but a more troublesome "type scene" (see Alter 1981,

37–62). What is dramatized is the cruel practice—attested from time to time in human society—to subject strangers and newcomers to homosexual humiliation as a way of impressing upon them their subordinate status (see Lance 1989, 143). Thus the particular act threatened in vv. 4-9 is that of a proud and self-righteous citizenry (cf. v. 9).

A comparable and even more barbaric example of such a pattern is preserved in the story of the Levite's concubine (Judg 19:22-26).

That the messengers' urge Lot to warn members of his family of the imminent destruction—a warning that falls on deaf ears (v. 14)—may be to show that not as many as ten righteous people could be found, whose presence might have spared the city (cf. 18:32). The skepticism of Lot's *sons-in-law, who were to marry his daughters* (v. 14a) insures their own doom and, in turn, becomes the rationale for the subsequent incest between Lot and his daughters (vv. 31-32).

19:15-29. Destruction of Sodom and Gomorrah. An "act of God"—in the modern use of that phrase for a natural disaster (earthquake, flood, volcanic action, or the like)—destroyed Sodom and Gomorrah and the other cities of the plain (cf. 13:12; 14:1-12). This does not preclude understanding it as an act of God in the sense of judgment, which is the way it is interpreted in the present tradition, principally for didactic purposes (see Wiles 1990).

In spite of the brevity of her cameo appearance in the story, Lot's wife, who *looked back* and *became a pillar of salt* (v. 26), is more remembered in tradition than Lot himself. That this is "an old tradition to account for bizarre salt formations in the area" (NOAB v. 26n.) may well be true, but artistically and theologically not especially relevant to J's use of it here. The "looking back" and the "salt" suggest tears and a heart of compassion.

It is possible, further, that by bracketing his story of Sodom with the reference to Lot's wife on the one hand, and to Abraham's intercession for Sodom (18:22-33) on the other, the J writer himself conveys discomfort with the tradition in chap. 19 about Sodom's destruction.

19:30-38. Birth of Ammon and Moab. That the account of the birth of sons to Lot's daughters by incest with their father is placed so closely alongside the prediction of the birth of Isaac to Sarah and Abraham invites a comparison of the traditions with each other. It is hard not to see it as intended by the narrator to be an invidious comparison favoring Israel, descended miraculously from Abraham and Sarah, over the nations Ammon and Moab, descended from Lot and his own daughters, who have been pushed to desperate measures for the sake of their father's posterity.

20:1-18. Sarah as Abraham's sister, again. This brief narrative puzzles readers. *Gerar* is identified as the cite of Abraham's encouter of *King Abimelech*, but GERAR is very difficult to locate in the ancient world. Similar problems surround the king; nothing is known beyond what is said about him here, in 21:22-34 and chap. 26.

Whether these citations all refer to the same person is not clear because the personal name is fairly common in West Semitic literature.

This particular tradition is clearly a variant (attributed to E) of the like tradition in 12:10-20 (attributed to J). Both are somehow related to another such episode involving Isaac and Rebekah (26:6-11). Each such encounter finds Abraham or Isaac misrepresenting a wife as a sister because the husband believes his life to be in danger.

In all three cases it turns out, however, that the husbands' lives were not in danger, because when it is discovered that the women are their wives, no harm befalls the husbands. On the contrary, they acquire wealth and protection from their hosts (20:14; cf. 12:16; 26:11-14).

The true point of these particular stories seems to be that Abraham and Isaac, by pretending that their lives are in danger, shrewdly use their wives to place persons of power and wealth in the husbands' moral debt (20:6, 9; cf. 12:18-19; 26:10). The stories reflect the shrewd wisdom of the ancestors who are viewed as having been able to dupe the rulers of the land into enriching them. There may well be here an ironic play on the proverbial admonition: "Say to wisdom, you are my sister" (Prov 7:4).

Abraham is identified as *a prophet* (v. 7). This is the first canonical mention of the prophetic office in the OT (see commentary at 15:1-6).

21:1-7. Birth of Isaac. The report of Isaac's birth combines brief notations from each of the three major sources. That Sarah conceived and bore Isaac *at the time of which God had spoken* (v. 2) recalls 18:10 (J). Reference to Isaac's circumcision recalls 17:9-14 (P). Wordplay between the name Isaac and "laughter" occurs for the third time (cf. 17:17; 18:12-15) but with a theocentric reference, in contrast to the derisive laughter in the previous occurrences: *"God has brought laughter for me; everyone who hears will laugh with me"* (v. 6; see commentary at 18:9-15). This appears to be from the E source.

21:8-21. Expulsion of Hagar and Ishmael. The threat to the life of Ishmael in being exposed to the elements (vv. 15-16) parallels the threat to the life of Isaac in being bound on the altar (chap. 22; both traditions bear the characteristics of E). On both occasions, the threat arises when God tells Abraham to do that which will endanger the son—send Hagar and Ishmael away (v. 12), and offer Isaac on the altar (22:2). On both occasions, the threat is resolved at the last moment by the miraculous provision of *a well of water* for Ishmael to drink from (v. 19), and *a ram caught in a thicket by its horns* to be substituted for Isaac on the altar (22:13).

The two traditions exhibit a striking differences between themselves also: the women, Sarah and Hagar, are the primary human actors in the drama of Hagar's and Ishmael's expulsion, and Abraham is merely compliant (v. 14). In the story of the binding of Isaac (chap. 22), however, Abraham is the chief actor, and Sarah, who would seem to have a stake in what will happen to Isaac, is not even mentioned.

Nothing is said of Abraham's emotions or inner thoughts as he prepares to sacrifice Isaac; Hagar, on the other hand, says to no one in particular, *"Do not let me look on the death of the child,"* and sitting a long way off, *she lifted up her voice and wept* (v. 16).

Except for references to his descendants (see commentary at 16:15) and to his helping Isaac with the burial of their father (25:9; see commentary at 25:8-10), no more is told of Ishmael than the brief details here. Living *in the wilderness of Paran* (v. 21) locates the tribe or clan, of which Ishmael is the eponymous ancestor, in a region somewhere between the southern end of the Dead Sea and the northern border of the Wilderness of Sinai. Ishmaelite caravaneers will appear in the story of Joseph, where they buy Joseph from his brothers as a slave to be sold in Egypt (Gen 37:25-28).

21:22-34. Abraham's covenant at Beer-sheba. The name *Beer-sheba* can be translated as both "well of seven" (cf. the thrice-repeated *seven ewe lambs* [vv. 28-30] and "well of the oath" [v. 31]). The like-sounding words in Hebrew both derive from the same verbal root, so that to take an oath concerning something may be said, as it were, to "seven" it—the number is believed a good omen.

The tradition is essentially an etiological tale con-cerning the founding of BEER-SHEBA, a major urban center today on the northern edge of Israel's NEGEB which dates back at least to the Iron II period (i.e., ca. 1000 B.C.E. and later). Based on available archaeological evidence, its association as an urban center in the ancestral period would seem to be traditional but lacking historical support (Sarna 1989, 389).

The name for God as *the Everlasting God* (v. 33) appears only here in the OT. Thought originally to have been the name of one of the ancestral pre-Israelite deities worshipped in Canaan, it is now made an epithet of Yahweh: *the LORD, the Everlasting God* (Alt 1966, 10–11, 34). The *tamarisk tree* that Abraham plants is presumably a memorial to the covenant with Abimelech (v. 32); it may also have been a sacred tree, in the context of Abraham's worship.

Abimelech and *Phicol* appear again in the doublet of this tradition at 26:26-33, where the naming of Beer-sheba is associated with Isaac. It is possible that these are not personal names but titles, for it seems unlikely that both men could be associated with both Abraham and then, considerably later, with Isaac. More likely is it that the two stories are simply doublets of each other in the tradition.

22:1-19. The binding of Isaac. The belief narrated here, that Abraham was commanded by God to offer Isaac as a burnt offering, is traditionally referred to in the Jewish tradition as "the binding of Isaac," or simply as "the *Akedah.*" Several important features of the way this tale is told have been mentioned above in the comparison of it with the story of the expulsion of Hagar and Ishmael (see commentary at 21:8-21). Coming mainly from the E source (vv. 1-13, 19, although vv. 14-18 appear to be J), this narrative is a showcase example of the classically laconic, allusive, and introverted style of Hebrew narrative in the OT.

Paradoxically, in the absence of reference to the characters' emotions, the laconic reporting of a word or a gesture (e.g., vv. 1, 3, 7-8) forces the reader-listener to reflect on what must be happening emotionally "behind the scenes." The narrator relies heavily on the involvement of audience imagination (for a study of the impact of the narrative style in this passage see Auerbach 1953, 7–12).

No further identification of the site of the Akedah is given other than *the land of Moriah* (v. 2). Identification is made more of a puzzle by the literal wording in Hebrew: "the land of *the* Moriah." Later biblical tradition associates MORIAH with the temple site in Jerusalem (2 Chr 3:1), as does Islamic tradition. Samaritan tradition holds that the altar for Isaac was on Mount Gerizim, above Shechem.

God tested Abraham (v. 1) makes it explicit that the command to offer up Isaac is from God. The syntax of this Hebrew sentence has "God" in the emphatic position, that is, before the verb. Usually in Hebrew the noun-subject follows the verb.

The story sets forth and explores the enigma that God claims the offering up of the very life he has given. That it is meant to show that sacrifice of the firstborn human is not finally God's wish, is a possible and understandable way of reading it. Yet if God is willing to forgo such an offering, it remains troublesome that Abraham's faith should be measured by his willingness to offer up Isaac if called to do so (vv. 15-18). The story can also be interpreted to mean that God alone can ask for such a sacrifice, in which case the lesson is directed against humanity's readiness to sacrifice its children on some lesser altar such as the nation in war.

Søren Kierkegaard's extended and profound meditation on the import of God's testing of Abraham, and the meaning of Abraham's faith in being prepared to obey, found in *Fear and Trembling*, offers a classic perspective on this difficult story.

That at the end of the story Abraham rejoins his servants and returns with them to Beer-sheba, but nothing is said of Isaac's return, led some Jewish interpreters to the disturbing speculation that this perhaps implies that Isaac was indeed sacrificed by Abraham after all. (On this view, and for a comprehensive history of Jewish and Christian interpretations of the tale, including Christian interpretations of it as pointing to the sacrifice of Jesus Christ, see Spiegel 1967.)

22:20-24. Descendants of Nahor. The inclusion in this genealogy of *Bethuel . . . the father of Rebekah* suggests that the twelve sons of Abraham's brother Nahor are included at this point in anticipation of the story of Isaac and Rebekah that will follow shortly (chap. 24).

23:1-20. Death and burial of Sarah at Hebron. Although it contains dialogue more animated than is elsewhere found in the P source, this story seems on the whole to be in the style of P (careful attention to detail in general, and legal procedural detail in particular).

Kirath-arba is an older name for *Hebron* (v. 2), located about nineteen miles south of Jerusalem. HEBRON would later become the first capital of the Davidic kingdom, before David moved his capital to Jerusalem (2 Sam 2:1-4).

The *Hittites* (v. 3) are literally "children of Heth." These are not the HITTITES of Anatolia (the region of modern Turkey), but "a late and very minor element in the ethnic mix of Iron Age Canaan" (Dever 1990a).

The cave of Machpelah (v. 9) is the burial site not only of Sarah, but, in due course at their deaths, of Abraham, Isaac, and Jacob. Two of the other three matriarchs, Rebekah and Leah will also find rest here (49:29-32; 50:13). Rachel would be buried near Bethlehem (35:19-20) or, according to another tradition, in the territory of Benjamin north of Jerusalem (1 Sam 10:2). (For a concise overview of the importance of MACHPELAH in the tradition, see Sarna 1989, 156–57.)

Isaac and Rebekah. 24:1–26:35

24:1-67. Betrothal of Isaac and Rebekah. This lovely story from the J source speaks for itself and requires little explanation. A wife for Isaac is not to be found not among the Canaanites, viewed as corrupt and idolatrous, but from Abraham's *country* and *kindred* (vv. 3-4). Abraham (and later Isaac; 28:1-2) remains oriented to the Mesopotamian lands of his origin even as he consolidates residence in the land of Canaan.

Consistent with tradition, it will be an arranged marriage—Isaac takes no part in the mission of Abraham's steward, who brings negotiation with Rebekah's family successfully to conclusion. Before the betrothal is finally agreed to by the family, however, Rebekah is asked whether she is willing to go with Abraham's servant. Her response, *"I will,"* (24:58), matches in both its faith and its brevity of expression Abraham's own ready response (*and he went*; 12:4) when called to leave his *country and . . . kindred* to go to Canaan (12:1).

The story thus marks the transition between the generation of Abraham and Sarah and the generation of Isaac and Rebekah. At the story's beginning, Abraham inaugurates the action; at its consummation, with the servant's return, having carried out Abraham's wishes, Isaac and Rebekah are in the foreground, and Abraham is not mentioned (24:62-67). The name *Rebekah* in Hebrew may mean "link" or "connection" between people (Noth 1966, 10).

The phrase describing the servant's oath-taking—he *put his hand under the thigh of Abraham* (v. 9)—is a euphemism meaning that he touched Abraham's genitals. Such a gesture was apparently a traditional sign signifying that the person's life will be served faithfully by the oath-taker's fulfilment of the oath. The sign in this case underscores the importance of finding a wife for Isaac (cf. 47:29).

The home of Rebekah and her father, Bethuel and brother, Laban is *Aram-naharaim* (v. 10). The name means "Aram of the two rivers"; the region would therefore appear to be somewhere in northern Mesopotamia. It is apparently synonymous with Paddan-Aram (25:20).

25:1-18. Abraham's many lines of descendants, at his death. This genealogical list, cited along with notice of Abraham's death and burial (vv. 8-10), recalls the covenant promise to Abraham that his posterity would be as many as *the stars* of heaven (15:5). The citation also intends to confirm, however, that Isaac and his posterity, not other descendants (or their posterity), are the true heirs of Abraham (v. 5).

25:8-10. Abraham's death and burial. On *the cave of Machpelah* (v. 9) see commentary at 23:9. An affecting detail in this citation is the reference to fraternal collaboration between Isaac and Ishmael in the burial of their father.

25:12-18. Descendants of Ishmael. The names found here reflect the earlier material from 16:15 (see commentary there). These verses bring closure to the story of Ishmael (he will be mentioned in passing when Easu arranges to marry one of Ishmael's daughters [28:9]) in a manner that preserves his heritage and dignity. Although he is the "son of right" and not the "son of promise" (Brueggeman 1982, 203) Ishmael is assured a place among the descendants of Abraham.

25:19-28. Birth of Esau and Jacob. Whereas the list of Ishmael's descendants brings closure to his role in Genesis, the mention of Isaac's offspring heaurlds the beginning of an important new phase of the partriarchal story. Isaac's sons, Esau and Jacob, are the ancestors, respectively, of Edom and Israel (25:30; 36:1; 32:28); hence the oracle to Rebekah, *"Two nations are in your womb"* (25:23). By the late postexilic period and in NT times Edomites have moved from Transjordan into southern Judah where the region becomes referred to by the Roman (Latin) form of the name Edom—Idumea. Herod the Great, at the end of whose reign Jesus was born, was Idumean.

The tradition that Israel and Edom are brother nations is widely attested and is unlike any relationship claimed with other nations or peoples in the OT (cf. Deut 23:8; Numb 20:14; Obad 10; Mal 1:2). Edom is the only people that shares with Israel the same ancestral parents. It is possible that buried in the tradition is a memory that somewhere in their early history the two peoples shared a common cultic tradition.

A number of references to Yahweh in the OT associate God positively with the region of Edom (or Seir, another name for Edom; cf. Gen 36:9)—see, for example Judg 5:4; Deut 2:5; 33:2; Hab 3:3. It is possible, but not demonstrable, that the name of the Edomite deity *Qos* (or *Qaus*) appears in the priestly name Kushaiah (1 Chr 15:17), which, if so, would imply the existence at some point in history of a community that identified *Qos* with Yahweh.

The folk etymology of Jacob's name plays on the similarity in Hebrew between the word *heel* and the name *Jacob*, which means "he supplants." The oracle predicting Jacob's ascendancy over Esau (v. 23) is already being fulfilled. Similarly, the name *Esau* is related to his redness at birth; that etymology is underscored in the following passage where Esau trades his heritage for some *red stuff* Jacob had prepared (25:30).

25:29-34. Esau sells his birthright. Sibling rivalry is anticipated by parental favoritism: *Isaac loved Esau . . . but Rebekah loved Jacob* (v. 28). The oracular prediction to Rebekah that *the elder shall serve the younger* (v. 23) is complemented by the narrator's moralizing observation that *Esau despised his birthright* (v. 34), the inheritance rights of the eldest son. The implication is that Esau didn't deserve his birthright. This judgment about Esau becomes embedded in later tradition (cf. Heb 12:15-17).

26:1-5. Promise of the land reaffirmed to Isaac. Here and in the rest of chap. 26 Isaac's experiences repeat in a relatively close way those of Abraham earlier. Since it is unlikely that Isaac's career would have been in lockstep with Abraham's, the respective duplications must be variants of each other—one variant featuring Abraham; its doublet featuring Isaac. Which narrative in each of these cases is the earlier cannot be determined with any certainty.

Editorial awareness that variants are being dealt with is suggested by reference to *a famine* besides the one in Abraham's day (v. 1) and by the seemingly gratuitous admonition to Isaac not to *go down to Egypt* (v. 2).

King Abimelech of the Philistines (v. 1) is probably the same figure mentioned in 20:1-18. Reference to the PHILISTINES, who did not enter the region until after the ancestral period, is anachronistic—unless it is taken vaguely to mean merely the people who lived where the Philistines at the time of the recording of the narrative.

My charge, my commandments, my statutes, and my laws (v. 5) is the conclusion of a long quotation attributed to Yahweh (beginning at v. 2). This particular combination of technical terms for divine law in Israel appears only here in Genesis, but with small variation is typical elsewhere in the Pentateuch and the historical books of the OT of the legal language of the D source (for "Deuteronomist"; cf. Deut 7:11; 11:1; 1 Kgs 6:12; see also Gregory 1990). This is the source responsible for the editing of Deuteronomy and the so-called Deuteronomistic History (Joshua–2 Kings).

Genesis 26:5 may be the one place in Genesis rather clearly attributable to the D source—probably by way of editing by P.

26:6-33. A pair of doublets. These passages are doublets of the previous stories about Abraham and Sarah. See commentary at 20:1-18 and 21:22-34.

26:34-35. Esau's Hittite wives. See commentary at 23:3.

Jacob, Rachel, and Leah, 27:1–36:43

27:1-46. Jacob steals Esau's blessing. Besides having induced Esau to surrender his birthright (25:29-34), Jacob—pushed by his mother Rebekah's initiative—now tricks Isaac into bestowing on him the blessing that was rightfully Esau's.

As the story now stands it is more than a little contrived. Jacob's disguise (vv. 15-16) would scarcely appear capable of fooling anyone, even one whose *eyes were dim*, like Isaac's (v. 1). Isaac's credulity, especially in the face of his own suspicions (vv. 20, 22, 24), seems a bit improbable. Contrived or not, the narrative is very entertaining.

The story may originally have carried a merely chauvinistic and perhaps comic thrust, expressing ancient Israel's delight over a story of a rival people or ancestor outwitted by one of their own. It was probably firmly planted in the tradition before its appropriation by the J writer, who uses it now to show how Israel's destiny under

God according to the oracle in 25:23 was working itself out in the relationship between the brothers. On the blessing and curse formula in v. 29b, see commentary at 12:3.

The notion that a blessing (or for that matter, a curse), once uttered, cannot be withdrawn or transferred to another (v. 33, 35), reflects a general view held in the OT literature of the gravity and power of the spoken word. Thus when Isaac responds to Esau's pleas for a blessing it is only a dark saying (vv. 39-40), not a blessing like the eloquent invocation of success and prosperity spoken to Jacob (vv. 27-29). Neither is it a curse, however (vv. 39-40). What is said to Esau hints at some future recovery of Esau's (and Edom's) fortunes (v. 40b)—the J writer here perhaps alluding to events in the days of Solomon or later (cf. 1 Kgs 11:14-22, 25; 2 Kgs 8:20-22).

Esau's plan to kill Jacob in revenge for what he has done comes to the attention of Rebekah, who warns Jacob to flee to her own family in Paddan-Aram (vv. 43-44). Rebekah then advises Isaac that she will not have Jacob marry *one of the Hittite women* (v. 46). The purity of the stock of Abraham is once again assured (cf. 26:34-35 and commentary at 23:3).

28:1-22. Jacob's journey to Paddan-aram. This narrative is a conflation of the J and E sources, with an introduction by P (vv. 1-9). P's form of Isaac's blessing is less ebullient than J's (27:27-29) and brings the blessing explicitly into line with the Abrahamic tradition (v. 4). P's citation of Esau's desire to please his father by not marrying *one of the Canaanite women* (vv. 6, 8) is probably motivated more by P's dislike of the Canaanites (or of what they represent for him) than by a desire to treat Esau sympathetically.

Jacob's dream at Bethel (vv. 10-22) is an etiological legend associating the founding of the temple at BETHEL with Jacob. It is a mixture of the sources J (vv. 10-11a, 13-16, 19) and E (11b-12, 17-18, 20-22). Bethel is also one of the places where Abraham built an altar to Yahweh on his inital exploration of the land of promise (see 12:8).

The Hebrew word for *ladder* also means "stairway" or "ramp" (v. 12, NRSV mg.) Rather than a runged ladder, therefore, what Jacob sees in his dream may indeed be steps leading up a steep incline like that leading up the side of a ziggurat or temple tower (see commentary at 11:1-9). Consistent with the foregoing observation, the *angels* in Jacob's dream would not be winged celestial beings (who would not need a ladder or stairway), but quite possibly would be priests in temple service.

The heart of this narrative appears to be the reaffirming to Jacob of promises made to Abraham (vv. 13-16). The renewal establishs Jacob, later named "Israel," as heir to the promises to Abraham and Isaac.

The Hebrew name for God at this point is *elohim*—not *el*, as in the name *Bethel* (v. 19). It would appear that the E writer is concerned not to imply that Jacob worshiped the Canaanite god El. It is the J writer who associates Bethel explicitly with God in Jacob's dream.

29:1-14. Jacob meets Rachel. In contrast to the story of Isaac's betrothal to Rebekah (chap. 24), the story of Jacob's winning of Rachel moves relatively quickly and with passion. Unlike Isaac, who remained offstage while Abraham's servant arranged everything, Jacob represents himself, and would appear to have swept Rachel off her feet (vv. 9-12). The source is J.

29:15-30. Laban rewards Jacob with Leah, then Rachel. Here the source is E—note the introduction of Rachel as if for the first time (v. 16), ignoring her appearance earlier (vv. 9-12).

Laban's deception of his nephew in substituting Leah for Rachel on the wedding night (v. 23) lends a touch of the farcical to the narrative—*when morning came, it was Leah!* (v. 24). The narrative suggests poetic justice for Jacob who had substituted himself for Esau (27:18-29). The entire saga of Jacob's and Laban's relationship (chaps. 29–31) will prove to be a battle of wits, which Jacob ultimately wins.

29:31-30:24. Birth of Jacob's sons and daughter. To these announcements of the birth of Jacob's first eleven sons and his daughter, *Dinah* (30:21), must be added the later report of the birth of *Benjamin* (35:16-18). The several traditions more or less speak for themselves and need not receive special comment.

It is generally recognized that the traditional list of the twelve tribes represented here by their eponymous ancestors is an "official" list, and somewhat artificial, coming from some time during the monarchic period (see Devries 1990, 932–33).

What may be less obvious on the printed page, however, is that the sons (or the tribes of which they are the eponymous ancestors) that are descended from Jacob's wives—Leah and Rachel, and their respective servantmaids Zilpah and Bilhah—can be seen on a map (e.g., MDB Plate 11, or Gottwald 1985, 130) to form rough geographical groupings according to the particular mothers by whom they are related in the genealogical passages under consideration.

The Rachel tribes—Joseph (subdivided between Ephraim and Manasseh) and Benjamin—form together the major territorial region north of Jerusalem. The Leah tribes—Reuben, Simeon, Judah, Issachar, and Zebulon (omitting Levi, who has no territory)—together frame the Rachel tribes to the north and south of the latter, with Judah and Reuben sharing the whole region south of Jerusalem, on either side of the Jordan. The Zilpah tribes—Gad and Asher—are separated from each other and are relegated to the northern and eastern fringe of Israel. The Bilhah tribes—Dan (after the migration northward; cf. Judg 17–18) and Naphtali—lie at the northern extremity of Israel.

The correlations are imperfect or incomplete at some points, but marked enough to suggest that the Genesis writers have sought to order the birth narratives artificially by associating the mothers with particular geographical regions.

Dinah, whose birth is noted in v. 21, is identified with no tribe. Her place in the narrative is apparently to prepare for the story of Dinah and Shechem in chap. 34. She is mentioned after that only in Gen 46:15.

30:25-43. Jacob acquires wealth through magic. Once more an element of farce is injected into the narrative. In a spirited contest between Laban's mendacity and Jacob's skill with magic, Jacob outwits his uncle. Agreeing between them that Jacob's wages shall be only the *speckled and spotted* among the sheep and goats, and *every black lamb* (v. 32), Laban proceeds to remove all such animals from his flock and sends them off with his sons three days' journey away from Jacob.

Using "sympathetic magic" (the peeled rods are presumed somehow to influence genetically the color of the animals when they breed at the watering trough where Jacob has placed the rods) Jacob builds his own flock, which he sequesters from Laban's (vv. 37-44).

The acquisition of wealth ascribed here to Jacob is hyperbolic (v. 43) and seems to exemplify a heightened stage in a programatic movement through the whole of Genesis from the initial blessing of Abraham (12:1-3) to what will become finally the spectacle of Joseph administering the wealth of *all the world* (41:57).

31:1-18. Jacob departs for Canaan. Jacob's explanation to Rachel and Leah (v. 4) of how he came by his wealth constitutes E's version of the preceding account from J. There the outcome depended altogether on Jacob's cleverness; here it is ascribed to the working of God (vv. 9-13). His wives support Jacob's decision (vv. 14-16), and Jacob sets out for Canaan with his family and herds.

31:19-42. Rachel's theft of the household gods. The story of Rachel's theft of Laban's images of the household gods, and her prevention of Laban's discovery of them—by sitting on them and declining to rise, claiming that she is in her menstrual period (v. 35)—is clearly designed to discredit the gods in the eyes of those who worship them.

31:43-55. The covenant at Mizpah. Laban's frustrated capitulation to Jacob's manifest success (v. 43) leads him to propose a covenant between himself and Jacob. Laban's invocation, *"The LORD watch between you and me, when we are absent one from the other"* (v. 49), is not a kind of benediction commending the parties to divine care while they are apart. Rather, as the context requires (vv. 50, 52) it is a warning not to do any harm to one another's interests while out of each other's sight. It is a covenant between parties who remain suspicious of each other.

32:1[MT 32:2]-33:17. Jacob makes peace with Esau. The cycle of stories now returns to unfinished business. Jacob had been sent away to escape Esau's wrath; now that he is returning, he must confront his brother. While the narrative plot is not complicated, there are certain wordplays apparent in MT that seem to lend a mystical dimension to the story, which are not preserved in translation, as follows:

The Hebrew word translated as *angels* (32:1) is the same word that is translated *messengers* in 32:3, 6 (see commentary at 16:7-14). Thus, Jacob is met by God's messengers, and sends his own messengers to meet Esau.

The Hebrew word translated *camp* (32:2) is the singular form of the same word that is left here untranslated, *Mahanaim*, which in turn is the same word that is translated as *two companies* in 32:7, 10. Thus *God's camp* is paralleled by Jacob's *two companies.* Jacob and his family will later be divided, with his family on one side of the Jabbok (32:23) and he alone on the other, to wrestle with God (32:24, 30).

Peniel (32:30) literally means "face of God [*el*]." As Jacob gives this name to the place, he declares, *"For I have seen God [elohim] face to face, and yet my life is preserved."* When Jacob finally meets his sibling rival, Esau, he declares, *"To see your face is like seeing the face of God"* (33:10). Jacob's struggle with Esau (cf. 25:22) is paralleled by his wrestling with God (vv. 24-26) and in both instances Jacob has prevailed. The mysterious wrestler summarizes the story: *"You have struggled with God and with humans, and have prevailed"* (32:28). At this point, *Jacob* is renamed *Israel* (32:28).

Verses 25 and 31 bracket Jacob's struggle with the reference to his limping, because of his hip, struck by the wrestler (32:25). This may be an etiological element from an earlier form of the tradition to account for a limping dance performed at the site sacred to the Canaanite god El. In the present use of the tradition, it implies Jacob is marked by his struggle. The reference to the dietary tradition (32:32) is an etiological footnote, possibly placed there by the narrator to deflect attention from his more serious purpose—in the nature of metaphorical understatement.

Following the intense description of Jacob's struggle the narrative shifts to a scene of reconciliation. Esau appears to have forgiven Jacob, or at least to have been so impressed by the size of his family and his herds (cf. 29:10) that he prudently gives up further thought of revenge. Jacob, however, remains distrustful or fearful of Esau—he clearly wants to avoid having Esau or his men accompany him (33:12-15). Like the peace with Laban (31:43-55), Jacob's peace with Esau is uneasy. Esau was quick to relinquish his birthright (25:29-34) and now seems equally eager to offer forgiveness.

<u>33:18-20. Jacob at Shechem.</u> These verses stand out as a crude seam at the intersection of two rich patches in the Jacob stories. There are two ways to read this brief account of Jacob settling in Shechem. It may be the conclusion to the narrative that began at 32:1. If so, the account of purchasing land and building an altar punctuates Jacob having come full circle since his dispute with Esau (25:27-34; 27:1-45; see Westermann 1985, 527–30). Because the following narrative is set in Shechem some would see these verses as an introduction to a new movement in the Jacob stories (see Brueggemann 1982, 275).

Whether the ending of one narrative or the beginning of another, vv. 18-20 present puzzles of their own. *Shechem* is a son *of Hamor* from whom Jacob buys land (in 34:2 Hamor is further identified as *the Hivite, prince of the region*). Shechem must be understood as the eponymous ancestor of the region; the attentive reader will also know that Jacob is the eponymous ancestor of Israel.

Also curious is the altar that is called *El-Elohe-Israel.* The altar building recalls Abraham's survey of the land in Gen 12–13, suggesting that Jacob now lays claim to the land. If *Israel* is a specific reference to Jacob (cf. 32:28) then the altar is an outpost. If *Israel*, however, is taken as a reference to all the people of God, then the altar "is the beginning of a permanent cult of the God of Israel" (Westermann 1985, 529). Both readings are appropriate.

34:1-31. The rape of Dinah. The narrative is less about Dinah than it is about the total destruction of the city of Shechem by Simeon and Levi. The rape of Dinah leads to what follows and seems to be an etiological explanation for the Shechem's destruction.

By the time of the J writer—the source for this tradition—the tribe of Simeon has become more or less scattered within the territory of Judah, and the tribe of Levi has no territory but has been reduced to the status of servant priests. Consequently this must be a very old tradition that preserves the memory of a time well before the Israelite monarchy, when Simeon and Levi were marauding bands to be reckoned with. This is consistent with their portrayal in Gen 49:5-7, where their cruel violence is recalled and their ultimate decline predicted.

35:1-15. Jacob's return to Bethel. In its present form this section is something of an appendix to the narrative cycle up to this point. The *foreign gods* (vv. 2-4) in Jacob's household recall those brought to Canaan by Rachel (31:19-42). The hiding of them *under the oak that was near Shechem* (v. 4) may be a tendentious thrust against Canaanite cults at Shechem; the events of chap. 34 seem unrelated here. Verse 9-15 contain P's version of God's reiteration to Jacob of the covenant promises made to Abraham (cf. 17:1-8).

35:16-20. Birth of Benjamin; death of Rachel. Rachel's death in childbirth as she bears Benjamin (v. 18) suggests somehow a status apart for Rachel, Jacob's most-loved wife (29:30) and for Benjamin, Jacob's youngest son and the only one to be born in Canaan. Benjamin will be a significant figure in the story of Joseph and his brothers (cf. 43:1–44:34). Rachel is the only one of the matriarchs and patriarchs of Israel not to be buried at Machpelah (see commentary at 23:9).

35:21-22a. Reuben's immorality with Bilhah. Why this brief notice should be placed just here seems a bit arbitrary, except that it does prepare the way for the allusion to this event in Jacob's deathbed "blessing" of Reuben (cf. 49:1-4; cf. Deut 33:6). The tradition may reflect the memory of a sortie in earliest times by the Reubenites against one or both of the small Bilhah tribes.

35:22b-26. The twelve sons of Jacob. This somewhat perfunctorily offered list is apparently from P. The inclusion of Benjamin among *the sons that were born to [Jacob] in Paddan-aram* (v. 26b) ignores or overlooks what appears the much more authoritative tradition concerning Benjamin in 35:16-20.

35:27-29. Death of Isaac. *Esau and Jacob* assist each other at the burial of their father Isaac, as Isaac and Ishmael had done at the burial of Abraham (25:9). By this point in the narrative we have grown comfortable with Jacob's importance over Esau. For that reason the naming of Esau first in the burial narrative is a jolt. Since 25:23 we have expected the brothers to fight. Now they are reconciled in the face of a solemn task.

36:1-43. Descendants of Esau. The genealogy is a combination of several lists, the sources of which are not easily recognized (see Speiser 1964, 280–83). What is remarkable about this genealogy is that the Jacob stories conclude with a thorough acknowledgment of Esau! Even though the narratives from Gen 25–33 make it plain that the son of right (Esau) is not the son of promise (Jacob), this list of Esau's descendants serves as a caution to Israel to avoid an arrogant appropriation of their ELECTION (see Brueggemann 1982, 285–87).

Joseph and His Brothers, 37:1–50:26

The story of Joseph and his brothers is the longest single narrative unit in Genesis. In form it is a *novella*—a short prose tale that typically stresses moral teaching. It is a composite work, combining the sources J and E, with a few brief insertions by P (presumably the final redactor; see Gottwald 1985, 151–53).

Certain distinctive literary and theological features that set the story of Joseph apart from what precedes it call for preliminary commentary that helps frame the story. There are two notable absences in the Joseph stories and four points of correlation with the rest of the book.

(1) The absence of a matriarch. Although in the story Joseph marries the daughter of an Egyptian priest, *Asenath* (41:45), who bears him *two sons* (41:50-52), Asenath does not otherwise play a role in the narrative. Thus, in spite of the prominence of Joseph, the story has no matriarch among its cast of characters—unlike the typical ancestral traditions surround Abraham and Sarah, Isaac and Rebekah, and Jacob, Rachel, and Leah.

(2) Absence of THEOPHANY. A more striking feature is that unlike the patriarchal experience, and in spite of Joseph's many and sincerely pious references to God (e.g., 39:9; 40:8; 50:19), nowhere in the Joseph story is Joseph explicitly addressed by God. Neither does God appear to him directly. Whatever Joseph's inner experience, there is no explicit theophany for Joseph in the story. God does address Jacob (Israel) *in visions of the night* (46:2-4), but this is a true case of the exception proving the rule. God remains in the background in the Joseph narratives. In every episode it is Joseph as a human being who is in the foreground.

The relation of the Joseph story to the primeval history (Gen 1–11) raises the question of the overall unity of Genesis. Granted that the whole work has a composite character, there is the assumption that there is an interior logic to the work in its present redaction. The end, therefore, must somehow answer to the beginning. Affirmations made in the beginning must somehow be confirmed or validated (or exposed as invalid) by the way things turn out at the end. Questions raised or problems posed at the start must be shown as dealt with by what happens at the finish. When this is undertaken with Genesis, evidence for the book's unity emerges at four points.

(1) Joseph and the Eden story. In the oldest of the two creation accounts (2:4b–3:24 [J])—and its exploration of the mystery of human sin and guilt—the dialogue between the serpent and the woman is prominent. The serpent says to the

woman, *You will not die; for God knows that when you eat of [the forbidden tree] your eyes will be opened, and you will be like God, knowing good and evil* (3:4-5).

It seems more than coincidence that in the concluding chapter of Genesis, when the brothers appeal to Joseph for forgiveness, he responds as follows: "Do not be afraid! Am I in the place of God? As for you, you meant evil against me, but God meant it for good, to bring it about that many should be kept alive, as they are today" (50:19-20 RSV, a more accurate rendering of the MT than the NRSV).

Here then is a significant correspondence between beginning and ending. The serpent had declared, *You will be like God*; Joseph exclaims, *Am I in the place of God?* The serpent had promised, . . . *knowing good and evil*; Joseph declares, "You meant evil against me but God meant it for good" (RSV). The serpent had said, *You will not die*; Joseph declares, "God meant to bring it about, that many should be kept alive as they are today" (RSV).

The use of these specific words in Joseph's conversation with his brothers, in which he seems to speak to the serpent's argument (3:4-5) point for point, is intended to serve as a dramatic theological reversal of the Eden scene. Thus the Joseph story serves as a resolution of the human situation exposed in Eden.

(2) Joseph as opposite in character to the primeval ancestors. In the early narratives, the human ("Adam") was entrusted with caring for the earth (1:26-28; 2:15) but is described as forfeiting the trust (e.g., 3:17-19; 6:1-4). Humans in the primeval history fail to meet the responsibilities demanded of them. By contrast Joseph, who has become the manager of Egypt's economy and to that degree a savior of the world (41:53-57; 47:13-26), is seen to be the kind of human being the first ancestors were intended to be but fell short of becoming.

(3) Joseph and the ancestral history. The blessing of the patriarchs, seen in its universal aspect as meant for all the peoples of the earth (*In you all the families of the earth shall be blessed* [12:3b; cf. 18:18; 22:18; 28:14]), is for Abraham, Isaac, and Jacob a promise for the future. In the Joseph story, this promise is being fulfilled—*The LORD blessed the Egyptian's house for Joseph's sake* (39:5; cf. 41:53-57; 50:20b).

(4) Joseph as model for humankind. The question, finally, is not whether Joseph is psychologically or socially a universally appealing or likeable human character, but how he or the tradition about him is used to express what the compilers of the Genesis narratives are trying to say. The Joseph story is integrated in an artful way with the events and theological affirmations of the preceding Genesis material and serves as its artistic and theological culmination.

A work that began with troublesome humankind's infidelity to the Spirit by which it was created—a universal situation (chaps. 1–11) to which God responds with the call to Abraham and his posterity (chaps. 12–36), finds its end in the career of Joseph. Joseph is represented in Genesis as an ideal for Israel and the human race, and it is toward the incarnation of this ideal in Joseph that the whole Genesis narrative moves. Pharaoh himself sums it up, as he exclaims rhetorically: *Can we find anyone else like this—one in whom is the spirit of God?* (41:38).

A book that began promisingly with humankind made in the image of God (1:26-28), after many trials and adventures ends redemptively with a portrayal of that humanity finding itself in the person of Joseph. To his story we now turn.

37:1-36. Joseph sold into slavery. The beginning the Joseph story recapitulates certain elements of the story of Cain (4:1-12), although without its unhappy outcome. Joseph's brothers *hated him* (v. 4) and *conspired to kill him* (v. 18). Strife between brothers is a motif running through the whole of Genesis.

As "helper" to the Bilhah and Zilpah tribes, Joseph, ancestor of what are territorially the two largest tribes (Manasseh and Ephraim; cf. 41:50-52) enters the story being associated with the four smallest tribes, which are immediately to the north of the Joseph tribes. These, apparently, are the brothers who hated him and conspired to kill him.

Reuben (vv. 21-22) and *Judah* (vv. 36-37)—ancestors of the two large tribes to the south of the Joseph tribes—try in different ways to save Joseph from death at the hands of the other brothers. Trouble between Joseph and his brothers in the story, then, would seem to parallel historical rivalries and relationships among the tribes of Israel.

The Hebrew phrase translated *a long robe with sleeves* (v. 3) or "a coat of many colors" (KJV) is problematic as to whether the second term means "colors," "sleeves," or something else. In the OT it occurs only here and at 2 Sam 13:18. The Hebrew word for robe, however, occurs only one other place in Genesis: in the expression *garments* [or robes] *of skins* in Gen 3:21, referring to the garments made by God for Adam and Eve after their expulsion from the garden.

Joseph's dreams (vv. 5-11) foreshadow the events to follow. The brothers' grain-sheaves bow down to Joseph's sheaf (vv. 5-8), and the sun, moon and stars bow down (vv. 9-10)—apparently portrayed in the dream either as gods, or as the animal representations among the signs of the zodiac (cf. commentary at 1:14-19). The meaning of the dreams is plain to Joseph's brothers, his father, and the reader. Since dream interpretations are from God (40:8), Joseph's eventual ascendancy over his brothers and father is determined from the beginning of the story.

The itinerary of Joseph's search for his brothers (vv. 12-17)—from Hebron in the south of Canaan to Dothan (ca. sixty mi. to the north of Jerusalem) covers the three largest tribal territories of Israel. The detail may intend to suggest Joseph or the Joseph tribes EPHRAIM and MANESSEH) as the bond between Judah in the south and the other tribes in the north.

That two different ethnic identifications (vv. 25-28, *Ishmaelites* and *Midianites*) are made of the caravaneers or traders that purchase Joseph may be due to the juxtaposition of the E and J sources. On the other hand, the shift in names could be an indication that the narrator understands them as ethnically more or less synonymous. The two groups were "half-brothers," the *Ishmaelites* being descended from

Abraham through Hagar (16:15) and the *Midianites* being descended from Abraham through Keturah (25:1-2).

The brothers' deception of their father Isaac by presenting him with Joseph's blood-stained coat—to make it appear that he had been killed by a wild animal (vv. 31-35)—recalls Jacob's analogous deception of Isaac with the clothes of Esau (27:18-29).

38:1-30. Judah and Tamar. The story of Judah and Tamar would seem to be intrusive in the Joseph story. Certain motifs tend to associate it, however, with what precedes and follows it in the Joseph narrative. A comprehensive and insightful treatment of the analogies between this interpolated chapter and the Joseph story in which it is now imbedded is offered in Alter (1981, 5–12). Judah, for example, figures prominently in the Joseph narrative, at the beginning (37:26-27), in the central narrative (chap. 44), and at the end (48:8-12). The tribes Judah and Ephraim-Manasseh are to be the dominant tribes shortly before and during the period of the monarchy. It is not surprising, therefore, that Judah receives attention in this romantic novel dealing the Joseph. It is not entirely clear, however, just what Gen 38 most wants to convey concerning the patriarch Judah, the ancestor of King David.

This narrative portrays, once again, how a resourceful and determined woman finds a way to uphold the demands of tradition in the face of personal tragedy and unfair treatment at the hands of the responsible male leader of the community. The story is in four parts, skillfully woven together: vv. 1-11, Judah and his family in the region of Adullum; vv. 12-23, Tamar takes the initiative to provide a male heir for her dead husband; vv. 24-26, Judah learns of his and Tamar's misdeeds; and vv. 27-30, Tamar bears twins.

As is often the case in these narratives of Genesis, the characters are vividly drawn, in very few words, enabling hearers and readers to reflect on complex human problems in which the question of who is right and who is wrong finds no easy solution.

Adullum is a town northwest of Hebron in the territory of Judah. Settling there, Judah marries an unnamed Canaanite woman, known only as "Shua's daughter" (see v. 2). Judah is not criticized for having done so, just as Joseph will not be criticized for marrying an Egyptian (41:50). But there may be in implied criticism in the account of the conduct of Judah's sons. Judah especially will be shown to be at fault for not having followed the tradition of the levirate marriage—that is, arranging for another family member to provide an heir for a man who dies without a son (see Deut 25:5-11 for the later form of the practice, now presented as a part of the law of Moses). Judah feared the loss of his third and only remaining son, *Shelah* (v. 5), if the latter should marry this unfortunate widow.

But what is Tamar to do? Both her standing and that of her dead husband are endangered if the widow Tamar is not allowed to build up a family. To be a mother in Israel and to provide one's husband with a son are both of critical importance.

Judah's wife (still unnamed) dies, is mourned, and still Tamar remains a widow without a child. At sheep-shearing time, a time for festivities and family visits, Tamar takes matters into her own hands. Pretending to be a prostitute, she bargains with her father-in-law, lies with him, and becomes pregnant. Unwittingly Judah has done what he was unwilling to let his youngest son do, but in doing so, he has endangered the life of Tamar, not that of his son.

Tamar's pregnancy exposes her to death by burning (v. 24; stoning in Deut 22:21), but Judah, on seeing the items he gave as a pledge to the *prostitute*, acknowledges that Tamar is more in the right than he is. He did not give Tamar his third son to provide her and her dead husband with a family.

Like Rebekah, Tamar has twin sons (v. 27). Popular etymologies of the two sons probably developed to explain the prominence that the clan *Perez* was to have in Judah. From this clan King David was to come, and the Gospels trace Jesus' lineage back through this son of Judah and Tamar.

While this story fits loosely into its context within the Joseph narrative, it probably owes its place in the Joseph narrative to the importance of Judah in the story soon to be unfolded and the place that Judah will occupy alongside of the sons of Joseph in the later tribal traditions (see Gen 48–49).

39:1–40:22. Joseph's life as a prisoner in Egypt. Now the story of Joseph resumes. Ishmaelites, rather than Midianites (37:36; see 37:28), sold Joseph to *Potiphar . . . captain of the guard* (v. 1) of Pharaoh, and in Potiphar's house Joseph prospered greatly. It was the LORD who was guiding the career of Joseph, with the result that soon Joseph was the overseer of Potiphar's household and responsible for all of the goods of his Egyptian master. But trouble awaited, in the person of the wife of Potiphar—again, a woman known only through the name of her husband.

The story unfolds in five scenes: 39:1-6a, Joseph enters the household of Potiphar as a slave; 39:6b-18, Potiphar's wife tries to seduce Joseph; 39:19-23, Joseph, falsely accused, is imprisoned; 40:1-19, Joseph interprets the dreams of Pharaoh's imprisoned officials; 40:20-22, Joseph's interpretation of the two dreams proves true.

Potiphar the Egyptian discovers quickly what a treasure has fallen into his hands. Everything that Joseph does is a success, and soon Potiphar can entrust into Joseph's hands all of his affairs. The striking abilities and good fortune that had made his brothers jealous now prepares the way for Joseph to confront a new peril.

The familiar story of the efforts of Potiphar's wife to have sexual relations with Joseph and of Joseph's steadfast rejection of her advances (39:6b-18) became a classic story of virtue in the face of temptation. In the pseudepigraphical work, *The Testament of the Twelve Patriarchs*, the testament devoted to Joseph strongly underscores Joseph's patient endurance of suffering at the hands of those who were jealous of him and his untarnished moral qualities. This struggle between Joseph and Potiphar's wife greatly enhances the aura of romance that surrounds Joseph throughout Jewish history and literature. The Book of Proverbs portrays the wicked woman who seeks to entice the unwary; here a married woman is simply overwhelmed by her lust for an innocent and virtuous man who is determined, even as a slave, to be loyal to his master.

Potiphar's wife quickly recovers from her obsession with Joseph when she sees that he is adamant. Having Joseph's outer garment in her possession as Joseph flees from his encounter with her, she uses the garment as evidence that it was Joseph who tried to seduce her, thereby betraying his master. She calls him *a Hebrew* (39:14), a term used frequently as the designation of an Israelite by foreigners (see Wilson 1990 for the origin and basic meaning of the term).

Joseph, falsely accused, is imprisoned (39:19-23). Potiphar is of course enraged at Joseph's apparent betrayal and has him imprisoned in the place where state prisoners are kept. There, once more, the LORD causes all of Joseph's affairs to prosper, even though he must remain a prisoner. He becomes second in command in all of the circumstances in which he finds himself: with Potiphar first, now with the chief jailer, and soon with Pharaoh himself.

Life in the court of Pharaoh was like that in any imperial, authoritarian court—precarious! It was easy to fall out of favor, and often the return to favor occurred capriciously. In our story, a *chief cupbearer* and a *chief baker* (40:2), both probably much higher offices than the terms might suggest, come to grief and end up in prison. Their jailer is Joseph's jailer, although the *captain of the guard* (v. 3) is not identified as Potiphar. Joseph serves these high-standing officials of Pharaoh's court, and Joseph hears their dreams after each has had a dream during a single night.

In Gen 37 Joseph's own dreams are presented with such clarity that there can be no doubt of their meaning. Here too, while Joseph is tested as an interpreter of dreams, he hears dreams that do not seem to be too difficult to understand. Even the more complex dreams of Pharaoh (chap. 41) may suggest their general meaning. As an interpreter of dreams, Joseph does not appear in quite the role that his later counterpart, Daniel must fulfill. Daniel was required both to repeat the dream of his master and then interpret it (Dan 2)!

The interpretation of dreams in the ancient Near Eastern world was a part of the task of seers and prophets who were charged to assist the rulers in governance. Dreams served along with other phenomena as means by which the gifted person might gain important insight or knowledge that was not available through other means. Frequently, the interpreter of dreams would enable the ruler to see that the outcome of an impending battle was either likely to be favorable or likely to be disastrous. Or a dream could offer clues to other aspects of the future. The dream provided a window on the as yet unrealized future, giving at least a clue as to what lay in store. In our day, dreams too are avenues by which to secure insight and knowledge that is not readily available otherwise, but primarily in order to gain understanding of the past and present, not to predict the future (see Brueggemann 1982 for a detailed discussion of the importance of the dream as a clue to the whole import of the Joseph narrative).

Joseph's interpretation of the dreams of Pharaoh's out-of-favor officials centers entirely on the question whether they will be restored to favor in Pharaoh's court. He promises the chief cupbearer that he will be restored, but he must say that the chief baker is shortly to lose his life.

Very soon, Pharaoh does indeed lift *up the head*—publicly calling the attention of the court—both the chief cupbearer and the chief baker, restoring the former to office and ordering the execution of the latter. But the spared official does not carry out Joseph's plea (40:14-15) for justice; once the chief cupbearer is back in office, he gives no thought to the part that Joseph's interpretation of the dream might have played in his return to favor or to the injustice Joseph has suffered. A day will come, although well into the future, when the chief cupbearer will have occasion to remember Joseph. And all the time, the Lord is holding Joseph in readiness for great deeds yet to be accomplished.

41:1-45. Pharaoh's discovery and elevation of Joseph. The narrator now turns to the central part of the narrative: Joseph's rise to authority in Egypt, and the peaceable settlement of the people of Israel in Egypt as a result of Joseph's position, and in accordance with God's purpose all along. George Coats (1983) has pointed out how the Joseph narrative serves well to link the earlier promises of God to Abraham, Isaac, and Jacob to the tradition of oppression in Egypt and deliverance from slavery there. Joseph preceded the Israelites into slavery and rose to high rank. His descendants again fell into slavery and were brought to freedom through God's massive intervention.

This linkage is clear as the story of Pharaoh's dreams unfolds. In Egypt, a land that is the "gift of the Nile," great plenty is coming, but it will be followed by terrible privation. How is Pharaoh to handle such a future? Will he squander the goods in the time of plenty, giving no thought to the future? Or will he learn to be a prudent ruler, recognizing God's provident gifts in times of plenty and doing his own part to make those gifts available for the welfare of his whole land and people? The promise of the seven rich years and the predictions of the seven lean years offer to Pharaoh a test of leadership.

Joseph quickly says to Pharaoh that interpretation of dreams is God's business, not that of human beings. But Joseph dutifully fulfills his part in God's interpretation, being God's voice to Pharaoh. Joseph does not simply say what is about to happen; it is his task also to say how Pharaoh is to confront the coming events. Pharaoh likes what he hears, assigns Joseph to take charge of affairs in Egypt, using the prosperous years to prepare for the lean ones, and in general serving as a just ruler under Pharaoh's overall sovereignty.

The story does not fail to give Joseph all the trappings of wealth and glory that he had been denied by the action of his jealous brothers, by the false accusations of Potiphar's wife and Potiphar's uncritical acceptance of the truth of her charges, and by the ingratitude of the chief cupbearer. Joseph even receives as wife a *daughter of Potiphera* (v. 45), identified as a priest at the religious center of lower

Egypt, the city of On, or Heliopolis. This daughter of a chief official of the religion of Egypt now joins the household of a descendant of Abraham, through whom the God of Israel has promised blessing to the whole world. Joseph is God's instrument in the bringing of that blessing, and so of course is *Asenath*, the Egyptian *daughter of Potiphera*. She and Joseph will rear a family that will take its place in the community destined later on to undergo oppression, gain freedom, and enter the land of the promise as Israel, the people of the covenant.

41:46-57. Egypt and the world saved from starvation. At the age of thirty years, Joseph now becomes the savior from famine of all Egypt and of many other peoples. The narrator portrays Joseph as a shrewd administrator in the time of famine, selling grain both to Egyptians and non-Egyptians. The narrator does not mention gifts from the royal granaries for the destitute, but such largesse must surely have been understood to have been a part of state policy. Later on (47:13-26), Joseph is said to have claimed all the land and all its population for Pharaoh and then to have returned it to them, reserving for Pharaoh one-fifth of the produce of the land. The narrator's attention was to portray Joseph as representing at once the best interests of Pharaoh and those of the people of Egypt.

42:1–44:34. Joseph, unrecognized, deals with his brothers. The story abruptly shifts to Canaan, where Jacob and his family are apparently still located in the region of Hebron, suffering from the same famine, which had not been confined to Egypt alone. We see that Joseph is the savior of the entire world; word of the availability of grain in Egypt is spreading to all the affected lands. And the very brothers who sold this dreamer into slavery must now appear as supplicants before him. Joseph's ability to interpret dreams had enabled him to rescue those who, despising the dreamer, had disposed of him.

Much of the remaining material in the Joseph narrative is devoted to exchanges between Joseph and his brothers. The narrator wonderfully presents Joseph's demand for the punishment of those who have wronged him, while displaying the family love that overrides his hunger to settle accounts. And in the background is the love of the patriarch Jacob for the whole family as they sort out their differences and find reconciliation.

The story unfolds in six distinct parts. Joseph recognizes his brothers but he keeps his identity hidden from them, treating them harshly and pretending to be suspicious of their intentions. The brothers are bewildered. They have constantly before them what they did to Joseph and how deeply Jacob still mourns Joseph's death. But they must have grain, or they will die, and that means that they have to do what the tyrant Joseph demands, even as they seek to reassured their aged father that he will not be required to lose yet another son.

42:1-5. Jacob sends ten sons to buy grain in Egypt. The famine has struck even in one of the richest parts of southern Canaan: the Hebron HILL COUNTRY, famous for its grapes and other fruits. Jacob hears that there is grain available for purchase in Egypt, and he thus unknowingly begins the process that will bring about reconciliation among his sons and joy to his own heart. He orders ten of his sons to go to Egypt to bring back grain, keeping the youngest, Benjamin, Joseph's full brother, with him at home.

42:6-28. Joseph meets his brothers. The first encounter of Joseph and his brothers seems marked largely by anger and resentment on Joseph's part. The narrator skillfully withholds any statement of Joseph's affection for them, his longing to see Benjamin, and above all, his hunger for reunion with his aged father. Joseph remembers past mistreatment and addresses the brothers *harshly* (v. 6). He accuses them, knowing that the charge is false, of having come down to spy out the land for some enemy of Egypt. The brothers protest their innocence, and readers are intended to recognize the irony of the governor of all Egypt being worried about the threat that these shepherds and farmers from Canaan might pose to Egypt.

The narrator shows the brothers protesting their innocence and in the process saying entirely too much: they tell Joseph that another brother of theirs is still at home with their aged and grieving father. Their father lost one son already. And so Joseph is quick to demand that one of them return and bring the youngest son, as a demonstration of their truthfulness and good faith, while all the other brothers remain in Egypt as prisoners.

After three days, Joseph allows the brothers to return home, with grain they have purchased, and with Simeon only kept in Egypt. Joseph is almost overcome as he hears Reuben speaking to the brothers about the wrong they had done to their other brother, Joseph. Reuben sees this current misfortune as a direct consequence of their having sold Joseph into slavery (v. 22).

With their grain and with their purchase money also in the sacks of grain, the brothers journey home. One brother discovers the money, and all are fearful of what that can possibly mean.

42:29-38. The brothers return to Jacob. When they arrive home they discover that *all* of the purchase money has been returned, and they are all the more mystified. What are they to do? Jacob is adamant that Benjamin will not go to Egypt; even if Simeon cannot be saved, Benjamin must not be lost also. There is grain for a time, and Jacob and his sons know that the story has not yet reached its conclusion. And meanwhile, Joseph is in Egypt, with Simeon in prison, and Joseph must often remember the scene when Reuben spoke of the wrong that they had done to Joseph.

43:1-34. The brothers, including Benjamin, go back to Egypt. Jacob cannot maintain his resolve. Famine drives him to abandon his resolve never to part with Benjamin. Judah becomes the spokesman for the brothers, challenging Jacob to recognize the choices they face: either Benjamin goes with them to Egypt, or the brothers will not go, and there will be no grain. The narrator skillfully unfolds more of the scene between Joseph and the brothers as Judah tells of that encounter. Why had they mentioned Benjamin? Because Joseph had quizzed them in detail about their homeland, their family, and they had no choice but to mention Benjamin.

Judah pledges his own life as surety for Benjamin's safety. Judah also boldly criticizes his father for having delayed so long: they could have been and returned twice in the time that they have waited before going back to Egypt with Benjamin. Jacob relents, but carefully arranges to placate the Egyptian governor with rich gifts, with the return of the original purchase price, and with double payment for the new grain.

What follows is a story of extraordinary artistry and psychological depth. When the men arrive in Egypt, Joseph has them brought to his own house, and privately orders preparation for a great feast. The brothers are in terror; the man must be intending to punish them for having left with the money in their bags. They speak to the steward of Joseph's household and are reassured. The steward says that God must have placed the money in their bags, since he was paid in full (v. 23). He releases Simeon to them, and they all prepare for the coming feast.

The vivid description of the feast intensifies the drama. Joseph is still determined to make the brothers repentant over their mistreatment of him, but his love for them and especially for Benjamin almost overwhelms him. He greets Benjamin, and has to excuse himself as the tears come to his eyes. Once he has composed himself, the banquet proceeds, and a fivefold serving from Joseph's table is sent to Benjamin.

44:1-13. The brothers leave for Canaan but are arrested and returned to Joseph as thieves. Joseph once more arranges for the brothers to be put in the wrong. Their money is once more placed in their sacks of grain, and into Benjamin's sack is placed Joseph's silver cup that he used for divination, that is, for gaining answers about the future and the meaning of things by studying the pattern formed by wine poured onto the ground from the cup or by studying the pattern formed in the bottom of the cup by the dregs of the wine. The loss of such an important object would of course arouse the wrath of Joseph and spell doom for one accused of stealing it.

When the brothers are brought to Joseph as criminals, and when the cup is found in Benjamin's sack, Judah once again seeks to plead their cause, this time only able to confess and hope for mercy. Joseph insists that only the youngest son is to be punished. He must become a slave, but the other brothers may return to their father. And again Judah speaks, rehearsing in great detail the events concerning this son of Jacob and also what had happened to the other son. Judah asks that he be taken in place of Benjamin, so that their father will not die of grief at the loss of the youngest son. We can see here how the Joseph story fills in the character of Judah, which may help to explain the inclusion within the Joseph narrative of the account of Judah and Tamar in chap. 38.

45:1-15. The reconciliation. Judah's plea for Benjamin is too much for Joseph. Joseph has had enough of retaliation for the wrong done him, and love of family now override his toying with his brothers and his determination to teach them a lesson. Sending all of the Egyptian attendants away, Joseph identifies himself and immediately puts the question that must have been bursting to be asked: *"Is my father still alive?"* (v. 3). One can feel the anxiety in that question: has Joseph spent so much time paying back his brothers that he has forfeited the possibility of seeing his father?

The brothers are speechless, unable to believe what they are hearing, and no doubt fearful of further reprisals by this wronged brother. But Joseph reassures them, calls them closer, and provides, through the theological reading of the narrator, an explanation of the whole sweep of their life together. The brothers were jealous of Joseph (how could they not have been?) and they let their jealousy lead them into a terrible act. But God was in the act, bringing life and good out of what could only appear to be a crime against love and family. Just as Jacob's conniving against Esau and his trickery with Laban had brought blessing and wholesome consequences for Jacob's family, so the misdeeds of Jacob's sons have worked to the benefit of humankind in general and the promise of God to Israel in particular.

45:16-28. Jacob hears the news. Arrangements are quickly made to transport Jacob and his entire household from Canaan back to Egypt, where Pharaoh and Joseph stand ready to receive them and assure their protection and prosperity in the land. In the second year of the famine, Joseph sends lavish presents to Benjamin and to his father. The text notes that a parting word of Joseph to his brothers is, *"Do not quarrel along the way"* (v. 24), which could also be translated, "Do not be agitated [or: anxious] along the way" (the Heb. verb is *ragaz*). The former seems likely, since the brothers might well be tempted to shift blame from themselves to others, or they might want to take credit for having been more in the right than others. Not even Judah, whom the narrator has presented with such power and eloquence, is given a special place among the reconciled brothers. Joseph's counsel may also be intended to prevent their being jealous of Benjamin's favored treatment.

The brothers report to Jacob as a group; neither Judah nor Reuben nor the favored Benjamin appears as leader. Jacob is hard pressed to believe such good news, but the evidence convinces him, and his next concern is to make his way to Egypt to see Joseph before Jacob's day of death dawns.

46:1-47:12. Israel's Descent into Egypt. This section contains more diverse material than any treated thus far in the Joseph narrative. It opens with a remarkable THEOPHANY, an appearance of God in a night-vision to Jacob before he leaves Canaan for Egypt (46:1-4). This is followed by a brief narrative telling of the start of Jacob's journey to Egypt (46:5-7), which in turn is followed by a list of the seventy members of Jacob's family who were understood to have gone into Egypt during the time of Joseph's governorship (46:8-27). The children are identified by naming which wife of Jacob bore them: the children of Leah and Rachel, and the children of Zilpah and Bilhah. We note that Benjamin has the largest number of children (ten), once again an indication of how the youngest son was favored.

This family (actually a tribal) list is followed by the resumption of the narrative, relating the meeting of Joseph and Jacob and Joseph's preparation of his father to meet Pharaoh (46:28–12).

46:1-4. Jacob's theophany. Note that *Jacob* and *Israel* have now become alternate names for the patriarch. God's promise that Abraham's descendants will receive the divine blessing (Gen 12:1-3) has now become God's promise to Israel, the new name borne by Jacob since his meeting with God at the Jabbok ford (Gen 32:22-32). This section gives prominence to *Beer-sheba*, closely associated with Jacob's father Isaac, and long a center of Israelite worship (see Amos 5:5). The expression *God of your father* (v. 3) is familiar from the Abraham and Isaac traditions and has already appeared in the Jacob traditions as well (see esp. Gen 28:13, 31:53, and 32:9). The meaning of the theophany is clear: Jacob is again about to leave the land of the promise; he does so only with the approval and under the explicit command of God. Canaan remains the place where the promise of God will find its realization, but Egypt, during this period, is the site where the blessing will also come to pass. Jacob also leaves with the implicit blessing of his dead father Isaac, the one from whom he once received a blessing by deceit.

46:5-27. Jacob's descendants who entered Egypt are carefully identified. The list serves the function of making clear the extent of God's blessing upon Jacob's family. Entering Egypt as the family of a single man (including children and grandchildren), Israel would return as a great multitude, preserved by God, enabled to prosper, and even to multiply in numbers during the time of oppression and enslavement.

46:28-34. Joseph and Jacob meet. Finally, Joseph and Jacob meet, embrace, and affirm their joy at being reunited. Jacob is now ready to die, he says for he has seen his lost son alive and prospering. Joseph offers instruction to his family when they meet Pharaoh: they must not speak of themselves as *shepherds* (v. 34). The instruction is puzzling, since it seems clearly not to have been followed, although Pharaoh does explicitly ask for tenders of livestock, not for shepherds, from among Jacob's family (47:6). The best explanation for the warning that they not identify themselves as shepherds but as herdsmen is suggested by Speiser (1964, 345). The popular etymology of the term HYKSOS, one of the occupiers of Egypt in the late eighteenth- and seventeenth-centuries B.C.E., was "shepherd-kings"; perhaps this is a reference to that time.

47:1-12. Jacob and Pharaoh meet. Joseph very carefully prepares for the meeting of his family with Pharaoh. He first brings the news to Pharaoh that his family has arrived, not saying that it was his, Joseph's own doing that brought them. They are settled, Joseph says, in the land of GOSHEN, apparently territory in the eastern delta region of Egypt, close to the site of later building activities in the Nineteenth Egyptian dynasty (fourteenth century and following). Then he presents five of his brothers to Pharaoh, who answer Pharaoh's question as to their occupation with what would appear to be the forbidden answer: "We are shepherds"

(v. 3). But clearly, these shepherds are not a part of the remnant of the invading Hyksos of an earlier time; they are no threat to Pharaoh or to Egypt.

Pharaoh offers them their choice of land—for example, the land where they already are settled, Goshen. He invites any specialists in livestock among them to join in the care of his own herds.

Finally, Joseph presents his father to Pharaoh. Jacob is now a very old man—according to the tradition, 130 years of age. But such an age does not compare favorably with the years of his ancestors' lives; really, Jacob says, his days have been few and hard. While this may simply be courteous and conventional speech in the Egyptian court, it may also be intended to convey the demands of a life in the service of the promise of God. After this brief but weighty exchange, Jacob joins his family in the land of Goshen, while Joseph continues to administer affairs for Pharaoh, as the famine continues.

47:13-26. Pharaoh's power over Egypt owed to Joseph. This section presents Joseph as a shrewd and almost unfeeling overlord of Egypt, seizing the opportunity presented by the famine to enrich Pharaoh and the administration of the empire at the expense of the Egyptian population at large. Joseph, on this view, could be said to have helped prepare the way for the later oppression of his own family, the Israelites in Egypt. There may, however, be another intention in this story of Joseph's impoverishing and eventually enslaving the population of Egypt. The narrative is probably reminding the Israelites that though their ancestors were subjected to slavery in Egypt, their ancestor Joseph had already, with God's blessing, dealt the Egyptians an equally severe blow. Back in the days of the famine, Joseph had demanded all their money, then all their goods, and finally their landholdings as well.

Then the story makes clear that Joseph was not just a ruthless oppressor in the service of Pharaoh. He also provided for the needs of the Egyptians, returning to them four-fifths of the goods they produced and only claiming one-fifth for Pharaoh. Even so, as Brueggemann points out (1982, 356-58), the Joseph of the narrative skirts dangerously closely to being taken in by the opportunities presented by the exercise of absolute power over the lives of others. Is Joseph going to be a faithful son of the promise made to the ancestors? Or will he be corrupted by the opportunities opened up to him by God's favor? Eventually, Joseph is seen to have remembered why he had been sent by God into Egypt: it was not for Pharaoh's sake, and not for Joseph's sake either. It was in order that God's purpose to preserve a great multitude might be realized (see 45:7-8 and 50:19-20).

47:27-31. Jacob's approaching death. The story draws toward an end. The family of Jacob, now called *Israel* regularly, settled in the region of Goshen and prospered greatly. Jacob has seventeen more years to live and reaches the age of 147 years when he realizes that his death is imminent. One thing he asks of his influential son Joseph: that he not be buried in Egypt but that he be taken back to the land of Canaan and buried with his ancestors. The tradition has in mind the cave of MACHPELAH (Gen 23), where Abraham and Sarah and Isaac and Rebekah and Leah already lie buried (see Gen 49:29-32). Rachel's tomb is elsewhere, either near Ramah in the north (see Jer 31:15-17 and 35:16-21, which may presuppose a burial site near Ramah on the way to Bethlehem), or (perhaps more probably) just north of Bethlehem at the site still identified as "Rachel's tomb." Joseph too is said to have been buried in the north, near the ancient city of Shechem (Josh 24:32). But Jacob is destined to sleep with his ancestors in the vicinity of Hebron, in the cave purchased long before by Abraham as a place to bury his wife Sarah.

48:1-22. The blessing of Ephraim and Manasseh. On Joseph's insistence that Jacob, in blessing Ephraim and Manasseh, place his right hand on the head of the younger and his left on the elder—contrary to the convention of primogeniture and to Jacob's wishes (48:13-14). What began with the stories of Ishmael and Isaac, Esau and Jacob, and even Joseph and his brothers, continues here: the rights of the first-born are superseded by the promises to the later-born.

49:1-28. Jacob's blessing of his sons. The introduction (v. 1) and long poem that follows is difficult to fit with the narrative blessing that precedes and the solemn narrative of Jacob's death that follows (see Brueggemann 1982, 365–67). Except for the important mention of the *scepter* of Judah (vv. 8-12), and the pronouncement over Joseph (vv. 22-26), the poem offers more characterizations of the tribes than it does blessings.

Jacob says of Judah, *The scepter shall not depart from Judah* . . . "until he comes to whom it belongs" (v. 10 and NRSV mg.). "To whom it belongs" is obscure in the MT, which reads "until Shiloh comes" (cf. NRSV mg.). In this case the literal translation seems more likely the correct one. That Judah would rule in Israel "until Shiloh comes" seems to allude to the prophet Ahijah the Shilonite, who instigated Jeroboam's rebellion—which ended the rule of Judah over the Northern Kingdom (1 Kgs 11:29-31; 12:15).

The only one of the "blessings" in the poem that is indeed a pronouncement of blessing (vv. 25-26). It is also the single one that associates its recipient with God—in this case with *Shaddai* (*the Almighty*; v. 25), which is a wordplay on the Hebrew word for *breasts* in v. 25.

49:29–50:14. Death and burial of Jacob. Jacob's life is no dangling sentence. With calm and dignity the narrative reports that the patriarch assumes full responsibility for his last days and final rest. Coming at the end of the long and glorious account of Israel settling into Egypt, the story of the death of Jacob underscores and punctuates that Jacob dies as a son of promise. Although all of Egypt mourns his death Jacob did not die as an Egyptian. Jacob dies *gathered to his people* (v. 29) and is returned to Canaan (see Brueggemann 1982, 367–69).

50:15-21. The brothers are reconciled. The scene of reconciliation between Joseph and his brothers reveals the theological kernel of the whole story (and, perhaps, all of canonical Genesis; see above introduction to the Joseph stories). What some would term an irony of history is interpreted simply as God's providential care for those whom bear the promise. Following the death of Jacob the brothers of Joseph retreat to their former methods of conniving and lying: Jacob did not tell them seek forgiveness from Joseph. Joseph's response comes from genuine transformation. He knows that the evil intent (v. 20; cf. RSV) of his brothers has been redeemed by God's goodness.

50:22-26. Death and embalmment of Joseph. With the kernel of the story disclosed the narrative quickly ends. Joseph secures his brothers' oath to bring his bones out of Egypt when they return one day to Canaan. The promise is a necessary link to the narratives to follow in the OT (and is carried out, as described in Josh 24:32).

Works Cited

Alt, Albrecht. 1966. *Essays on O.T. History and Religion*.
Alter, Robert. 1981. *The Art of Biblical Narrative*.
Andrews, Stephen J. 1990. "Patriarch," MDB.
Auerbach, Erich. 1953. *Mimesis*.
Bailey, Lloyd R. 1989. *Noah: The Person and the Story in History and Tradition*.
Barrois, Georges A. 1952. "Chronology, Metrology, Etc.," IDB.
Bethge, Hans-Gebhard, et al. 1988. "On the Origin of the World," in *The Nag Hammadi Library in English*, 3rd ed., ed. Robinson.
Bjornard, Reidar B. 1990. "New Year's Festival," *MDB*.
Brown, Raymond E. 1978. *The Gospel according to John*. AncB.
Bullard, Roger A. 1990a. "Hypostasis of the Archons," MDB. 1990b. "Origin of the World, On the," MDB.
Childs, Brevard S. 1960. *Myth and Reality in the O.T.*
Christensen, Duane L. 1990. "Chronology," MDB.
Coates, George W. 1983. *Genesis, with an Introduction to Narrative Literature*.
Dahlberg, Bruce T. 1990. "Hunting," MDB.
Dalley, Stephanie. 1989. *Myths from Mesopotamia*.
Daube, David. 1969. *Studies in Biblical Law*.
Dever, William G. 1990a. "Hittites," MDB. 1990b. "Shechem," MDB.
Devries, Lamoine. 1990. "Tribes," MDB.
Gottwald, Norman K. 1985. *The Hebrew Bible: A Socio-Literary Interpretation*.
Gregory, Russell L. 1990. "Sources of the Pentateuch," MDB.
Gunkel, Hermann. 1901; repr. 1964. *The Legends of Genesis*. 1997. *Genesis*.
Hayes, John H. 1990. "Covenant," MDB.
Heidel, Alexander. 1951; repr. 1963. *The Babylonian Genesis*. 2nd ed.
Jacobs, Joseph. 1901. "Yezer Ha-ra," *EncJud*.
Kierkegaard, Søren. 1954 (orig. 1841). *Fear and Trembling*.
Knight, Douglas A. 1990a. "Cosmology," MDB. 1990b. "Genre in the OT," MDB.
Lance, H. Darrell. 1989. "The Bible and Homosexuality," *ABQ* 8/2 (June): 140–51.
Laughlin, John C. H. "Canaan," MDB.

Layton, Bentley, trans. 1988. "The Hypostasis of the Archons," in *The Nag Hammadi Library in English*, 3rd ed., ed. Robinson.
Niditch, Susan. 1985. *Chaos to Cosmos: Studies in Biblical Patterns of Creation.*
Niebuhr, Reinhold. 1941. *The Nature and Destiny of Man.* Vol. 1.
Noth, Martin. 1928. *Die israelitischen Personennamen.*
O'Brien, J. Randall. 1990. "Babel, Tower of," MDB.
Oppenheim, A. Leo, trans. 1969. "The Sumerian King List," ANET.
Rad, Gerhard von. 1972. *Genesis.* 3rd ed. rev.
Redditt, Paul L. 1990. "Genealogy in the OT," MDB.
Rosenberg, David, and Harold Bloom. 1990. *The Book of J.*
Sarna, Nahum M. 1989. *Genesis.* JPSTC.
Speiser, E. A. 1969. "Akkadian Myths and Epics," ANET. 1964. *Genesis.* AncB.
Spiegel, Shalom. 1967. *The Last Trial.*
Trafton, Joseph L. 1990a. "Genesis Apocryphon," MDB. 1990b. "Jubilees, Book of," MDB.
Trible, Phyllis. 1978. *God and the Rhetoric of Sexuality.* 1984. *Texts of Terror.*
Van Seters, John. 1992. *Prologue to History: The Yahwist as Historian in Genesis.*
Vermes, G. 1987. *The Dead Sea Scrolls in English.* 3rd ed.
John Keating Wiles. 1990. "Sodom/Gomorrah/Cities of the Plain," MDB.
Wellhausen, Julius. 1885. *Prolegomena to the History of Israel.*
Westermann, Claus. 1985. *Genesis 12–36: A Commentary.*
Wilson, Johnny. 1990. "Hebrew/Habiru/Apiru," MDB.
Wintermute, O. S. 1985. "Jubilees," in *The Old Testament Pseudepigrapha*, vol. 2, ed. Charlesworth.
Wyatt, Nicolas. 1993. "The Darkness of Genesis I.2," *VT* XLIII, 4:543–54.

Exodus [MCB 127-55]
John I Durham

Introduction

The Book of Exodus is the book of departure for the Bible. This is so because of its content even more than because of its narrative. Exodus presents the themes that permeate the entire canon of scripture, in both retrospect and prospect. As the second book of the TORAH, Exodus is a part of a continuing story. But as a repository of major biblical motifs, Exodus is the primary book of the OT and, in general terms, of the entire Bible.

Exodus presents the account of the birth of God's people as his people, the account of the first of his two great salvation-acts, the account of his covenant with humankind, and the account of his mercy after the first of what has become a long succession of betrayals. Above all, Exodus burns with the conviction that so undergirds the whole of OT and NT theological assumption: that God is vitally present among his people. In terms of theology, Exodus begins the Bible.

The Name of the Book of Exodus

The canonical Hebrew name of Exodus is וְאֵלֶּה שְׁמוֹת "And these are the names," that is, the names of the sons of Jacob, the theoretical progenitors of the twelve tribes of Israel. It was also given the name, "the book of the departure from Egypt," and it was this name, translated and abbreviated by the LXX, that has given us the English name, Exodus.

The Text of the Book of Exodus

There is no question of the availability of the original text of any OT book. The earliest textual witnesses to any part of the OT are centuries removed from any autograph, even an autograph of the "final" compilation of so composite a book as Exodus. The most a commentator can hope for is the most accurate version of the text that specialists can provide, and as scholars keep learning, that text is always a moving target.

The text of Exodus has for the most part been well preserved, owing chiefly to the fact that this book achieved what was effectively canonical status very early in the history of the growth of the OT.

The language of Exodus is classical or biblical Hebrew. For the most part it is uncomplicated and generally devoid of philological and grammatical problems. Most of Exodus is prose, either as straightforward narrative or as lists of laws and detailed sequences of cultic specification. Exodus 15:1b-18, 21 and 32:18b-e are in poetic form, and these verses are generally regarded as among the oldest parts of the book. It is also possible, at least, that some sections now rendered as prose were originally in poetic form: the Decalogue, for example, expanded in the received text from its original form as "ten words," or early recitations of the deliverance from Egypt and the sustenance in the wilderness. Later examples of such poetic originals may be found in Pss 105:24-45; 106:1-23; 136:10-16.

Composition and Compilation of the Book of Exodus

Despite the antique reference to Exodus as the second of the five "Books of Moses," MOSES cannot be defended as the author of the Exodus we know. Nor, for that matter, can any other author of Exodus be identified. The OT does not assign an author to the Book of Exodus, nor to the other four books of the Pentateuch to which Exodus is related, by content or by this title.

Tradition has assigned these five books to Moses, both because of his significant role in five of them and on the basis of such references as Deut 1:1, 2 Kgs 14:6, Ezra 6:18, 2 Chr 25:4, and Mark 12:26. This traditional view was forwarded both in early Jewish literature (PHILO, JOSEPHUS, the Talmud) and by the early Christian Church. It has had its critics almost from its inception; but it remained the dominant theory until the eighteenth century.

With the rise of what might be called modern critical study of the OT, a painstaking isolation of anachronisms, repetition, conflicting accounts, an extensive array of discrepancies, several differing conceptions of God, and at least four distinct styles of writing has led the majority of modern scholars to the view that the Pentateuch is neither a unity nor in any sense a composition of Moses.

More than a century and a half of critical study of the Pentateuch, and of Exodus within it, has led rather to the view that these five books are the product of a complex compilation of oral, written, and redactional source material. In still more recent years, this study has been further augmented by the isolation of the distinct literary forms that are recurrent not only in the Pentateuchal books but in the OT as a whole.

A combination of the results of source-research and form-analysis has suggested a theoretical literary history of the OT. The isolation and review of recurring traditions and the study of rhetorical patterns and characteristic structures have aided the understanding of what may be called the interior of the text. And the interpretation of the biblical books by the Bible has increased our appreciation of those books as works that have a life of their own, quite apart from the sources and forms that may lie behind them.

All these approaches, however, despite their obvious and contributing value, have tended to draw our attention to the *pieces* of the Book of Exodus, to what might be called the speculative Book of Exodus, and therefore away from the Book of Exodus no one can deny, the one we have in our Bibles. That Book of Exodus is being taken more seriously, and, in result, Exodus is now being read more as a whole, and as the product of a literary organization governed by a theological purpose, a purpose effectively achieved by a dramatic presentation.

The Historical Content of the Book of Exodus

The historicity of the events described in Exodus, and indeed the historicity of the persons and peoples involved in those events, is hardly to be doubted. That there was an Egyptian bondage, an exodus from it, and a special revelation at a wilderness mountain, in each of which events an extraordinary Israelite with the Egyptian name Moses is present is not to be doubted because of a lack of extrabiblical evidence.

The fact remains, however, that there is little extrabiblical information about the historical context of the events described in Exodus, and absolutely no extrabiblical corroboration for even one of them. The historical content of Exodus must therefore be described in terms of probabilities, not certainties. Once this point is understood, certain historical facts can be adduced that give support to the general background of the Exodus narrative. These facts do not however give verification to any specific details of that narrative.

The sojourn in Egypt and Joseph's rise to power are made quite plausible, for example, by either the period of HYKSOS domination (1720–1550 B.C.E.) or the rule of Akhen-aton (1370–1353 B.C.E.) in the AMARNA period (1406–1353 B.C.E.).

The rise of *a new king . . . who did not know Joseph* (1:8), and the oppression in connection with an extensive public works program in the Delta region are made credible by the rise of the Nineteenth Dynasty of Egypt and the building projects of its first two Pharaohs, Seti I and Rameses II.

The presence of a mixed group of migrant workers, mercenaries, and displaced persons known in extrabiblical sources as *habiru/'apiru* in Egypt and the ancient Near East generally during the second millennium B.C.E. lends credence to both the presence and the need of a group such as the one led by Moses.

The array of ancient Near East law codes (Ur-Nammu, 2050 B.C.E.; Eshnunna, ca. 1925 B.C.E.; Lipit-Ishtar, ca. 1875 B.C.E.; Hammurabi, ca. 1725 B.C.E.; Middle Assyrian, ca. 1400–1100 B.C.E.) and the larger body of covenantal and legal literature they represent clearly reflect the context from which some of the covenantal and legal material of Exodus is derived.

Archaeological evidence in Transjordan as well as in the central Palestinian plain confirms both a powerful Edomite presence in Transjordan and the fall of certain strategic cities in central Palestine/Canaan during the last part of the thirteenth century B.C.E. This is the very period when, in sequence to the narrative of Exodus, the Israelites would have been deflected by the Edomites, and would have fallen upon such cities as LACHISH, HAZOR, BETHEL, and DEBIR. It is also the period of the famous victory stele of Merneptah, which mentions Israel in a list of victim peoples in Palestine/Canaan.

All such evidence, however, offers confirmation only to the context and general background of Exodus. No single event in the book and no single person mentioned in its narrative is known in any extrabiblical record discovered thus far. Indeed, the question of the historicity of Exodus, a question of such acute concern to the commentators who wrote about the book in the sixty years following 1875, is the wrong question for the commentator to ask of a book so clearly and repetitiously theological and religious in its purpose. Exodus is a book about the Presence of God and the meaning of that Presence for the whole human family. To ask it to be history or biography or geography or sociology or ethnography is to misuse and therefore to misunderstand it altogether.

The Theology of the Book of Exodus

The unity of the Book of Exodus in its canonical form is a unity of theological purpose. The compilers of Exodus were intent on presenting a story of revelation and response. Every piece of the book is a deliberate statement of a single theological assertion: that God comes to his people and rescues and guides them.

The narrative sequence of Exodus, the covenantal/legal sequence, and the symbolic/liturgical sequence are each and all together expressions of this essential and central confession.

What appears at first to be an uneasy and disjointed jumble of text turns out to be, on a more careful reading, a marvelous interweaving of story sequence, requirement sequence, and memory sequence. Even the most arcane law, even the most exotic tabernacle decoration, and even the most apparently discontinuous turn of narrative all have a direct function as expressions of this central theme: God is here; God is, here.

The sequence of story, a continuation of the story of the ancestors told in Genesis, strains forward to the moment when God's Presence will be known to all his people, then describes that moment and its double aftermath. The sequence of requirement sets forth the protocols of behavior in the Presence of God, in terms of both everyday life and special-situation circumstances. The sequence of memory brings to the present the action of the sequence of story, in the acts, the spaces, and the symbols of day-to-day and special-event worship.

Exodus is of course not the sole biblical presentation of this theme, which is the theme in a way of the entire Bible. But Exodus is the first and fundamental sourcebook of the theme, and the singleness of its text is both representative of and an anticipation of what makes the Bible a whole, despite the wide diversity of its content.

For Further Study

In the *Mercer Dictionary of the Bible*: COVENANT; EXODUS; EXODUS, BOOK OF; GOD, NAMES OF; MOSES; PLAGUES; PRESENCE; RED SEA/REED SEA; TORAH.

In other sources: L. Brisman, "On the Divine Presence in Exodus," *Exodus*, ed. H. Bloom, 105–22; D. Daube, *The Exodus Pattern in the Bible*; J. Durham, *Understanding the Basic Themes of Exodus*; M. Goldberg, *Jews and Christians Getting Our Stories Straight*; M. Greenberg, *Understanding Exodus*; S. Herrmann, *Israel in Egypt*; N. M. Sarna, *Exploring Exodus*; S. Terrien, *The Elusive Presence*.

Commentary

An Outline

I. Israel in Egypt, 1:1–13:16
   A. The Family, the Oppression, the Deliverer, 1:1–2:25
   B. The Deliverer's Call, Command, and Response, 3:1–7:7
   C. Ten Wonders and the Exodus, 7:8–13:16
II. Israel in the Wilderness, 13:17–18:27
   A. The Route and the Rescue, 13:17–15:21
   B. Provision, Protection, and Complaint, 15:22–17:16
   C. Jethro, Worship, and Law, 18:1-27
III. Israel at Sinai, 19:1–40:38
   A. YHWH's Presence and Covenant, 19:1–24:18
   B. YHWH's Plan for the Spaces and Symbols of Worship, 25:1–31:18
   C. Disobedience and Its Consequences, 32:1–34:35
   D. Obedience and Its Blessing, 35:1–40:38

Israel in Egypt, 1:1–13:16

The Family, the Oppression, the Deliverer, 1:1–2:25

1:1-7. The names and the many. The beginning of the Book of Exodus presupposes the events described in Gen 38–50, whereby the family of ISRAEL came to be in EGYPT in the first place. The providential nature of their migration to and consequent prosperity in Egypt is in view. So also is the gradual unfolding of the promise to the patriarchs of a numberless progeny and a wide land to hold and to be held by such a progeny.

As Exodus opens, the progeny is present already, in great, even teeming numbers graphically suggested by the use of a verb (שׁרץ, 1:7) used elsewhere in the OT to describe the swarming multiplication of fish or frogs. That *seventy* (v. 5) could become so many so soon in circumstances so difficult is the first hint in Exodus of an array of miracles about to take place.

This fulfillment of the first part of the covenant promise to ABRAHAM (Gen 12:2, 15:5, 17:4-22) becomes a blessing that causes problems in Egypt and makes necessary the fulfillment of the second part, the promise of land (Gen 12:1, 15:7, 18–21, 17:8).

1:8-22. A new king and a new policy. Thus it is God's multiplication of Israel that rouses Egyptian fears and makes the family of Jacob *persona non grata* in a land that has been their home for more than four decades. The new king was the beginning of a new dynasty. Previous treaties, agreements, and obligations were null and void. Israel was an obstacle to new and grandiose building plans. Israel's growing numbers represented a threat that might just be turned into an asset.

Thus did Pharaoh attempt to deal with these numerous "Hebrews," first by the enslavement of unremitting toil in the construction of the two supply-cities, *Pithom and Rameses* (v. 11; and, according to LXX, "On, which is Heliopolis"). Incredibly, this policy had no effect on the Israelite population explosion, even when the forced labor was increased to bitter proportions, and the Egyptians "came to have a sickening dread because of the presence of the sons of Israel" (v. 12, author trans.).

So it was that the Pharaoh turned to a policy of genocide as a means of controlling the "Hebrews." He required the "Hebrew" midwives to put to death every male child and spare every female child born to his rapidly expanding Delta slave population. The term "Hebrew" is used in this narrative as an Egyptian epithet for the Israelites, and is not a name they use of themselves (cf. Gen 14:13).

Pharaoh's first method of genocide has an air of quiet conspiracy about it. The midwives could have carried out his order with some degree of secrecy, reporting stillbirths or at least a strange rash of infant deaths following birth.

The midwives, however, protected by the privacy of the circumstances Pharaoh hoped to profit by, refused to cooperate. They did so perhaps because they too were "Hebrew," but most of all because they believed in God. When the Pharaoh called them to account, they gave him a witty retort. And Israel continued to increase in number and so in strength, and the midwives themselves were blessed with families.

Thus Pharaoh turned to open genocide, with the order that every male "Hebrew" child be cast into the Nile, an order required of every citizen of Egypt. How many Israelite boys were drowned as a result of this order, we are not told. The thrust of this narrative would suggest not many. As 1:7, 9, 12, and 20b make clear, *God* is behind the growth of Israel, and any attempt by Pharaoh or by anyone else to thwart that growth can only end in failure. *What* the result of Pharaoh's attempts will be is not in doubt; *how* that result is to be achieved provides an element of rising tension. And that tension is resolved by the arrival of the Deliverer, Moses.

2:1-10. The deliverer is born. The story of the birth of Moses is told directly and without elaboration. The fact that the parents of Moses are unnamed suggests their names were unknown in the earliest sources. In time, as the memory of Moses became more and more important, the names of his parents came to be supplied, perhaps even invented, by the priestly writers (6:20; Num 26:59; 1 Chr 23:12-13).

The sister of Moses is also unnamed here. Although MIRIAM has traditionally been assumed to be the *sister* of v. 4, she is actually called the sister of Moses only twice in the OT: in Num 26:59 and in 1 Chr 6:3. At the earliest appearance of her name, she is called the sister of AARON, and she is primarily associated with Aaron in the OT (see esp. Num 12). This fact, and the often arbitrary addition of Aaron to the Moses narratives, has led to the suggestion that both Miriam and her brother Aaron became related to Moses only in the later layers of the Moses traditions.

The essential emphasis of this birth account is presented by the manner in which this Israelite baby boy's life is preserved, and the delightful irony of Moses' rescue, nurture, and education at the expense of the very hand that sought to slay him. Indeed, the stratagem succeeds even to the extent of getting the little boy's mother onto Pharaoh's payroll, for performing the one duty she most wanted in all the world to undertake. More ironic still, the Pharaoh of Egypt and his daughter become the unwitting saviors of the Deliverer who will bring Egypt to humiliating defeat.

This account is the epitome of the folksy story at which the early sources of Genesis and Exodus excel. It even includes a characteristically homespun—and inaccurate—name-etymology. The name Moses is Egyptian in origin, the Hebrew equivalent of an Egyptian noun meaning "son, boy-child." It occurs often in Egyptian names, as for example Tuthmose, Ahmose.

Unaware of this, the author of v. 10 turned Pharaoh's daughter into a Hebrew etymologist, and explained the name by a connection of assonance with the Hebrew verb meaning "to draw up, out" (משה; cf. 2 Sam 22:17b). As Griffiths (1953, 229-31) has pointed out, Moses' Egyptian name may well present the most significant testimony of the Egyptian context of this story. It is certainly of far greater importance than the frequently mentioned parallel narratives of Sargon and other heroes exposed in infancy (Childs 1965, 109-22; Redford 1967, 209-28, has collected thirty-two such accounts).

2:11-22. The deliverer's flight and homecoming. The security of Moses' youth and upbringing thus provided for, the details of the early years are left to the reader's imagination. They are not important to the purpose of the story, which is after all not really about Moses, but about God and his coming to and for Israel.

When Moses next appears, therefore, he is a grown man, and by an instruction we are left to imagine, he is aware of his Israelite heritage and deeply concerned about the plight of his people. Thus when he comes upon an Egyptian beating one of his people, he intervenes and strikes the Egyptian a mortal blow. The same verb, "strike" (נכה), is used of the Egyptian's action and the action Moses takes. It is a verb that connotes violent and intense action, of the kind that always results in harmful, often fatal, damage (Gen 37:21; Exod 12:29; Lev 24:17, 18, 21, Num 3:13).

Despite his precaution, turning to look *this way and that* (v. 12), Moses soon learned that word of his crime was among the people. His precarious position is brought home to him vividly by one of his own people: "Who set you up as judge and jury?" (v. 14). In justified fear, Moses thus fled Egypt, under Pharaoh's sentence of death, to Midian, a land beyond Pharaoh's jurisdiction.

This flight to Midian does not appear to have been the result of a random choice. Moses escaped Pharaoh, and *settled in the land of Midian* (v. 15). The Midianites with whom Moses settled appear to have been in the main a nomadic people. Recent archaeological surveys of the area east of the Gulf of Aqaba have suggested, however, a complex and fixed-dwelling dimension of Midianite culture (Mendenhall 1992, 4:817-18). At a later period, they were at enmity with Israel (Num 22–25; Judg 6–8). They are connected, however, with the prehistory of Israel through Keturah, whom Abraham married following the death of Sarah (Gen 25:2).

One may reasonably assume that Moses had been made aware of distant family ties among the people to the east of the Egyptian Delta. If so, his connection with the family of Jethro may even be considered something of a homecoming. As Moses himself says, in explanation of the name he gives his firstborn son, Gershom ("stranger there"), *I have been an alien residing in a foreign land* (v. 22).

As the narrative makes plain, Moses has fled a foreign land with strange gods for a land made familiar by the worship there of the God of his fathers. For the first time in his life, Moses is at home among a people whose ancestors are his ancestors, and as he is shortly to find out, he is at home in the land of the God of his fathers. From a place where he did not belong, he has come to a place where he does belong. Thus the Moses-Midianite connection is a theological one, and the attention given it in this theological narrative reflects that fact.

The story of Moses' entry into the family of JETHRO is charmingly told, including as it does deft reminders of Jethro's sonless status and the high standard of ancient Near Eastern hospitality. Moses' father-in-law is called REUEL here and in Num 10:29, Hobab in Judg 4:11, and Jethro ten times (Exod 3, 4, and 18). There is confusion about Hobab in Num 10:29 and a mistaken spelling, "Jether" (Exod 4:18), but given the greater frequency of Jethro, and the fact that only that name is used with the title "priest of Midian," "Jethro" is the preferred name for the father-in-law of Moses. Despite many attempts, this names confusion remains without a satisfactory explanation.

2:23-25. The oppression in Egypt: a further note. These three verses provide an important connection with the beginning of Exodus, and the real beginning of the drama now unfolding, and an important shift in the story that opens the way to what is to come. Exod 1:1-7 list the names of the sons of the father, the grandfather and the great-grandfather who are themselves mentioned now in v. 24. The death of the Pharaoh whom Moses fled brings no letup to the suffering of enslaved Israel. And hearing their increasing cry for help, the God of Israel remembers his covenant promise to the fathers even as he is experiencing their agony (note the use of the verb "know by experience," NRSV *took notice*, in 2:25). Thus are we prepared for what now is to come.

The Deliverer's Call, Command, and Response, 3:1–7:7

3:1-22. God's arrival and Moses' call. The account of Moses' call is a composite of narrative from at least two sources. The name *Horeb*, by which the mountain of God's arrival is identified here, is the name given in two strands of tradition. The name SINAI is given to the same mountain in at least two others.

A great many proposals have been made fixing the location of this mountain, in the southern and the northern sections of the Sinai peninsula and outside the Sinai peninsula altogether, and even across the Aravah from Petra (Har Karkom, Anati 1986) and in Saudi Arabia (Davies 1979, 63-69). No firm location has so far been established. The traditional location, Jebel Musa in the southern range of mountains in the Sinai peninsula, dates from Byzantine times. The OT nowhere gives any information on this special mountain's location.

Moses was ranging far with his flock, searching, according to the Targum of Onkelos, for choice grazing for his family's flock. Suddenly, he was encountered by the Presence of God. The symbol of that Presence was a bush all aflame but strangely unconsumed.

There is no merit in the attempts to determine the species of a bush that might give the appearance of being afire, or to discover some natural phenomenon by which an illusion of a burning bush might have been impressed upon Moses. Fire is one of the recurring symbols of God's THEOPHANY in the OT. The essential element in this narrative is the real Presence of God in the place, not the flaming bush, which is but one symbol of that Presence. As the text makes clear, the bush is no more than the medium of the appearance of the messenger of God. The fascination with the bush began at least with Deut 33:16, which refers to the "kind favor of the one settled in the thornbush."

The visible manifestation of the theophany is followed immediately by an auditory one. Moses hears first his name, then special instructions, then the identification of the source of the fire and of the voice. The place has been made holy by the Presence of God, and Moses must take the precautions made necessary by the danger of the Presence before the experience can continue, lest it end prematurely and disastrously.

Once these instructions have been issued, and met, the real identity of the messenger is disclosed. As so often in the OT (Gen 18, Judg 6), the fluid interchange between symbol, representative, and God himself is suggested. The strange fire becomes God's messenger, who in turn soon becomes God himself. The moment is an electric one, and a fearful one.

Only after the authority of the speaker has been established, by the theophany and by the self-identification that Moses has heard God declare, does the call of the deliverer come. It is a pattern Moses himself is to repeat in Egypt: identification, establishment of authority, and call. Yahweh relates himself to the fulfillment of the covenant promise of progeny by referring to Israel as *my people* (v. 7). No more need be said, as Moses well knows their plight. But God, who begins to be called

"YHWH" in this chapter in Exodus, refers to his people's humiliation and pain and announces his plan to "snatch them forth from the power of the Egyptians and to bring them forth from that land to a good and roomy land, to a land gushing with milk and honey" (v. 8, author trans.).

Albrecht Alt many years ago pointed out (Alt 1966, 11-15) the complex way in which early and later traditions are intermingled in Exod 3, noting the conscious attempt to identify the God known variously to the Fathers with the God of the theophany to Moses. This identification at first seems to satisfy Moses (v. 6), but is apparently judged by him to be insufficient for Israel in Egypt (v. 12).

The question, however, is not a question of identity. That has been resolved already. It is rather a question of authority. Moses is satisfied as to who the God who speaks to him is. So also, it must be assumed, will the people of Israel be satisfied, so far as the God's identity is concerned.

The crucial question is what can be done in the face of the apparently impossible difficulties in Egypt, and who will do it. The God of the Fathers, in various times and places and under various conditions, had proved himself to the Fathers. But Egypt and bondage there present a new situation. Egypt is a world power. The people of Israel in bondage are in no way the peers of their oppressors. Their situation is quite unparalleled in the history of the Fathers, who after all had to contend with local groups and local rulers, not to mention local gods.

Further, if Israel in Egypt knew the tradition of the God of the Fathers, they surely knew also that it was by his act and direction that they came there in the first place. And their very situation there seemed to discredit his ability to help, whatever his intention. The Egyptians possessed, or were possessed by, a magnificent pantheon of gods, exerting a cooperative lordship over every aspect of life and granting international influence to Egyptian power.

Moses' real questions are therefore what can be done and who is able to do it. When he is told that he is to be sent to "bring out" the people, a commission that answers his first question, he asks the second question, quite unconvinced of his own ability to carry out such an order.

The answer given to Moses is the recurrent biblical answer to the humble called to great tasks: his wisdom, his strength, his special ability are to come from the Presence with him of God (note also Judg 6:12, 16; 1 Sam 1-2; 17:41-54; Jer 1:5-10). And it is this answer, finally, that brings the dialogue to its climax and the revelation to its essential point. In effect, Moses says "So I am to go. So the God of the Fathers is with me. The people will want to know 'What is his name?'"

The literal translation of this crucial question is insufficient to suggest its real impact. Moses by his own admission will certainly have given his people in Egypt the name that satisfied him, *the God of your father* (v. 6). Thus the question שְׁמוֹ מַה is not one of identity but one of authority. What the people will want to know, says Moses, is what the God of the Fathers is really like; who he really is; how he can hope to accomplish the impossible.

The question Moses anticipates from Israel is the theological question the Book of Exodus is calculated to ask and to answer, and the question we may well imagine to have been in Moses' own mind in such circumstances. What is this God's credentials for what he is promising to accomplish? What is there in his reputation (see Num 6:27; Deut 12:5, 11; 14:23, 24; 16:2-6; Pss 8:1; 74:7) that lends credence to the claim inherent in his call? How, suddenly, does he expect to deal with a host of powerful Egyptian deities against whom he has for so many years apparently been ineffectual?

The question Moses poses can thus be rendered, less literally and more specifically, "What can *He* do?" (v. 13, author trans.) Only against some such understanding of the question can the significance of the much-discussed answer to it be seen. When Moses poses the question of his authority to accomplish an apparently impossible command, God replies simply, אֶהְיֶה אֲשֶׁר אֶהְיֶה, "I am the One who always is" (v. 14). That is to say, "I am the one who really exists, whatever may be said of the gods of Egypt or any other gods."

In response to the question "What is he really like?" God replies "I really AM," and proceeds to instruct Moses, *Thus you shall say to the Israelites, "I AM has sent me to you"* (v. 14). The clue to what has been made into a very difficult formula thus lies in its essential simplicity.

Moses is to say to the people of Israel that he comes on the authority of the one who really is, the one who gets things done. And so that they may never forget the nature of the authority they will have questioned (down all the generations), God gives to Moses to give to them as his special name a name formed from the same root (היה, "to be") as the verbal form employed to explain who and how he really is, a verbal form (אֶהְיֶה) four times repeated in vv. 12, 14, the name יהוה, YHWH, NRSV's *the* LORD.

That this revelation of the name YHWH was subsequently sufficient for neither Israel nor the Egyptians is made clear in the continuation of the narrative. But that the essential meaning of the name is vindicated and that the authority sustaining it triumphs is made no less clear. Both Israel and the Egyptians come to learn that YHWH really *is*, as vv. 16-22 predict.

The key to understanding the insistent requirement that the people be permitted to go into the wilderness to sacrifice is to be found in the urgent desire of Moses, reflected in the present form of the text of Exodus for the first time at v. 12. Although Moses knew that Yahweh would be with him, he felt also the need to have the people feel at the holy mountain what he had first felt there. And their reason for going, as they are to advance it to Pharaoh, is that Yahweh has happened to them—they have encountered "the One who always IS," the "I AM."

This important name of God and this important explanation of the name are formatively influential on much of the remainder of the Bible, from the 6,823 occurrences of YHWH in the OT to the "I AM" sayings of Isa 40–55 and the Gospel of John.

In a way, all the remainder of the narrative of the Book of Exodus is a proof of the truth of the name YHWH.

4:1-17. The credentials of Moses and the mouth of Moses. Convinced that YHWH means business, Moses proceeds to protest that Israel will not believe that he himself has seen such a God. On the surface, his protest is a request for authentication as the spokesman of YHWH. At a deeper level, it is a variation of the question of v.13. The causative active form of the verb "trust" (אמן), the verb from which our word "amen" is derived, occurs five times (vv. 1, 5, 8bis, 9) in the first nine verses of this section, a vivid suggestion of Moses' concern. The Egyptians and Israel will not trust what Moses tells them, for they will have no basis for such trust.

Thus does YHWH provide three signs of Moses' authority, the first and the second of which are immediately demonstrated. Only the first and the third of the signs are actually employed in Moses' demonstration of his authority, and of course of YHWH's authority, in Egypt.

These signs leave no doubt about YHWH's authority, so Moses turns his protest to his own inadequacy, about which he has no doubt whatever. To this point, Moses has really been occupied with the question of the authority of the God who has made what seems so rash a command, and with the power of this God to support such a command.

Moses comes not for the first time to a serious consideration of his own lack of fitness for the job he is being given. His query in 3:11, at least a hint in the same direction, was answered only by reference to the gift of God's Presence. Having satisfied himself as to God's role, Moses raises now the question of his own limitation. Indeed, his protest of personal inadequacy assumes the preceding proof of YHWH's adequacy.

In what almost amounts to a correction of God, Moses states that he is not a man of words, adding in a threefold repetition that this condition is one of long standing, persistent up to the moment of their meeting, and as much in evidence as ever since. In effect, Moses says "You are clearly all that you claim. But I am the same old Moses, heavy-lipped and thick- tongued."

The answer of YHWH is properly indignant. He is the one who has put a mouth on a man, and he gives or withholds the ability to speak, to hear, to see. It is up to Moses to get on with the task, and depend in his weakness on YHWH who will be with him. This answer of course is the one Moses has already been given, and it calls forth from him his real concern: he does not want to go.

Whether the proposal that Aaron accompany Moses as his *mouth* is original to this narrative is disputed. Since the publication in 1948 of Noth's *A History of Pentateuchal Traditions* (1972), the extraneous nature of the Aaron traditions has been often recognized. As already indicated, it seems unlikely on the basis of the OT text that Aaron and MIRIAM are to be considered the actual brother and sister of Moses.

Whatever the original shape of the pieces that make up the composite that is our Exodus, however, the composite in its received form has a statement of its own.

And Moses' concern about his deficiencies as a speaker is treated by YHWH for what it plainly is, an excuse. YHWH promises to be "I AM" with the mouth of both Moses and Aaron, and the discussion is finished.

The postscript about the staff with which Moses is to do the signs is a further indication of the fact that it is YHWH, not Moses *or* Aaron, who is in charge.

4:18-31. The deliverer returns to Egypt. This section of the narrative of Exodus is transitional. The next stage in the dramatic proof by YHWH of his powerful Presence must necessarily take place in Egypt, and these verses move the action from Sinai to Egypt, albeit with Sinai as the ultimate destination.

Moses is not depicted here as having told JETHRO the real reason for his desire to return to Egypt, a fact that seems to be borne out by the account of 18:1-9. There is a minor difficulty in the conflict between vv. 20-26 and 18:6 that 18:2 does not fully resolve. Apparently Zipporah and Gershom went at least part of the way to Egypt with Moses, but the fact that they are never mentioned as being there, or as being on the return journey to Sinai, suggests that Moses committed his family to the care of his father-in-law prior to the final and dangerous leg of the trip into Egypt. The reference in v. 20 to "sons" seems, in the light of 2:22 and 4:25, to be at least premature at this point, and perhaps a scribal error. A second son of Moses is mentioned elsewhere in the OT only at 18:4 and by the Chronicler at 1 Chr 23:15 and 17.

The mighty "wonders" that are to be called forth by YHWH's own "firming up" of Pharaoh's heart are anticipated in YHWH's further words to Moses and perhaps also in Moses' tutelage of Aaron (v. 28), who meets Moses at the command of YHWH at Sinai. These forthcoming mighty wonders, called "signs" (אתות) in 4:8, 9, and 17 and "extraordinary deeds" (נפלאות) in 3:20, are here (v. 21) called "wondrous deeds" (מפתים) for the first time (see also 7:3, 9; 11:9, 10). They are the important proofs of YHWH's Presence in Egypt, to both the Egyptians and Israel. Verse 21 mentions the wonders Moses has been given power to do, and v. 23 mentions the climactic wonder YHWH will do, the one that will bring about Israel's release by the reluctant Pharaoh.

The strange narrative of vv. 24-26 is difficult to translate, and more difficult still to understand. A part of this difficulty is presented by the ambiguity of antecedent for the pronouns "he" and "him." Moses is not mentioned by name anywhere in these three verses (in spite of an unauthorized insertion of his name into v. 26 of earlier printings of my own translation by an anonymous gremlin-editor; see Durham 1987, 52, and cf. 53n.25a.). In v. 26, who lets whom alone?

Despite a great many learned and lengthy efforts, the passage remains a murky one. The best to be made of it is the reasonable guess that the rationale for the inclusion of these verses by the compilers of Exodus is the rite of circumcision. The Egyptians practiced a partial circumcision, one referred to in Josh 5:9 as "the disgrace of Egypt." Either according to tradition or assumption, Moses had to have this "disgrace" remedied before his arrival in Egypt as the spokesman of YHWH. Given the urgency of his journey, the act is performed vicariously on his son, so that Moses might not be incapacitated at a critical moment.

The eventual arrival in Egypt of Moses and Aaron is strangely laconic, and out of keeping with the dramatic nature of the commission and its consequences. There is good reason to think of it as a transitional synopsis, an addition to fill the gap between the last wilderness appearance and the first audience with Pharaoh. The passage presents Aaron in the best possible light, not only speaking for Moses but also doing the portentous signs for the people. Moses and Aaron confer first with the elders, and having convinced them, they represent their case to the people. The instant belief and worship in response they meet, particularly in view of Israel's subsequent paroxysms of doubting, are a further indication of the secondary nature of 4:29-31.

5:1–6:1. The first encounter with Pharaoh. In their very first encounter with Pharaoh, Moses and Aaron present, as a request transmitted directly from YHWH (*Thus says the LORD, the God of Israel* [5:1]), the need of Israel to be free to *celebrate a festival . . . in the wilderness*. Pharaoh refuses, on the grounds that he does not know any YHWH. The refusal, so stated, is a dramatic preparation for the establishment of identity and authority that the reader already knows to be coming. Pharaoh's imperious reply is also a preparation, one dripping with irony, for what is to take place: "Who is YHWH, that I should give attention to what *he* says, and so send forth Israel? I have no knowledge of YHWH, and I am not *about* to send Israel out!" (v. 2, author trans.).

The result of the first petition of Moses and Aaron is an intensification of Israel's arduous labor by a Pharaoh who thinks they have too much time on their hands if they are paying attention to such distractions, which he terms *deceptive words* (5:9), from Moses and Aaron.

When the new and onerous demands are put into effect, the people complain, and the section-leaders bring their protest directly to Pharaoh. His response is unsympathetic: *You are lazy, lazy* (v. 17). Thus do these work-bosses turn on Moses and Aaron, waiting to learn the outcome of this further audience with Pharaoh. They call upon YHWH, whose name they have apparently accepted, to judge Moses and Aaron for making them odious to Pharaoh's supervisors and so to Pharaoh himself.

Thus for the first time since Sinai, Moses doubts. Hurt by the people's accusations, he repeats them to YHWH, then asks why he was ever sent to Egypt. YHWH, he charges, has not even begun any escape for his people. This charge is a perfect preparation for a further prediction by YHWH that the promised authentication is on the way. Before he is finished, Moses will see what he is up to, and Pharaoh will send Israel out with *a mighty hand* (6:1).

6:2-13. YHWH's promise and YHWH's rescue. The compilers of Exodus have interrupted their ongoing narrative here with a sequence of material paralleling the account of 3:1–4:17. This is not the record of a second experience of call, prompted by Moses' discouragement and consequent doubt, but a parallel account of the call and commission with an emphasis on covenant instead of theophany. These verses are from the hand of the Priestly redactors, and they are set here for the practical reason that they cannot logically come after the beginning of the narrative of the wondrous deeds of YHWH.

Of particular interest are the special Priestly emphases: the introduction of the TETRAGRAMMATON (i.e., the four-letter name YHWH) in a self-confession formula, the stress upon the promises of YHWH's covenant, and a characteristic descendants-list. Unlike the Yahwistic narrators, who date the use of the name YHWH from the time of Seth (Gen 4:26), the Priestly narrators avoid using the name until it has been revealed to Moses in this experience of call and commission.

The Priestly narrators have God reveal his special name to Moses with no preparation, no theophany, in the meaning-filled self-confession, "I am YHWH." It is a basic assertion of OT theology, one about which Zimmerli (1982, 20) has written: "All that Yahweh had to say and to declare to his people appears to be a development of the fundamental assertion, 'I am Yahweh'."

The phrase occurs with great frequency in OT passages linked especially with Priestly interests, as a declaration of the authority upon which requirement is made. Here in v. 2 it is precisely that, and the authoritative nature of the name YHWH is enhanced by its relation to the ancient title "God Almighty" (אֵל שַׁדַּי, El Shaddai), identified as the name known to the Fathers, to whom the promise of progeny and land was made as a promise of covenant. That promise was of course the promise of YHWH, whatever name was attached to it, and that promise YHWH is now about to fulfill (vv. 4, 8), and that fulfillment means rescue.

Moses' further protest of inadequacy ("the sons of Israel paid no attention to me, how is Pharaoh going to pay attention to me, especially with my stumbling speech?" v. 12, author trans.) is ignored. YHWH gives him and Aaron a direct order to get on with his commission.

6:14-27. The family line of Aaron (and Moses). The obvious dominance of Aaron in this genealogical list is a priestly attempt to establish Aaron as entirely worthy of his place in the Exodus narrative as Moses' assistant. At the same time, the genealogy—beginning with the same three sons of Jacob as does Exod 1:2 and the "Blessing of Jacob" in Gen 49:3-7—functions as another connecting link in the composite of Exodus as a whole. I have elsewhere referred to it as one of seven "sequences of memory" designed to bring to the present Israel's significant religious past (Durham 1990, 97-104).

Moses' parents are named in this section for the first time, but there is no mention of Miriam as his sister. Both Moses and Aaron are designated as descendants of Levi through Kohath to their father Amram. Aaron is referred to first (and not merely as the eldest) and at length, and Moses is only mentioned. Aaron's wife and sons (and even one of his grandsons) are named, yet there is no mention of Moses's wife and children.

The reason for this emphasis on Aaron is to be seen in the need to establish Aaron as the brother of Moses, and to trace the lineage of both of them to the priestly family of Levi within the descendancy of Jacob/Israel.

6:28–7:7. A preview of things to come. The genealogy justifying Aaron is followed by a brief summary of the call and commission of Moses as it is described in 6:2-13, and that account is resumed with a repetition (v. 30) of Moses' objection (see 6:12). YHWH then declares that he will present Moses to Pharaoh as a god (אֱלֹהִים, 7:1, not NRSV's *like God*) and Aaron as Moses' prophet. Even when confronted by so impressive a legation, however, YHWH predicts that Pharaoh will pay no attention, precisely because YHWH intends to "firm up" Pharaoh's mind in order to provide a cause and a setting for the ultimate proof of his Presence.

The first confrontation with Pharaoh is thus recounted in the divine prediction of how it will be. The end result of this display will be the exodus, and that will give the Egyptians (and by inference Israel) the knowledge by experience that "I am YHWH." And at the time it takes place, Moses is eighty, and Aaron, eighty-three. Thus quite handily, Exodus 6:28–7:7 sums up the narrative from 3:1 to this point in Exodus, and anticipates what is to come through 15:21.

Ten Wonders and the Exodus, 7:8–13:16

The narrative of the ten wonders that prove that YHWH is powerfully, even dominantly, present in Egypt is a skillful composite of material from three of the major tetrateuchal sources, usually designated J, E, and P. These three sources recount in common only the first wonder and the tenth. Of the others, J and E include the seventh, eighth, and ninth in sequence; J and P, the second; J alone mentions the fourth and fifth; and P alone, the third and sixth. Each source proceeds with its own vocabulary, its own formulae, its own emphases, even its own heroes (J emphasizes Moses; P, Aaron), but the three have been woven together to produce a dramatic and logically progressing account. And as intriguing as a comparison of identifiable source layers is, the composite of the Exodus we have, unified by its emphasis upon YHWH as the central figure, must remain at the center of our attention.

The relating of the first nine of the ten wonders to natural phenomena connected with the river Nile and Egypt's Delta has often been noted. Any attempt to explain these wonders as exaggerated natural events does a disservice, however, to the theological purpose of Exodus. The ten wonders are presented quite deliberately as miracles. The terms that describe them, the timing and ferocity and extent with which they fall, and above all their much-stressed role as proofs of the Presence of YHWH all assert their miraculous nature in the concept of the authors of the Book of Exodus.

The sequence of the ten wonders is a dramatic one. They move forward in an upward progression of seriousness towards their terrible climax. Pharaoh is first competitive, then aggravated, then discomfited, then dealt both fiscal and physical reverse, then finally faced with extinction, literally a fate worse than death, as in the ancient Near East sonlessness was death before death, the ultimate oblivion.

The fundamental purpose of the wonder accounts is the enhancement of the staggering implication of what appears (4:22-23) to have been the earliest wonder, and is now the tenth and most serious of them. Contrary to all past experience of and every present appearance to Israel in Egypt, it is only YHWH who really is, and YHWH who is thus alone supreme. In his Presence, the Pharaoh and all his advisers and officers and wizards, even all his magnificent pantheon of gods, are as nothing. All of them together are bested and defeated in every issue.

And the issues on which attention is focused are the very issues on which the Egyptians are supposed to have been most experienced, and so most capable of controlling. YHWH repeats with Pharaoh, and simultaneously with his people, the pattern he followed with Moses: identification, establishment of authority, and command. Pharaoh's complacent ignorance (5:2) turns first to limited respect (8:8,25), then guarded cooperation (9:27-28; 10:7-8), then fearful obedience (12:29-32).

7:8-13. The rod and the great snake. For the first time in the Exodus narrative, a request from Pharaoh for a proving wonder is anticipated. The wonder that is provided is the first of the signs given to Moses at Sinai, but it is repeated here with a significant difference. In 4:1-5, Moses' staff, thrown upon the ground, becomes a dangerous serpent (נחש, from which Moses ran away). Here, the staff is called Aaron's, and it becomes a "terrifying snake" (תנין, translated δράκων by LXX; see Gen 1:21; Ps 74:13; Isa 27:1; Job 7:12).

This portent loses its impact when it is repeated by Pharaoh's team of wonder-workers, and this impact is only partly recovered when Aaron's staff devours all their staffs-become-reptiles.

The implication of this introductory passage thus is that weightier and more consequential portents are to be required if Pharaoh is to come to know YHWH and respect his authority. The ten wonders thus become unavoidable by Pharaoh's own recalcitrance, a recalcitrance we already know will be reinforced, when it appears to be weakening, by YHWH himself.

7:14-25. The first wonder. Each one of the first nine wonder-narratives presents an identical conclusion. In each of them, YHWH attempts to prove his Presence, to Pharaoh, to the Egyptians, and to Israel. In each of them, the Pharaoh refuses to believe, although from the sixth wonder on, YHWH is directly involved in that disbelief to the end that Israel may come to a certain belief.

The first wonder is anticipated in 4:9, where Moses is told, in the provision of a third sign for Israel, that he may dip water from the Nile onto dry ground, where it will turn to blood. In J's account of the first wonder, the entire Nile turns to blood. In P's account, every body of water in Egypt and even the water in buckets and jugs becomes blood. The term used throughout, with no qualification of any sort, is דם, which can only mean blood in such a context.

The report that Pharaoh's wizards duplicated the wonder wrought by Moses and Aaron creates a problem if *all* the water in Egypt has been turned to blood, since the wizards would be augmenting the discomforts already created by the pollution of YHWH's wonder, and without any water at that. There is an ironic touch here, in that the Pharaoh's competition with Moses and Aaron, really a competition with YHWH, makes matters *worse*, not better, for Egypt. The Egyptians search everywhere for potable water, *for they could not drink the water of the river* (v. 24). This statement is reminiscent of a text from Egypt's Middle Kingdom that refers to the water of the Nile as blood, and notes that it must be rejected "as human," despite a thirst for water (*ANET* 3, 441, ii 10).

8:1-15. The second wonder. The second wonder is an extraordinary abundance of frogs from the Nile. As in the account of the first wonder, the extent of this blow against Egypt is multiplied in the later version of the tradition, so that there are frogs not only in the Nile, but also in its tributaries, and even in the irrigation trenches and ponds of Egypt. The picture of frogs in beds, ovens, and mixing bowls and even leaping up onto the august persons of Pharaoh and his courtiers is characteristic of the wit of the J traditions.

Once again, Pharaoh's wizards match YHWH's feat, presumably adding still more frogs. For the first time, however, Pharaoh recognizes both the existence and the power of YHWH, and promises to let the people go if YHWH will remove the frogs. This promise is soon enough seen to be a ruse, however, for when the frogs die, Pharaoh's mind remains "firmed up," just as YHWH has predicted.

8:16-19. The third wonder. This blow of YHWH consists of a transformation of the dust of the earth, an obviously inexhaustible supply of raw material, into gnats (כנים, stinging gnats, even mosquitoes or sand flies). For the first time, Pharaoh's wizards are stumped. Unable to duplicate this wonder, they confess to Pharaoh that they are up against an act of a god (אלהים, 8:19).

This wisdom of his wizards has no effect on Pharaoh, however, who remains as unmoved as ever. And the reader simply must by this point begin to wonder about such an extraordinarily stubborn response.

8:20-32. The fourth wonder. Some commentators have argued that the fourth wonder is only a variant version of the third. This wonder too involves insects, although a different and apparently more general term is used to designate the variety of insect: ערב suggests a mixture of flying insects, hence NRSV's *swarms of flies*. There is no conclusive evidence for combining the third and fourth wonders into a single account, however.

Indeed, the best single argument for treating them as separate wonders is the fact that the compositors of Exodus did so. The two wonders are best taken as sequential, and the fourth wonder is best understood as a different, more intensive blow of YHWH. Each wonder in the sequence is more severe than the one before, as each wonder is intended to make the proof of YHWH's presence progressively more convincing.

Nothing is said in this section about the stuff whence these flying bugs come, only that they are "heavy" in number, to which adjective the Samaritan Pentateuch adds "exceedingly," and that they blanket the ground and devastate the land.

In this wonder, reference is made for the first time to the fate of the Israelites. That part of Egypt in which they are dwelling, designated for the first time in v. 22 as *the land of Goshen*, is exempt from the presence of the *swarms of flies*. This exemption is emphasized to Pharaoh as a further testimony to YHWH's authority, that the Egyptians (and obviously the "Hebrews") "may know by experience that I am YHWH." (v. 21, author trans.)

Also for the first time, Pharaoh agrees to permit the people of Israel to make their sacrifices, but with the proviso that they do so on Egyptian territory. Moses sticks adamantly by his (YHWH's) original requirement: three days' journey into the wilderness. And Pharaoh once again makes a false promise to gain relief. While there is no reminder this time of YHWH's prediction of Pharaonic intransigence, a sense of its inevitability has been established by the recurring narrative pattern.

The protection of Israel from the insect swarm is a convincing proof of YHWH's powerful Presence to Israel, and of course it is Israel that is the real target of this sequence of proving wonders. Pharaoh learns enough to negotiate, but never enough to believe—but Pharaoh and his people are not the objects of YHWH's evangelism in Exodus.

9:1-7. The fifth wonder. A severe epidemic among Egyptian livestock comprises the fifth wonder of YHWH. Once again, the Israelites are spared the effects of the devastation, in a further proof that YHWH is in charge of events.

Protests that a reference to camels in v. 3 is an anachronism fall into the same category as questions about whether an enslaved people such as Israel in Egypt would possess herd and flock animals on any appreciable scale, and proposals of a "naturalistic" basis for the "plagues." The wonder-events are *not* "plagues," except from an Egyptian point of view, and this account is *theological* in nature as in purpose. Whether there were camels in Egypt in Moses' time or whether the epidemic suffered by the Egyptians' animals was anthrax was irrelevant to the compositors of Exodus.

This time, Pharaoh asks no relief and makes no promises, although he does send out to GOSHEN to check on conditions there. And still, as we fully expect, his mind remains "heavy and dull."

9:8-12. The sixth wonder. With the sixth wonder, Moses is instructed to alter the usual prediction of what is to come. Instead, he is to scatter towards heaven (הַשָּׁמַיְמָה in v. 8, not *in the air*, as in NRSV) double handfuls of furnace-ash (פִּיחַ כִּבְשָׁן; note Gen 19:28 and Exod 19:18) in full sight of Pharaoh. The result is a widespread and virulent pustulous condition of the skin, afflicting humans and animals alike.

Pharaoh's wizards are now completely cowed, and they withdraw from the contest, unable to stand up to Moses and Aaron and covered with boils. Pharaoh remains as immovable as ever, and for the first time in the narrative, the prediction of 4:21 is specifically described as having come to pass. Heretofore, Pharaoh has apparently been stubborn on his own. Now, YHWH is said to make Pharaoh's mind obdurate. And the reader is left with the suspicion that something of the sort has been happening all along: how else are Pharaoh's actions to be understood?

This motif, present in each of the tetrateuchal traditions, is far more than a description of YHWH's manipulation of Pharaoh as an unwilling but ultimately helpless puppet. This Pharaoh has disclaimed even any knowledge of YHWH, it is true. But YHWH's own people, the children of Abraham in Egypt, have manifested a lack of confidence in him.

YHWH, therefore, must prove his powerful Presence, and hence his authority, irrefutably. YHWH's influence on Pharaoh's stubbornness is implied from 3:19-20 forward, stated by inference in 4:21, 6:1, and 7:13, promised in 7:3-5, and now stated directly. A premature capitulation by Pharaoh would frustrate this irrefutable proof. We must not lose sight of the fact that this sequence in the narrative composite of Exodus was important to Israel's confessional worship for many years; Pss 78 and 105 are alone enough to establish such a usage.

9:13-35. The seventh wonder. The seventh wonder is a devastating hailstorm accompanied by furious lightning. It is begun with an explanation of the reason for all the wonders. YHWH tells Moses to announce to Pharaoh that his sending of such annoyance and devastation upon Egypt is to the end that they "may know by experience that there is none like me in the whole earth" (v. 14, author trans.).

For the first time, some provision is made for those Egyptians who, in contrast to their Pharaoh, are convinced. This detail is a brilliant touch, one that increases the dramatic tension of Pharaoh's recalcitrance and enhances the extent of YHWH's self-proof. Those who heed the warning instruction are spared at least the loss of the animals left to them, and at most, their own lives.

Once again, the Israelites in Goshen are wholly spared. Over the rest of Egypt, there is an awesome obliteration of all unsheltered life, human, animal, and vegetable. The poet of Ps 78:48 expands even this tradition of decimation by attributing the death of some of the Egyptian cattle to bolts of lightning.

Pharaoh is depicted not only as agreeing to let Israel go, unconditionally, but also as confessing his own sinfulness, YHWH's righteousness, and the Egyptians' collective guilt. Moses remains unconvinced (9:30), both because of YHWH's promise (4:21; 7:13, 22; 8:15; and elsewhere), and also because the sequence of mighty wonders by which YHWH is proving himself is by no means finished.

But the wonders have now for the first time brought death to the Egyptian people. The implication is full of dread. The progressive tension is intensified. A point of no return has been passed.

10:1-20. The eighth wonder. This wonder is introduced in an aside of YHWH to Moses that repeats, in direct terms, the reason for all that is happening. Specifically mentioned is the continuing obduracy of Pharaoh as the basis for the continuing and intensifying disasters, an obduracy for which YHWH takes full responsibility. Moses is reminded that he is to "recount again and again" (תְּסַפֵּר, v. 2) what YHWH has done, to his children and his grandchildren, the plainest statement to this point of the proving motive of the wonder sequence. In producing his portents among the Egyptians, YHWH says he has made a plaything of the Egyptians (cf. Num 22:29; Judg 19:25; 1 Sam 31:4) to the end that Israel may know "that I am YHWH."

In a lengthy prelude to the wonder itself, promised to be a locust-horde of unprecedented extent, Pharaoh, under pressure from his advisers, offers a compromise that is unacceptable, that the men alone be permitted to go out to worship YHWH. Moses and Aaron of course refuse, and are thrown out of the palace. Immediately, under YHWH's command, Moses sets the locust swarm in motion, and the vegetation that survived the hailstorm is quickly devoured.

Once again, when the wonder is in full progress, Pharaoh moves quickly to bring it to an end, confessing his mistake, and adding for the first time a request that his sin be "lifted away" (v. 17). The awful severity of the swarm of locusts is vividly accented by Pharaoh's desperate plea: *remove this deadly thing from me.*

Moses' prayer to YHWH brings a diverted west (or sea) wind, removing every one of the locusts brought in such number by the east wind. Once more, however, YHWH makes Pharaoh's mind obstinate, and he does not permit Israel to leave.

<u>10:21-29. The ninth wonder.</u> Although this wonder ostensibly causes less actual physical harm than any other single blow of YHWH against Egypt, it brings a terror more awesome in a thick, eerie darkness, *a darkness that can be felt* (v. 21). This is owing in part to a cumulative effect, and in part to an element of suspense aggravated by mystery. The Egyptians had suffered dreadfully from disasters that were visible—who could tell what the black darkness might hold?

Israel, presumably in Goshen, had light, although the implication is that it was in their homes, בְּמוֹשְׁבֹתָם, *where they lived* (v. 23).

For three days the Egyptians were in a terror of blindness in this extraordinary darkness, a cancellation of their "eternally rising sun." So Pharaoh again capitulates, with a condition, but with the weakest one thus far stated, that Israel's flocks and herds remain behind.

Moses of course refuses. YHWH "firms up" Pharaoh's mind once again, and Pharaoh's intransigence brings the negotiations to a halt. No further mention is made of the darkness, not even in a request by Pharaoh that it be removed. And Moses is expelled without the privilege of reentry, upon pain of death.

<u>11:1-10. YHWH replaces Moses.</u> These ten verses function as a transition sequence, providing the movement from the first nine wonders in which Moses and Aaron act as YHWH's intermediaries to the tenth wonder in which YHWH acts for himself. Indeed, from this point forward, Moses fades increasingly into the background of the action except in the narratives of rebellion in the wilderness and at Sinai. The tenth wonder is predicted, in grim detail, and the fleeing theme is introduced to suggest just how glad the Egyptians are finally to be rid of Israel. Only near the end of the section, at v. 8, is this passage linked to Pharaoh's presence. That reference suggests that death and despoilation are introduced in the angry "final" exchange between Moses and Pharaoh. *And in hot anger he left Pharaoh* (v.

8); yet again, Pharaoh's divinely-stimulated obstinacy is stated, with the sonorous repetition of a chorus in a Greek tragedy.

12:1-28. YHWH's Passover, reminder, and protection. These verses are an interruption of the story of YHWH's proof to Israel of his Presence in Egypt, but an appropriate interruption. They provide important directions for the rituals of remembrance whereby the momentous events about to take place are to be brought perpetually to the present of Israel's consciousness.

The first of these rituals, PASSOVER (vv. 1-13), probably originated in a nomadic celebration connected with flock and herd birthing in springtime. The second of them, Unleavened Bread (vv. 14-20), probably has an agricultural origin. The directions for the two celebrations are from the Priestly tradition, and therefore represent a developed application of the original intent of each, in terms of the tenth wonder and the exodus from Egypt.

Anything more than reasonable speculation about the background and time of origin of these two rituals is not possible. Certainly by the time of the compilation of Exod 12:1-20, they were time-honored in both direction and significance. No two festivals in the ancient ritual calendar of Israel could more appropriately have commemorated the totality of YHWH's great deliverance of his people than these two, the one from the past, recalling the nomadic days of the fathers, the other from Israel's new future as a people, associated specifically with the settled, agricultural life of CANAAN. In a way, they symbolize the exodus experience in its historical totality.

The Passover may well have been connected with the Exodus from the very beginning, in part because of its apotropaic element, in part because of its nomadic character. Much as some festive features of the ancient Roman celebration of the winter solstice have been absorbed into the modern Christian celebration of Christmas, features of the Passover that predated the Exodus perhaps came with time to be expressly symbolic of it.

Subsequently, after the arrival in Canaan, the Feast of Unleavened Bread, that is, new bread from the new crop at the beginning of the harvest, was joined to the Passover ritual. The Feast of Unleavened Bread fell at the same time of year as Passover, marked a new beginning, and was naturally related through the ancient Passover requirement of unleavened bread and bitter herbs to be eaten with the paschal lamb. Joined to the Passover celebration, it became symbolic of the completion of the Exodus cycle begun in Egypt. This association was probably made early in the period of the settlement in Canaan.

The reference to the month of Passover celebration as *the beginning of months* (v. 2) is a statement of theological import as well as a specification of an agricultural CALENDAR such as the one found at GEZER. Passover marked the beginning of Israel as a people rescued by God as well as the beginning of a new undertaking of God, and thus it was an appropriate time for the start of a new year.

The marking of the doorposts and lintels of the houses in which the people of Israel were eating Passover (v. 7) is an anticipation of the protection (v. 13) Yahweh is to give them when the judgment against *all the gods of Egypt* (v. 12) falls in the tenth wonder.

The unleavened bread cakes are a keeping of remembrance, the ritual means of reminding Israel of the time, the event, and above all the rescue of YHWH's intervention on their behalf. Together with the ordered ritual of Passover, the seven days of unleavened bread were intended as a means of making the experience of exodus real to every successive generation of Israelites.

Thus also is the protection of Israel explained in this inserted sequence. It is a protection that in preparation augurs the nature of the tenth wonder, and anticipates and explains the requirement of the dedication of Israel's firstborn specified in 13:1-16. YHWH's "destroyer" is to pass throughout Egypt, including the Delta area where Israel lives, and the blood of the Passover lamb on the doorposts and lintels of Israel is the means of their protection. This act becomes another means of actualizing the past in each new present, and a further testimony of the proof of the Presence of YHWH to Israel in Egypt and so to Israel wherever they may come to be, in any period of history.

12:29-36. The tenth wonder. Thus at last the final proof of YHWH's identity and authority is presented. It has been made inevitable by Pharaoh's divinely encouraged stubbornness. It is reminiscent, at the very least, of Pharaoh's slaughter of the "Hebrews' " sons early on in the oppression (1:15-22).

As Moses had angrily predicted to Pharaoh, Egypt's firstborn, of men and cattle alike, are slain. Only one explanation is possible for Pharaoh and his subjects, and, of course for Israel, whose firstborn have been spared. YHWH, whose name and power the Egyptians and the Israelites have now come to know by experience, has struck the deadly blow. The report of it is chilling still: *there was a loud cry in Egypt, for there was not a house without someone dead* (v. 30).

Numbed and brought beyond resistance by the catastrophe, Pharaoh forgets his command ostracizing Moses (10:28-29), summons Moses and Aaron in the middle of the night and commands them to be gone as they desire, without condition. YHWH's prediction (6:1; 11:8) comes true, as the Egyptians urge Israel to leave in a hurry. The fleecing of the Egyptians so eager to be rid of these people whose God has brought them such suffering is a further fulfillment of prediction (3:21-22; 11:2). Articles of silver and gold and clothing are willingly given to the departing Israelites by their benumbed and entranced Egyptian neighbors.

12:37-51. The exodus. Thus finally does the Exodus, the saving event of such central importance in the faith of the OT, take place. The notice of it in vv. 37-39 seems anticlimactic and almost laconic. The people travelled hastily and haphazardly, ill-prepared for their journey despite (or perhaps because of) their long anticipation of it. As a result, the first leg of their journey was evidently a brief one. Neither *Rameses* nor *Succoth* can be located with any certainty (see Herrmann 1973, 23-28, and Uphill 1968, 1969), although the narrator's intention was probably to provide a clear record of the route of Israel's departure from Egypt.

The figure 600,000 for the number of "strong men on foot" leaving Egypt with their families is generally regarded as an impossible exaggeration. Whether this number represents the male population of Israel during the monarchy, or a number that has been incorrectly transmitted or translated remains a matter of academic debate.

The period of 430 years for the sojourn in Egypt is also a number difficult to reconcile with the information we have in the OT. It is in conflict with Gen 15:13, and even more, with Gen 15:16; Exod 6:16, 18, 20, and passages in Leviticus and Numbers that imply an exodus four generations from the generation of Jacob. Like the census figure for the males in Exodus, it may be an exaggeration, even one dictated by that inflated figure.

The narrative of the Exodus itself is rounded out by a repetition of the command to keep Passover, the means by which the redemptive event is to be kept real to every successive generation of Israelites.

13:1-16. Remembering in ritual. The narrative of the tenth wonder and the Exodus it made possible is rounded out with yet another sequence of ritual instructions designed to make the story real to Israel yet to come. Because YHWH spared Israel's firstborn, of family, of flock, and of herd, those same firstborn are to be given to YHWH, either in fact or by vicarious ransom.

Reminding symbols are mentioned, albeit somewhat ambiguously here (vv. 6, 16), and the keeping of the reminding festival of unleavened bread cakes (note 12:14-20).

All this is to the end, once again, that the all-important exodus event be actualized, made a real event, to each new generation of Israelites, by keeping ritual, by symbol, and above all by personal cost. Israel has been ransomed by YHWH. YHWH commands of Israel a response.

Israel in the Wilderness, 13:17–18:27

The Route and the Rescue, 13:17–15:21

13:17–14:4. The route. The flight of Israel from Egypt appears to have been directly southeast from Succoth, although the uncertain location of the places mentioned in the account renders impossible any precise plotting of the route, either in its initial stages or later, to and from Sinai. The references in 13:17 and 14:1-3 make plain that the more direct and obvious route was divinely eliminated, and that YHWH himself determined the route Israel was to take.

Both this divine guidance and the columns of cloud and fire (13:21-22) are testimony to the divine Presence in the midst of Israel. This Presence, whose effective authority and power the Exodus narrative has to this point sought to demonstrate, becomes henceforth the essential hub around which all of the remainder of Exodus turns and from which its cultic and legal requirements stem.

The uncertainty of the identification of the place-names mentioned in the account of the Exodus make an identification of the site of the great deliverance at the sea as impossible as the fixing of the route to it. Without a doubt, the place-names were provided to do the very thing they cannot now do, because we no longer know where the places are, or were.

Two facts however emerge: (1) the initial direction of the march was set to get Israel out of Egypt and thus beyond the authority of Pharaoh by the quickest and most direct route possible; and (2) the change of direction once the border had been crossed was designed to move Israel toward the only immediate goal Moses could conceive, the mountain of YHWH's special revelation. The distinction between the crossing of the Egyptian border and the crossing of the sea is not always made, but it is nonetheless an important one.

The moment of the Exodus is noted in 12:37-38. The crossing of the Egyptian border must have occurred between *Succoth* and *Etham*, *on the edge of the wilderness* (13:20). The deliverance at the sea comes still later in the journey, after the departure from Etham, as 14:1-2 make plain.

By any tracking we can imagine, since the places mentioned have yet to be located, the route in which YHWH guides Moses and the Israelites is an eccentric one. The third camp of the fleeing Israelites is even a turning back, one designated by not less than four points of reference: *in front of Pi-hahiroth, between Migdol and the sea, in front of Baal-zephon* (14:2).

The reason for this maneuvering is made clear by the return, at the beginning of Exod 14, to the motif of YHWH's making obstinate the mind of Pharaoh. Pharaoh's decision to pursue Israel will be the result of more work on the part of YHWH, who is still proving his Presence to Israel.

14:5-31. The rescue. Pharaoh's pursuit of Israel is presented first of all as a decision of the Egyptian cabinet made on economic grounds: Egypt was losing an invaluable source of slave and semi-slave labor. The gathering of forces for avoiding this loss reflects their sense of its serious nature. Pharaoh gathers around himself 600 crack chariots as an attack force, to be supported by a still larger force of three-man chariots, each commanded by a שָׁלִישׁ, the "third" who coordinated the driver and the weapon wielder completing his team. Such a mode of attack is frequently attested in Egyptian battle art from the very period in which the exodus is most likely to have occurred (Yadin 1963, 86-90, 104-105). Pharaoh himself is depicted as in command of the advance force, with the support force operating as an independently commanded backup.

This extraordinary force emphasizes the hopeless plight of Israel, on foot and largely weaponless, and, at the same time, dramatizes the inevitable victory of YHWH. The dismay and panic of the people of Israel upon learning of the Egyptian pursuit is all the more understandable when it is seen as a prospect beyond which Israel believed themselves utterly removed. They are presented as having thought themselves beyond Pharaoh's authority and interest. He had, after all, sent them out. He was, they had believed, a beaten man. Yet suddenly here he was again, with a crushing, irresistible force. Their frightened expectation was death, and they longed for the slavery they had left so gladly.

Moses attempts to encourage the people with the assurance that YHWH will himself do battle on their behalf, predicting the complete removal of any threat to them of the Egyptians advancing toward them. YHWH instructs Moses to bring the staff into play once again, to manipulate the waters of the sea and to enable Israel to cross on dry ground. He adds that he is about to make Pharaoh obstinate once more, so that "the Egyptians will know by experience that I am YHWH in my winning glory for myself" (v. 18, author trans.).

Next YHWH sends the "attendant [NRSV *angel*] of God" (מַלְאַךְ הָאֱלֹהִים, v. 19; note 23:23-30) from a position of guidance before the people of Israel to one of protection behind them, also moving the daytime pillar of cloud as an obscuring cover between the encamped Israelites and the oncoming Egyptian force. As night falls, the pillar of fire, a source of light in the dark, is absent for the first time. Through the night, the two groups remained separate.

The "sea" Israel crossed the next morning, the "sea" the Egyptians were prevented from crossing remains a subject of indeterminate discussion (see Wiles 1990). A wide range of seas, rivers, and marshlands has been proposed, and "reed sea" has become a more popular translation for יַם סוּף than "Red Sea," a translation influenced by LXX and Vulgate. No location thus far suggested, however, is convincing.

The miracle of the crossing lies not in the crossing so much as in the deliverance of Israel from the forces of Pharaoh. The first part of this deliverance is the protective interposition of "God's attendant" and the pillar of cloud. The second part comes with YHWH's "confounding" or "driving to panic" the Egyptian pursuers, a divine maneuver characteristic of the HOLY WAR (Durham 1987, 336), accomplished here by YHWH's Presence looking down toward the Egyptian force and misguiding their chariots' wheels. This panic in the pursuit affords the people of Israel time for a careful crossing even as it brings the Egyptians to chaotic confusion.

The third part of the deliverance is the manipulation of the waters of the sea. This miraculous control of the waters, so obviously an echo of the creation and flood narratives of Gen 1 and 7, makes the Israelite crossing more direct and more safe, and brings disaster to the Egyptians who attempt, already in confused disarray, to follow.

Verses 30-31 are an apt summary of the events of the rescue at the sea. YHWH made the rescue. *Israel* saw displayed once more, and more convincingly than ever, the great power of YHWH. And thus in awe of YHWH, Israel *believed* in YHWH, just as their father Abraham had in a time of testing much earlier (Gen 15:6, where the key verb, as here, is אמן).

<u>15:1-21. Victory celebration.</u> At least three hymns celebrating the deliverance at the sea are preserved in Exod 15. The brief song of MIRIAM (v. 21) is generally held to be the very ancient, perhaps contemporaneous kernel from which the longer

song of Moses (vv. 1-12) was developed (cf. vv. 1 and 21). To these has been added another poem, celebrating the further victory of the conquest and settlement of Canaan (vv. 13-18).

A variety of dates has been proposed for the separate poems, as well as for their present arrangement. No date can be defended as certain, but the tendency in recent years has been towards an earlier date (Cross 1973, 176-78).

The hymn as it stands in Exod 15 is thus an evolved work, the oldest elements of which date from the experience at the sea, with additional lines added in a succession of decades, if not centuries. These verses are therefore neither a poetic unity nor a chronological unity. They are rather a theological unity, bound together by praise of the incomparable YHWH whose saving Presence is so undeniably real to his people.

Exodus 15:1-21 thus remains a happy combination of at least three psalms, two of which are connected directly with the climactic deliverance at the sea, and one of which is sequential to that deliverance, bridging the gap between it and the eventual settlement of the promised land. In part, at least, these verses incorporate some of the oldest poetry in the OT.

The emphasis upon YHWH's incomparability and potent Presence sung so eloquently here is in a way an excellent summarization of the whole of Exodus. YHWH, who has made the exodus necessary by the fulfillment of his promise, has himself brought it off against everything the Egyptians could do, and even against the disbelief and the objections of his own people. Having fulfilled his promise of progeny, he has carried them through every interpositioned obstacle toward the eventual fulfillment of his promise of land.

And his incomparable Presence, connected with the fathers before (v. 2) and the Temple to come (v. 17), is the basis of his ritual and covenantal expectations, woven with such skill into the exciting narrative of the Book of Exodus. Indeed, the ultimate basis of the three hymns, as of Exodus as well, is the permanent effective reign of YHWH (v. 18), who rescues his people, then protects, then establishes them. There are overtones in these lines of the celebration of a victory of YHWH much greater than his victory over Pharaoh, greater even than his victory over those who opposed Israel on the way to and in Canaan itself. The *waters* (מַיִם) and *floods* (נֹזְלִים, better "currents") of the immediate event suddenly become the "ancient deeps" (תְּהֹמֹת, vv. 5 and 8; NRSV's rendering, *floods* in v. 5 and *deeps* in v. 8, is misleading), the chaos-waters brought under control at the time of creation (Gen 1:2; Ps 93:1-4; Ezek 26:19-20; note Reymond 1958, 167-79, 182-94). And in v. 16, YHWH's people are referred to as "this people you have created" (author trans.; see also Deut 32:6; Pss 74:2; 78:54; 139:13), a further suggestion that Exod 15:1-21 celebrate YHWH, even more than his victory and his victories.

Provision, Protection, and Complaint, 15:22–17:16

15:22–17:7. YHWH provides, Israel grumbles. When Moses and the people of Israel departed from the vicinity of their sea crossing, apparently on the day of their deliverance, they headed directly for SINAI, which was for Moses the primary trysting-place with YHWH's Presence. Unfortunately, a fully satisfactory location for Sinai/Horeb has yet to be found. And the location of the various oases and stopping places *en route*, equally uncertain, leaves similarly obscure the route of travel that Moses and Israel followed.

When all the possibilities (see commentary on Exod 3:1-22, above) have been considered, the traditional location, Jebel Musa in the southern Sinai peninsula, remains most satisfactory. Thus despite the difficulties involved, particularly by conflicting OT sources, the best assumption is as direct as possible a southerly route from the crossing-place to Sinai.

The narratives of the journey to the place of YHWH's theophany to Moses, an experience he expects to be repeated for Israel (see 3:12), are moved forward through a tension of complaint and provision. Israel feels put to the test, and in return Moses and YHWH himself are put to the test.

The complaining and testing motifs occur not only in these narratives, but also in the narratives of Numbers and by allusion elsewhere in the OT (Coats 1968). They are introduced by such catchwords as *bitter* (15:23), *complained* (16:2), *fleshpots* (16:3), and *quarrel* and *test* (17:2, 7).

The text in its present arrangement presents even the cursory reader with what seems a hodgepodge of overlapping and sometimes self-contradictory narrative. The purpose of the compilers of this account is clear enough, however. They intend to make it clear that, whatever Israel's need and criticism, YHWH is more than equal to every problem, and that with each solution the effectiveness of his Presence is proven more and more. What we have in this section is a compacting of a series of stories of wilderness crises involving water, food, and hostile peoples set at an appropriate point in the narrative of the proving of YHWH's Presence with his people Israel.

The water crises are two in number, the one involving nonpotable water, the other involving a complete lack of water of any kind. Both situations are common enough to such an arid region as the Sinai peninsula, where water is very scarce and often too alkaline for consumption when it is present.

In the first instance, Moses is shown by YHWH an herb that sweetened the alkaline water (15:25). In the second, YHWH indicates to Moses a rock from which a spring gushes when Moses' rod is used to strike it (17:6). Both instances, whatever explanations may be given them, even correctly so, are plainly depicted in Exodus as miraculous events. They are therefore a continuation of the wonders done in Egypt and in the rescue at the sea.

The point at issue in these further miracle narratives, since YHWH has abundantly proved himself powerful, is whether he is still present with his people (17:7). The question is natural enough, but it attests a lack of faith, and so the place of *the rock at Horeb* (17:6) is called *Massah and Meribah*—"Testing and Dissatisfaction" (17:7; cf. Ps 95:8-9).

According to Exod 16, there is a single food crisis which is met by the supply of two foodstuffs. Comparison of this account with Num 11 indicates that the OT gives us a tangle of traditions related to YHWH's provision of food for his people in the wilderness. The crises in Exodus occur on the way to Sinai; in Numbers they occur on the way from Sinai. Their importance, in either instance, even in the assumption that there were two sets of crises, is theological, not historical or chronological.

Exodus 16:1-12 is an introduction to YHWH's miraculous feeding of his people, and 16:13-36 then records the miracles themselves. A definite emphasis is placed on the manna (מָן הוּא, the *What is it?* [16:15]), *bread from heaven* (16:4), as the space given to its arrival, its collection and its lessons for Israel show.

The appearance of the manna in the morning, its lasting beyond one day only on the sabbath, and the arrival of the quails in the evening are miraculous keepings of YHWH's promise, to the end that the people *shall know that I am [YHWH] your God* (16:12). Here in the wilderness as in Egypt, YHWH is proving his powerful Presence. Twice in Exod 16, YHWH's *glory* is mentioned (vv. 7 and 10), and when it appears, the glory appears in a cloud in the direction of the wilderness (v. 10), that is, Sinai/Horeb.

The food crisis separates the two water crises in the present text of Exodus, and immediately following the second water crisis, there is an account of YHWH's provision of protection. *Rephidim* can no more be located in connection with this narrative (17:8-16) or the second water narrative (17:1-7) than can any of the other sites mentioned in the journey of the exodus. The Amalekites were a nomadic people whose territory included the southern NEGEB and the Sinai peninsula, and their attack upon Israel may well have been more of a defensive action than an aggressive one. There is another reference to this battle in Deut 25:17-19.

The defeat of Amalek, like the defeat of the Egyp-tians at the sea, is attributed directly to YHWH, although Israel this time does play more than a passive role. The mention of the rod of God, the importance of Moses' uplifted hand, and the construction of an altar commemorating the victory all emphasize YHWH's further proof of his Presence to Israel, this time through protection instead of provision.

JOSHUA appears in 17:9 for the first time. His abrupt and very brief introduction may imply the omission of additional Joshua-traditions at this point as unnecessary to the compiler's purpose. He is presented as someone we should know already.

Jethro, Worship, and Law, 18:1-27

18:1-12. Meeting Jethro. Chapter 18 has often been considered out of place in the narrative sequence of Exodus, because of the account of Deut 1:9-18, which seems to place the events of Exod 18:13-27 at the departure from Sinai, and because of Exod 18:5, which seems to refer to Israel at Sinai before the actual arrival there, recounted in Exod 19:1-2.

There is however a theological logic that overrides story logic in Exodus, as throughout the OT. The compilers of Exodus are concerned to reconnect the two branches of the family of ABRAHAM-ISAAC-JACOB/ISRAEL *before* their experience of YHWH's Presence at his mountain. From Abraham's time, the SARAH-ISAAC-JACOB-JOSEPH side of the family has been separate from the Hagar-Ishmael-Esau-Midian side of the family. It is important that the family be reunited *before* the events at Sinai, and thus this story of reunion is placed here, despite the fact that the long sequence dealing with the application of YHWH's laws to the needs of the people thus comes *before* those laws are actually given (Durham 1987, 240-46).

The priority given to JETHRO, both as the leader of worship despite the presence of both Moses and Aaron, and also as the instructor of Moses regarding the management of the people has given rise to an array of theories about Midianite faith and its influence on Israel. Jethro's role in this chapter hardly sustains the theory that he is a new convert, and although it is too much to claim that he introduced YHWH to Moses and the Joseph-tribes, Exod 18 clearly accords him a significant tutelary role. Elated at Moses' account of YHWH's wonders in Egypt and the exodus, he says, "Now I know for certain that YHWH is greater than all the gods" (v. 1, author trans.). And in the ensuing celebratory worship, it is Jethro who presides.

18:13-27. Leadership and Law. The account of Jethro's advice on leadership in the application of YHWH's law, and Moses' implementation of the old priest's counsel must be read alongside Deut 1:9-18. What is apparent in the content of both passages is that the situation in view is reflective of a period in history long after the time to which the two passages are assigned in the Exodus narrative.

Even so, however, there is little reason to doubt that the precedent for such a division of cases into "important" and "minor" categories, those requiring an ORACLE and those capable of settlement by extant legal precedent, may have been given to Moses by Jethro. The procedure of inquiring (דרש) the will of God in matters not provided for in extant law is based upon the theology of YHWH's Presence that appears to have originated at Sinai and that became the very basis of the theology of the Jerusalem cultus.

The principal assertion of this narrative of the beginnings of Israel's legal system is that YHWH is the source and therefore the authority of Israelite guidance in relationship. Moses is an important intermediary, as are the "able men and honest" who are called forward to represent the people and to extend Moses' wisdom and strength. But the law giver and the law definer and the law sustainer is YHWH. On such a view, there is no such thing in Israel as "secular" law. Every law, whatever its concern, is sacral, because every law, ultimately, is YHWH's.

That such a concept did not prevent abuse of the law is plain from the preaching of the prophets alone. But that it presented a high view of law, and of the motivation for obedience of law, cannot be doubted.

Israel at Sinai, 19:1–40:38

YHWH's Presence and Covenant, 19:1–24:18

19:1-25. YHWH comes to Israel. Certainly the single most important passage in the Book of Exodus is the dramatic and graphic account of the theophany on Sinai/Horeb. This is so because the THEOPHANY is the effective visible announcement of the advent of YHWH to speak to, and to be with, his people. The theophany motif is the one theme from Exodus most recurrent in the remainder of the OT, amid so many consequential motifs and traditions.

The importance of the Sinai theophany may be understood when the essential nature of the theology of the Presence of YHWH is recognized. Moses' call is predicated on such a basis. The authority Moses declares to Israel in Egypt is established by it. The sequence of wonders and the culminating victory at the sea are a direct result of it. Provision for the people in the jejune barrenness of the wilderness is guaranteed by it, as is their protection from the threatened and so threatening Amalekites. And the basis of the commandments, laws, and cultic instructions and requirements that occupy most of the rest of Exodus is, purely and simply, the immanent Presence of YHWH.

Immediately after the brief notice of Israel's arrival at Sinai, Moses received from YHWH for repetition to the people a magnificent summary of covenantal theology, often called the "eagles' wings" speech (19:4-6). These lines, probably composed for liturgical use at covenant renewal ceremonies, have been inserted here as both recital and conditional prologue to the revelation of YHWH's Presence and the giving of the law.

As such, they stand as the first of a series of insertions that form the bulk of the remainder of the Book of Exodus, insertions wonderfully woven into the narrative, and presenting the reader with a remarkably symphonic whole, but insertions all the same that interrupt the story sequence. In broad terms, the flow of that story sequence can be broadly reconstructed by a reading, *seriatim*, of the following passages: 19:1-3a, 10-19a; 20:1-21; 24:1-18; 32:1–34:35 (Durham 1990, 56–81).

Such a reading, while it makes the story of Exodus easier to follow, nevertheless does disservice to the Book of Exodus as it stands in the OT. The theological purpose of the compilers who brought Exodus to its present form is celebration and obedience. The gift of YHWH's self-revelation to Israel, with the provision, protection, and assurance that brings, is celebrated. And the gift of YHWH's guidance for living, for shaping personal lives and the national life in harmony with YHWH's intention for his people is held up as the opportunity for obedience.

All of this is summed up in vv. 4-6, which in its present location in Exodus is a passage of recollection *and* a passage of anticipation. The deliverance from Egypt is recapitulated in a moving metaphor of protective love, one developed more fully still in Deut 32:11-12. YHWH's personal direction to the mountain of his special Presence is stressed. Then the conditions of the covenant, attention to and integrity in covenantal promises are juxtapositioned against YHWH's own promises: if Israel hears him and obeys him, they will be his prized treasure, his nation of priests, his people set apart.

YHWH's theophany is anticipated, first in prediction (v. 9), then in an ordered preparation involving isolation of the place of his appearance and ritual purification of the people who await it (vv. 10-13).

The description of the theophany is lean of simile, and dramatically and convincingly drawn. The violent mountain storm, along with fire and thick smoke, is a frequent accompaniment of OT theophany and therefore not to be taken as suggestive of a volcanic eruption. In the midst of the fury of this entirely unnatural storm, the loud blast of the unmusical *shophar* signals the imminent arrival of YHWH. The people are assembled by Moses. YHWH descends in the fire that accompanies his Presence (note Pss 18:7-15; 50:1-7; 97:1-5), causing the entire mountain to shake violently. The *shophar* blasts yet louder, that is nearer at hand, indicating the approach of YHWH's Presence.

YHWH has come to Israel at Sinai/Horeb, as Moses knew he would. Israel is experiencing in this special place what Moses experienced there, as he hoped they would. The way is prepared for the revelation of his expectation, his guidance, that is now to be delivered to Moses in Israel's hearing.

20:1-21. YHWH's Ten Words and Israel's fear. The TEN COMMANDMENTS in their present form have obviously been expanded from their original terse form as "ten words" of YHWH (Exod 34:28; Deut 4:13, 10:4). This expansion does not however justify the excision of the commandments from the Exodus narrative, any more than the Sinai traditions can be separated from the Exodus traditions (Durham 1970, 197–99).

The commandments in their briefest form should be assumed as a part of the Exodus narrative that begins with 19:1-19a and continues from 20:1 through v. 21, giving a sequence reading something like: "The sound of the ram's horn meanwhile was moving, and growing very strong. Then God spoke all these words, saying, 'I am YHWH, your God, who brought you forth from the land of Egypt' " (19:19a and 20:1-2b, author trans.).

The Decalogue has been transmitted with a different numbering in variant Christian and Jewish traditions, although the final number of commandments has nearly always been ten. The sequence followed here is: first commandment, v. 3; second commandment, vv. 4-6; third commandment, v. 5; fourth commandment, vv. 8-11; and fifth through tenth commandments, one verse each, vv. 12 through 17.

The Exodus Decalogue must be considered along with the parallel version of Deut 5:6-21, but contrary to an earlier view, the version in Exodus must now be thought of as the earlier OT version. Behind both versions, there lie still earlier, more terse versions, and there is no convincing reason to deny that the earliest "ten words" are to be associated with Moses.

A probable relationship in form between the Decalogue and the state treaties of the Hittites and other ancient Near Eastern peoples has been established, although the parallels must not be pressed too rigidly. The Ten Commandments follow the apodictic form of the requirements listed in such documents, and like them are begun with a prologue justifying that list of expectations.

The point of such a prologue (v. 2 and Deut 5:6) is not identification: Moses and the people of Israel would have known with whom they were dealing, as surely as the Hittite and other vassals would have known the name of the protective overlord whose strength made a covenant desirable or even necessary to them.

The point is rather a declaration of the authority that is the basis for the covenant, an authority established by experienced reality. Without this reference to such authority, the stipulation of requirements that follow would in effect be largely meaningless—a list of requirements without reason or authority and to no purpose.

The prologue to the Ten Commandments is thus to the same point as the revelation and explanation of the name YHWH at the bush aflame in the narrative of Moses' call. Here as there the question is not one of the identity of the commanding deity, but one of the authority behind the command and its implications. And here the wonders in Egypt and the Exodus rescue are cited in historical retrospect, as there in promised prospect.

In sequence, the commandments prohibit (1) the worship of other gods, assumed as a reality at least for the people; (2) the creation and use of images of any sort in worship, a commandment that is testimony to the fact that such images were made and employed in Israel's worship; (3) the profanation or vain use of YHWH's name, the equivalent of his Presence, in false covenanting, insincere swearing, or magical rites; (6) killing a fellow-member of the community in covenant with YHWH; (7) adultery; (8) theft; (9) lying or distortion of the truth that maligns persons, specifically perjury; and (10) unbridled desire for that which belongs to another, the lust to have that can lead to legal or illegal theft.

Two commandments, four and five (vv. 8-11 and v. 12) are stated not as prohibitions but as positive commands: (4) respect for the sabbath, as a special day set aside for rest and worship; and (5) appropriate esteem for parents.

The considerable expansion of commandments two, four, five and ten suggest how much trouble the people of Israel had keeping them. To the fifth commandment alone, a promise and an implied warning have been attached, an indication that this commandment may have been the most abused of them all.

The Ten Commandments not only set forth the essential priorities of life in relationship with YHWH; they also suggest in their sequence the proper arrangement of those priorities: God first, his worship next, and concern related to the human community last. The commandments must also be thought of, however, as a totality: each impinging upon all the others, and all of them together providing the general outline of Israel's covenantal obligation. The violation of any one of them by any one member of the covenantal community was a weakening of the entire group's relationship with YHWH.

The implication of the narrative of 19:1-20:21 is that the people of Israel were themselves a part of the experience of both YHWH's advent *and* his revelation of his expectation of them in covenant. 19:9 states that the people are to hear YHWH's speaking; 19:17, that Moses brought them out from the camp to encounter God; 19:21 implies the presence of the people just beyond the boundary established at the foot of the mountain; and in 20:18 the people react with fright, trembling and drawing back, and then they say to Moses, "*You* speak with us, and we promise we'll hear—but don't let God keep speaking with us, lest we die" (20:19, author trans.).

This implication is borne out by the parallel account in Deut 5:22-27 and the questions of Deut 4:32-33. It is also sustained by Moses' answer to the people's request. He seeks to allay their fear by telling them that God's coming on this momentous occasion is for their benefit, that they may have a firsthand experience of his Presence so that their joining in covenant with him may be memorable and have lasting effectiveness.

Such is certainly the result of the theophany, whether the revelation of the Decalogue be thought of as audible to the people or not, and they move some distance away, leaving Moses to venture alone into the dense cloud to encounter YHWH's Presence further.

20:22–23:33. Applying YHWH's commands. This section, which is called *the book of the covenant* in Exod 24:7, has long been recognized as an entity in its own right. Like much of the content of Exod 20–40, it is disruptive of the story sequence into which it has been set as a part of a sequence of requirement (Durham 1990, 81–95). And like the similarly disruptive sequence of memory (Durham 1990, 97–101), it pulls apart the Exodus narrative. It does so, however, in a most appropriate way: for the sequence of requirement and the sequence of memory give a continuing present tense to a story that would otherwise not be experienced (and so believed and so heeded) by the succession of Israel's generations.

The Book of the Covenant is a mixture of requirements and regulations governing worship and "judgments," case decisions, governing what today would for the most part be called civil matters. In ancient Israel, all behavior was under religious aegis, and all law was theocratically based. Most of the judgments are casuistic in form, but alongside them are apodictic requirements that are always applicable, that require no special set of conditions to make them relevant.

The antiquity of the Book of the Covenant, once seriously doubted, has in recent years been more generally accepted, particularly in view of the parallels provided by an assortment of law codes from the second millennium B.C.E. (see introduction, above). Not surprisingly, there is material in the Book of the Covenant that reflects the settled agricultural society of life in Canaan, and there is material that reflects the nomadic life of the wilderness.

This section is thus best considered as having its origin in a premonarchial collection of laws, one perhaps even begun by Moses as an expansion and application of the Ten Commandments and as a cumulative body of precedents in judgments rendered on the "lesser cases" that Jethro had advised Moses to delegate to carefully selected "honest men." Such a collection would have had authoritative weight from its inception, and may have been circulated along with the Decalogue it was intended to apply and supplement. To it, extant laws from the oldest periods of Israel's past, new laws revealed at Sinai and in the wilderness, and laws encountered and adapted in the contact with new cultures and new situations would readily have been attracted.

The disorganization of the Book of the Covenant suggests the authoritative antiquity of some of its parts. Material on similar subjects is not always together, and there is an arbitrary and disjointed arrangement that suggests sections were added to units that already had the sanctity of long use. When the Book of Exodus was in compilation, what more logical place for this collection than between the Decalogue it was intended to supplement and the narrative of the actual ratification of the covenant it delineated in such detail?

The first sequence of laws (20:23-26) is connected with worship, and can readily be recognized as supplemental, in part, to the first two commandments. The specification that altars be earthen or of unhewn stone reflects an early period. The connection between the altars used in worship and the theology of the Presence of YHWH is strongly stressed in 20:24.

The second sequence of laws is begun (21:1-2) with an introductory statement that indicates the beginning of a collection of "judgments," that is, precedents, governing "lesser cases." This introduction governs an indeterminate number of sequences of precedents extending through 22:17.

First, there are cases that arise in connection with the ownership of slaves (21:2-11). These judgments are humanitarian in emphasis, and designed in each case to protect the familial and personal rights of the slaves in a series of situations that are certain to have been recurrent. 21:6 apparently specifies a kind of scarring or "brand" as a physical mark of the permanent attachment of a slave.

Next there are two sections dealing with harm, chiefly physical harm, willfully inflicted upon others. Cases that carry the death penalty are appropriately set first (21:12-17). A distinction is made between premeditated murder and an unplanned slaying, and a physical blow or a curse against one's parents is, along with slave-stealing, considered as heinous a crime as premeditated murder.

Cases involving injury, whether by intention or through negligence, are provided for next (21:18-36). Punishment is required, although not specified, for killing one's slave. That this punishment appears to have been less severe than in the case in which a free man is killed is owing in part to the lesser status of the slave, but more to the fact that such a killing would not in the nature of things be premeditated, as the slave was valuable and expensive property (21:21b).

If a slave should be struck and maimed (even by the loss of a tooth), he is to be freed: this action is both a reparation for the injury and a guarantee that it would not occur. If someone should be killed by a violent ox because its owner had been negligent, the owner would be subject to the death penalty, although with the right of redemption.

The fifth sequence of judgments treats instances involving thievery (22:1-4 [MT 21:37–22:3]). NRSV's reordering of these verses to 1, 3b, 4, 2, 3a is unnecessary and perhaps misleading. As Daube (1969, 74–77, 85–89) and others have pointed out, collections of legal material grow by subject more than by logical sequence.

The sixth sequence (22:5-15 [MT 22:4-14]) deals with damage or loss because of negligence. Of special interest is the provision of a ceremony (22:10-11 [MT 22:9-10]) to guarantee lack of evil intention on the part of the responsible party.

The seventh sequence (22:16-17 [MT 22:15-16]) provides for the expectation of compensation to a father whose virgin daughter has been compromised. The virgin in this context is treated not as a person, but as property valuable to her father. Thus these two judgments have been placed with other precedents governing the loss or damage of property.

With the beginning of the eighth sequence of laws (22:18-20), there is a shift to the apodictic form in the statement of the laws. This shift has often been taken to indicate a collection originally separate from the predominantly casuistic collection of 20:22–22:17. Most of the remainder of the Book of the Covenant is in apodictic form, with what appear to have been explanatory addenda in the casuistic "precedent" form here and there (22:25-27 [MT 22:24-26]; 23:4-5).

This eighth sequence specifies the death penalty for sorcery, copulation with animals, and violation of the first and second commandments of the Decalogue. The ninth sequence (22:21-27 [MT 22:20-26]) commands protective concern for the alien and the dispossessed: the widow, the orphan, and the poor.

The tenth sequence (22:28-31 [MT 27-30]) requires an appropriate respect for God and the נָשִׂיא, the leader or representative of the tribe. Specifically, in this case, the "honest man" whose job it was to help out with the lesser case decisions is probably intended. The effectiveness of YHWH's system of justice was after all dependent upon the acceptance by the people of the rightness of the oracle-decisions and the precedent-judgments. Connected with this respect are such other means of its expression as offerings from the harvest, dedication of the firstborn (by means specified elsewhere), and by rigid standards of cultic probity.

The eleventh sequence of laws (23:1-9) concerns honesty in legal matters, specifically those that involve case decisions that affect other persons. Perjury, prejudicial testimony, bending to dishonest pressure, false charges, bribery and disregard for the poor and the stranger are all strictly forbidden.

The twelfth sequence (23:10-13) is concerned with the rest of the seventh year and the seventh day. The summary statement in v. 13 probably indicates a conclusion, at some earlier point in its development, of at least a subsection of the Book of the Covenant. Verse 13 is related in theme to the first commandment, and to the beginning of the Book of the Covenant at 20:23 and to 22:28 in the tenth sequence.

The thirteenth sequence (23:14-17) is, along with Exod 34:22-23, the oldest ritual calendar in the OT, specifying as it does the three occasions in the year on which the men of Israel were to appear with gifts in the Presence of YHWH: the first harvest of grain, the harvest of the remainder of the cereal crops seven weeks later, and the final harvest of all crops in the autumn.

The fourteenth and final sequence of laws (23:18-19) lists four cultic regulations, the fourth of which occurs also in 34:26 and in Deut 14:21.

The conclusion to the Book of the Covenant (23:20-33) is a sort of epilogue, and a parallel to the beginning of the collection, at 20:22-23. It amounts to a promise-appendage similar to the conclusion of the Holiness Code in Lev 26 and the Deuteronomistic Code in Deut 28. The promises it offers, of a guiding, protecting, intervening and fighting Presence of YHWH, are in effect the reward promised for keeping the laws and the precedents just set forth.

These promises are specifically appropriate to Israel at Sinai, looking forward to the fulfillment of the ancient promise to the Fathers of land, and insecure at the prospect of encounter with unfriendly peoples. The extent of the land to be possessed is described here (23:31), as at so many places in the OT, in terms descriptive of the Davidic-Solomonic empire. And YHWH's part in the displacement of the inhabitants of the land of promise is described in the language of the HOLY WAR.

24:1-18. The covenant is made. The narrative of the making of YHWH's covenant with Israel represents a kind of "happy ending" to the Exodus story, an ideal conclusion to the story of the birth of Israel as YHWH's special people. It brings together the themes anticipated in the "eagles' wings" speech of 19:4-6, and it provides a natural point of departure for the detailed sequence of instructions for the spaces and the symbols and the arrangements for worship that follow in chaps. 25–31 and 35–40.

This "ideal" end is not however the "real" end of the Book of Exodus, as the conclusion of the Exodus narrative in chaps. 32–34 shows. It is for that reason that the covenant made here has to be remade in 34:10-28, and for that reason, in part, that Exod 24 has such a patchwork arrangement.

The making of the covenant is thus described as taking place on two levels. The first involves the people and Moses (vv. 3-8). The second involves Moses and his assistants, Aaron, Aaron's sons Nadab and Abihu, and seventy of the elders of Israel (vv. 1-2, 9-11).

The people enter into the covenant upon the instructions of Moses, who acts as the intermediary of YHWH. The Presence of YHWH is symbolized by the altar, and the symbol of ratification is the blood of the "completion-offerings" (זְבָחִים שְׁלָמִים, NRSV *offerings of well-being*), half of which is dashed upon the altar, and half upon the people.

In between these two symbolic manipulations of the blood, the Book of the Covenant, the revelation of the requirements and expectations of YHWH, is read aloud to the people by Moses. This ceremony takes place at the foot of the mountain, just beyond the appointed boundary (v. 4).

Moses and the leaders of Israel enter into this covenant, along with the people, but there is a further covenant ceremony for them as well. They are invited by YHWH to ascend Sinai/Horeb. They do so, and they experience there a theophany and share a meal of communion.

Ratification of the covenant here is at least suggested in the meal as well as in the appearance of God. Verses 10 and 11 employ different terms for the experience of Moses and his assistants: the term in v. 10 is ראה, "see, understand," and the term in v. 11 is חזה, "behold, gaze"; NRSV has *saw* and *beheld*, respectively.

What actually was seen by Moses and his companions is far from clear. The description of v.10 is of the appearance of what lay at God's feet, not of the appearance of God himself. Even so, the experience is unique in the OT. The statement in v. 11 that the company suffered no harm (*He did not lay his hand on the chief men of the people of Israel*) is a further indication of the special nature of the experience (see also 3:20 and 9:15 for the stretching out of YHWH's hand in harm, and Ps 138:7 and Ezek 8:3 for the stretching out of YHWH's hand in beneficial action).

Immediately following the making of the covenant, Moses is commanded to come to the place of YHWH's Presence on the mountain to receive *the tablets of stone, with the law and the commandment* (v. 12) written for Israel's instruction. Precisely what was written on the tablets is ambiguous (cf. 34:1 and 34:27-28). The way is prepared, however, for the extended revelation that is to follow as YHWH is described as settling down upon the mountain in a cloud shielding his glory (כָּבוֹד, which along with שֵׁם, "name," is the equivalent of Presence, פָּנִים, in the OT.

YHWH's Plan for the Spaces and Symbols of Worship, 25:1–31:18

25:1-9 (=35:4-9). Israel's offering. The instructions for the spaces, the symbols, the personnel and the acts by which YHWH's Presence and interventions are to be called to mind are the contribution of the priestly circles. In broad summary, they are set forth in terms of instructions, 25:1–31:18, and the implementation of those instructions, 35:1–40:38, a thirteen-chapter sequence of memory (Durham 1990, 112-26).

These two sections are a near thing to a mirror image of each other, although there are differences in order and a few differences in detail. This being so, the parallels in the second of the two sections will be listed in this commentary on the first section, to avoid a needless repetition.

The raw materials for the media of Israel's worship are called for, in an instruction that makes clear that they are to be given freely by the people, by *all whose hearts prompt them* (v. 2). The materials specified are precious and semi-precious metals, yarns and fabric, skins, lumber, oil, spices, and precious and semi-precious gemstones. Only the best is to be employed in the preparations to follow.

25:10-40 (=37:1-24). The Ark, the Table, the Lampstand. These three objects are special symbols of the Presence of YHWH, and so it is appropriate that the instruction for their construction should come first in YHWH's plan. The Ark and the Table were to be made of acacia wood, a hard and durable material, which in both instances is to be overlaid with pure gold.

The Ark was to contain the "testimony" (עֵדֻת, NRSV *covenant*, 25:21), probably the tables of stone on which the "Ten Words" were recorded (on the parallel practice in the ancient Near East, see Sarna 1991, 160-61). The Table was to provide a resting-place for the Bread of the Presence, the incense, and the drink offering.

The lampstand and its accessories were to be made of one talent (approx. 75 lbs.) of pure gold, in the form of a growing tree, probably the almond tree, the "wake-up" tree of Jer 1:11-12. It was to hold seven lamps, one for the trunk of the tree and one for each of its six branches.

The Ark, the Table, and the Lampstand were each a symbolic reminder of the Presence of YHWH, and their nearness to the place of his immediate Presence dictates the material of their construction.

26:1-37 (=36:8-38). The Tabernacle. The Tabernacle was the most holy shelter of the Presence of YHWH. Its arrangement and its materials involved a gradation of movement from the most holy place, where the Ark, the special symbol of YHWH's nearness (note 26:32, and such passages as 1 Sam 4:4; 2 Kgs 19:15; Ps 80:2; and Isa 37:16), stood, to the one opening to the courtyard in front of the Tabernacle. It was also constructed to be readily portable, an indication that YHWH is a Presence in motion, not to be considered captive to a single location. This emphasis is an important one, not least in material from the Priestly source, for what it suggests about the conservative view of the Temple in Jerusalem that Jeremiah attacked so vigorously (Jer 26).

The question whether the wilderness Tabernacle really existed or is a retrojection of a Jerusalem priesthood eager to justify the Temple of Solomon (or even a reconstructed Temple) is beside the point of the description in Exodus, which has a theological point, not an historical one, in view.

27:1-21 (=38:1-7, 9-20; Lev 24:1-3). The Altar, the Courtyard, and the Light. The instructions for the altar for burnt offerings are more ambiguous than any of the instructions concerning the media of worship. It too was to be portable, and the direction that it be made of wood, albeit overlaid with copper, seems to be somewhat in conflict with its function, as also with the instructions of Exod 20:24-26. The use of copper for the altar and its accessories aids our understanding of its location, in the area farthest from the holiest space where the Ark stood.

The Courtyard that surrounded the Tabernacle and the activities in front of it was formed by an also entirely portable arrangement of columns and draperies. The space thus enclosed was 150 ft. by 75 ft., and the draperies blocked the view of any activity that did not rise higher than 7.5 ft.

The instruction for pure olive oil extracted by pounding the olives is an additional specification that only the finest substances were to be used in the place of YHWH's Presence. Such oil was nearly smokeless, and gave off a brighter light than the easier to obtain pressed oil.

28:1-43 (=39:1-31). The Priests' clothing. The special garments to be worn by AARON and his sons are described in detail, both as to design and material, although the specifications set forth deal primarily with the vestments of Aaron, who is presented as the prototypical high priest. Provision is made for an ephod (vv.6-14) set with two stones of onyx engraved with the names of the twelve tribes of Israel, and for a kind of vest (vv. 15-30) containing a pouch for the oracular device of the sacred lot, and decorated with twelve semiprecious stones symbolizing, again, the twelve tribes.

By means of this latter garment, worn across the breast and containing the instruments of oracular decision, "Aaron" was to keep Israel before YHWH and to have Israel's judgment ever *on his heart* (v. 29) whenever he entered the Presence of YHWH.

These high-priestly vestments were completed by a robe equipped with bells (vv. 31-35), apparently for an apotropaic purpose; by a golden *rosette* (vv. 36-38) symbolizing Aaron's special status as one uniquely consecrated to YHWH's service; and by a coat, a turban, and an embroidered waistband (v. 39).

That such an elaborate array of splendid vestments represents the end of a long and cumulative evolution is more than probable. Further, this evolutionary process no doubt incorporated into the high priestly attire some elements of the king's ceremonial dress as, with time, his own role in the leadership of cultic worship decreased.

The garments to be worn by the ordinary priests (vv. 40-43) are much simpler and more practical, and are probably closer to what was actually worn by all priests on most occasions. The Hebrew idiom for ordination, "fill the hand" (NRSV *ordain*, v. 41 and in chap. 29), probably means "to complete the power of" or "to grant full authority to" the person set apart for the appointed round of sacral duties.

The vestments may be thought of as having a double significance: they were a reminder of both the priests' authority and of the source of that authority, the immanent Presence of YHWH.

29:1-46 (=Lev 8:1-36). The Priests' ordination. From the implements of cultic worship, including the apparel of the priests, the instructions are now turned to the personnel of the cult. This transition is a natural one in the present arrangement of the text of Exodus, as the description of what the priests are to wear leads directly to the directions for the consecration of the priests for sacral service.

Unlike most of the specifications of Exod 25:1–31:18, the ceremony of the ordination of Aaron and his sons is not actually carried out in Exodus, but in Lev 8. This fact, plus some inconsistencies between what is recorded about the priestly garments in chap. 28 and chap. 29, and the fact that chap. 29 contains in its final third additional material not directly connected with its central theme (vv. 38-46), suggests that chap. 29 is a collation of variant traditions about ordination, some early and some late. The chapter is closed by a summary reference to the theme underlying all the instructions in Exodus, the insistent confession that YHWH is present.

The ceremony of ordination is an elaborate one requiring extensive sacrifices and gifts and a period seven days in length. There are three stages in the ceremony: the rites of anointing, rites granting authority, and rites of setting apart (note 28:41; 29:1, 7, 9, 21, 29). The order of these rites is unclear, and they may not have been sequential but simultaneous.

The rites include ceremonial ablutions, donning the vestments, anointing with special oil, smearing the priests and sprinkling their vestments with sacrificial blood, and a communion meal in which YHWH and the ordinands are specially bound together by the manipulation of "the ram of ordination." The sacrifices include a young bull as a sin offering, and two rams— one as an offering wholly consumed before YHWH, and the other as the sacrifice of communion.

30:1-38 (30:1-10 =37:25-28; 30:17-21 =38:8). The incense altar, the atonement money, the laver for washing, and the anointing oil and the special incense. Elaborate specifications are given for the construction and placement of the altar of incense (vv. 1-10) of the inner sanctuary. This altar both symbolized and augmented the large altar of burnt offerings in the courtyard of the Tabernacle.

A special head-tax on adults (vv. 11-16), called *the atonement money* is commanded, as the means by which the financial requirements of keeping up the cult fabric may be met. There is nowhere in the OT a passage that records the fulfillment of this instruction.

The bronze laver for ceremonial ablutions (vv. 17-21), the special formula anointing oil (vv. 22-33) and the special formula incense (vv. 34-38) are ordered and precisely described. The sanctity of the oil and the incense is strongly stressed: they must never be put to any profane use. While the making of the laver is reported (38:8), there is not in the OT any narrative of the blending of the special oil or the special incense.

31:1-18 (31:1-11 =35:10-19 and 35:30-36:1; 31:12-18 =35:1-3). The artisans and the Sabbath. The equipment of worship specified and described, the one matter yet lacking is the provision of an artisan and a capable assistant to direct the work of creating that equipment. Verses 1-11 are given to this subject, and Bezalel is designated as the man divinely endowed for the task. He is to be assisted by Oholiab; together they are to carry out the instructions of YHWH to the letter.

In the face of so much to be done, in so worthy a cause, an emphatically expanded version of the fourth commandment (vv. 12-17) provides a conclusion to the chapters of instruction, making it clear that no cause is so important as to take precedence over YHWH's specification of a day of rest.

Exodus 31:18 then serves both to close YHWH's instructions regarding the media of worship and also to anticipate the narrative section that follows immediately, in which *the two tablets of the covenant, the tablets of stone* have so important a role.

Disobedience and Its Consequences, 32:1–34:35

32:1-35. Israel's first disobedience. The account of Israel's disobedience of their covenant promises, a disobedience that comes all too soon, is the continuation of the narrative that was interrupted by the insertion of the priestly instructions regarding the media of Israel's worship in the Presence of YHWH. The interruption is a logical one, of course, as also is the continuation of the narrative describing Israel's betrayal of YHWH, *after* the instructions for worship have been given but *before* they are implemented and *before* such worship can actually take place.

The people of Israel, impatient in Moses' lengthy sojourn on the mountain and insecure because of the awesomeness of their surroundings and the uncertainty of their future, make the first of what can only have been many demands for a visible object of worship. Aaron gives in all too readily to their request, and asks for their jewelry of gold, a move strikingly parallel to Israel's own fleecing of the Egyptians.

From this gold, Aaron creates a cast and carved bull-calf, and identifies it with the power that wrought their deliverance from Egypt. The people respond with a feast, which Aaron proclaims in honor of YHWH, with sacrifices, and with wanton celebration. That the worship is the worship of YHWH is not in question. The problem is that it is the worship of YHWH on *Israel's* terms rather than on YHWH's terms.

Thus YHWH immediately communicates to Moses what has happened, then lapses into a sharp condemnation of the people's disregard of their promise of obedience, and threatens to obliterate them. This catastrophic decimation is prevented only by the intervention of Moses, who reminds YHWH of his promise to the Fathers, and of what the Egyptians will think, if Israel has been freed only to be destroyed.

Moses heads immediately down the mountain with the tablets of stone, picking up JOSHUA on the way. When they draw near to the camp and Joshua mistakes the sound of celebration for the sound of battle, Moses replies sadly,

> Not the sound of heroes exulting,
> not the sound of losers lamenting,
>   the sound of drunken singing is what I hear! (v. 18, author trans.)

Moses flies into a furious rage. He casts the stone slabs containing the commandments to the ground, breaking them. He seizes the calf, burns it, grinds it into powder, and mixing it with water, he makes the people drink it. He confronts Aaron, who blames the people, and even disavows his own role in the making of the idol: *I threw it [the gold] into the fire, and out came this calf!* (v. 24).

Moses calls the people to their covenant responsibility to YHWH on YHWH's terms. He is joined by the sons of Levi, with whom he wreaks judgment on the idolaters. How the guilty are separated from the people at large is not indicated, only that about 3,000 are put to the sword. The narrative both describes how Moses brought what had become a mob under control and glorifies the Levites as the sacerdotal tribe.

Again declaring to the people of Israel the terrible gravity of their sin, Moses returns to the Presence of YHWH, apparently on Sinai/Horeb, to intercede for them. Once in YHWH's Presence, he does not excuse the people, but asks forgiveness for them, and begs to be identified with them, even in judgment. YHWH declares that the guilty must suffer, and that the people's punishment is yet to come.

Moses is to lead the people according to the guidance of a divine emissary; for the moment, at least, the people's disobedience has so profoundly shaken YHWH's relationship to them that he is unwilling to resume his chosen place among them. And *when the day comes for [their] punishment* (v. 34), YHWH promises that he "will punish them for their sin." The punishment already meted out, having to drink their ground-up idol and losing to the sword 3,000 of their number, is not the punishment referred to in this composite Exodus narrative.

33:1-11. Israel and YHWH's Presence. What that punishment is to be, hinted at by 32:34, is now made clear. The covenant that was to have cemented the people's relationship with YHWH, and his to them, has been violated. They have been judged by him and ordered to leave Sinai/Horeb (32:34), the mountain of his Presence. And he now declares that what has happened has made it impossible for him to go himself with them: he can only send an emissary to guide them (vv. 2-3, 5, as in 32:34).

Thus do vv. 1-6 elaborate the theme of 32:34: YHWH will still keep his promise to the Fathers, but he can no longer come amongst Israel, for fear his anger will get the better of him and mean their destruction. Thus will he send a guiding emissary, in his place.

This prospect is a doleful one for the people of Israel. They realize more clearly than ever how their fortunes have been linked to YHWH's Presence in their midst. They remove, at YHWH's command, the *ornaments* (or "festive dress") that recalled their worship of the calf. This action is indicative of their depression at the prospect of their departure from YHWH's Presence and, worse still, at the prospect of his departure from them.

At this point, the narrative of disobedience and its consequences is interrupted by the insertion of a block of material dealing with the "trysting tent" (אֹהֶל מוֹעֵד, vv. 7-11) of YHWH's Presence. This material, important though it is, is completely out of place at this point in what is otherwise a tightly suspenseful account.

The compilers' purpose in placing these verses here was probably to give emphasis to the terrible isolation of the Presence of YHWH by declaring that he is no longer in the midst of encamped Israel, but outside the camp, and accessible only to Moses and his select helpers (Joshua, Aaron, Miriam and carefully picked leaders; note Num 11:16, 24-26; 12:4).

In doing so, the compilers have given us a very early tradition concerning the advent of YHWH's Presence in a tent. Indeed, this trysting tent of the Presence is not only separate from the wilderness TABERNACLE and the Ark; it very likely preceded them both, and may well be the sole tent-manifestation of the Presence in the entire wilderness period.

On such a view, the Ark would be the natural evolution in the progressive development of the theology of YHWH's Presence, and the Tabernacle, in its earliest form, a portable shrine for the Ark. The elaborate Priestly Tabernacle of chap. 26 and the ornate Priestly Ark of 25:10-22 would then be retrojections into the past of the Ark and the Tabernacle of Davidic-Solomonic times, but not retrojections without precedent.

The compilers' use of the tradition of the trysting tent to expand the theme of the departed Presence of YHWH is thus at best somewhat misplaced. And the tent may be thought of as the first post-Sinai palladium of YHWH's Presence, and so perhaps as the symbol of the fulfilled promise of 33:14.

33:12–34:9. Moses asks and YHWH answers. This continuation of the narrative of Israel's disobedience and its consequences is best read immediately following 33:6. Following YHWH's declaration of the removal of his Presence, Moses argues the total insecurity of the people he is to lead and his own total inadequacy for such a task under such conditions. His request of vv. 12-13 amounts to a rhetorical question: how does YHWH plan to accomplish his promise without granting his Presence, the very Presence that has brought every victory and every blessing the people have thus far enjoyed? YHWH's answer (v. 14) indicates some relenting. Moses presses his advantage, raising a second rhetorical question (vv. 15-16) in which he connects his own fate with that of the people he leads. Without YHWH's Presence, any further movement forward is futile, and doomed to fail. Moses' argument is incontrovertible, and YHWH agrees to his request, because *you have found favor in my sight, and I know you by name* (v. 17).

Thus encouraged, Moses asks the personal favor of a special revelation of YHWH's Presence: *Show me your glory, I pray* (v. 18). Such a request cannot of course be granted because of the danger involved (v. 20). Yet YHWH does grant Moses a special privilege: he manifests his goodness to Moses, and calls out to him his name, thus revealing to Moses as much as he can know of the essential divine self. This wondrous and mysterious experience of Moses is described, awkwardly, as a vision of where YHWH has passed (NRSV *my back*, 33:23). How else, indeed, could it be described?

YHWH's answer to this further request of Moses (34:1-9) is parallel to his response to Moses' request in 3:14-15. Here, as there, YHWH confesses the reality of his Presence by calling out his name, the name that means "the One who always is," "the I AM." There, YHWH began his story with Moses by giving him this name. Here, YHWH repeats that name, twice, then describes *how* he is "I AM" (34:6-7). Moses' response is to prostrate himself in worship. No other response would have been appropriate.

34:10-35. The covenant renewed, and Moses vindicated. Following the promise of the return of the Presence of YHWH, the logical conclusion to the whole episode of disobedience and disaster is the renewal of the covenant that Israel's idolatry had broken. There is no attempt to duplicate the dramatic narrative of chap. 24, or to list, even in summary, the conditions of relationship set forth in the TEN COMMANDMENTS. The attention here is on the sin that caused the disobedience, the embrace of divided loyalty.

Thus the commands of 34:12-26 all have to do, in one way or another, with the first commandment, *you shall have no other gods before me* (20:3). No covenant renewal ceremony is described, beyond the words of YHWH in v. 10, *I hereby make a covenant*, and the narrator's report in v. 28, "And he wrote on the tablets the words of the covenant, the ten words" (following the more literal marginal reading of NRSV).

With the covenant thus remade, Moses' leadership, rejected by the defection of the people of Israel (note 32:1), is reaffirmed by a visible sign of his special relationship with YHWH. He descends Sinai/Horeb with a shining face, the result of his close communion with the Presence of YHWH. Where his previous descent (32:15-35) was to a scene of wild idolatrous orgy, this descent meets awed and reverent respect.

This shining of Moses' face has stimulated commentators to write about cultic masks, priestly veils, radiant skin, bull-calf connections, and so on. It prompted Jerome to the famous translation *cornuta esset facies sua*, and Michelangelo Buonarroti in turn to carve horns on his *Moses*. The emphasis is really on YHWH, not Moses, as the unique use of the verb קרן, "shine," makes clear (only here, vv. 29, 30, 35). Moses has been vindicated by YHWH himself. His shining face is a reflection, no more, of the dazzling brightness of YHWH's Presence.

Obedience and Its Blessing, 35:1–40:38

As I have noted above, this section is, by and large, a mirror image of the section of instructions in 25:1–31:18. There, the directions of YHWH are given; here, they are carried out. There are a few differences in order and even a few additions here. But the major purpose of this section is to report that, after disobedience, its consequences, and covenant renewal, YHWH's instructions are finally carried out.

The parallel passages in the earlier section are as follows:

35:1-3 = 31:12-18	37:25-28 = 30:1-10
35:4-9 = 25:1-7	37:29 = 30:22-25, 34-36
35:10-19 = 31:6-10	38:1-7 = 27:1-8
35:30–36:1 = 31:1-6	38:8 = 30:17-21
36:8-38 = 26:1-37	38:9-20 = 27:9-18
37:1-9 = 25:10-22	39:1-31 = 28:1-43
37:10-16 = 25:23-30	39:32-43 = 31:7-11; 35:11-19
37:17-24 = 25:31-40	

Beyond these close parallels, there are expansions and additions. A command against kindling a fire on the sabbath for domestic purposes, a prohibition that is not found elsewhere in the OT, appears in 35:3. The call for workmen is broader in 35:10-19, and the response to the call for raw materials is met with so much enthusiastic generosity that Moses has to call a halt to the giving (36:2-7).

Exodus 38:8 adds a mysterious note about the material for the base of the bronze laver, connecting it with the mirrors of certain women *who served at the entrance to the tent of meeting*. These women are not elsewhere mentioned in the OT, and the matter remains obscure.

Exodus 38:21-31 records an inventory of the gifts of metal, with large amounts listed and the notation that the inventory was taken by Ithamar (mentioned elsewhere in 6:23 and 28:1).

A final inventory of the objects made is given in 39:32-43, and the Book of Exodus is brought to a close with an account of the setting up of the Tabernacle, the arrangement and consecration of its furnishings, the cleansing of the priests, and the settling of the Glory, the Presence of YHWH, into the Tabernacle in the midst of his people Israel (40:1-38).

With that settling, the ideal of Exodus is reached. In that settling, the theology of Exodus is summarized. By that settling, the hope of Exodus is confessed.

The remainder of the story occupies all the rest of the Bible, and is still being worked out beyond it. The Presence of YHWH is still available to all who are open. The human family is still resisting the loyalty that Presence demands and deserves. YHWH's self-proclamation, "I AM YHWH your God" has become the self-proclamation of Christ: "I AM the Way, the Truth, and the Life." We have not yet come to the Promised Land, but God comes still to us, showing us still the way.

Works Cited

Alt, Albrecht. 1966. "The God of the Fathers," in *Essays on O.T. History and Religion*, 3–77.

Anati, Emmanuel. 1986. *The Mountain of God*.

Childs, B. S. 1965. "The Birth of Moses," JBL 84:109–22.

Coats, G. W. 1968. *Rebellion in the Wilderness*.

Cross, F. M., Jr. 1973. "The Song of the Sea and Canaanite Myth," in *Canaanite Myth and Hebrew Epic*, 112–44.

Daube, David. 1969. *Studies in Biblical Law*.

Davies, G. I. 1979. *The Way of the Wilderness. A Geographical Study of the Wilderness Itineraries of the Old Testament*.

Durham, John I. 1970. "Credo, Ancient Israelite," *IDBSupp* 197–99. 1987. *Exodus*. WBC. 1990. *Understanding the Basic Themes of Exodus*.

Griffiths, J. G. 1953. "The Egyptian Derivation of the Name Moses," *JNES* 12:225–31.

Herrmann, Siegfried. 1973. *Israel in Egypt*. SBT 2nd ser.

Mendenhall, G. E. 1992. "Midian," *AncBD* 4:815–18.
Noth, Martin. 1972. *A History of Pentateuchal Traditions.*
Pritchard, J. B., ed. 1969. ANET. 3rd ed.
Redford, D. B. "The Literary Motif of the Exposed Child," *Numen* 14:209–28.
Reymond, P. 1958. *L'Eau, sa Vie, et sa Signification dans L'Ancien Testment.*
Sarna, Nahum M. 1991. *The JPS Torah Commentary. Exodus.*
Uphill, E. P. 1968 and 1969. "Pithom and Raamses: Their Location and Significance," *JNES* 27:291– 316 and 28:15–39.
Wiles, John Keating, "Red Sea/Reed Sea," MDB.
Yadin, Yigael. 1963. *The Art of Warfare in Biblical Lands.*
Zimmerli, W. 1982. "I Am Yahweh," in *I Am Yahweh*, 1–28.

Leviticus
James W. Watts

Introduction

Leviticus, the third book of the Pentateuch (see TORAH), usually receives less attention from readers than its neighbors, probably because it contains mostly ritual instructions and legal regulations. Yet Leviticus makes vital contributions to both the theology and the plot of the Pentateuch. Its instructions and regulations spell out the practical implications of the promise (Exod 29:42-45; 33:14) that God will live *with* the people of Israel. And its narratives, although few in number, include the fulfillment of that promise in the dedication of God's dwelling, the TENT OF MEETING or TABERNACLE, by supernatural fire (Lev 9:22-24). Thus Leviticus interprets the significance of God's COVENANT with Israel in the concrete terms of regular worship and daily life, while also illustrating the unpredictable nature of life in the presence of God.

Leviticus in Context

The Pentateuch presents itself as a continuous narrative, within which the division into five books may seem superficial. Leviticus in particular continues the setting (at Mt. Sinai) and situation (MOSES receiving divine instructions) of the latter part of Exodus.

Boundaries of the book. Nevertheless, the narrative does separate the material of Leviticus from its surroundings by several markers. Exodus concludes with the completion of the Tabernacle, which in the last scene is occupied by God's GLORY in the form of a cloud (Exod 40:34-38). Then Leviticus begins with the statement that *The LORD summoned* [or called] *Moses and spoke to him from the tent of meeting* (Lev 1:1), which establishes the Tabernacle, rather than the mountain, as the setting for the divine instructions that follow. The book concludes with several summary statements (Lev 26:46; 27:34) to the law of Sinai (i.e., all God's instructions, whether given on the mountain or in the Tabernacle pitched at its base; see the commentary below). The Book of Numbers begins with a census in preparation for the people's departure from Sinai. Within the Pentateuchal narrative, therefore, the boundaries of Leviticus are marked by the completion of the Tabernacle on the one hand and the organization of the Israelite camp on the other.

Leviticus within Exodus 25–Numbers 10. Yet, the book is clearly part of a larger unit concerned with creating and preserving the divine-human community. The material in Leviticus falls into two thematic parts that generally mirror the context on either side of the book. Leviticus 1–10 describe the sacrifices and rituals conducted in the Tabernacle, whose construction and furnishings are described in Exod 25–40. Leviticus 11–27 contain, for the most part, instructions for holy living that affect all members of the Israelite camp, whose organization and features are described in Num 1–10. By analogy with modern computers, the contents of Leviticus can be thought of as the "software" for use in the "hardware" described in the surrounding material (Blum 1990, 302n.56).

Leviticus within the Pentateuch. The book's meaning, however, is shaped by an even wider narrative context. When God first encountered Moses at the burning bush, God predicted Israel would worship on that mountain (Exod 3:12). Upon their arrival at the mountain, God declared that Israel would become "a priestly kingdom and a holy nation" (Exod 19:6). Leviticus narrates the fulfillment of these promises in the inauguration of sacrificial worship in the Tabernacle (Lev 8–9). By surrounding this story with chapters of instructions on ritual worship (Lev 1–7) and holy living (Lev 11–27), the book also emphasizes that God's presence with the people, symbolized by the Tabernacle in the middle of the camp, affects most aspects of their lives. However, the story's unexpected climax—a supernatural fire consuming the sacrifices (Lev 9:24)—is a reminder that, despite the importance of ritual, living with God remains an unpredictable endeavor.

Leviticus periodically refers to events within its wider narrative context, especially the EXODUS from Egypt and the coming conquest of Canaan. But the book's narrative role within the Pentateuch is more complicated than such references to past and future events might suggest. Exodus 19–24 have already narrated the creation of the covenant community at Sinai, complete with ritual instructions (20:22-26; 23:10-19), civil and criminal laws (21:1–23:9), and sacrifices inaugurating the covenant (24:3-8). What is the purpose of going over similar ground again in Leviticus?

Obviously, the material in Exod 25–Lev 27 adds many instructional details lacking in the much shorter account of Exod 19–24. But Leviticus is more than a collection of supplemental details. It recounts the events at Sinai from a different perspective. Exodus 19–24 emphasizes the historical event of making the covenant and accepting its stipulations. Leviticus instead organizes the experiences of the people's daily lives to conform to the fact of God's presence in their midst. Where the first account points to a singular event and its historical consequences, the second points to an eternal reality—God's holiness—and its consequences for anyone who comes in contact with it.

Leviticus, together with the Tabernacle account in Exod 25–31 and 35–40, is therefore a doublet for Exod 19–24, that is, a parallel narrative of events at Sinai from a different perspective. In the establishment of the worshiping community at

Sinai, the book portrays a partial restoration of the divine-human community intended at creation. It describes an orderly reality separating the distinct spheres of life, in which any invasion of one sphere by another must be isolated, lest it threaten the relationship between God and Israel that this separation makes possible. This "religious organization of reality" was summarized by Leon Wieseltier (1987, 33):

> Structure for the reception of the unstructured: this is the subject of Leviticus—indeed, of the Torah. The organization of the world for sanctity proceeded by the increasing specification of ordained structure. Cosmic differentiations (between light and darkness and so on, in Genesis) led to historical differentiations (between the children of Abraham and others, in Genesis and Exodus), which led to the differentiations of holiness (most thickly and systematically in Leviticus).

Ritual in Leviticus

Modern readers may be tempted to dismiss much of Leviticus as "meaningless ritual," but the ancient writers of this book would have found that phrase self-contradictory. It is through ritual that they create and communicate religious meaning. In Leviticus, belief cannot be divided from action. Instead, ritual action defines the symbolic meaning of Israel's relations with God, other nations, the natural world, and itself.

Offerings and Sacrifices. Offering gifts to God is a pervasive feature of ancient and modern religious observance. In an agricultural economy such as ancient Israel's, religious gifts naturally took the form of grain, fruits, and domestic animals, although their equivalent could be paid in precious metals (Lev 27). Israel, however, also believed that certain offerings were not gifts, but belonged to God by right. Offerings of *new grain* (23:16), *first fruits of . . . harvest* (23:10), firstborn animals (27:26-27), and *tithes* (27:30-33) acknowledge God's ownership of the land and the people's status as God's *tenants* (25:23).

Although gifts and tithes persist in today's religious observances, animal sacrifices do not. The practice of blood sacrifice may have arisen partly to compensate for the guilt of slaughtering animals for food (Milgrom 1991, 440–43). Priestly theology reflects such ideas in its depiction of animals and humans as originally vegetarian (Gen 1:29-30) and of a divine command allowing humans to slaughter animals for food (Gen 9:2-6). Consequently, all slaughter is sacred and must be performed as a sacrifice (Lev 17:3-4) to make atonement before God (17:11; see below on atonement). Slaughter for food thus becomes a sacrifice of well-being and the consumption of flesh a sacred meal (Lev 7:11-18).

Some of Israel's sacrifices, however, do not produce food for the worshiper or even the priests (e.g., the *burnt offering*, Lev 1). Their meaning stems from Leviticus's understanding of the relationship between God and Israel, and involves processes of purification and atonement (see below). Sacrifice preserves the conditions necessary for God's presence in Israel's midst by providing formal and repeatable means for divine-human reconciliation (Mann 1988, 121).

Blood sacrifice is an ancient religious ritual far older than the priestly theology of Leviticus, so it is unlikely that any one explanation will account for all of Israel's sacrificial practices. Nevertheless, the issue of the meaning of sacrifice must play a central role in any interpretation of Leviticus. Ritual exists to give symbolic expression to religious reality. In Leviticus, the meaning of sacrifice determines the form of its performance. In subsequent Jewish and Christian interpretation of Leviticus, the meaning of sacrifice overshadows and replaces its performance (see below).

Holy and Common, Clean and Unclean. The priests' job, according to the programmatic statement in Lev 10:10, is *to distinguish between the holy and the common, and between the unclean and the clean.* These categories pervade the theology of Leviticus and determine part of its literary structure: the sacrificial regulations in chaps. 1–7 focus on the separation of the holy from the common, and the dietary and purification laws of chaps. 11–15 classify the clean and the unclean.

The two pairs of opposites are not equivalent, but they do affect each other. God is "holy," which means that God is completely separate, different, and other than humans and the natural world, that is, the "common." People or objects that are dedicated to God's use—such as priests, the Tabernacle, and sacrifices—derive their holy status from God and are removed from common use (see HOLINESS IN THE OLD TESTAMENT).

The labels "unclean" and "clean" distinguish between people, animals, or objects on the basis of ritual purity, not hygiene. Interpreters debate the meaning of the various purity laws of Leviticus, but it is clear that the distinctions reflect the symbolic structure of Israel's world view (Douglas [1966] 1985). Israel is called to holiness by distinguishing itself from other peoples (Exod 19:5-6; Lev 18:3-5; 20:25-26), which it partly accomplishes by eating only a limited number of "clean" animals distinguished from the rest of the animal world (Lev 11) and by temporarily separating Israelites rendered "unclean" by genital discharges, diseases, etc., from contact with the holy (Lev 12–15; CLEAN/UNCLEAN).

The four categories partially overlap. What is clean may be either holy or common, and what is common may be either clean or unclean. But what is holy cannot be unclean, or vice versa. Holiness and uncleanness are dynamic; they try to expand into their static antonyms, the common and the clean (Milgrom 1991, 732). Thus in OT thought, the unclean and the holy oppose each other, and Leviticus orders Israel's world to diminish the former power and maximize the latter.

Atonement. Leviticus frequently describes the purpose of sacrifice as "atonement" (כפר). The Hebrew word ranges in meaning from the concrete notions of "rub" and "cover" through "ransom" to the more abstract "purge" and "expiate" (see ATONEMENT/EXPIATION IN THE OT; Milgrom 1991, 1079-84). Leviticus applies it not only to sacrifices for sins (chaps. 4–5, 16) but also to purification rites (e.g., after childbirth, 12:7) and to the all-purpose *burnt offering* (1:4; Wenham 1979, 57-62).

Atonement removes impediments to communion between humans and God, whether they be sin or unavoidable impurity. Through sacrificial atonement, Israelites move from an unclean to a clean state and some, the priests, from common to holy status. In Leviticus's thinking, God's residence with Israel requires a pure community surrounding a holy sanctuary. Atonement preserves the conditions necessary for a divine-human community.

The Priestly Traditions and Editors

The contents of Leviticus belong to the Priestly (P) layer of the Pentateuch. Despite considerable reevaluation in recent decades of the Documentary Hypothesis of the Pentateuch's composition, the identification and isolation of P remains virtually unchallenged. P's distinctive interests (e.g., the priesthood, the Tabernacle, rituals, holiness) and style (e.g., careful use of technical vocabulary, repetitive structure) make it the most recognizable layer in the Pentateuch (see PRIESTLY WRITERS).

Authorship. P's interest in liturgy, sacrifice, and the Tabernacle as Israel's only shrine points to its origins among the priests of the Jerusalem Temple. The narrative context of P's laws presents them as divine instructions given through Moses to the people encamped at Mt. Sinai. The Pentateuch, however, presents Mosaic Law in a threefold form consisting of instructions from the mountain top (Exod 19–40), instructions from the Tabernacle (most of Leviticus and part of Numbers), and instructions from the plains of Moab (end of Numbers and Deuteronomy). Differences in style, content, legal particulars, and theology, as well as narrative setting, distinguish the three from each other (although their boundaries do not exactly correspond to those discerned by modern interpreters; see LAW IN THE OT). Yet all three blocks are presented separately and together as the divine Torah given to Israel through Moses.

The result is a document that openly presents a variety of Israelite legal traditions as authentically representative of Mosaic law. It thereby affirms the proposition that the God who initially inspired Moses continued to inspire the development of Israel's institutions in subsequent centuries and through various groups. One of the groups claiming Mosaic legal authority consisted of the priests who formulated, elaborated, and edited the P regulations in Leviticus.

Editing. Although all of Leviticus stems from P, it nevertheless shows signs of development over time. For example, the regulations regarding sacrifices in Lev 1–7 divide into two versions. The rituals described in Lev 1:1–6:7 are portrayed in somewhat different terms in Lev 6:8–7:38. The latter passage refers to the more detailed account of the former, but also adds to it additional regulations and concerns. It seems, therefore, to be a later supplement to the instructions in Lev 1:1–6:7. Another example is the block of material in Lev 17–26, which stands out stylistically and thematically from the rest of the book. Many scholars have concluded that it was originally a separate document, the "Holiness Code," which was incorporated into the larger context of Leviticus.

A close examination of Leviticus therefore suggests that the material was not composed by a single author at one sitting, but rather developed and grew over time. Some passages show the characteristic features of oral tradition, composed and handed down by word of mouth. Others show the signs of editorial activity, which adjusted separate documents to fit side by side. Thus P seems to have been the product of a community of teachers, authors, and editors who shared the priestly outlook on Israel's history and religious institutions.

Date. Dating the composition of P is much more difficult than identifying and isolating P from the rest of the Pentateuch, and current scholarship is divided over the problem. Efforts to date P linguistically by comparing its language with that of other Hebrew texts have produced contradictory results. Attempts to place P's institutions within the history of Israel's religion have not been very convincing, aside from showing that they are not Mosaic (e.g., see TENT OF MEETING).

The most promising evidence for dating P rests on its literary relationship with the rest of the Pentateuch. Despite a number of assertions to the contrary, it still appears that P was the last layer to be added to the Pentateuch. P structures and shapes the rest of the material. P seems to consciously react to and reinterpret older non-P material in the Pentateuch.

When this literary observation is combined with the historical observation that P seems to have had no literary influence on other Hebrew literature until the postexilic period (fifth and fourth centuries B.C.E.), we can conclude that P was combined with the rest of the Pentateuch and published at this time. However, observations regarding editorial activity within Leviticus (and the rest of P) suggest that much of P's material is considerably older than this date of publication. Thus it seems that P consists of materials from preexilic as well as later times that were made part of the Pentateuch and published only in the postexilic period.

Leviticus in Jewish and Christian Interpretation

Leviticus has influenced the beliefs and practices of generations of Jews and Christians, although often in different ways. As part of scripture, the book contributes to a wide network of religious ideas. Its significance cannot be fully understood apart from that larger context.

The Old Testament. Although Leviticus directly influenced only the later OT books, many of its ideas pervade the OT literature, which develops them further. For example, Leviticus considers both ritual and ethical legislation necessary for the divine-human community. The prophetic books define the relationship between ritual and ethics more closely by arguing that without justice and mercy, sacrifice and festivals are useless (Isa 1:10-17; Jer 7:1-15; Amos 5:21-24). Again, Leviticus distinguishes between unclean and clean on ritual and symbolic grounds. Outside the Pentateuch, these terms usually describe a general religious or moral condition (e.g., 2 Sam 22:21-25; Isa 6:5-7). On a larger scale, the historical and prophetic books interpret Israel's history as the outworking of the blessings and curses in Lev

26 and Deut 28, that is, as a consequence of Israel's fidelity to or rebellion against the covenant (e.g., cf. Ezek 22 and Lev 20). Leviticus's vision of the requirements for divine-human community thus finds echoes and elaborations throughout much of the OT.

Second Temple Judaism. The Second Temple period (515 B.C.E. until 70 C.E.) witnessed the completion of the OT and the publication of a wide variety of other religious works. These extrabiblical writings develop Leviticus' ideas in a variety of ways. WISDOM LITERATURE increasingly equates the law of Moses with divine wisdom and expounds on legal texts through proverbs (Sir 24:23; on Sir 19:13-17 as an interpretation of Lev 19:17, see Kugel 1986, 91). Under Hellenistic influence, some Jewish writers allegorize the ritual legislation to signify moral and intellectual virtues: for example, parting the hoof and chewing the cud (Lev 11:3, the criteria of clean land animals) symbolize the rational virtues of ethical discrimination and thoughtfulness in the *Letter of Aristeas* (see ARISTEAS, LETTER OF; and, on Philo, see PHILO). But the anti-Hellenistic writers of the Qumran TEMPLE SCROLL also revise Pentateuchal legislation on the basis of their own ritual concerns and attack particular practices at the Jerusalem Temple (Milgrom 1991, 558–66). Thus, concern for the interpretation and application of Pentateuchal law pervades a wide variety of later Second Temple writings.

Rabbinic Judaism. Legal interpretation, called *halakhah*, plays an even more crucial role in the classical rabbinic literature (second to fifth centuries C.E.; see RABBINIC LITERATURE). Although the Mishnah's rulings rarely depend on scriptural citations, *Sifra* uses midrash (see NT USE OF THE OT) to explicate the themes of Leviticus and anchor rabbinic rulings more firmly in scripture. *Leviticus Rabbah* reinterprets Leviticus' priestly and sacrificial rules as the means to sanctify the whole people of Israel. Along with the other rabbinic writings, these texts take laws that originally addressed the conditions of Palestine and its Temple and apply them to a people without land or temple. All the people are now priests, and prayers are their sacrifices. Despite the change in conditions, the law can be obeyed and Israel made holy.

The New Testament. Concern for interpreting law spread to early Christianity as well. The NT interprets the laws of Leviticus in two different ways. On the one hand, it singles out the commandment of love for neighbor (Lev 19:18), along with love of God (Deut 6:5), as the essence of the Mosaic law (Matt 22:37-40; Mark 12:29-31; Luke 10:27; Rom 13:8-10; Gal 5:14; Jas 2:8; see LOVE IN THE NT). On the other hand, it relaxes the requirements of many Pentateuchal purity regulations (Matt 15:11; Acts 10:9-16; Rom 14:14-23) and ritual laws (Acts 15:1-35; 1 Cor 7:19; see CHURCH AND LAW). Alongside such legal discussions, the NT also interprets the law typologically (see INTERPRETATION, HISTORY OF) as foreshadowing Christ's work. Hebrews casts Jesus as the high priest on the Day of Atonement (Lev 16), who offered his own blood instead of animal sacrifices to purify from sin (Heb 9:1-14). Like Leviticus, the NT emphasizes the ideal of close communion between

God and humans, but that communion is symbolized, not by the presence of the sanctuary in the middle of the camp as it is in Leviticus, but by its *absence* (Rev 21:22). This image at the end of the NT aptly represents the conscious continuity of theme and discontinuity of practice in NT interpretations of Leviticus.

Early Christianity. Christian commentators continued to distinguish ritual laws as nonbinding on Christians, while searching every part of the OT for typological and allegorical significance. This approach was shaped on the one side by Jewish criticisms of Christians for not obeying the law and on the other by Gnostic attacks on the OT's status as Scripture. Christian interpreters defended the scriptural status of law by showing typologically how it foreshadows Christ, while also maintaining that it was completed and superseded by the new covenant. However, controversy over the status and meaning of Mosaic law marks every period of Christian history, and continues in the present.

Summary. Jewish and Christian interpretations of Leviticus have always struggled with how to apply this book's legislation to changing times and circumstances. The two communities have for the most part adopted opposite approaches to OT law: traditional Jewish interpretation usually attends to every regulation by reinterpreting them to apply to different conditions, while traditional Christian interpretation promulgates the love commandment as the essence of and replacement for all the rest. The results of either approach may seem far removed from the national and liturgical concerns that permeate the text of Leviticus. But God's people, with or without land or Tabernacle, have much to learn from a book that confronts a wilderness generation (Lev 7:38) with the ideal of a divine-human community and promises God's continuing faithfulness to their descendants in exile (Lev 26:44-45).

For Further Study

In the *Mercer Dictionary of the Bible*: BLOOD IN THE OT; COVENANT; LAW IN THE OT; LEVITICUS, BOOK OF; PRIESTLY WRITERS; TABERNACLE; TENT OF MEETING; WORSHIP IN THE OT.

In other sources: D. Damrosch, "Leviticus," in *The Literary Guide to the Bible*, 66–77; J. E. Hartley, *Leviticus*, WBC; J. L. Kugel and R. A. Greer, *Early Biblical Interpretation*; T. W. Mann, *The Book of Torah*; J. Milgrom, *Leviticus 1–16*, AncB; N. H. Snaith, *Leviticus and Numbers*, NCB; G. J. Wenham, *The Book of Leviticus*, NICOT; L. Wieseltier, "Leviticus," in *Congregation*, 27–38.

Commentary

An Outline

I. Regulations for Sacrifices and Offerings, 1:1–7:28
   A. Introduction, 1:1-2
   B. Burnt Offerings, 1:3-17
   C. Grain Offerings, 2:1-16
   D. Offerings of Well-Being, 3:1-17
   E. Sin Offerings, 4:1–5:13
   F. Guilt Offerings, 5:14–6:7
   G. Priest's Instructions regarding Offerings, 6:8–7:36
   H. Summation, 7:37-38
II. Inauguration of Worship, 8:1–10:20
   A. Ordination of Priests, 8:1-36
   B. Inauguration of Worship, 9:1-24
   C. Priestly Practice and Malpractice, 10:1-20
III. Unclean and Clean, 11:1–15:33
   A. Edible and Inedible Animals, 11:1-47
   B. Purification after Childbirth, 12:1-8
   C. Growths on Skin, Clothing, and Houses, 13:1–14:57
   D. Genital Discharges, 15:1-33
IV. The Day of Atonement, 16:1-34
V. The Holiness Code, 17:1–27:34
   A. Rules for Sacrifice and Slaughter, 17:1-16
   B. Sexual Relationships, 18:1-30
   C. Rules for Holy Living, 19:1-37
   D. Penalties for Religious and Sexual Sins, 20:1-27
   E. Rules for Priests, 21:1–22:33
   F. Annual Calendar, 23:1-44
   G. Miscellaneous Regulations, 24:1-23
   H. Sabbath Years and Jubilee, 25:1-55
   I. Blessings and Curses, 26:1-46
   J. Appendix on Vows and Tithes, 27:1-34

Regulations for Sacrifices and Offerings, 1:1–7:38

Exodus 25–31 and 35–40 narrated the building of the TABERNACLE and its furnishings, but gave few instructions as to their use. Leviticus 1–7 supplies these instructions. The sacrifices and offerings described here are the essential elements in the Tabernacle (and Temple) services. They are presupposed in the following (Lev 8–10) story of the inauguration of the priests and the Tabernacle services.

Leviticus 1:1–6:7 describes five offerings by means of divine instructions given through Moses to the people as a whole, according to headings at 1:1-2 and 4:1-2. These offerings are described again in 6:8–7:21, instructions whose intended recipients are *Aaron and his sons* (i.e., the priests) according to 6:8-9 and 24–25. Differences in style and details of the contents, together with the change of recipients, suggest that the two sets of instructions were originally distinct. Leviticus 6:8–7:21, however, presupposes the elements of the preceding instructions, and Lev 7 ends with prohibitions aimed at the whole people (7:22-36). These observations indicate that the priestly instructions have been edited for their present context and are now intended for a larger audience (Hartley 1992, 94–95).

The style of Lev 1–7 illustrates all the distinctive features of P literature. The use of specialized vocabulary shows P's concern for accuracy and detail. Formulaic repetition calls attention to analogous cases, especially in Lev 1–3, but small variations prevent total redundancy in either style or contents. The results convey a sense of order and completeness in the Tabernacle service, a sense strongly reminiscent of the story of creation in Gen 1:1–2:4a—another example of P's unique literary style and theological perspective.

Introduction, 1:1-2

The phrase *the LORD summoned* marks the start of something new. In Exodus, God invariably summons or calls MOSES from Mount Sinai (Exod 3:1-4; 19:3, 20; 24:16) to hear a major new revelation. The phrase indicates the same intention here, except that now God speaks *from the tent of meeting* (אהל מועד; this is the usual term in Leviticus, although in Exodus and Numbers it is frequently called a dwelling or tabernacle, משכן). This tent, whose construction and furnishings are described in Exod 25–31, 35–40, is a mobile sanctuary of worship that can move with Israel on the journey to Canaan (see TABERNACLE; TENT OF MEETING). With only a few exceptions, it replaces Mount Sinai from this point on in the Pentateuch as the place from which God reveals the Law.

The summary command in 1:2 specifies that *offerings* (a broad term covering all gifts made to God, whether animals, grains, or precious metals) of livestock should consist of domestic animals only. This command introduces the subject that dominates chaps. 1–7, although the list of offerings also includes birds (1:14-17; 5:7-10) and grain (2:1-6; 5:11-13).

Burnt Offerings, 1:3-17

The instructions for the burnt offerings appear in three sections (vv. 3-9, 10-13, 14-17), one for each category of sacrificial animal (herd animals, flock animals, birds). Each section begins with the conditional *if*, describes the steps of the ritual in similar terms (although abbreviated in the second and third accounts), and concludes with *a burnt offering, an offering by fire of pleasing odor to the LORD*. The formulaic repetition gives the chapter a rhythmic cadence, which may reflect its origins in the priests' oral teaching of the people.

The Hebrew word עלה which is translated *burnt offering* means literally something which "goes up, ascends," presumably referring to the fire and smoke of the sacrifice. Another traditional translation is "whole offering" (REB), which points to the essential difference between this and other sacrifices: the whole animal is burnt in this offering; nothing is left to be eaten by either priests or worshipers.

The purpose of the burnt offering is not described in this chapter. Its results are merely alluded to: *acceptance* of (v. 3) and *atonement* for (v. 4) the worshiper before God. Since other offerings are described later to deal with particular sin (Lev 4:1–5:13) and restitution (5:14–6:7), the burnt offering's purpose seems to be less specific. This is confirmed by the fact that in other texts, burnt offerings are described as occurring on a variety of occasions: regular observances (Num 28–29); royal sacrifices (2 Sam 6:17-18; 1 Kgs 9:25); as accompanying prayers of petition (Ps 20:3) and thanksgiving (Ps 51:19); and celebrations of all sorts (1 Sam 6:14; Lev 12:6-8). Burnt offerings, then, seem to have been the ordinary means for smoothing the relationship between humans and God.

The burnt offering, whether cattle, sheep or goat, must be *a male without blemish* (vv. 3, 10). Both specifications emphasize this animal is to be of high value, although the option of substituting a moderately valued sheep or goat or even an inexpensive bird for the high-priced bull enables every Israelite to participate in sacrificial worship (Lev 5:7, 11). The worshipers lay hands on the animal to establish ownership of it and claim the benefits of the sacrifice for themselves (see Milgrom 1991, 150-53, and Hartley 1992, 18–20).

The worshipers are responsible for slaughtering the bulls, sheep, and goats, and helping the priest prepare them for the altar. As in all Israelite sacrifice or slaughter, the *blood* requires special treatment (cf. Gen 9:4-6; Lev 3:17; 7:22-27; 17:11). It must be drained from the carcass and offered to God, no matter what use the rest of the animal is put to.

The burning sacrifice is described as *an offering by fire of pleasing odor to the* LORD (vv. 9, 13, 17 and throughout Leviticus and P sections of Exodus and Numbers). God's pleasure at smelling the sacrifice and the resulting divine mercy towards humans is depicted in Gen 8:21. P, however, usually avoids strong anthropomorphic imagery for God, which suggests that *pleasing odor* is here simply a technical term for God's acceptance of the offering.

Grain Offerings, 2:1-16

The Hebrew word מנחה translated *grain offering* has a wide range of uses in the OT. It can refer to gifts from one person to another (Gen 32:13) or tribute paid to a king or ruler (1 Kgs 4:21). When used of offerings to God, it sometimes includes animal sacrifices as well as grain (Gen 4:3-5). Within ritual instructions, however, the word refers to offerings of grain that usually accompanied the burnt offerings of animals. The underlying notion of gift or tribute suggests that grain offerings may represent the worshipers' recognition of God's ownership of the land, an idea reinforced by the connection to first fruits in vv. 14-16.

2:1-10. Procedures. As with the burnt offerings, grain offerings should be of good quality. Hence the emphasis on *choice flour*, *oil*, and *frankincense* (a kind of INCENSE). The priest burns a *token portion* (אזכרה, often translated *memorial*) on the altar. The remainder goes to support the priests. Grain offerings can be presented in a variety of forms, so long as the quality of the ingredients remains high (vv.4-8).

2:11-13. Leaven, honey, and salt. The reasons for prohibiting *leaven* (yeast) and *honey* (probably fruit nectar as well as honey) in grain offerings are not explained here or in other prohibitions of leaven in sacrifices (Exod 23:18; 34:25). They may be offered to God as a "first fruits" offering (v. 12, RSV for ראשית; NRSV, NJV *choice products*), but cannot be burnt on the altar. On the other hand, *the salt of the covenant* is to be included with every grain offering. Salt is a symbol of a covenant's permanence (Num 18:19; 2 Chr 13:5), so its presence in the offering reminds worshipers of the perpetual covenant between Israel and God.

2:14-16. First fruits. Israelites were expected to give to God an offering from the first harvest of the year as thanks for giving them the land (Deut 26:1-11). These *first fruits* (בכורים; ראשית in v. 12) are offered like the other grain offerings. Lev 23:9-20 associates this offering with the festivals of Unleavened Bread and Weeks.

Offerings of Well-Being, 3:1-17

Sacrifice of well-being is the NRSV and NJV rendering of זבח שלמים, elsewhere translated "sacrifice of peace offering" (KJV, RSV), "shared offering" (REB), and "fellowship offering" (NIV). The root of the crucial term is related to שלום *shalom* "peace, prosperity, well-being." The translations all point out the key feature of this offering: the sacrificial animal is divided between God, the priests (Lev 7:31-36), and the worshipers, and the worshipers eat the meat in a sacred meal (7:11-18). The offering of well-being is essentially a meal celebrating the relationship between God and Israel. Its performance marked many of the high points of Israel's history (Exod 24:5, 11; 2 Sam 6:17-19; 1 Kgs 8:64-65).

Like the regulations governing the burnt offering in Lev 1, Lev 3 divides into three sections (vv. 1-5, 6-11, 12-16) on the basis of the type of animal sacrificed (cattle, sheep, and goats respectively), and each part repeats the same instructions with only minor variations. The ritual follows many of the same procedures as that for burnt offerings, except that male or female animals may be used and only part of the animal (the fat and some internal organs) is burnt on the altar.

The ritual instruction to burn the fat on the altar is expanded in the chapter's conclusion (vv. 16b-17) into a prohibition against eating any fat. It is not clear why fat is added here and in 7:23-27 to the more usual dietary prohibition against blood (v. 17; cf. Gen 9:4; Lev 17:10-16; 19:26; Deut 12:16, 23; 15:23). *Fat* is used metaphorically in Gen 45:18 and Ps 81:16 for the best of something, so perhaps the reasoning is like that behind the first fruits offering: the best of the land's produce, whether vegetable or animal, belongs to God.

Sin Offerings, 4:1–5:13

Sin offering (חטאת) is sometimes translated as "purification offering" (REB), which more accurately describes its nature. Burnt offerings and guilt offerings also atone for sin (Lev 1:4; 5:16); the unique benefit of sin offerings is that they purify the sanctuary from the polluting effects of unintentional sins (4:2; 5:1-4; Milgrom 1991, 254-61). These instructions presuppose and cite previous descriptions of offerings (4:10, 26, 31; 5:10, 13).

4:3-35. Kinds of sin offerings. Lev 4 legislates the procedures to be followed for different categories of sinners: the high priest (vv. 3-12), the community as a whole (vv. 13-21), a ruler (vv. 22-26), or an ordinary person. This last category is subdivided into offerings of goats (vv. 27-31) and sheep (vv. 32-35). The first section is the longest and most explicit; subsequent sections presuppose the first (v. 21) and omit some steps. Except for the first, each section concludes with the formula *the priest shall make atonement for them/him/you and they/he/you shall be forgiven.*

The anointed priest (הכהן המשיח, found in OT only in Lev 4 and 6) is a rare term for the high priest, who was anointed during his ordination (see below on 8:12).

מָשִׁיחַ "anointed one," transliterated as "Messiah," is normally used in the OT for the king. A *ruler* (נָשִׂיא, v. 22) is a tribal leader (Num 2:3, 5, etc.).

Sins of the high priest or whole community defile the sanctuary more than do sins by other individuals, and so require a more valuable sacrificial animal, a bull, and more thorough purification procedures. The blood is sprinkled in front of *the curtain of the sanctuary*, which separated the innermost part of the Tabernacle (the Holy of Holies), and on the *altar of fragrant incense* that stood in front of it (vv. 6-7, 17-18), rather than just on the altar of burnt offering at the Tabernacle entrance (vv. 25, 30, 34).

5:1-6. Examples of unintentional sins. Unintentional sins include acts done ignorantly, unconsciously, by accident, or even omissions due to a lack of nerve. Leviticus 5:1-4 provides examples: failure of a witness to testify in court; contact with unclean animals or humans (cf. Lev 11–15); rash oaths (Lev 19:12). Once realized, the problem is corrected by confession and a sin offering (vv. 5-6).

5:7-13. Alternative offerings for the poor. Poverty should prevent no one from making offerings, so alternative sin offerings of two birds or *one-tenth of an ephah of choice flour* (v. 11; approximately six and one-half pints) are permissible.

Guilt Offerings, 5:14–6:7

Guilt offering (אָשָׁם) is sometimes translated "reparation offering" (JB, REB). This offering is prompted by an act of *treachery* (מַעַל, 5:15; 6:1; NRSV's "trespass" is too weak) and accompanied by compensation for the loss plus one fifth (5:16; 6:5). Three examples of treachery form the contents of this section: misuse of God's *holy things*, i.e., anything dedicated to the sanctuary or the use of the priests (5:14-16); any violations of law (5:17-19); and acts of deceit, fraud, and robbery (6:1-7). This mixture of specific and general examples, together with the passage's failure to describe the guilt offering ritual (cf. 7:1-7) as earlier chapters have done, may indicate that it was originally separate from what precedes it. As the text now stands, however, the formulas of atonement and forgiveness (4:20, 26, 31, 35; 5:6, 10, 13, 16, 18; 6:7) unite the descriptions of the sin and guilt offerings.

Like sin offerings, guilt offerings atone for *unintentional* sins (5:15, 17). Yet the last set of offenses (6:1-3) includes flagrant acts. The OT's sacrificial system otherwise makes no provision for intentional sins. Milgrom argues, however, that heartfelt repentance and confession could reduce the severity of transgressions from flagrant to unintentional, "thereby qualifying them for sacrificial expiation" (1976, 119). Thus confession and restitution (6:4-5) are preconditions for atonement and forgiveness (6:6-7), even of willful sins.

Priest's Instructions regarding Offerings, 6:8–7:36

God now instructs Moses to address the priests, *Aaron and his sons* (6:9, 25), rather than the whole people as in 1:2, 4:2, 7:22 and 28. The instructions cover the same five offerings discussed in 1:1–6:7, but in a different order and with particular attention to the rights and responsibilities of the priests. The phrase, *this is the ritual of* (the word translated "ritual," תּוֹרָה *torah*, means "instruction, law, teaching"; see LAW IN THE OT), introduces each offering.

These differences in audience, issues, and phraseology suggest that 6:8–7:21 were originally separate from 1:1–6:7 and may have originated in the Temple as instructions for priests. In their present context, however, they supplement the earlier chapters and have been adapted to instruct the whole people, as indicated by the second person pronouns in 7:12ff., the digression on dietary prohibitions in 7:22-27, and the summation in 7:38.

6:8-30. Burnt, grain and sin offerings. Presupposing the descriptions of these offerings in chaps. 1, 2, 4–5, these instructions focus on the responsibilities (maintaining perpetual fire on the altar) and rights (to portions of the sacrifice) of the priests. Verses 19-23 describe a previously unmentioned grain offering offered daily by the high priest. Unlike ordinary grain offerings, those of priests are burned completely (v. 23); none can be eaten by priests who would otherwise be consuming what they themselves had given to God.

7:1-10. Guilt offerings. The guilt offering is described more fully than the previous three offerings, apparently to provide details omitted in 5:14–6:7.

7:11-21. Offerings of well-being. Verses 11-21 shift the address and focus from the priests to the worshipers. Most of this offering is eaten by the worshipers, so the primary concern here is with rules for its proper consumption. There are three categories of offerings of well-being: *thanksgiving* for a specific divine act, *votive* in fulfillment of a vow, and *freewill* for general celebration.

Since lay persons as well as priests will be handling the meat, they must be as careful as priests to protect it from defilement. Failure to do so can result in the severest divine penalty known to P, being *cut off from one's kin* (vv. 20, 21), which probably means loss of offspring and perhaps loss of afterlife (Milgrom 1991, 457-60).

7:22-27. Prohibition on eating fat and blood. God now addresses all Israel explicitly. On *fat*, see comments on 3:17. Verses 22-27 limit the prohibition on eating fat to those species of animals suitable for sacrifice, *ox or sheep or goat* (v. 23), and to carrion (v. 24), implying that the fat of game animals may be eaten. The prohibition on eating blood, however, remains absolute.

7:28-36. Priest's portions of offerings of well-being. The discussion of offerings of well-being continues after the interruption of 7:22-27 by specifying that the fat belongs to God, and the breast and right thigh belong to the priests. Raising portions of the sacrifice as an *elevation offering* (vv. 30, 34) dedicates them to God (Milgrom 1991, 461-81). The rest is returned for the worshipers to eat.

Summation, 7:37-38

The sacrificial regulations conclude by listing the six priestly *rituals* or instructions of 6:8–7:36, which God gave Moses on *Mount Sinai*. At the same time, the directions on how the *people* should *bring their offerings*, found in 1:2–6:7, were given *in the wilderness of Sinai*, i.e., from the Tabernacle (1:1). Despite the Tabernacle's existence and use for divine-human communication (cf. Exod 33:7-11), the site of revelation in Leviticus sometimes reverts to the mountain (Lev 25:1; 26:46; 27:34).

Inauguration of Worship, 8:1–10:20

After seven chapters of sacrificial regulations, the narrative now resumes where it left off at the end of Exodus. Moses, having built the Tabernacle (Exod 35-40), offers the first sacrifices in it and ordains *Aaron and his sons* as priests (Lev 8). They then take over responsibility for the Tabernacle (Lev 9), and all the plans detailed in Exod 25 to Lev 7 are finally realized: the sanctuary and its rituals enable God and Israel to live together (Exod 29:42-45). Divine fire displays the fulfillment of this promise (Lev 9:24).

Leviticus 10, however, immediately dampens the excitement of chaps. 8–9 by narrating stories of priestly disobedience and disagreement. God's presence in the sanctuary turns dangerous when taken too lightly. The center of the chapter summarizes the priests' responsibilities in terms of sobriety, discernment, and education of the people (10:8-11).

Ordination of Priests, 8:1-36

Moses acts in this chapter in accordance with *what the LORD has commanded to be done* (v. 5) in Exod 29 regarding ordination of priests. The refrain, *as the Lord commanded Moses*, echoes throughout the passage. God's instructions could not be carried out until after the Tabernacle was built (Exod 35-40) and the sacrificial regulations were given (Lev 1–7), since the priests require both to perform their duties.

The priests' vestments (vv. 7-9) symbolize their office and are to be worn when serving in the Tabernacle. Exodus 28 and 39 describe their construction in detail (see DRESS; EPHOD; URIM AND THUMMIN).

Moses consecrates both the Tabernacle and Aaron, the high priest, by anointing them with holy oil (for its composition, see Exod 30:22-33). Although oil is later sprinkled on the other priests (Lev 8:30; cf. Exod 40:15), only the high priest is anointed, as his other title, *the anointed priest* (Lev 4:3), shows. The OT uses this title, "anointed one" (משיח, often transliterated "Messiah"), more commonly for Israel's kings, who were anointed upon their accession. The act of anointing separates the recipients from common life and makes them sacred, although its implications are different for kings and for high priests (see Milgrom 1991, 553-55; ANOINT; MESSIAH/MESSIANISM).

Moses performs the sacrifices in close accord with the instructions in Exod 29, although there are some differences in order and detail. A sin offering of a bull (vv. 14-17) is followed by the sacrifice of two rams, one for a burnt offering (vv. 18-21) and the other, called the *ram of ordination* (v. 22), for an offering of well-being (vv. 22-29, 31-32). Blood is daubed on the altar and on the priests to purify them of contamination (vv. 15, 23-24), and is sprinkled together with oil on the priests and their vestments to consecrate them (i.e., make them holy; v. 30). The ordination ceremony lasts seven days, with at least some of the sacrifices repeated daily (Exod 29:35-41).

Inauguration of Worship, 9:1-24

In chap. 8, Moses acted as priest for Aaron and his sons. *On the eighth day* (v. 1), Aaron takes over and the people bring him their offerings, responding to the promise that on this first day of regular worship, *the LORD will appear to you* (vv. 4, 6).

Aaron offers the full range of required sacrifices, first for himself (vv. 8-14), then for the people (vv. 15-21). The account is abbreviated, but frequent references to Lev 1–7 (*as the LORD commanded* [v. 10]; *according to regulation* [v. 16]; *as Moses commanded* [v. 21]) make it clear that Aaron carries out faithfully every detail of the instructions.

The service ends with a blessing, perhaps that recorded for the priests' use in Num 6:24-26. Blessing is not simply the conclusion but the goal of the entire service: it is God's response to the people's worship, a statement that the divine relationship with Israel has been restored (see CURSE AND BLESSING).

This first time, however, there is a surprise ending. As promised at the beginning of the chapter, *the glory of the LORD appeared* (v. 23), probably in the form of a cloud and lightning (Exod 24:15-18; 40:34-38). Then comes the unexpected finale to this meticulously planned service: divine lightning hits the altar, devouring the already burning sacrifices. Thus human liturgy sets the stage for divine spontaneity, and the people meet God in worship.

Priestly Practice and Malpractice, 10:1-20

The same divine fire, however, destroys those who presume upon "a familiarity with the divine" (Wieseltier 1987, 33). Aaron's sons, Nadab and Abihu, bring *unholy fire* ("alien" NJV; "unauthorized" NIV; "strange" KJV; i.e., coals from a profane source instead of the altar; cf. 16:12) into the sanctuary, perhaps into the Holy of Holies *before the LORD*. A divine saying interprets their deaths as showing God's holiness and glory (v. 3), a idea found in other accounts of divine punishment (Num 20:13; Ezek 28:22; 38:16). God's separate (holy) and pure nature is revealed by intolerance for pollution of any sort.

Leviticus 10 is written artfully to balance the sudden tragedy in vv. 1-3 with another account of priestly malpractice in vv. 16-20. The latter story, however, has a very different conclusion: Aaron, who *was silent* in v. 3 and prevented from mourning in vv. 6-7, now defends the practice of his younger sons and convinces Moses that his interpretation is correct. (The problem is that the priests are supposed to eat the people's sin offering according to 6:24-30, but apparently Aaron argued that Nadab and Abihu's sin or deaths had transformed it into a burnt sin offering, like those in 8:14-17 and 9:8-11. See Milgrom 1991, 635–40.)

Furthermore, the center of the chapter contains (vv. 8-11, in a divine speech to Aaron, not Moses!) a summary of the priests' responsibilities that emphasizes sobriety in the performance of their liturgical duties, discernment in distinguishing between *the holy and the common* (specified in Lev 1–7) and between *the unclean and the clean* (specified in Lev 11–15), and the people's education in the Mosaic law. Thus the chapter as a whole emphasizes that priests should know, obey, and teach the law, and that failure to do so can result in drastic penalties; at the same time, it endorses the use of reason in the law's interpretation.

The two stories of priestly malpractice anchor instructions for disposing of corpses (which are unclean—Lev 22:4; Num 19:14-16) in the sanctuary and for the distribution of the priests' portions of the sacrifices. A five-part CHIASM therefore structures the chapter, with the narratives at the beginning and the end bracketing the two sets of instructions, which in turn surround the summary of priestly responsibilities at the center (Hartley 1992, 128-29).

Unclean and Clean, 11:1–15:33

On the categories "clean" and "unclean," see the introduction above and CLEAN/UNCLEAN in MDB.

Edible and Inedible Animals, 11:1-47

Leviticus 11 divides the animal world into five categories: land animals (vv. 2-8), water animals (9-12), birds (13-19), flying insects (20-23), and land swarmers (41-43; cf. the three categories in Deut 14). Criteria of purity and examples are provided in two cases (vv. 2-8, 20-23), but for water animals the criteria (fins and scales) appear without examples while the reverse is true of the list of unclean birds. Verses 24-40 digress into the transmission of impurity to those who touch dead animals. Along the way, the section adds another criterion for unclean land animals (v. 27) and provides examples of land swarmers (vv. 29-30) omitted from vv. 41-43.

The OT does not explain why certain animals should be considered clean and others unclean. The most credible explanation relies on anthropology to argue that the CLEAN/UNCLEAN distinction is Israel's symbolic means of structuring the world. Clean animals stay in their own sphere (land, water, air) and move in a way appropriate to that sphere (walking, swimming, flying). Unclean animals cross between the spheres and use inappropriate locomotion (Douglas [1966] 1985). Many of the unclean animals are carnivores who break the vegetarian order intended at creation (Gen 1:30; cf. 9:2-6; Carroll [1978] 1985). Israel, then, affirms God's original plan by eating only those animals whose behavior is appropriate and limited to their own sphere.

11:2-8, 26-27. Land animals. This category covers most quadrupeds, except for the reptiles and small mammals that are classified as land swarmers (vv. 29-30). Four species fail to meet the criteria of being cleft-hoofed and chewing the cud (vv. 4-7). Verse 27 adds a third criterion, walking on paws, which makes carnivores such as cats, dogs, and bears unclean and inedible for Israel.

11:9-12. Water animals. The criteria of fins and scales declares unclean all water animals except fish. The adjective *detestable* (v. 11) emphasizes the repugnance with which Israel regarded shellfish and amphibians (cf. vv. 23, 42).

11:13-19. Birds. Unclean animals of the air are named without any criterion of selection, and some cannot be identified with certainty. All those which are known seem to be carnivores or scavengers.

11:20-23. Winged insects. Insects that fly and walk mix the spheres of land and air and are unclean. It is not clear why they are described as *walking on all fours* (insects have six, eight, or more legs) nor why four kinds of grasshoppers or locusts are clean and edible (e.g., Mark 1:6).

11:24-40. Transmission of uncleanness. All carcasses, whether of unclean (v. 24) or clean (v. 39) animals, transmit impurity when they touch people or human artifacts (vv. 31-38).

11:29-30, 41-43. Land swarmers. *Swarm* describes the movement of small multilimbed creatures on the land (v. 41) or in the water (v. 10), including rodents, reptiles (vv. 29-30), and nonflying insects. All swarmers are unclean.

11:44-47. Motivation and summary. Israel should avoid unclean foods to identify with God, just as God identified with them by saving them from Egypt. *You shall be holy, for I am holy* (v. 45) is the central principle of chaps. 17-26 and links these diet laws with the rules for holy living found there.

Purification after Childbirth, 12:1-8

Leviticus 12 and 15 both treat impurity due to genital discharges and crossreferences (vv. 2, 5) connect them. Since genital discharges of blood or semen convey impurity (Lev 15), the loss of blood in childbirth makes a mother unclean (Lev 12). The periods of impurity and blood purification last a total of forty days for a male child, and eighty for a female, but both require the same sacrifices (vv. 6-8). The *sin offering* purifies; it does not make restitution for particular sin, so there is no suggestion here that childbirth or sex are sinful acts. It is the loss of blood, which in the OT symbolizes life itself, that requires temporary separation and rites of purification. See further on chap. 15, below.

Growths on Skin, Clothing, and Houses, 13:1–14:57

Scaly growths on skin, clothing, and houses represented the onset of death to ancient Israelites (e.g., Num 12:12; Job 18:13). They therefore render the affected persons or objects unclean. As the parallel diagnoses and treatments for skin, clothing, and buildings show, the issue in these chapters is not contagious disease but rather ritual impurity. Scaly or peeling skin and fungal growths in cloth or house conjure up images of decomposing corpses. Such growths are therefore unclean like corpses, and contact with them conveys impurity (cf. Num 19:11-22).

13:1-46. Unclean skin growths. Seven kinds of skin growth are described together with procedures for their diagnosis (vv. 2-44). Medical identification of these skin diseases remains elusive (see LEPROSY), but one thing is clear: the traditional translation of צרעת as "leprosy" (i.e., Hansen's disease) is wrong. The priests do not perform medical treatment, but rather determine an individual's status as clean or unclean. The unclean person's appearance resembles that of a mourner, reinforcing the connection with death (vv. 45-46; cf. 10:6; Ezek 24:17, 22). Banishment of individuals or objects with persistent growths is necessary to keep the community ritually clean and protect the Tabernacle from impurity. Contagion from growths represents a more severe threat to the community in Leviticus than that from genital discharges (cf. Num 5:2-3, which ostracizes those with discharges as well as those with skin growths).

13:47-59. Growths in clothing. Mold or fungal growths on clothing are treated like skin growths. Clearly, the concern is with impurity, not disease.

14:1-32. Purification after healing. If the priest certifies that the skin has healed, the individual can be readmitted to the camp. Some of the ceremonial procedures for cleansing resemble those for consecrating priests (Lev 8–9), since both solemnize a significant change in status.

14:34-53. Growths in houses. Fungal growths in houses, such as mold, mildew, and dry rot, threaten Israel's purity as much as skin growths. Graduated measures for dealing with the problem range from a one-week quarantine to destruction of the building. The contents, however, may be removed and kept (v. 36).

Genital Discharges, 15:1-33

Semen and blood represent life in the OT. Their loss implies a loss of life. This symbolic affiliation with death characterizes all of the causes of impurity in Lev 12–15 (but not the unclean animals of chap. 11). Genital discharges therefore make a person unclean, while urinating and defecating do not (although feces must be properly disposed of, Deut 23:12-14). The issue is not sex and procreation, but their fluid byproducts. Leviticus 15 describes the impurity and purification procedures for discharges of semen, both abnormal (vv. 2-15) and normal (vv. 16-18), and of blood, normal (vv. 19-24) and abnormal (vv. 25-30).

15:2-15. Abnormal discharges of semen. Secretion of mucus (v. 3) is a symptom of gonorrhea, and renders a man unclean as long as the discharge continues. He transmits impurity to things under him, to utensils, and by touch to other people. If the secretions cease and do not recommence for a week, bathing and a small sacrifice will make him clean (vv. 13-15).

15:16-18. Normal discharges of semen. Emissions of semen, whether during sexual intercourse or not, cause impurity that requires bathing and lasts until nightfall. Normal discharges of semen or blood do not require sacrifices.

15:19-24. Normal discharges of blood. A menstruating woman is unclean *for seven days*. She transmits impurity to things under her and to those who touch her, and more severe impurity (and divine punishment according to 20:18) to a man who has intercourse with her. Unlike a gonorrheal man, however, her touch is apparently not considered contagious, probably so that she can continue to work during menstruation (cf. Num 5:2-3).

A fear of menstruating women is common in many societies around the world (for a survey, Milgrom 1991, 763-68, 948-53). Folk wisdom frequently portrays menstrual blood as having demonic power. Leviticus opposes such magical interpretations of reality, and so subordinates this fear to its system of unclean and clean, death and life. Menstrual blood, like semen, represents loss of life and is therefore unclean. Nevertheless, male anxiety about menstrual blood contributes to the lower status of WOMEN IN THE OT.

15:25-30. Abnormal discharges of blood. Women with continuous or irregular flows of blood remain unclean as long as the problem persists. Once the bleeding stops, the purification rites are the same as for gonorrheal men.

15:31-33. Motive and summary. In Leviticus, the Tabernacle is the underlying reason for distinguishing unclean from clean. God's holiness is intolerant of impurity. Since God resides with Israel, the unclean must be recognized and separated to avoid disaster.

The Day of Atonement, 16:1-34

The ritual fail-safe in Israel's system of sacrificial worship is the Day of Atonement, familiarly known by its Hebrew name *Yom Kippur*. The observances of this day atone for all impurities or sins that were overlooked by Israel throughout the year (see ATONEMENT, DAY OF; on atonement, see introduction above and ATONEMENT/EXPIATION IN THE OT).

The heading dates these instructions *after the death of the two sons of Aaron* (v. 1), i.e., after the events of chap. 10. Their appearance in chap. 16 illustrates the thematic arrangement of Leviticus: just as the inauguration of worship (chaps. 8–9) presupposed sacrificial instructions that therefore precede it (chaps. 1–7), so also these purification procedures presuppose the system of impurities detailed beforehand in chaps. 11–15.

The attention in Lev 16 is focused on the innermost part of the sanctuary and particularly on the MERCY SEAT, the golden cover on the ARK of the covenant. The Hebrew word כפרת *kapporet*, usually translated "mercy seat" or "cover," is from the same root as כפר *kippur* "cover, atonement," so the same idea identifies both the day and the place. This place is most holy, for God *appears in the cloud upon the mercy seat* (v. 2). As the locus of God's presence in Israel's midst, the ark's cover must be kept clean and holy. The rites of the Day of Atonement assure that it is.

Most of the sacrifices in Lev 16 follow the usual procedures detailed in chaps. 1–7, and serve to purify the sanctuary from the people's sins and impurity (v. 16). Confession (v. 21) permits sacrificial atonement even for flagrant offenses (see above on 6:1-7). However, only this occasion employs a goat *for Azazel* (vv. 7-10, 20-22). The word "Azazel" is obscure and has been translated as "scapegoat," as "a rocky place," or as the proper name of a demon. The goat's role is clear, however: it *shall bear on itself all their iniquities to a barren region* (v. 22). Thus the observances of the Day of Atonement not only purify the sanctuary; they also free Israel from sin's power.

The chapter's concluding verses turn from describing the high priest's actions to addressing the people, who are to fast and rest on the Day of Atonement (vv. 29-34). Verse 29 fixes this annual observance on the tenth day of the seventh month. If the ambiguous sentence, "and he did as Yahweh had commanded Moses" (v. 34, author trans.), means that Aaron performed these instructions immediately, there is a temporal problem. This date does not fall within the month between the erection of the Tabernacle (Exod 40:2, 17) and Israel's departure from Sinai (Num 10:11)—further indication that Lev 1-16 is arranged topically rather than in narrative sequence.

The Holiness Code, 17:1-27:34

For more than a century, many scholars have identified Lev 17-26 (27) as a separate law code, usually termed "the Holiness Code." These chapters distinguish themselves by their distinctive sermonic style containing frequent self-introductions (*I am the LORD your God*), exhortations to obedience (e.g., 18:4; 19:36) and holiness (e.g., 19:2), and a preponderance of categorical (as distinct from case) laws. Such features are not unique to Lev 17-26, but they do occur here with much greater frequency than elsewhere in the Pentateuch. Recent studies have tended to dispute the unity of the Holiness Code and its separation from P (for a review of research, see Hartley 1992, 251-60).

Whatever their history, these chapters contain the rhetorical climax of Leviticus. Here religious and ethical instructions unite to describe how Israel should become holy, and thus fit for communion with a holy God. Together with the purity rules in Lev 11-15, these holiness instructions set forth standards of behavior for the whole community (see Blum 1990, 321-23). Thus the book is unified by one overarching theme: the people as well as the priests must preserve the conditions for God's residence with Israel.

Like other OT law codes, the Holiness Code begins with sacrificial regulations (Lev 17; cf. Exod 20:22-26, Deut 12). The main body of the code is in three parts: the first consists of laws governing sexual relationships (Lev 18, 20) surrounding a miscellany of ethical and ritual rules (chap. 19); the second contains priestly instructions (chaps. 21-22); and the third consists of calendar instructions (chaps. 23, 25) surrounding another miscellaneous collection (chap. 24). The code climaxes in chap. 26 with a series of blessings and curses that spell out the consequences of Israel's obedience or disobedience (cf. Deut 27-28). The book concludes with an appendix on vows and tithes (chap. 27).

Rules for Sacrifice and Slaughter, 17:1-16

The theme of blood unites the sacrificial and dietary regulations in Lev 17. Blood represents life (vv. 11, 14) and belongs to God. Therefore blood may not be eaten but must be given back to God through sacrifice.

17:3-9. Location of slaughter and sacrifice. Concerns about idolatry (v. 7) motivate these restrictions on the location of slaughter (vv. 1-7) and sacrifice (vv. 8-9). Animals suitable for sacrifice (*an ox or a lamb or a goat* v. 3; cf. v. 13 on game animals and birds) must be offered as sacrifices at Yahweh's sanctuary. Verse 4 equates slaughter apart from a proper sacrifice with murder! (On the penalty of being *cut off*, see above on 7:20.)

These rules conflict with Lev 1–4 and 22:18-25, which prohibit blemished animals from the altar although they are apparently edible, and with Deut 12:15-27, which permits nonsacrificial slaughter for food. Some commentators therefore interpret vv. 3-7 as referring only to sacrifice, not to profane slaughter. But these verses do not make that distinction, identifying all slaughter outside the Tabernacle as idolatrous sacrifices. Ancient Israelites apparently held various views on slaughter, which these discrepancies reflect (see SACRIFICE).

17:10-16. No consumption of blood. Prohibitions on eating blood appear seven times in the Pentateuch, four of those in Leviticus. Only v. 11, however, connects the blood prohibition with blood sacrifice. Leviticus identifies blood with life, so offering blood means offering the animal's life for the sake of human life (see BLOOD IN THE OT; LIFE IN THE OT; Hartley 1992, 273–77). The law reserves blood exclusively for this atoning role. The blood of nonsacrificial edible animals must be poured out on the ground (v.13). Since animals dead of natural causes have not been properly drained of blood, eating them conveys temporary impurity (vv. 15-16).

Sexual Relationships, 18:1-30

Leviticus 18 lists prohibited sexual acts (vv. 6-23) surrounded by warnings against imitating the practices of Canaanites. The punishments for breaking these laws appear in chap. 20.

18:2-5, 24-30. Avoidance of Canaanite practices. Some ancient religions used ritual sex in attempts to ensure fertility for humans, livestock, and land. The OT, however, strips sexuality of any religious connotations, restricting it entirely to the secular realm. Leviticus 18 emphasizes this difference by explaining the Canaanites' expulsion from the land as punishment for their sexual practices, and threatening Israel with a similar fate if it imitates them (vv. 24-30).

18:6-18. Incest taboos. These examples of prohibited relations all derive from the general principle: *none of you shall approach anyone near of kin to uncover nakedness* (v. 6). The phrase *uncover nakedness* refers to sexual intercourse whether within marriage or apart from it. The speech addresses male heads of households, implicitly enjoining them not only to observe but also to enforce these laws.

18:19-23. Five offenses. Four of these prohibitions clearly concern sexual practices: intercourse with a menstruating woman, adultery, homosexual intercourse (see ADULTERY IN THE OT; HOMOSEXUALITY IN THE BIBLE), and bestiality. Menstrual blood conveys impurity (see above on 15:19-24). The other three kinds of intercourse blur the distinctions between families, between the sexes, and between humans and animals. Leviticus strives to maintain such symbolic categories (cf.

above on chap. 11) because their erosion threatens Israel's communion with God. On the prohibition of MOLECH sacrifice (v. 21), see below on 20:2-5.

Rules for Holy Living, 19:1-37

Leviticus 19 contains a collection of brief commandments and longer instructions that in style and themes resemble the contents of the TEN COMMANDMENTS (Exod 20:2-17; Deut 5:6-21). As in every other OT law code religious concerns permeate the chapter, from observance of SABBATH (vv. 3, 30) and prohibitions on IDOLATRY (v. 4) through SACRIFICE regulations (vv. 5-8, 21-22; see above on chaps. 3, 5) and prohibitions on mixing animals, grain, or cloth (it blurs symbolic categories, v. 19; cf. above on chap. 11) to injunctions against ritual acts associated with Canaanite religions (vv. 26-28, 31), particularly rituals for the dead. MOURNING RITES could include shaving hair and gashing skin (Lev 21:5; Jer 7:29; 16:6), actions that may also have played a role in divination with ancestor spirits. The OT prohibits all MAGIC AND DIVINATION, because Yahweh is God (v. 28); turning for advice or help to any other spirit is idolatry.

Concern for justice also permeates Lev 19, ranging from judicial issues such as theft, fraud, perjury, and impartiality in judgment (vv. 11-13, 15-16) through honest business practices (vv. 35-36) to issues of social justice, such as prompt payment of wages (v. 13) and respect for the disabled (v. 14) and the elderly (v. 32). Through these specific examples, the chapter illustrates the central claim of justice: one standard should apply to all.

Leviticus 19, however, balances the impartiality of justice with the partiality of love. General commandments to love both the neighbor and the stranger as oneself (vv. 18, 34) are made concrete by orders to revere one's parents (v. 3), to make provision for the poor (vv. 9-10), to correct but not hate or take vengeance on a neighbor (vv. 17-18), and to treat aliens like citizens (vv. 33-34). The protection of women suggested by the injunction against forcing a daughter into prostitution (v. 29) and by the guilt offering required from men who had sex with a betrothed slave (vv. 20-22) seems minimal by current standards of morality. But in the patriarchal culture that Israel shared with all its neighbors, any limits placed on men's arbitrary power over women are welcome. The power of biblical ethics derives from the hope that the general love commandment (vv. 18, 34) will continually find expression in better concrete instructions.

Penalties for Religious and Sexual Sins, 20:1-27

The penalties prescribed in this chapter for religious and sexual offenses are extremely severe. By modern standards, only child sacrifice might qualify as a capital offense. Leviticus, however, views religious and sexual misconduct as a threat not only to the social order but also to Israel's tenure in the land (v. 22). Thus severe penalties on individuals protect the community from divine punishment.

20:2-6. Molech sacrifice and divination. Interpreters disagree on the identity of MOLECH. *Molech* was probably not the name of a god, but rather a term for child sacrifice. Genesis 22:1-14 and Judg 11:29-40 show that sacrificing children to Yahweh was not unknown in Israel. In attacking this practice, however, Lev 18:21 and 20:2-5 turn Molech into a proper name and thus characterize the practice as idolatry. A play on the Hebrew word זרע, which means both "semen" (in the phrase translated *sexual relations* in 18:20) and *offspring* (vv. 2-4; 18:21), and the equation of idolatry with *prostituting themselves* (vv. 5, 6) probably accounts for the appearance of this prohibition in the context of sexual taboos. On *mediums and wizards* (20:6, 27), see above on 19:31.

20:9-21. Sexual offenses. The appearance of a penalty for cursing parents (v. 9) at the beginning of a list of sexual offenses indicates that the writers saw both as threatening a family's integrity. The community punishes capital offenses (vv. 9-16). Other penalties (*subject to punishment, cut off, die childless* in vv. 17-21) can be exacted only by God. From ancient Israel's perspective, the latter are probably no more lenient than the former.

20:7-8, 22-26. Motivation. Because Yahweh is Israel's God, the people must be holy. God sanctifies the people, but Israel must protect that holy status from defilement (vv. 7-8). Otherwise, history will repeat itself and the land will *vomit you out* (v. 22), as it did the Canaanites. Verses 24-26 contain the motivation for the entire priestly system: because God separated Israel from the nations, Israel must separate itself to be holy to God. All the laws of Lev 11-27 are dedicated to this end.

Rules for Priests, 21:1–22:33

Chapters 21–22 instruct the priests (21:1, 17; 22:2) regarding personal conduct and their acceptance of sacrificial animals. But the people also hear the instructions (21:8, 24; 22:18) so that they understand the priests' limitations and privileges. People and priests share the responsibility to sanctify God *among the people of Israel*, for God has sanctified them (22:32).

21:1-15. Protecting priests from impurity. Since priests come into regular contact with a holy sanctuary and holy sacrifices, they must observe special restrictions. The *anointed* high priest (v. 10), who enters the holiest areas of the Tabernacle (Lev 16), has even more restrictions placed on his activities.

Contact with corpses makes one unclean (Num 19:11). Therefore priests must avoid funerals except for close family members. (On the mourning customs prohibited in v. 5, see above on Lev 19.) Injunctions against priests marrying prostitutes (vv. 7, 14) and having daughters who are prostitutes attack the practice of sacred prostitution (see WOMEN IN THE OT; and above on 18:2-5) by arguing that, far from sanctifying the participants, such practices defile them (v. 9). The other restrictions on who priests, and especially the high priest, can marry probably involve concerns over succession to the priesthood: since the office is hereditary, care is necessary to ensure a legitimate heir.

21:16-23. Priests with physical anomalies. Physical impairments or anomalies disqualify priests from service in the sanctuary, just as "blemished" animals cannot be offered as sacrifices (22:18-25). In priestly thinking, wholeness is commensurate with holiness. Disqualification on physical grounds, however, does not make the priest unclean and therefore does not impair his livelihood (v. 22; cf. 22:4-6).

22:2-16. The priests' income. The priests' livelihood derived in part from their portion of the sacrifices (2:3, 10; 7:28-36), so it is natural that the priests' families and slaves eat them (vv. 11-13). Since the portions are holy, however, unclean persons must not touch them. Lay people (outside the priests' households) cannot infringe on the priests' rights (vv. 10, 14-16).

22:17-25. Animals with physical anomalies. Like priests (21:16-23), sacrificial animals must be *without blemish*. On the possible implications of this rule for eating blemished animals, see above on 17:3-9.

22:26-30. Three rules for sacrifices. Laws restricting slaughter involving a mother animal (or her milk) and her young (v. 28) are widespread in the Pentateuch (Exod 23:19; 34:26; Deut 14:21; 22:6) and are probably attacks on Canaanite religious practices. On eating sacrifices of well-being, see 7:15-18 and 19:5-8.

Annual Calendar, 23:1-44

Calendars of annual festivals appear five times in the Pentateuch: Exod 23:12-17; 34:18-24; Lev 23; Num 28–29; Deut 16:1-17. Exodus and Deuteronomy command Israel to observe three festivals: Unleavened Bread, Weeks, and Booths. The P writers of Leviticus and Numbers mention five, adding New Year's Day and the Day of Atonement to the other three (see FEASTS AND FESTIVALS).

23:3. Sabbath. Most of the festival calendars include commands to observe the weekly SABBATH. *Sabbath* (שבת) comes from a verb meaning "cease, rest" which aptly sums up the essence of the observance: *complete rest* (v. 3).

23:5-14. Passover. Detailed instructions for observing PASSOVER (Heb. *Pesah*) and UNLEAVENED BREAD are contained in the Exodus story itself (Exod 12–13). Leviticus 23 focuses only on the festival's date and duration. Immediately following the feast of Unleavened Bread comes the offering of *the sheaf of the first fruits of your harvest* (v. 10). The land belongs to God, not Israel. Therefore the people cannot eat of the land's harvest until they have first offered a portion to God (v. 14).

23:15-22. Weeks. Seven weeks or fifty days later comes the festival of WEEKS (Heb. *Shavuot*; Gk. *Pentecost*, "fiftieth"), which concluded the harvest season. After the detailed instructions on offerings (vv. 17-21), v. 22 repeats almost verbatim from 19:9-10 the command to leave grain in the fields for the poor and aliens, so the produce of God's land is shared among all the people.

23:23-25. New Year's Day. The special sabbath at the beginning of the seventh month goes unnamed in vv. 23-25. From at least postexilic times, it was celebrated as New Year's Day (Heb. *Rosh Hashanah*; NEW YEAR'S FESTIVAL), despite the placing of Passover in the "beginning of months" (Exod 12:2). Ancient Israel likely had several calendars at different times, and the Talmud acknowledges four different New Year's Days in the Jewish CALENDAR (Strassfeld 1985, 96).

23:26-32. Day of Atonement. Leviticus 16 instructs the high priest how to observe the Day of Atonement (Heb. *Yom Kippur*). Here the people are told of the day's status as a *sabbath of complete rest*, threatening severe penalties for transgressors (vv. 29-30).

23:33-36, 39-43. Booths. The festival of booths or tabernacles (Heb. *Sukkot*) commemorates the wilderness wanderings of Israel's ancestors (v. 43; TABERNACLES, FESTIVAL OF). The original calendar notice about Booths (vv. 33-36) has apparently been supplemented by an appendix to the chapter (vv. 39-43) that provides more details on how the festival should be celebrated.

Miscellaneous Regulations, 24:1-23

24:2-9. Lamps and bread. The sanctuary requires regular supplies of oil and flour for the lamps and bread *before the Lord*. The instructions regarding lamp oil repeat the contents of Exod 27:20-21, but the description of the bread is more detailed than in Exodus (25:23-30; 40:23-32). Continual light represents the presence of God. The twelve loaves eaten by priests symbolize the communion of Israel's twelve tribes with their God.

24:10-23. A case of blasphemy. Aside from regular speech headings (i.e., *the LORD spoke to Moses*), this story is the only narrative in chaps. 17-27. The account is unconnected with the larger story of Israel in the books of Exodus through Numbers. It appears here because of its legal implications, and illustrates how case law arises out of concrete situations in Israel's life.

The offense occurs when a half-Israelite *blasphemed the Name in a curse* (v. 11). *The Name* refers to the divine name Yahweh (= LORD; see TETRAGRAMMATON and GOD, NAMES OF), whose use is restricted by the third commandment (Exod 20:7; cf. 22:28). The writers use this circumlocution to avoid any risk of reproducing the blasphemy themselves. Their restrained description of the incident obscures the exact nature of the crime.

Due to his parentage, the offender's legal status is uncertain and requires a *decision of the LORD* (v. 12). The ensuing divine speech upholds one standard of punishment for all (vv. 15-16, 22), so the community administers the death penalty (v. 23; on capital punishment, see above on Lev 20). The speech also advances the law of RETALIATION (*lex talionis* vv. 17-21; cf. Exod 21:22-25; Deut 19:19) which, although irrelevant to blasphemy, emphasizes the universality of law. Punishment should be proportionate to the offense, not to the status of the offender.

Sabbath Years and Jubilee, 25:1-55

Leviticus 25 promulgates a multiyear calendar of sabbath years and weeks of years. The land and its crops should rest in the seventh "sabbath" year just as humans and animals rest on the seventh day (v. 4; cf. Exod 23:10-11). God promises a bumper crop in the sixth year large enough to last until the harvests of the ninth year (vv. 20-22). Verse 18 provides the motivation to obey the fallow law: *that you may live on the land securely*. The following chapter makes clear that either Israel will allow the land to rest or else Israel will be driven off the land, which will then rest undisturbed (26:34-35).

The fiftieth year (after *seven weeks of years* [v. 8], i.e., forty-nine) is a year of release for debts, slaves, and land. The three topics are related, for in the ancient Near East, indebtedness was usually the reason for selling both one's land and oneself. (On the name *Jubilee*, see JUBILEE, YEAR OF.) The laws described in Lev 25 would have a revolutionary impact on Israel's economy: ownership of land and slaves can be transferred only temporarily and then is subject to redemption by relatives (vv. 25-33, 48-52; Ruth 4:4-6; Jer 32:6-8), prices must be set with reference to the coming Jubilee (vv. 14-17; 27:16-25), and capital cannot be accumulated because lending at interest is prohibited (vv. 35-37; Exod 22:25-27). The chapter's overriding concern is for the poor and their treatment: *you shall support them* (v. 35). This legislation prevents poverty from having permanent effects and preserves the ideal of all Israelites as God's tenants on the land (vv. 23, 38, 55).

There is, however, little evidence that Jubilee was ever more than an ideal in Israel. There is no mention of its observance in the OT, and even sabbath years seem to have been ignored in the preexilic period (2 Chr 36:21). Furthermore, Deut 15:1-18 contradicts Jubilee legislation by providing for release for debts and slaves every *seventh* year, but also for voluntary permanent slavery. Thus concern to protect the equality of Israelites before God and each other seems to have given rise to several legislative programs, but reality rarely lived up to them. The ideals of Jubilee nevertheless inspired prophetic hopes for "the year of the LORD's favor" (Isa 61:1-3).

Blessings and Curses, 26:1-46

The conclusions of ancient Near Eastern law codes and treaties usually contain lists of blessings and curses (see COVENANT; CURSE AND BLESSING), which make the consequences of obedience and disobedience clear. Such lists conclude OT law codes for the same reason (Exod 23:23-33; Lev 26; Deut 28).

26:1-2. Idolatry, sabbath, and sanctuary. This summary of the most prominent religious commands reminds readers what kind of *statutes and commandments* (v. 3) the blessings and curses presuppose. These three stipulations symbolize the whole priestly law.

26:3-13. Blessings. Prosperity (vv. 4-5, 10), security (vv. 6-8), and growth (v. 9) await those who keep the covenant stipulations. Most of all, God will live with Israel (vv. 11-12). The statement, *I will walk among you*, describes a divine-human relationship closer than any since primordial times, when God walked in the garden (Gen 3:8) and Enoch and Noah "walked with God" (Gen 5:22-24; 6:9; Blum 1990, 326). All the regulations of Leviticus aim towards this goal: recreation of the communion intended by God from the beginning.

26:14-39. Curses. Disobedience, however, will result in God's enmity. Drought, war, and plague will ravage the land and ultimately the people will be conquered and scattered "among the nations" (v. 33). There they will still be harassed by enemies (vv. 36-39). A reversal of the previous description of close communion emphasizes God's enmity: rather than *walk among you* (v. 12), God will now "walk contrary to you" (vv. 24, 28, 41, author trans.; NRSV *continue hostile*).

26:40-45. Reconciliation in exile. The exiles' confession and repentance (v. 40) will cause God to *remember in their favor the covenant* (v. 45). Remarkably, Lev 26 does not predict a return to the land. It rather emphasizes that, despite the loss of the land, Israel's covenant with God remains in force (v. 44). The result, for readers of the Pentateuch in the postexilic community, is that Leviticus identifies them with the wilderness generation with whom God made the covenant. It reminds them that the divine-human community described in this book was first experienced *outside* the land in the wilderness, and that God will preserve that covenant community regardless of location. Thus Leviticus incorporates the people's historical successes and failures, summed up in the blessings and curses, into a broader vision of God's perpetual faithfulness to Israel.

Appendix on Vows and Tithes, 27:1-34

Chapter 26 forms the rhetorical and theological conclusion to Leviticus, as the summary in 26:46 shows. The additional case laws in chap. 27 therefore come as a surprise. Verses 17-24, however, presuppose the Jubilee legislation of Lev 25, so the arrangement may owe more to legal logic than to literary considerations.

27:1-25. Assessments. Israelites consecrated people, animals, or land to Yahweh as gifts or to fulfill vows. Clean animals were sacrificed (vv. 9-10); the rest must be assessed and the equivalent paid in silver or gold (v. 25). (For earlier practices of dedicating humans to temple service or even sacrifice, see 1 Sam 1 and Judg 11:29-40.) The Jubilee year would complicate the assessment of land values (vv. 17-24; 25:13-17).

27:26-33. Exceptions. Certain people, animals, and crops already belong to God, and therefore cannot be replaced or redeemed by cash payments. The first offspring born to animals or humans belongs to God (Exod 13:2; 34:19-20), as does one-tenth (a "tithe") of the agricultural produce: clean animals must be sacrificed, the rest may be redeemed at 120% of their value (vv. 26-27, 30-33). People and property may also be *devoted to destruction* (vv. 28-29) as spoils of holy war (Josh 6:17-21) or as punishment for idolatry (Exod 22:20). The prohibition on selling or redeeming such people or property eliminates the profit motive from holy war and judicial sentencing.

27:34. Subscript. This summary statement, along with that in 26:46, encompasses all the laws from Exod 20 through Lev 27. It locates the origins of the whole corpus on *Mount Sinai*, although Leviticus' superscription describes the setting as the Tabernacle (1:1; but cf. 7:37-38 and 25:1). Since Numbers begins with preparations for Israel's departure from Sinai, the summaries in Lev 26:46 and 27:34 may not intend to distinguish the mountain from the tent. Instead, they contrast the law given in and around Mt. Sinai with law revealed later in the wilderness journey (Numbers and Deuteronomy).

Works Cited

Blum, Erhard. 1990. *Studien zur Komposition des Pentateuch*. BZAW 189.

Carroll, Michael P. 1985 (1978). "One More Time: Leviticus Revisited." *Anthropological Approaches to the Old Testament*, ed. B. Lang, 117–26.

Damrosch, David. 1987. "Leviticus." *The Literary Guide to the Bible*, ed. Alter and Kermode, 66–77.

Douglas, Mary. 1985 (1966). "The Abominations of Leviticus." *Anthropological Approaches to the Old Testament*, ed. B. Lang, 100–16.

Hartley, John E. 1992. *Leviticus*. WBC.

Kugel, James L., and Rowan A. Greer. 1986. *Early Biblical Interpretation*. LEC.

Mann, Thomas W. 1988. *The Book of Torah: the Narrative Integrity of the Pentateuch*.

Milgrom, Jacob. 1976. *Cult and Conscience*. SJLA. 1991. *Leviticus 1–16*. AncB.

Strassfeld, Michael. 1985. *The Jewish Holidays: A Guide and Commentary*.

Wenham, Gordon J. 1979. *Leviticus*. NICOT.

Wieseltier, Leon. 1987. "Leviticus." *Congregation: Contemporary Writers Read the Jewish Bible*, ed. D. Rosenberg, 27–38.

Numbers

Jack G. Partain

Introduction

The Book of Numbers stretches like a canal across a great desert, linking the narratives of the Exodus with that of the conquest of Canaan. The Book of Exodus, with its story of the LORD's great salvation of the Hebrews from Egyptian bondage— and the account of the covenant at Sinai—sets the tone for the high drama that matures in the narratives surrounding Joshua and the judges. Between those epic accounts are sandwiched the final three books of the Pentateuch. Leviticus is code or law, which has a numbing effect on the excitement that precedes it; Deuteronomy is intentionally reflective and, therefore, tends to systematize the events and interpretations of the Exodus. Nearly lost in the flow of the canon is the story of the first glimpses of the gift of a promised homeland, and the trials faced by a newborn Israel.

There is no wonder that many readers are tempted to rush through the Book of Numbers (pausing, perhaps, to enjoy the talking donkey story). Three lengthy chapters are devoted to census reports, including their fantastic totals. The story line, if one can be found, is persistently interrupted: long accounts of cultic regulations; a detailed list of offerings repeated twelve times verbatim; a description of an ordeal to expose an unfaithful wife by using water tinctured with ashes from a red heifer that had been burned; a grisly story of a zealous priest who impales on his spear an Israelite and his foreign wife; a remembrance of a day when Sheol opened up and swallowed alive a rebel and all his followers; and a report of the extermination of tens of thousands of Midianites, including women, children, and the elderly. Not, at first glance, terribly edifying reading.

Although the Book of Numbers may not be every reader's idea of religious literature, it has an important place in the Torah.

Content

The epic story that is the basic fabric of the Book of Numbers explains why the generation of Israelites who came to know Yahweh in the Exodus did not inherit the LAND God had promised them.

The Book of Numbers is set "In The Wilderness" (the Hebrew title of the book). After elaborate preparations at Mt. Sinai, including the first censuses, Israel moves toward Canaan like a great religious procession. Early complaining turns into outright rebellion when a scouting party does not give a positive report of the land Israel is to occupy. The LORD condemns the rebellious generation to wander and die in the desert. Little is said about those wanderings. Almost half the book tells of the passing of that generation and their leaders, of renewed preparations to invade Palestine, and of early successes in violently settling the east bank of the Jordan. A new generation, hardened and purified by years in the desert, stands ready for the great invasion itself.

Interspersed in this narrative are various religious plans and regulations. These materials communicate several of the priestly ideals for postexilic Israel as they reconstitute themselves the people of God, this time a holy people, with a new temple and a proper priesthood.

Structure

A glance at the suggested outline reinforces the impression that the traditions used in the Book of Numbers are diverse. Traditions from various periods in Israel's history, on a variety of topics, have been included in each section of the book by the ancient editors. The rationale for selecting and placing the various legal and cultic traditions is not easily discerned. Efforts to impose some further order on the book seem subjective. Martin Noth thought that the Mosaic tradition was used as a fabric onto which the diverse clan traditions were embroidered, giving the book its unity (1968, 4–11).

The outline is traditional, grouping the materials around three places prominent in the story: Mount Sinai, the desert (especially the oasis at Kadesh), and the Transjordan.

Authorship and Sources

Numbers is the work of priests during the Babylonian Exile. They use traditions both oral and written, from various periods of Israel's history and from diverse perspectives, giving the impression of a heterogeneous book. There is wide agreement about which materials are YAHWIST and/or ELOHIST traditions and which traditions or compositions come from the PRIESTLY WRITERS. Over three fourths of the book may be traced to the priestly writers. Some of the poetry seems quite ancient (6:24-26; 10:35; 14:18; 21:15, 17-18). Even scholars who wish to see Mosaic compositions in the book understand Numbers, in its present form, as composite (e.g., Thompson 1970, 168).

Themes

The wilderness years that Numbers remembers were formative years in Israel's history. During that era the LORD created a people and their institutions. The creative process is recorded as less complex than it probably was. Various groups joined "Israel" in the desert, others during the invasion and settlement years. From this unpromising raw material Yahweh creates a "holy nation" (cf. Exod 19:5-6), uniquely set apart and prepared to be his covenant society.

Some of Israel's most valued convictions are expressed in Numbers: Israel's faith and institutions are rooted in their concrete history. The LORD has chosen to bestow God's awesome Presence on and in the midst of Israel. God's Presence demands holiness of the covenant people, including uncompromising ceremonial cleanliness. Among God's gifts to the people are the land of Canaan, the law (Torah), and the Aaronite and Levitical priesthood. God's covenant loyalty to the people can be violated, but it cannot be set aside by Israel's rebellions.

All of these convictions became precious to people trying to learn the lessons of their destruction and exile, and hoping to get it right the second time around.

For Further Study

In the *Mercer Dictionary of the Bible*: ATONEMENT/EXPIATION IN THE OT; BALAAM; CALENDAR; CONQUEST OF CANAAN; CURSE AND BLESSING; ELOHIST; HEIFER, RED; LAND; LEVI/LEVITES; MANNA; MARRIAGE IN THE OT; NUMBERS, BOOK OF; ORACLE; PRIESTLY WRITERS; PRIESTS; SOURCES OF THE PENTATEUCH; VOW IN THE OT; WEIGHTS AND MEASURES; WORSHIP IN THE OT; YAHWIST.

In other sources: P. J. Budd, *Numbers*, WBC; R. de Vaux, *Ancient Israel: Its Life and Institutions*; M. Noth, *Numbers*, OTL; D. T. Olson, *The Death of the Old and the Birth of the New*.

Commentary

An Outline

I. Preparation at Sinai to Move to Canaan, 1:1–10:10
   A. First Census of the Tribes of Israel, 1:1-54
   B. The Sacred Camp, 2:1-34
   C. Census and Duties of Priests and Levites, 3:1–4:49
   D. Miscellaneous Laws and Observations, 5:1–8:26
   E. Final Preparations, 9:1–10:10
II. Days in the Desert, 10:11–21:20
   A. Israel on the March to Canaan, 10:11-36
   B. On the Way to Kadesh: Complaining, 11:1–12:16
   C. Reconnaissance of Canaan, 13:1-33
   D. Rebellion and Condemnation, 14:1-45
   E. Cultic Laws and Regulations, 15:1-41
   F. Revolts of Korah and Others, 16:1-50
   G. Aaron's Budding Staff, 17:1-13
   H. Duties and Support of Priests and Levites, 18:1-32
   I. Laws of Purification: Death, 19:1-22
   J. Last Days at Kadesh: Moses' Sin and Edom's Blockade, 20:1-21
   K. March Towards Transjordan: Aaron's Death, 20:22-29
   L. On the Way: Victory and Suffering, 21:1-20
III. Conquests and Settling In, 21:21–36:13
   A. Defeat of Two Kingdoms: Sihon and Og, 21:21-35
   B. Balaam and Balak, 22:1–24:25
   C. The Peor Affair, 25:1-18
   D. A Second Census, 26:1-65
   E. Daughters of Zelophehad, 27:1-11
   F. Joshua's Commissioning, 27:12-23
   G. Laws Concerning Offerings and Festivals, 28:1–29:40
   H. Laws Concerning Women's Vows, 30:1-16
   I. Holy War Against Midian, 31:1-54
   J. Settlements in Transjordan, 32:1-42
   K. An Exodus Itinerary, 33:1-49
   L. Ideal Boundaries of the Promised Land, 33:50–34:29
   M. Levitical Cities and Cities of Refuge, 35:1-34
   N. Protecting Tribal Property: Women as Heirs, 36:1-13

Preparations at Sinai to Move to Canaan, 1:1–10:10

The Book of Numbers begins where Exodus and Leviticus conclude. Israel is still camped near Sinai. Following the meeting with God and the gift of the covenant at Sinai, several kinds of preparation of the former slaves that will allow them to become the people of God have been described: the gift of the *torah* (instruction for covenant living), the construction of a portable sanctuary (the TABERNACLE), and the institution of Israel's religious system (the cultus), especially sacrifice (see Exod 21–40 and Leviticus).

Numbers completes the description of those preparations, beginning with a census of all able-bodied men of fighting age, and concluding with the Israelites east of the Jordan, beginning to inherit the promised LAND of Canaan.

First Census of the Tribes of Israel, 1:1-54

When readers of the Book of Numbers open the book they are in the midst of action. Like a movie-goer who comes into the theater as the projectionist begins the second reel, readers soon discover that some of the crucial events in the story have already been told.

God has rescued the Israelite people from Egypt—by means of a series of extraordinary events. Out in the Sinai desert, at "the mountain of God," the LORD was revealed to Israel and their leader, Moses. The LORD and the people have been bound together by the COVENANT. Despite eruptions of Israelite rebellion (which gave the covenant relationship an uncertain beginning), God has already shown that the divine purposes will not be deterred.

Modern readers may not be enticed by the way the Book of Numbers begins. Following the divine command to count the males able to go to war, there is a list of the twelve tribes, with the names of the headmen and their fathers; statements about the actual enrollment; a long recital of the results, tribe-by-tribe; a summary and total; and a section about the role of the Levites. The opening of the book is certainly not very exciting.

Among the several transitions that take place between the departure from Egypt and the arrival at the brink of the promised land of Canaan is Israel's transformation from a disorderly, "mixed crowd" (Exod 12:38) to an efficient fighting force. Discipline and order are the primary values that emerge during the transition narratives. If these people are to occupy Canaan they must become the army of the LORD. Thus, this census is the first in a series of preparations taken to ready the Israelites for what lies ahead—conquering Canaan and becoming a holy nation (Exod 19:5-6).

The account of the census is straightforward, but the alert reader should look for certain features of the narrative. Note the central role of Moses (along with Aaron). Moses is the sole mediator through whom Yahweh communicates with Israel. As will become obvious later, the leadership responsibility Moses carries is sometimes an odious burden to him, and an unacceptable centralizing of authority to others.

Moses receives the ORACLE of leadership not, as in the Book of Exodus on the holy mountain (Sinai), but in the recently assembled TENT OF MEETING. Exod 25–40 offers a detailed description of the construction of this portable shrine. Interest in the tent of meeting points to a central theme in Numbers, i.e., the presence of Yahweh among his people.

The Book of Numbers assumes a kind of idealized socio-political structure, even during these beginning months in the desert: all of Israel is united as a religious community made up of tribes (*the whole congregation*, v. 2), which are made up of *clans*, which are made up of *ancestral houses* (i.e., extended, patriarchal families), which are made up of individuals (with males being the ones of significance). We cannot be sure what some of the terms used referred to; meanings probably changed with time. Some terms seem to be interchangeable in this passage (v. 16).

With the list of tribes (vv. 5-15, repeated with variations in vv. 20-43) compare other lists in the OT (Judg 5; Deut 33; Gen 49; and esp. Num 26:5-50). The differences between the lists suggest that the groups themselves changed, with various tribes coming to prominence, dividing, and/or blending with others. The twelve-fold structure, however, remained the ideal through Israel's history. In this list the tribe of Levi is counted separately, as are the "Joseph tribes" (i.e., Ephraim and Manasseh, vv. 32-35).

The carefully done census reports 603,550 Israelite males, twenty years old or older, able to go to war. At the least that suggests a total population of more than two million! The figure in chap. 26 is only slightly less—after thirty-eight years of desert ravages.

What is one to make of such huge numbers? Because it would take far more than the miracles of MANNA, quail, and water for two million people to live in the Sinai desert, some dismiss the totals as a fiction. The common explanation looks for another meaning for the term translated *thousand* (*eleph*). What is referred to, the explanation goes, is a small military (perhaps tribal) unit of varying size. Thus, for example, the census of Gad reports forty-five *eleph*, a total of about 650 men (assuming fourteen to fifteen men in an *eleph*).

If this explanation fits this census, the priestly editor did not know it. And the explanation misses the point (in Numbers and in Exod 12:37). God has kept his promise. He has multiplied Abraham's seed as the sand on the shore. And he can provide for this great people in a barren place. The picture of such a great host will add bleak irony to the unfavorable report brought back by the majority of those sent to spy out Canaan for invasion in chap. 13.

The Levites do not have a military role, so they are counted separately (cf. 3:1-4). They are charged with guarding, caring for, and transporting the portable shrine (*tabernacle of the covenant*, v. 50). They also prevent other non-levitical Israelites (*outsiders*, v. 51) from coming into contact with the dangerous, Holy Presence at the tabernacle. More on the Levites' duties is found in 3:21–4:49.

The Sacred Camp, 2:1-34

Following the census, we read of Israel's camp layout and order of march, organized like a solemn assembly (cf. Lev 23:33-36). The camp resembles a square, with a lead tribe on each side, with other tribes flanking the lead tribe left and right or before and behind, and with the Levites sheltering the tent of the Presence in the center.

The description reads as though it had been generated by a computer, but it is intended to convey a stirring picture of Israel at its best. Everyone is in perfect order, as God has instructed. God's Presence is at the very center of life. The holiness that characterizes God's Presence is carefully guarded. God's rule and Israel's submission to it foster solidarity among what would otherwise be a loose conglomeration of people. This formation portrays an obedient theocracy. *The Israelites did just as the* LORD *had commanded* (v. 34, cf. Ezek 48). The atmosphere crackles with expectation, and provides sharp contrasts with the complaints and revolts that follow.

This chapter locates *the tent of meeting*, along with *the camp of the Levites*, in *the center* of the gathered people (v. 17). In another tradition the tent of meeting was outside the camp (Exod 33:7-11). The discrepancy is beyond explanation.

Judah has the favored position (to the east, facing the entrance to the tent) and leads, a different position than that described in Gen 25:22-26. One of the Joseph tribes, Ephraim, also leads. These positions may reflect the prominence that these tribes came to have later in Israel's history.

Census and Duties of Priests and Levites, 3:1–4:49

When the first census was taken (chap. 1), the tribe of Levi was not included. Rather, the Levites were separated from the other tribes for roles related to the tabernacle (1:48-53). Those roles now are made more explicit.

3:1-4. The house of Aaron. With the formula *this is the lineage* (v. 1) the priestly writer signals that Israel's story has reached a new, significant stage. The installation of Aaron and the Levites is especially important. Aaron and his sons are *anointed priests, ordained* (3:3) to perform the various services at the *tent of meeting* (3:7), especially to offer the various sacrifices. Other Levites are *set . . . before Aaron* to serve as the priests' assistants.

3:5-39. Establishing the Levites. Yahweh instructs that the Levites now be counted (*enrolled*, v. 14). Whereas Israel was counted by tribes, Levi is to be counted by clans. Four different clusters of clans have four places in the march and camp, parallel with the four groups of tribes. Moses and Aaron, and Aaron's family have the place of honor, *in front of the tabernacle on the east* (v. 38). They also have the most sacred duties, the *rites within the sanctuary* (v. 38). The sons of Gershon have responsibility for the tabernacle, the screens, and similar furnishings (3:25-26). The sons of Kohath (i.e., the Amramite, Izharite and Hebronite clans) are entrusted with the most holy responsibility. They are in charge of the sacred equipment, *the most holy things* (4:4)—after the Aaronite priests properly stow it (v. 31; 4:5-15). The Merari clans have the least sacred task; they are responsible for the framework of the tabernacle. The census for Levi is smaller than for the other tribes, 22,000 (v. 39). Various explanations have been given for the fact that the three groups, descendants of Gershon, Kohath, and Merari, total 22,300.

3:40-51. Numbering the firstborn males. A third census is ordered to determine the number of *firstborn males of the Israelites* (v. 40). The figure arrived at, 22,273, is not easy to reconcile with a total male population over the age of thirty, given as 603,550 (cf. 1:46). Following God's great rescue in Egypt, all Israelite firstborn males were to be dedicated to the LORD. But since child sacrifice was unacceptable, the members of Levi become *substitutes* for the firstborn males (3:12, 41), one for one. For the 273 firstborn males with no Levitical substitute, money is paid (*the price of redemption*, v. 46). The counting (and substituting) of the firstborn underscores the conviction that the Levites represent all Israel in their service to God, and God to Israel.

4:1-49. Numbering the Kohathites, Gershonites, and Merarites. Three clans are set aside for service *relating to the tent of meeting* (vv. 4, 23, 30). Each of these three clans trace their lineage as *sons of Levi* (3:17). This section of the narrative provides details of the specific functions of the levitical servants in the tent of meeting.

The history of Israel's priesthood, and of the Levitical roles in particular, is complicated. After the reforms of JOSIAH in the late seventh century, and before the Babylonian Exile, the Levites saw their roles sharply curtailed (Ezek 44:10-14). What we read in Numbers seems to give expression to the ideals that animated many who shaped Judaism after the Second Temple (late sixth century and following).

Miscellaneous Laws and Observances, 5:1–8:26

Having described certain institutional or structural innovations Israel needed in order to live as the people of God (at the beginning, or during the new Exodus, which followed the Exile), the writer of Numbers lays out procedures that help insure that Israel is, at all times, a "holy nation" (Exod 19:6).

The material must be read with a lively historical and religious imagination. Basic themes (e.g., "holy," "unclean," "pure," "death," "blessing," "oath/vow," "sacrifice," "name") must be grasped and kept in mind.

The Israelite camp has been ordered in such a way that the divine Presence can take up residence in its midst. If the divine Presence resides in the midst of the camp, it is a dangerous place. Precautions must be taken to keep the camp morally and ceremonially clean.

5:1-4. Ceremonial cleanliness. Persons with skin eruptions or unusual bodily discharges are considered ceremonially unclean. Those contaminated by death, i.e., having had contact with a corpse, similarly are unholy. All such contaminations and contact are considered infected and must, therefore, be isolated—put out of the community. The reason? Because "the LORD *dwell(s) among* Israel," v. 4. Some interpreters suggest that the rationale is good community hygiene, but there is not a hint of that motive in these passages.

Leprosy probably refers to a variety of skin diseases, including but not limited to Hansen's disease. Death is referred to as almost a substance that can contaminate a person who touches or gets close to it.

5:5-10. Broken relationships. Wrongs against fellow Israelites also disrupt relationships. In Israel, the covenant society, sins against others not only violate community; they *break . . . faith with* Yahweh. God will not tent in a community where interpersonal conflicts are left unresolved.

The provisions for restitution and reconciliation between persons set out in Lev 19 and 25 are supplemented here to include cases in which there is no *go'el* (*next of kin* advocate, v. 8).

5:11-31. Instances of adultery. Cases in which adultery is suspected (without evidence) are dealt with in a way that seems strange to many moderns. If a jealous husband suspects his wife, she is put through a ceremonial ordeal. In Israelite society wives could not accuse their husbands of adultery. Sexual intercourse with another woman was considered adultery only if the other woman was married. The accused wife (implied to be pregnant) is taken to a priest who will take her *before the* LORD, in the Holy Presence. There she will be required to drink sacred water, tinctured with dust from the sanctuary and ink from an oath. If she is innocent, nothing will happen to her; if guilty, she will suffer dropsy (?) and become infertile (or have a miscarriage).

If this seems chauvinistic—and plainly it is—the reader should remember that in most trials by ordeal the presumption is that the accused is guilty.

The ordeal is tinged with connotations of magic. Superstitious Israelites would be trapped by the ordeal, if they felt guilty. *The water of bitterness* is believed to be *the water that brings the curse* and *cause(s) bitter pain* (v. 24). But the priestly writer sees Yahweh acting by means of this ordeal. It is God who *makes your uterus drop* (v. 21).

Conflicts in a marriage are not merely a private domestic matter. Festering relationships are to be dealt with, even when there are no witnesses nor any evidence. Such disruptions, unresolved, foul community. Yahweh will not dwell where such things are ignored. The ordeal presses the LORD himself to clear the wife of guilt and forces the husband to stop his accusations . . . or vice versa.

6:1-21. Regulating the Nazirites. From time to time readers of the Bible encounter stories of men and women who have taken *the vow of a Nazirite* (v. 2). Samson is the best-known example—even though his mother made the vow (Judg 13); Samuel is also described as being under a Nazirite vow made by Hannah (1 Sam 1:22). This section provides the fullest details in the Bible of what a Nazirite vow involved. NAZIRITES were to separate themselves from others in the community, were expected to renew their vow if they became contaminated, and had rituals to perform once their vow had been fulfilled.

Nazirites gave themselves (or were given) to God. As a mark of their separateness, they were to abstain from wine and all intoxicants, from cutting the hair on their head, and from any contact with dead bodies. No reason is given for this choice of prohibitions. Persons under the vow who accidentally violate it—by having contact with a *corpse*, for example—were provided ways to renew the vow (vv. 9-12). In a similar way, a series of offerings and symbolic debriefing actions (e.g., shaving the head and burning the hair) are prescribed for the time when the vow has been fulfilled.

6:22-27. The Aaronite Blessing. The Aaronite Blessing is perhaps the best known text in the Book of Numbers. The blessing is poetry-like. The three lines have parallel structures, made up of three words, five words, and seven words. Many think the blessing is very ancient. The words are both a prayer for God's favor (may [understood] *the LORD bless* . . .) and a declaration that God does bless his people (*The LORD bless you* . . .). The pronoun *you* is singular.

7:1-88. Offerings from the tribes. This chapter is the longest in the Bible; some would also identify it as the most tedious. The account begins with the tribes' representatives providing transport for the tabernacle, *six covered wagons* (carts) with two oxen to pull each (v. 3). No transport is provided *the Kohathites* because they are to carry the most sacred objects (*the holy things*) *on the shoulders* (v. 9).

Verses 12-83 record a procession of tribal leaders as each presents his tribe's offering for *the dedication of the altar* (vv. 10-11), one-a-day, for twelve successive days, including even the SABBATH. All twelve offerings are exactly the same. Every detail is recounted twelve times. The effect on the modern reader is numbing; the intended effect is probably an emphasis on Israel's unanimous and lavish offering to service at the tent, laid on with meticulous care. Such mundane commitment to the priesthood and to the service at the tabernacle is an essential ingredient in Israel's preparation to be the people of God.

The account climaxes with an inventory of all that was given (vv. 84-88). The offerings are to be used in worship events and include supplies for incense and grain offerings, as well as for the burnt offerings, the sin offerings, and the well-being offerings.

The order in which the leaders present themselves differs from place to place in Numbers. A descendant of Judah leads the list here, whereas descendants of Reuben lead lists elsewhere in the book (1:5, 20; 26:5). When the encampments and the marches are mentioned, Judah leads the list (2:3; 10:14).

7:89. The LORD speaks to Moses. Once the tabernacle was properly prepared and provided for, it becomes the place where Moses goes to hear *the voice speaking to him*, i.e., where Moses receives oracles. The promise of Exod 25:22 is now realized. God speaks to his people plainly and personally. The lesson is transparent: when God's people generously support the cultus, God communicates freely with them.

The *ark of the covenant* becomes the visible symbol of Yahweh's invisible presence in the midst of his people. The LORD communicates with the people from the shrine itself, an arrangement that may stand in contrast to uncontrolled prophetic inspiration.

Sphinx-like *cherubim* were fixed to the cover of the ark, their almost-touching wings hovering over the ark. Thus, the space above the ark came to be thought of as the LORD's throne, the place where God meets with his people, *the mercy seat*.

One final task is required to put Israel's life in order before the march, i.e., setting apart the Levites themselves. Those ceremonies signal that Israel is about ready to move toward Canaan.

8:1-4. Objects of the cultus. The construction and placement of the menorah, the traditional *lampstand* with *seven lamps*, is an example of final, detailed touches given the preparation.

8:5-26. Rituals of cleansing. Elaborate ceremonies *cleanse* the Levites and separate them for a distinctive service. First, they are "de-sinned" (*the water of purification*, e.g., is a unique expression). *They shave their whole body* (symbolically ridding themselves of their old life) and wash their clothes (cf. the rituals surrounding the consecration of priests in Lev 8).

With offerings for ceremonial uncleanliness in hand, the Levites are presented in front of the tabernacle. The community itself *lay their hands on the Levites* (v. 10), designating them as representative of the entire congregation. Israel serves at the shrine vicariously through the Levites. They are presented, as it were, as Israel's *elevation offering* (vv. 13, 15). They belong to God, as substitutes for *the firstborn* (v. 16; cf. 3:44–51), and they protect Israel from the Presence and the sacred objects in the tent of the Presence. They act as a protection, an *atonement* (v. 12), so that *there may be no plague* (v. 19).

Clearly, the Levites are being described in ways that distinguish them from Aaronite priests (cf. the consecration of priests in Lev 8). They have an important, sacred role. They are near to the people, but distinct from them. They are given to God, and he in turn gives them as *a gift to Aaron* (v. 19). Thus, their service to Israel and to God is equated with their *attendance on Aaron and his* descendants (v. 22).

Levites are only expected to serve at the tent of meeting between their twenty-fifth and fiftieth years (vv. 24-25). See the related commentary above at 4:3.

Final Preparations, 9:1–10:10

The essentials for constituting an Israel that is the LORD's holy nation, obedient in all matters to the God present in their midst, have now been described. Before Israel breaks camp at Sinai and heads for the LAND God has promised, the reader is told of three matters that anticipate their journey.

9:1-14. A Passover. Prior to the beginning of the journey Israel is instructed to observe a second PASSOVER, just as they had a year earlier on the night before they set out from Egypt. The date given for the Passover is one month earlier than the date given for developments described in chaps. 1–8 (esp. 1:1).

The festival of Passover reenacted the formative events in Israel's history. It was essential for their corporate identity. Everyone was to participate every year, without exception. The instructions recounted in Exod 12 are here presupposed.

Two specific excuses for nonparticipation are dealt with: one that could arise anywhere—ceremonial uncleanness; another that would arise once Israel was living in Palestine or the diaspora—being on a journey. Neither circumstance is a valid excuse. Provision is made for an alternate celebration a month late. Arrangements are to be made even for resident foreigners (*aliens*, v. 14) who wish to participate.

To underscore the indispensability of the Passover observance, Moses is instructed to ostracize, *cut off from the people* (execute?), anyone who did not participate.

9:15-23. The Cloud. Previous priestly themes, God's constant guidance of and the LORD's awesome Presence with the people, are here blended. The symbol of the

LORD's guidance from Egypt to Sinai, a column of fire or cloud, here becomes a cloud that *covered the tabernacle* or an *appearance of fire* (v. 15), a powerful symbol of God's residence in the middle of the camp.

The emphasis is upon God's daily guidance and Israel's unfailing response—no matter how unpredictable that guidance might seem to be. The description anticipates the ways the LORD will lead Israel in the days ahead.

10:1-10. Trumpets. The instruction to shape *two silver trumpets* (v. 2) leads to a description of the community called to action by them. The trumpeters call the entire community or its leaders to an assembly at the tent's *entrance* (v. 3); they sound an alarm in time of war; and they herald great cultic occasions. Thus the LORD's rule in Israel is communicated in the concrete action of the priest-trumpeters.

The trumpets were probably straight tubes, flared at the end; not to be confused with the *shophar*, a ram's horn. Such trumpets came into common use in the Second Temple.

Days in the Desert, 10:11–21:20

Israel's story now enters a new, decisive phase, as does the Book of Numbers. Yahweh has made a covenant with Israel at Sinai. After initial disorder and rebellion the life of an orderly, obedient covenant community has been described—sometimes in meticulous detail. All is ready. At last the march toward the land promised begins.

Israel on the March to Canaan, 10:11-36

10:11-24. On the move. Eleven months after arriving at Sinai and nineteen days after the census of the tribes, Israel moves. The signal to break camp is the lifting of *the cloud from over the tabernacle* (v. 11), the cloud being a symbol of the presence of the LORD. In a different way this is described as *the command of Yahweh by Moses* (v. 13). Perhaps the trumpets also sounded as a signal of the command.

The description conveys a sense of large-scale but disciplined activity, as, stage by stage, according to plan, the tribes move out. The emphasis on *the tabernacle* (v. 17), the placement of the *holy things* (v. 21) at the very center, and the leadership by *the ark* (vv. 33-36), all suggest a great liturgical procession—a holy nation off on a mission.

The configuration of the camp required in chap. 2 is here adapted to a march. The Gershonites and the Merarites go ahead of the Kohathites so that the tent will already be set up when the furniture and the ark arrive. The exact location of *the wilderness of Paran* (v. 12) in the Sinai peninsula is uncertain.

10:25-36. Offer to Hobab. The traditions dealing with Hobab and with the ark are usually considered to be quite old, probably part of the YAHWIST epic (last used by the PRIESTLY WRITERS in Exod 34).

Notice that each of these memories (v. 29 and v. 33) begin with the day of departure from Sinai and differ somewhat from the priestly version (e.g., *the ark* is some distance out in front of the march).

The point of Moses' request *(serve as eyes for us,* v. 31) is clear. This Kenite, Hobab, who presumably knows the desert and its hostile peoples, is asked to scout for Israel en route. He refuses, but seems to go anyway. *So they set out . . .* (v. 33).

That the passage, along with other passages (e.g., Judg 1:16; 4:11; 4:17), points to a close association of Kenites with Israelites during the years of the settlement seems clear. There may be a hint of a treaty.

But what is Hobab's relation to Moses? Assuming that JETHRO and Reuel refer to the same person in different traditions, the NRSV solves the riddle by taking *Moses' father-in-law* (v. 29) to refer to Reuel. But the phrase can also refer to Hobab, as in Judg 1:16, 4:11. And it may be translated "kinsman by marriage." Hobab/Jethro/Reuel is called both a *Midianite* (v. 29; cf. Exod 2:16, 18) and a Kenite (Judg 1:16; 4:11), groups closely associated in the OT.

Hobab's role as desert guide is not emphasized; guidance by the Presence is (vv. 33-34). The LORD's guidance is represented by *the ark of the covenant,* which is out ahead of the march (v. 33) rather than enclosed in the middle of the march (v. 21). *The cloud* of the Presence, which led Israel to Sinai and which seems to lead in 9:15-23, hovers over the march. The LORD both leads and stays with his people.

The Yahwist calls Mount Sinai the *mount of the LORD* (i.e., "the mount of Yahweh," v. 33), which is an unusual phrase ("mountain of God" in Exod 3:1).

Can the text mean that the ark traveled ahead *three days' journey* (v. 33)? The ancient Syriac version reads "one day's journey." Many think the phrase is a mistaken repetition and should be omitted.

The so-called "song of the ark" (vv. 35-36) contains lines of very ancient poetry. As quoted, it may reflect liturgical use in the Second Temple. But the song echoes a day when the LORD was thought to be enthroned on the ark and when the ark was carried into Israel's holy war battles (Josh 3–4, 1 Sam 4).

On the Way to Kadesh: Complaining, 11:1–12:16

The trek across Sinai did not go as intended. Once away from the holy mountain, the well-ordered, obedient people of God begin to complain and rebel. The abrupt change in Israel's response characterizes this entire period: one rebellion after another.

11:1-3. Murmerings. The journey has hardly begun, when the up-beat, positive mood is shattered. The *people complained* ("murmured," KJV). This paragraph introduces the complaining motif that will characterize much of the narrative that covers the next thirty-eight years.

Israel had been only three days away from Egypt on the way to Sinai when they first began to complain (Exod 15:24). In Exodus, Israel complained about genuine problems. Moses interceded. And God provided what was needed.

But in Numbers the complaining is understood differently. The grumbling is not caused by a bona fide physical need; its root cause is unfaith. Therefore, Yahweh lashes out in judgment that threatens to destroy the rebellious Israelites. Moses intercedes on their behalf, and God relents—somewhat.

God's Presence is often portrayed as *fire* (v. 3). The account gives no hint as to what phenomena might be intended.

11:4-35. Provisions. Three juxtaposed events are related in this section: the provision of quail meat, the choice of elders to share the burden of leadership with Moses, and the place of "unofficial" prophecy.

The complaint is specific: desert food. Certain riffraff (*rabble*, v. 4) incite the complaint; but soon the outcry is heard at every door in camp (v. 10): "*This manna stuff.* . . . We can't stand *to look at* it anymore. We're wasting away. Manna, manna, manna. Why can't we have some food for a change, something tasty—with *leeks* and *onions* and *garlic*? And why can't we have some real *meat to eat*?" So the people whined.

The tradition that parallels this one (Exod 16) interprets the complaint as legitimate; in response God graciously provides quail. In this telling, the complaint is tantamount to rebellion—*You have rejected the* LORD (v. 20).

The lengthy explanation about MANNA (vv. 7-9) prompts interpreters to identify it with droplets from the fruit of the Sinai shrub, *tamarix gallica*, which "bleeds" during May and June. These explanations do not fit precisely, and may miss the point.

When God instructs Moses to *consecrate* the people in readiness for a sacred occasion and to prepare to *eat meat* (v. 18), Moses expresses reservation. *The people number six hundred thousand*, he says. *Are there enough flocks and herds . . . [or] fish in the sea* (vv. 21-22) to satisfy them? The apparent hyperbole reflects Moses' exasperation. "They will eat meat—quail meat," the LORD replies, "until it comes out of their ears." (The metaphor is more literal: *You shall eat . . . for a whole month—until it comes out of your nostrils* [vv. 19-20], i.e., until it makes you nauseous.)

So, God's response to Israel's complaint—an abundance of meat—is actually a punishment. A *wind* blows in *quails from the sea* (v. 31). The Israelites seem to be in the quails' migratory path. Exhausted, the quail either fall around the camp three feet deep (the modern equivalent of *two cubits*), or they fly so low (three feet high) that they are easily taken. The meat-starved crowd harvest them by the homer full, no one gathering less than *ten homers* (v. 32), i.e., more than sixty bushels. Gorging themselves brings on some *very great plague* (v. 33) from which people died. The plague is interpreted as an act of God's judgment.

Israel's slave mentality ("Better the securities and provisions of Egypt than the risks and responsibilities of freedom and following the LORD") foreshadows an ongoing temptation in Israel's foreign policy: looking to foreign empires, especially Egypt, to save them, instead of trusting God (Isa 7–8 [esp. 8:5-8]; Jer 27).

Into the story of Israel's complaint and the LORD's answer, the writer weaves a complaint by Moses (vv. 10-15; cf. a similar tradition about Moses' leadership in Exod 18). Israel's whining is too much for Moses. From the beginning they have complained. Having sole leadership of such a crowd is a *burden* (v. 11). After all, he informs God, they are God's people, not his. He neither conceived them, nor gave them birth, nor suckled them (an interesting analogy for God's salvation; cf. Hos 11:1-9). He cannot take it any more.

Moses' complaint is legitimate. He is instructed to bring *seventy elders* to *the tent of meeting* (v. 16). There they will be anointed with some of the same *spirit* that empowers Moses to lead. Thus they can *bear the burden of the people along with* Moses (v. 17). The *spirit* is spoken of as almost a material substance that God can divide, taking *some of* it to *put on* the elders.

Beliefs integral to Israel's "theocratic ideal" are seen as present from these earliest days. The *spirit* designated Moses as God's choice to lead Israel as Yahweh's surrogate. When that spirit was *put on* the elders, *they prophesied*, i.e., they joined in some kind of ecstatic behavior. Two elders who had been *registered* (meaning selected to serve) but who *had not gone out to the tent* (v. 26) also experienced the phenomenon or ecstasy. JOSHUA, jealous for Moses' preeminence, urged that they be silenced (vv. 28-30).

During the days of the judges and the first two kings, such ecstatic behavior was thought to be an essential qualification to lead. ANOINTing with olive oil symbolized God's "anointing" the judge or king with the divine spirit (cf. 1 Sam 10:1-13; 19:18-24). Ecstatic demonstrations are called *prophesying* (v. 27), a reminder that Hebrew prophecy had its historic roots in groups who sometimes received their messages through ecstatic trances.

Moses' reply is classic: *Would that all* of Yahweh's *people were prophets, with his spirit on them* (v. 29). Plainly, more is intended than that all would become ecstatics. In bestowing spiritual gifts, God is not limited to certain institutions or ecclesial offices. Further, if there is to be any reality to match ideals like "the people of God," or "the kingdom of God," then *all* the people must be enabled and directed by God, not just certain leaders.

12:1-16. Controversy about Moses' leadership. In these paragraphs the uniqueness and supremacy of Moses are addressed, but not without tensions. The issue is not what it first appears to be. Miriam, Moses' elder sister, and Aaron speak out (the Heb. says "she spoke") *against Moses* because of his *Cushite* wife. The reason for Miriam's objection to the woman is not part of the story. Readers are left to speculate whether the *Cushite woman* is Zipporah (cf. Exod 2:21) or another woman. Perhaps the objection is related to her non-Israelite heritage. No reason is given. Nor does it seem that the real problem is Moses' choice of a wife.

Miriam and Aaron are really objecting—so it seems—to the singularity of Moses' role in Israel. They ask: *Has the LORD spoken only through Moses* (v. 2), suggesting the questions, "What about us? Are we not also prophets?"

In the previous leadership-related incident (11:16-30), elders were drawn into the leadership and prophetic inspiration was shared with others besides Moses. Does that not suggest that all the leaders are equally special?

The aside in v. 3 asserts that Moses is not interested in gaining an advantage over others. He is *humble*; that is, he is confident and strong enough not to be drawn into his siblings' power games (since v. 3 refers to Moses in the third person, it can hardly have been written by Moses [cf. Deut 34:10-12]).

Yahweh himself intervenes. *The three* are summoned to meet at the tent, where the *pillar of cloud* appears *at the entrance* (vv. 4-5). Yahweh's *words* contrast revelation to prophets with God's communication with Moses. Prophetic revelation is opaque and indirect. It requires interpretation, and may be ambiguous. It comes through *visions* and *dreams* (v. 6), a phrase that reflects the way prophecy was understood early in the history of Israel.

But with Moses—the communication is direct and personal (*face to face*, lit. "mouth to mouth"), unambiguous (*not in riddles*), and unique (v. 8). The anthropomorphism of the Yahwist tradition is striking. Moses is allowed to see *the form of the* LORD (v. 8; cf. Exod 33:17-23 and Gen 3:8-14 in contrast to John 1:18).

The issue behind this confrontation is, of course, authority in religion: the written revelation vs. an inward revelation, *torah* vs. prophetic messages (often understood as subjective). Or, more historically, is the test of prophecy to be Moses? Or does prophecy submit to Moses?

The rebels spark Yahweh's anger. The result is immediate. Miriam is left with *leprosy* (probably not Hansen's disease). Thus, she becomes ceremonially unclean (see 5:2). A major and privileged leader is thrust outside *the camp* (v. 15). Her disgrace is complete, as though her father had *spit in her face* (v. 14) as a child, putting a curse on her. She must be ritually cleansed. No explanation is given as to why only Miriam was punished. Moses the *humble* (v. 3) man intercedes for his sister; evidently, she is healed. After Miriam's seven days of purification, *the people set out* (v. 16) again.

Reconnaissance of Canaan, 13:1-33

All the preparations have been made. Israel's army has been numbered and organized. The cultus has been put in order. The people of God have moved to the borders, ready to occupy the LAND Yahweh has promised.

But the final step is not taken—at least, not for a long time (forty years, according to the narrative). The well-known spies' story and its aftermath tell why.

The account begins positively. The LORD himself orders reconnaissance of the land, the first military move in an invasion (Cf. the Deut 1:21-22 version). And a leader from each tribe is chosen and sent—a careful reader will note that the list of leaders is different from 1:5-16, 2:3-31, and 7:12-83.

Israel remains camped at *Kadesh*, about fifty mi. south of Beersheba, in the *Paran* desert. The charge to the spies is comprehensive: check out everything, every asset, every liability. And *be bold* (v. 20). Their reconnaissance begins in mid-late July (*season of the first ripe grapes*, v. 20) and lasts "a long time" (*forty days*, v. 25).

The scouting report betrays ambivalence. To these desert seminomads, Canaan appears attractive and fertile (*flowing with milk and honey*, v. 27). The scouts brought back fruit to show. It also appears to be formidable. The people are advanced and their towns are strongly fortified.

Despite the apparent disparities, one of the spies, CALEB, called for an immediate invasion: *We are well able to overcome it* (v. 30). But the majority dissented: *they are stronger than we* (v. 31). What appears to be a contrast between seeing Canaan realistically and seeing it through rose-colored glasses is, in fact, a contrast between faith and un-faith. The majority forget their huge numbers, all their preparations in the desert, and that they are the army of Yahweh. Their low opinion of themselves wins: up against such great people *we seemed like grasshoppers* (v. 33). The two perceptions depend on the data that faith takes into consideration, as opposed to the limited data considered by faithlessness.

The enigmatic phrase, *a land that devours its inhabitants* (v. 32), seems to suggest a barren, inhospitable place—in contrast to the tradition of fertility. References to *Anakites*, vv. 28, 33, reflect Israel's lore about a GIANT race, descendants of half-god, half-human *Nephilim* (v. 33; cf. Gen 6:1-4).

The PRIESTLY WRITERS seem to be using an ancient memory in which the spying mission included only the NEGEB, the semi-desert south of HEBRON, and southern CANAAN, centered around Hebron (cf. vv. 17, 22-24, 29). To this has been added v. 21, which enlarges the mission to include all of Canaan. *Rehob near Lebo-hamath* (v. 21) is far to the north.

Rebellion and Condemnation, 14:1-45

With chaps. 13 and 14 the EXODUS event (indeed the Pentateuch itself) comes to a climax. The promises to the ancestors are at the point of fulfillment. The goal toward which Israel was set free from Egypt and brought into covenant at Sinai is just over the horizon. The task for which the preparations described in the Book of Numbers should have equipped Israel is at hand. Israel has moved to the borders of the promised land. Spies have already checked it out. This is the moment in the ancient story—the moment when Israel is to "inherit" their homeland.

What was intended to be the beginning of Israel's glory, though, turns into abject shame. The climax fizzles. What was to have been a triumphal march into Canaan collapses in confusion, recriminations, failure, and condemnation.

14:1-4. A challenge. Most of the Israelites were convinced by the *unfavorable report* (13:32) brought back by a majority of the spies. "Canaan is a wonderful place, but there is no way that we can succeed in conquering it," they decided.

The report was a final straw for the easily discouraged ex-slave Israelites. People in the camp came unglued. They *raised a loud cry* and *wept* (v. 1). And they bitterly *complained*—again. Ever the victim, they blamed their leaders for liberating them. "After all we have been through, what does it come to? Our fighters will be cut to pieces. And our *wives and little ones* (v. 3) will be taken as spoils of war."

Let us choose a leader *(captain), and go* back where we belong, *back to Egypt* (v. 4). "Better the routines and securities of slavery than this!" The theme of the desire to return to Egypt is a common OT metaphor for apostasy (see Deut 17:16; Hos 7:11; Isa 30:1-7; 31:1-30; Jer 2:18; Ezek 17:15).

14:5-10a. The response of Moses and Aaron. *Moses and Aaron* recognize that matters have reached a critical juncture. All that God has done for Israel is on the line. They prostrate themselves in full view of *all the assembly* (v. 5). Joshua and Caleb urgently try to talk some sense into the crowd. They *tore their clothes* (v. 6), a sign of their shock and dismay at the people's disbelief. Not only is Canaan *an exceedingly good land*, they insisted (v. 7); defeating the natives will be "a piece of cake" because *the* LORD *is with us*. This talk of turning back is tantamount to insurrection or mutiny against Yahweh. But the irrational mob is in no mood to listen. They threaten *to stone* (v. 10) Joshua and Caleb on the spot.

Into this near-riot scene, Yahweh dramatically appears *at the tent* (v. 10). What Israel sees of his presence is *the glory*, understood as light that protects Israel from actually seeing God. The glory is sometimes associated with the column of cloud or fire (see v. 22; 16:19; Exod 16:6-7; 40:34; Ezek 11:23); it appears during times of crisis.

14:10b-38. The LORD **responds.** The message that God communicates through Moses is drastic: enough is enough. Yahweh has decided to *disinherit* (v. 12) and destroy these people and start over again, this time with Moses' family alone.

The root of the LORD's problem with Israel is described in two ways: they *despise* him and *they refuse to believe* (v. 11). Both phrases name an aberration of the heart and will, not just the mind only (in the NT the Gospel of John uses the phrase "believe in" in a similar manner: e.g., 3:15-16; 6:29, 47; 14:44). In his appeal to Yahweh on Israel's behalf, Moses begs God to remember the divine reputation and nature: "What will *the nations* think when you wipe out these people, and thus seem unable to do what you set out to do? Demonstrate your *power*, instead, by dealing graciously with Israel, as *you promised*" (cf. vv. 13-17; see also Exod 32:11-14; Deut 9:26-29).

The striking confession of faith about God's nature (v. 18) is probably from Israel's early worship (cf. Exod 34:6-7; Neh 9:17; Ps 103:8; Jer 32:18; Jonah 4:2). Moss appeals to God as a covenant-keeping God. The LORD is characterized by *steadfast love* (vv. 18-19), i.e., unwavering and unshakable fidelity to his covenant. God's covenant loyalty requires patience *(slow to anger)* and *forgiveness*—not only of *iniquity* (people's perverseness), but also deliberate rebellion *(transgression)*. What this nature does not require is that God shield the people from the consequences of their sin, even when those consequences play out to several generations.

Throughout the passage there is a sense of corporate sin and punishment. Yahweh agrees, once again, to forgive Israel, *just as* Moses *asked* (v. 20). But he swears an oath (*as I live*) that none of Moses' rebellious generation who have seen the LORD's *glory* and the signs he *did in Egypt and the wilderness* shall so much as *see the land* their ancestors were promised (v. 23)—only *Caleb* who had a *different spirit* (see below). With that, Yahweh orders Israel to turn back and to stay in the desert.

A priestly tradition (vv. 36-38) parallels the account of the LORD's refusal. Israel's lamenting wish (14:2) will be granted; their carcasses (lit.) will litter the desert. Everyone counted in the census (chap. 1) is condemned to a life of landlessness. They and their children will be shepherds (v. 33) or ass nomads. For *forty years* they will suffer the consequences of their whorishness (*faithlessness*, v. 33), i.e., alienation (*my displeasure*, v. 34) from the LAND and the LORD.

The spies who precipitated this turn of events bear a special condemnation. They all die of some unnamed *plague*, all except Joshua and Caleb. How quickly the ten spies died is not part of the narrative.

14:39-45. The people's response. Not unexpectedly, when *Moses told* Israel what God's new plan was, consternation broke out. It is almost as if the camp, with one voice, decided, "We did not really mean what we said. Rally round. Let's do that invasion—right now!" (v. 40).

Moses tries to warn Israel that their too-late enthusiasm and obedience are actually the same old rebellion that has been their downfall from the beginning. Any fight must conform to the rules of "holy war," that is, *the ark of the covenant*, signifying that *the LORD is . . . with* them, must head the formation (v. 42). When the attack is made, both *the ark* and *Moses* stay in the camp. The outcome is inevitable. The Amalekites and Canaanites cut Israel to pieces (cf. Deut 1:41-45).

Thus the great opportunity is aborted. History turns. Not for another generation will God's purpose be realized. And Israel will always know why the people who left Egypt with such high hopes wandered in the desert until they died.

Through hindsight this turn in events may not have been all bad. A generation arose who had not known the seductions of Egypt, who were toughened by years in the desert, who could be nurtured in the Mosaic faith—a generation more ready (perhaps) than their parents to be God's covenant people.

The reader will note in chap. 14 the editor's use of at least two traditions. The older tradition features Moses alone (e.g., vv. 10b-19) and speaks only of Caleb's survival and invasion (vv. 24-25). Many think that in this tradition only the south was spied out (13:22-33) after which a Caleb group settled there.

Cultic Laws and Regulations, 15:1-41

This priestly insertion into the account gives regulations about the quantities of flour, oil, and wine that are to accompany various animal sacrifices; about first-fruit offerings of cereal grain harvests; and about what to do about unintentional and deliberate sins, with an example of the latter.

The material illustrates how Jewish law developed in response to changing situations and needs. Most agree that this material is from the hand of priestly editors, and that it is late (as suggested by the parallels with exilic prophecy, e.g., Ezek 46). These editors are anxious to emphasize their faithfulness to the Mosaic tradition (vv. 1, 17, 22-23, 35, 37).

To the reader this passage (like 5:1–8:28) may seem an incongruous intrusion because it comes immediately after the dramatic events recounted in chap. 14. But, in fact, the introduction of these regulations is a reaffirmation of faith—faith that even though Israel had revolted against God and his covenant and rejected his offer of the land, Yahweh himself remained committed to his promises. Israel would surely *come into the land* and *inhabit* it (v. 2). They would surely have agricultural produce, cereal grains, olive oil, and wine to offer God. Only adult Israel had been defeated; the LORD had not. This passage may suggest, with Amos 5:25 and Jeremiah 7:22, that the sacrificial system did not mature until Israel became farmers.

15:1-21. Sacrifices and offerings. *An offering by fire* (v. 3) may have included those sacrifices burnt and those partially burnt and/or eaten. The vivid ANTHROPOMORPHISM, *a pleasing odor for the LORD* (vv. 3, 24), recalls a time when the effect of a sacrifice was understood more literally (cf. Gen 8:21 and the parallel in the *Gilgamesh Epic*). The phrase as it appears here merely suggests that the sacrifice is acceptable.

For each kind of animal sacrificed, a *lamb*, a goat (*ram*), or a *bull*, the amount of flour (*grain*) mixed with *oil* and the amount of *wine* (vv. 4-10) are specified. The WEIGHTS AND MEASURES mentioned can only be approximated by modern standards, e.g., *one-tenth of an ephah*≈four and one-half liters, and *one-fourth of a hin*≈one and eight-tenths liters. The regulations are to apply, without discrimination, to resident aliens as well (vv. 14-15, 26; cf. 9:14).

The *donation of the bread of the land* (v. 17) refers to cakes made from the first flour ground from the first grain harvested. As with all such offerings, this one acknowledges the LORD's ownership of the land and the farmers' dependence on God's control of the natural order. Note again the renewal of the promise inherent in the phrases, *after you come . . . and throughout your generations* (vv. 18, 21).

15:22-29. Atoning for inadvertent sins. Provisions are made both for inadvertent mistakes by the whole community or their leaders in carrying out the liturgy, and for unintended mistakes made by individuals (vv. 22-29; cf. Lev 4–5). Animal sacrifices, with the accompanying grain and drink offerings, are prescribed for *atonement* (vv. 25, 27) for each offense. The gifts that make up the sacrifice symbolize the reconciliation (at-one-ment) taking place. Covenant relations are restored.

15:30-36. Facing willful sin. No provision is made for atoning for highhanded sins, i.e., knowing, deliberate *affronts [to] the LORD* (v. 30). *Such a person shall be utterly cut off* (v. 31), having rejected the covenant community, which was in many cases tantamount to death. To be a person was to be in community.

Verses 32-36 illustrate a sin that is an affront to the LORD, a deliberate sabbath violation. The *whole congregation* is responsible for the indictment and for the execution by stoning (cf. Exod 31:14-15; 35:2).

15:37-41. Reminders for the forgetful. The old custom of attaching *fringes* to *garments* (v. 38) served as a continuous reminder that Israelites were a people of the law. The law, in turn, was a sign that they were a separated, unique (i.e., *holy*, v. 40) people.

Lest the reader forget, the motivation for obedience to the law is clearly stated in v. 41: Israel joyfully embraces the law out of gratitude for Yahweh's gracious acts on their behalf. Yahweh is their God, not as a result of their obedience, but as a result of what God did for them during the EXODUS. When the order is reversed—when the Exodus is understood as a reward for obedience—legalism or moralism results.

Revolts of Korah and Others, 16:1-50

The reader is immediately presented with another example of high-handed sin (cf. 15:30-36). Most scholars see in this section both the combination of the YAHWIST tradition with various priestly traditions, and a blending of three memories about revolts, the first led by Korah, the second led by Dathan and Abiram, and the third led by 250 lay Reubenites. It is very difficult to determine what lies behind the canonical accounts.

What is at stake is nonetheless clear. In chap. 14 we read of Israel's rejection of God's offer of the LAND. This chapter describes certain leaders' rejection of God's appointed leaders, Moses and especially Aaron and his descendants.

16:1-40. The revolts described. On its face, the rebels' complaint seems to have merit. *All the congregation are holy* (v. 3; cf. 15:40); therefore *you have gone too far when you exalt yourselves above the assembly of the LORD* (v. 3). The protesters seem to demand a democratization of leadership in general and the priesthood in particular. The ideal of a democracy seems harmonious with the conception of Israel implicit in 11:29 as a community of prophets who have the spirit of God.

Moses accuses Korah and his fellow Levites of being discontent with their place in the hierarchy, of seeking *the [Aaronite] priesthood as well* (v. 10). Dathan, Abiram and their followers reject Moses' leadership; he has not come through on his word and "lords it over" Israel, they complain.

To these challenges to the established order, Moses proposes a test. The test will show that Yahweh, not Moses and Aaron themselves, ordained Moses and Aaron's unique and supreme places. The challengers are told to act like priests, to burn incense *before the LORD* (at the TENT OF MEETING) and see if their service is acceptable to the LORD (vv. 16-18).

When the pretenders fulfill their part of the test, making sure the whole camp is present to see, Yahweh's *glory* appears, threatening to exterminate the whole crowd on the spot. Moses' intervention saves the people but not their leaders. To prove which side of the contention he is on, *the LORD creates* a creation (lit.), i.e., a singular disaster. The *ground opens its mouth and swallows them up* (v. 30). Korah, Dothan, Abiram, and their households, and all that they own fall down *alive into Sheol* (v. 33), the realm of the dead under the earth. The 250 would-be priests are consumed by fire from inside the tent as they enter to offer the incense.

Many scholars see all this as relevant to postexilic clerical conflicts, when a hierarchy was evolving (Budd 1984, 188–91). The position taken by the priestly editors is clear: *no outsider* (meaning Levite or layperson) *who is not of the descendants of Aaron* shall do priestly things (v. 40).

16:41-50. Aftershocks. When an angry crowd gathers to protest the wholesale killing of their rebellious leaders, once again God's *glory* (v. 42) appears. Again God threatens *the whole congregation* (v. 41). A plague breaks out (the nature of the pestilence is not described). Aaron is sent into the crowd, frantically to *make atonement* (v. 46, lit. "to cover," or "to protect" them from the plague). Carrying his priestly incense censer, forbidden to others, he takes his stand *between the dead and the living* (v. 48).

The point cannot be missed. Refusing to accept the supremacy of the Mosaic tradition and the Aaronite priesthood is tantamount to rebelling against Yahweh and his covenant. The punishment for such high-handed sins (cf. 15:30) is death.

Aaron's Budding Staff, 17:1-13

The lesson in chap 16 is negative. No one may act as priests in Israel except Aaron and his descendants. The point of the present passage is positive. Among all the tribes, the LORD has chosen Levi; and among the Levites, Aaron alone and supremely is to be priest.

Each tribe (*ancestral house*, v. 2) is instructed to bring the symbol of tribal authority, *the staff*, to Moses. The Hebrew text has a significant word play: the same word means "staff" and "tribe." The Levi staff is engraved with Aaron's name. That Levi is counted among the twelve tribes is unusual. All the staffs are left overnight *before the LORD* (v. 7), i.e., in front of the altar in *the tent of meeting* (v. 4). When the LORD causes only Aaron's staff to sprout and flourish, Israel takes it as a sign that Aaron is the LORD's choice as priest. The staff is stored in the shrine as a perpetual reminder of Aaron's role. The complaints are to stop. Israel recognizes that priests are essential protection; *everyone [else] who approaches the tabernacle of the LORD will die* (v. 12).

Duties and Support of Priests and Levites, 18:1-32

Following the reaffirmations of the Aaronite priesthood's role (chaps. 16–17), the priestly writer pulls together material that reaffirms the responsibility of the priests, establishes a theological rationale for the priesthood, defines the role of the Levites, and prescribes the means of support for both groups.

The priests are to protect Israel from the kind of dangers illustrated in chap. 16. Everything connected with the powerful "holiness" of God, especially the holy things at the sanctuary, is life threatening. *From now on* (6th or 5th century?) *the Israelites shall no longer approach the tent of meeting* (v. 22). Neither is any unauthorized person (*outsider*) permitted in the sanctuary (vv. 4, 7).

18:1-7. Duties of the priests and Levites. Aaron and his descendants shield Israel from the risks, serving in the tent of meeting as Israel's representative, *performing the duties of the sanctuary and . . . the altar* (v. 5). Further, they bear the responsibility if something is done incorrectly. The Levites cannot enter the shrine nor handle the sacred objects, but they serve the priests. Thus, they act as an outer buffer, protecting Israel, too. In these roles, the priests and Levites are *a gift* of Yahweh to Israel (vv. 6-7).

18:8-20. Support for the Aaronites. The rest of the chapter specifies how these clergy are to be supported. Since they have no inheritance (*no allotment in [the] land*, v. 20), they are to receive a portion of most offerings, plus an annual tithe. The reader is not told how this corresponds with the gift of cities and pastureland to the Levites in chap. 35:1-3.

The Aaronite priests are to live off the offerings given by Israelite farmers. Normally, these offerings are in kind, animals and/or produce. Burnt offerings are burnt up completely. Only the suet and some viscera of other sacrifices were burnt; the rest was eaten. "Peace" offerings (communions, or offerings of well-being) were eaten by the worshipers, after the right thigh and breast had been reserved for the priests. After they were consecrated, i.e., made "holy of holy," (*most holy*), most gifts became the property of the priests and their families, *holy to you*, i.e., set aside exclusively (vv. 9-10). Some offerings were restricted to the officiating priests only.

The plans for upkeep of the priesthood varied through Israel's history (cf. 1 Sam 2:12-17 and Deut 14:22-29). What is required in the Book of Numbers and in later Judaism is greater than before the Exile.

18:21-32. Support for the Levites. The Levites, whose role was subordinate to the Aaronite priests, were special as well. They were to be supported by annual tithes, i.e., one-tenth of all agricultural produce (cf. Deut 14:22-29). This was their *payment for* their *service in the tent of meeting* (v. 31). They, in turn, tithe *the best of all that is given them* to the Aaronite priests (vv. 29-30).

Laws of Purification: Death, 19:1-22

In animistic societies death is often understood as a thing, almost a substance. Death, therefore is considered dangerous. It can contaminate anything that it touches (cf. 5:2-3). Touching a corpse is a powerful taboo. Since touching corpses cannot be totally avoided, such societies devise elaborate rites to cleanse the contamination by some type of ritual.

As late as the priestly writer's time, Jewish belief and practice about death seems still to have retained some such associations. Acculturation issues, i.e., how one incorporates the essence of beliefs and practices into a more sophisticated religion without adulterating that religion, continue to be crucial issues.

The mystifying rite of the *red heifer* (v. 2) has always intrigued readers. Its purpose clearly is to provide materials and rites by which persons who have touched a corpse can be detoxified. A sacrifice seems to be made; a heifer is ritually slaughtered. But no priest does the slaughter. The sacrifice takes place away from the shrine—even *outside* the *camp* (v. 3). Every part of the animal is burned up, even *its skin* and *blood* (v. 5). The animal must be female, not male. It must be *red*. Various unusual materials are thrown on the fire (v. 6). The ashes are collected and stored. That which is to cleanse, the ashes, contaminates temporarily. And any *clean person* (vv. 18-19) may manipulate the *water for cleansing* (v. 9), not just a priest.

Israelites *who touch a corpse* (v. 13) are sternly warned and branded unclean for *seven days* (v. 14). Some of the ashes from the heifer are mixed with *running water* to make some "water of purification" (v. 17). On the third and seventh day of a person's ritual impurity, cleansing shall be effected by dashing the person with the water of purification.

Heifer is the traditional English translation, though "cow" may do as well. She must be without ritual defect and without previous service, v. 2. Why *red*? Both the heifer and the *crimson material* (v. 6, "stuff," or "*thread*") may suggest the use of blood (the seat of life) as a powerful antidote to death. Aromatic *cedarwood* and *hyssop* (NEB: "marjoram") also may have been thought to have cleansing powers (see Lev 14:4). Everyone who handles the ashes becomes temporarily unclean (vv. 7-8, 10).

In a day when the spread of deadly infection was not understood, many precautions were taken to avoid accidental contamination by death (vv. 14-16). No doubt experience had taught that death imperiled the entire community. Failure to cleanse it was taken seriously. The holiness of the community was at risk (v. 13). The penalty was isolation and thus death (vv. 13, 20). The location of these rituals just here is appropriate, following the description of so much death in chap. 14.

Last Days at Kadesh: Moses' Sin and Edom's Blockade, 20:1-21

20:1-13. Moses' offense. Having said little about events during most of the remaining years in the desert, the writer moves to two final incidents at *Kadesh* (v. 1).

Israel's first generation was a rebellious generation. The people themselves continually complained and lacked trust (chaps. 11, 12, and 14). The priestly clans were no better; they fought over position (chaps. 16 and 17). In this section we read of the rebellious nature of Moses himself.

The priestly writer has given distinctive shape to a memory about God's giving Israel water at a place called *Meribah* (v. 13). In Exod 17:1-9 the incident is told to underscore God's providing grace. Here the account explains why Moses was not permitted to enter the promised LAND of Canaan.

The litany of whining and complaint is familiar: "Why have you (Moses) done this to us? Liberating us? Putting us at risk?" The specific quarrel (the term used has legal connotations, v. 3; see also the NRSV note at v. 13 that gives "quarrel" as a possible translation for *Meribah*) is: *no water to drink* (v. 5). When Moses and Aaron prostrate themselves at *the tent*, God grants them another theophany. Moses is told to take *the staff* (v. 8), *the one before the* LORD (v. 9), and *command the rock*

... *to yield its water* (v. 8). Whether this is Moses' staff (Exod 17:5), or Aaron's budding staff (Num 17:1-11) is unclear.

Before Moses does as he is told, he makes a speech (v. 10). Is there rashness in what he says (see Ps 106:32-33)? When he strikes the rock, the congregation is given water *abundantly* (v. 11). Does Moses go beyond his mandate when he strikes the rock? When he strikes it *twice*? In the Exodus account (17:6), he is commanded to strike the rock. What he did or did not do is described as *rebellion* (v. 24; cf. 27:14). And he is told, *you shall not bring* Israel *into the land* (v. 12).

What did Moses do that was so odious? Does he claim credit for the miracle? Is that the rashness in his speech? Was he driven to exasperation by these people's impossible griping, so that his downfall is anger (see Deut 1:3; 3:26; 4:21)? The writer states the reason enigmatically: *You did not trust in me*, thus failing *to show* Yahweh's *holiness* (v. 12).

The traditions all agree that Moses did not take part in the settlement of Canaan. A reason for that is given. But nothing is said that could dislodge Moses from his central place in Jewish faith and history.

20:14-21. The message to Edom's king. With the request to *the king of Edom* (v. 14), Israel begins the move from the *Kadesh* area to the Transjordan. As part of the request to Edom, the writer includes a version of Israel's confession of faith—reciting the mighty acts of God in the Exodus. Note the use of first person pronouns by which later Israel expressed solidarity with that Exodus generation.

Israel requests and is refused passage through the area east of the ARABAH, *Edom*, along the caravan route up on the plateau, called *the Kings' Highway* (v. 17, not a constructed road, as it later would be). This incident reflects an ancient rivalry between brothers (Gen 25:19-26, the story that provides the point of departure for the subsequent struggles between ESAU and JACOB who become the eponymous ancestors for EDOM and ISRAEL). The fact that a settled and strong king controls Edom is often used as evidence in dating the Exodus. Israel must make a detour around Edom. Why Israel, off to the west of Kadesh, would request a south-north passage through Edom is not explained (cf. Deut 2:1-15; Judg 11:7-18).

March Towards Transjordan: Aaron's Death, 20:22-29

This paragraph heightens the sense of transition. The old, rebellious generation has died (or are dying off). The years in the desert at Kadesh are ending.

Israel's route and the location of *Mount Hor* (v. 22) cannot be determined. Ancient tradition put the mountain near Petra in Edom—much too far east.

When it became clear that Aaron was dying, Moses took him and his eldest son, *Eleazar*, to *the top of the mountain* (v. 28). Aaron's priestly *vestments* (see Exod 28; Lev 8:7-9) were taken from him and put on his son. Thus, continuity in the priesthood was insured, despite Aaron's rebellion (v. 24).

Aaron's death is described in ways that suggest an importance comparable with Moses'. He dies on a mountain; and he is mourned *thirty days* (v. 29), rather than the customary seven (cf. 33:38-39; Deut 10:6).

On the Way: Victory and Suffering, 21:1-20

21:1-3. Arad destroyed. The fight at *Hormah* (v. 3) seems to interrupt the sequence of events, as Israel moves east from Kadesh. The account may be another version of a Judah clan's successful settlement in the northern Negeb (see Judg 1:16-17). Recounting the incident at this juncture signals a change in Israel's fortunes. From this point, Yahweh enables a more responsive Israel to succeed. Many of the places named cannot be specifically identified (Noth 1968, 155, mentions the generality of the names). After some reverses, Israel vows complete loyalty to Yahweh. They promise to *utterly destroy* these *Canaanites* (v. 2), i.e., they put them under "the ban" and the battle is fought as a HOLY WAR. The verb *utterly destroy* and the place name *Hormah* derive from the same Hebrew root *ḥ rm*.

21:4-9. The journey south. Israel moves south, not north (vv. 1-3), this time on the RED SEA/REED SEA route (?), beginning their detour around Edom. On the long journey people grow *impatient* (v. 4) once more. Again they protest about the *miserable food* (cf. 11:4-6). The punishment for their lack of confidence in God is a plague of *poisonous* (lit. "fiery") *serpents* (v. 6). The name *seraphim* may refer to their burning bite or to their appearance (see Deut 8:15; Isa 6:2; 14:29).

When *the people* confess their sin (v. 7), Moses intercedes on their behalf. He is instructed to make an image of a *poisonous snake* (v. 8). The image is made of *bronze* (v. 9) and mounted on top of a pole. Those who look at the image are healed of their snakebites. An intimation of magic lurks under the surface (cf. 1 Sam 6:4); therefore, the episode often has been spiritualized, e.g., Wis 16:5-7 and John 3:14.

In Hezekiah's temple a bronze snake image called Nehushtan had become a magic fetish of healing to which Israel burned incense (2 Kgs 18:4). Nehushtan was attributed to Moses. Some think, instead, that the image was a Jebusite fetish incorporated into Israel's cultus (Snaith 1967, 280). Others think that the YAHWIST is accepting the Mosaic origin of the image, but making plain its original use—against any magical or cultic use (Budd 1984, 233, 235).

21:10-20. The journey north. Essentially, vv. 10-20 are an itinerary of Israel's movements after having skirted Edom. Again, the places listed cannot be identified. The itinerary ends at Mount Pisgah, east of the northern end of the DEAD SEA, with Israel poised to enter Canaan. Attempts to work out from the accounts one straightforward itinerary for Israel have been unsuccessful.

The two song fragments are inserted following catchwords: *Arnon* . . . *Arnon* (vv. 13, 14) and *Beer* (=well) . . . *well* (vv. 16, 17). The Hebrew text of the poetry is difficult to decipher. *The Book of the Wars of the* LORD (v. 14) is mentioned only here (cf. "the Book of Jashar," Josh 10:13; 2 Sam 1:18). The second piece of a song seems to celebrate a new well. Evidently, both songs had become traditional by the time of the composition of the Book of Numbers.

The purpose of this section seems to be to summarize Israel's advance from the borders of Moab, *the Arnon*, to those of Canaan, *the top of Pisgah*, accenting the LORD's provision on the way.

Conquests and Settling In, 21:21–36:13

Defeat of Two Kingdoms: Sihon and Og, 21:21-35

Israel's success on the battlefield, anticipated in 21:1-3, now occupies center stage. A desert-hardened generation is portrayed sweeping up the Transjordan, destroying everything in its path.

21:21-32. The defeat of Sihon. The first victim is *Sihon, king* of Jordan, between *the Arnon* and *the Jabbok* (v. 24; cf. Deut 2:26-37). The term Amorites may be a synonym for the general term Canaanites. Israel asks Sihon for passage and is refused. The wording is similar to the request put to Edom in 20:17. When Sihon tries to back up his refusal with force, *Israel put him to the sword, and took possession of his land* (v. 24). Israel's displacement is described as total: *all of the towns*, including the main site, *Heshbon, and all its villages* (v. 25). This is the first account of Israel's actually capturing territory and settling in it.

A traditional taunt song, perhaps of Amorite origin, is used to mock Heshbon in defeat, vv. 27-30 (see another version in Jer 48:45-56). "Look what has happened to Heshbon," the balladeer sings, "who once *devoured . . . Moab*, who made the Moabite god, *Chemosh*, seem a servant of Sihon." The Hebrew text of v. 30 is not fully intelligible.

The Yahwist's telling of the conquest raises, at this and subsequent points, at least two issues. First, the picture of total displacement of the Amorite natives and total control of the entire Transjordan is not easy to square with the evidence in the Book of Judges. The struggle took centuries. At first, Israel only controlled pockets of territory (cf. Judg 3:12; 10:17). Second, some of the sites mentioned were not occupied until later, e.g., Heshbon in the eighth century. A separate tradition about the conquest of an area a few mi. south of the Jabbok called *Jazer* is mentioned briefly (v. 31). *Moses* figures in this account.

21:33-35. The defeat of Og. The story of the dispossession of *Og*, the king of *Bashan* (vv. 33-35), seems to be paraphrased from Deut 3:1-7. The plateau north of the Jabbok was famous for its pasturelands and fine animals. Again, as in the case of Hormah (21:1-3), Bashan is put under the ban and *no survivor* is *left* (v. 35). Interestingly, property is not devoted to Yahweh. The point is transparent: when Israel trusts the LORD, when they obey him and the rules of holy war, they are victorious. Inheriting the promised land of Canaan has begun.

Balaam and Balak, 22:1–24:25

22:1-5. Into the Jordan valley. The conquest of the Transjordan, from the Arnon to Bashan, is complete. Israel is *camped in the plains of Moab*, i.e., in the Jordan's rift valley, poised *across the Jordan from Jericho* (v. 1) and Canaan's central highlands.

As a pause in the action, the narrator tells a fascinating story. The story of an eastern diviner, BALAAM, and a Moabite king, Balak, dramatically spotlights God's historic intentions in what is happening.

Evidently, Balaam was a common figure in near eastern folklore, like NOAH, JOB, and DANIEL. Using some of that folklore and some ancient prophetic oracles, the writer weaves a funny, satirical, enigmatic tale. And in the process he proclaims some of "the most far-reaching and positive visions of Israel's future found in the entire Pentateuch" (Ackerman 1987, 87).

The story line is easy to follow. Moab, seeing Israel's successes and numbers, hires a professional diviner with a fine reputation to put a curse on Israel. The diviner, Balaam, first refuses and then comes. Three times, elaborate preparations are made for his occult arts to work; each time Balaam blesses Israel instead. Completely exasperated, the king of Moab sends Balaam home.

Interpretations of the story have varied widely. Efforts to sort out YAHWIST and ELOHIST sources for the narrative have not been widely accepted. Discrepancies, however, are not easily papered over (e.g., God instructs Balaam to go with Balak's emissaries [22:20] but then is angry with him for going; Balaam leaves with those officials [22:21], but is accompanied by only two of his young servants [22:22]).

Is Balaam a true prophet of Yahweh or a self-serving shaman? The thrust of chaps. 22–24 is essentially positive, although at times ambivalent. But subsequent traditions portray Balaam as out for personal gain or in league with evil (see Num 25:1-18; 31:8, 16; Deut 23:3-6; Josh 13:22; 24:9-10; 29:9-10; Mic 6:5; Neh 13:2; 2 Pet 2:15-16; Jude 11; Rev 2:14).

Archaeological evidence from the sixth century suggests that Balaam was a popular figure from Transjordan. But 22:5 describes him as coming from Mesopotamia, *the land of Amon*, from a town called *Pethor*, i.e., Pitru near CARCHEMISH. His first oracle says that he was *from Aram* (23:7).

22:6-21. Negotiations. *Balak* summons Balaam to *curse this people for me* (22:6), so as to offset Israel's advantages against him. A belief in the efficacy of words in general and blessings and curses in particular lies behind the request. Because of his famous gifts as a diviner, Balaam's curses are expected to be especially effective (22:6). The representatives of the king are variously called *messengers* (22:5), *elders* (22:7), and *officials* (princes, 22:8, 13, 15, 21, 35, 40). They are sent off with the customary *fees for divination in . . . hand*. Balaam will not agree to go with them until he has consulted Yahweh (22:8), which he does at nighttime—presumably through dreams (cf. 22:20, 24:1). That a Mesopotamian diviner knows *the LORD* is not explained. Note the uses of the divine name, Yahweh, and the more generic Elohim, *God*, throughout the narrative.

The answer comes: do not go. *The LORD has refused* (22:14). Nonetheless, Balak persists. This time his emissaries are *more numerous and more distinguished* (22:15). They promise *great honor* (22:17, no doubt including a large fee). If that is how it is, Balaam wonders if Yahweh *my God* might not have *more to say* to him

(22:19)! This time the LORD agrees. Perhaps there is some wish-fulfillment in Balaam's dream?

22:22–24:25. The oracles of Balaam. Thus is the stage set for the popular story of Balaam's talking she-donkey. Interpreters naturally have difficulty with this story. Either they studiously avoid the talking part, or they soberly explain it, e.g., "men have sometimes sensed that God's creatures spoke to them" (Thompson 1970, 191). Israel plainly delighted in telling of the day a dumb donkey could see more clearly what God wanted than a famous Mesopotamian seer. The story is laced with irony and satire. The earnest conversation between Balaam and his donkey should not be read with a straight face.

The angel (lit., "messenger") is a manifestation *of the LORD* (v. 22) present. The angel speaking is the LORD speaking (cf. 22:35). That God is angry with Balaam for doing what he has just been told to do passes without comment. Triads are used as a literary device throughout the narrative: The angel appears three times, sacrifices are offered three times, Balaam pronounces three initial and three final oracles.

When Balaam finally sees what his beast has seen all along, the angel reveals that he (the angel) has come to Balaam as *an adversary* (Heb: "a satan"; cf. Job 1:6-9; Zech 3:1; 1 Chr 21:1) to divert him from his dangerous journey. Balaam offers to go back home, but the angel encourages him to go on, now that he has been vividly warned again to *speak only what I tell you to speak* (22:35).

When Balak and Balaam finally meet, Balak upbraids Balaam for being slow to recognize his opportunity, and Balaam responds by warning Balak that he may not get the curse he has ordered. *Do I have the power to say just anything?* (22:38) he plaintively asks. Balak pretends not to hear and prepares a great feast for everybody, 22:40.

The series of three great sacrifices, three revelations from Yahweh, and three oracles by Balaam (22:41-24:9) follows a pattern building up dramatic interest. Balaam is taken to different vantage points where he can see *part of the people of Israel* and, finally, *to the top of Peor* (23:28), where he *saw Israel camping tribe by tribe* (24:2). Each time *seven altars* are built and *seven bulls* and *seven rams* are sacrificed, presumably as part of the rites of divination. The reader recognizes that seven is a sacred number.

The first time Balaam consults Yahweh the seer is cagey: *perhaps the LORD will come to meet me* (23:3). God does *put a word in* his *mouth* (23:5). But it is not the *oracle* (a message a seer gets when he consults his god) that Balak wants. The LORD will not curse Israel, so Balaam cannot. Israel is not like other *nations*; their number is vast (23:9). The promise to the patriarchs has been fulfilled (cf. Gen 22:17, 32:12). The first oracle ends with a "so-help-me-God" oath (23:10b).

The keystone cops atmosphere increases the second time around. "What's going on?" Balak shouts. "I paid you good money. You're supposed to be cursing these people!" "What comes in is what goes out," Balaam retorts (23:12). This time

Balaam does not go to a remote place (23:3, *a bare height*) to seek the oracle. "You people wait here," he instructs. "I will *meet the* LORD *over there*" (23:15).

The second oracle (23:18-26) reinforces the first. *God is not a human being* (v. 19, Heb. "son of man") who will *change his mind*. Yahweh, Israel's *God*, is *acclaimed as a king among them* (v. 21). God's KINGSHIP is an elemental theme in the OT. God will not abandon his people. He is raw power (*like the horns of a wild ox*, v. 22) available to them. And they are like a bloodthirsty lioness/lion that has only begun to ravage. No amount of skilful *enchantment* or *divination* can stop them (v. 23). Balaam again pleads his own inculpability: *whatever the* LORD *says, that is what I must do* (v. 26).

After the third series of sacrifices, Balaam did not bother to go aside *to look for omens* (24:1). Nevertheless, this time *the spirit of God came upon him*.

In the early history of Israel such spirit possession often threw people into frenzies and/or trances. It was the sign of authentic prophetic inspiration. The first verses of the oracle speak of that kind of ecstatic state. The seer *falls down* (24:4), *but with eyes uncovered*, that is, able truly to see. In this heightened state *his eye is clear* (24:3; cf. 11:25-26, 29).

The ORACLE itself describes Israel as owner of the land, a land where water is abundant and exotic plants luxuriate, a land governed by a powerful king. Like a *wild ox*, God destroys all Israel's *foes* (24:8). And a final oracle is for Israel themselves:

Blessed is everyone who blesses you
And cursed is everyone who curses you (24:9b).

This is the final straw for Balak. In a rage he strikes *his hands together* (24:10, a sign of contempt) and bitterly dismisses his famous seer. Before he leaves, though, Balaam defends himself with an "I told you so" reflection on what had happened. Whether Balak wants it or not, Balaam also unburdens himself of a prediction about Israel (note the repeated oracle about prophetic inspiration, 24:15-16, emphasizing the authenticity of the message). An Israelite king (*a star . . . a scepter*) shall come to power and *crush* all Israel's nearby neighbors. This may be an allusion to the conquering David and his empire, or an allusion to the northern kingdom. Balaam has finally pronounced a curse—but it falls on Moab (24:17c).

The narrative ends with three short, obscure oracles about various peoples (24:20-24). The Amalekites and the Kenites were ancient opponents of Israel who lived to the south of Judah.

It is difficult to make out whom 24:23-24 refers to. The MT is obscure. The usual guess, picking up on the mention of *Kittim* (v. 24, Cyprus), is to read the oracle as a reference to the SEA PEOPLES. Most students think the oracles themselves to be examples of early Hebrew poetry, perhaps from the tenth century. Anticlimactically, *Balaam got up and went back to his place and Balak also went his way* (24:25).

Why were this lengthy story and these oracles included by the priestly writer? The pleasures of making fun of a famous Eastern seer who could not see, and of a foreign king who could not buy a curse he wanted cannot be dismissed. But more serious purposes may be at work, too. The best of Oriental occult arts is exposed as impotent when challenged by Israel's God. God's ancient promises to Israel are reaffirmed. Yahweh controls history. Israel's historic destiny is unstoppable. Their enemies are powerless. While Balak and Balaam go through their little charade off in the heights, Israel, oblivious of what is happening, readies itself for conquest. And, ironically, the unsurpassed words of praise and promise for Israel come from the mouth of Balaam of Pethor.

The Peor Affair, 25:1-18

While Israel is poised on the plains of Moab ready to enter the promised LAND, rebellion erupts once again. And a purging is once again necessary.

For the narrative, two different memories seem to be used (cf. vv. 1-5 and vv. 6-18). Did the writer know Ps 106:28-31 and Hos 9:10? Several of the phrases are quite obscure, using words found only here. Generally, the passage is a polemic against Palestinian fertility rites and a legitimation of Phinehas' priesthood (cf. Ezra 8:2; 1 Chr 9:29; 24:3).

Israel was always attracted to the various Canaanite fertility cults. Perennially they had problems coaxing their land to produce. To the superstitious, BAAL worship seemed to lessen the insecurities of farming in such a place. More basically, the fertility rites claimed to offer ways to get the gods to do what people needed/wanted—in stark contrast to the demands of Yahwism.

25:1-5, 16-18. Prohibitions against the Moabites. *Sexual relations* with foreign women are linked with participation in a foreign cultus, which is linked to a baal. Eating and *sacrifices* are virtually synonymous (v. 2). *The LORD's anger* against this apostasy demands punishment for the leaders (v. 4 *chiefs of the people*). Exactly what the punishment was is uncertain. *The judges* who carry out the sentences are only to target guilty individuals (v. 5). The word *yoked* is used only here (vv. 3, 5; cf. Hos 9:10; Ps 106:28).

This brief treatment of the troubles at Peor concludes with an explanation why the Israelites later attack Midian (see chap. 31).

25:6-15. The example of Phinehas. The story about Phinehas assumes a correlation between *the women of Moab* (v. 1) and *a Midianite woman* (v. 6). The sin of the Israelite man, later identified as *Zimri son of Salu*, may have been marriage to a foreign woman, *Cozbi daughter of Zur* (v. 14). More likely the sin was his defiant acts during a sacred lament over Israel's sin and punishment. There is also the impression that he is guilty of some cultic action in the midst of the camp. The word play between *the tent* (v. 8) and *the belly* (v. 9)—both words are derived from the same Hebrew root—suggests a relationship between the immorality at Peor and an assault on Israel's worship. *The tent* is an inner chamber or shrine.

Phinehas proves his *zeal* (= *jealousy*) for cultic purity by running through both of them with his *spear*, thus stopping *the plague* (v. 8), but not before *twenty-four thousand* people had died. He is said to have *made atonement for the Israelites* (v. 13), that is, he "covered" their guilt so that their relations with the LORD could be good again. As a reward Phinehas is granted *a covenant of peace*, interpreted to mean *perpetual* tenure in the *priesthood* (v. 13).

A Second Census, 26:1-65

The wilderness narrative began with a census of Israel in chap. 1; it ends with another one. If the first census represented the final stage in the constitution of Israel for its mission, this census represents a re-constitution. The generation of former slaves who failed the tests of fidelity have passed off the scene. A generation disciplined in the desert is now ready to occupy the land promised their parents.

The two censuses are alike and different. Both reckon military strength, *men from twenty years old* who are *able to go to war* (v. 2). The second also looks to an apportionment of the land. The tribes are listed in the same order as before, with the exception that Manasseh comes first this time. To this list are attached lists of clan names (cf. the list in Gen 46:8-27). The totals arrived at are little different from those in chap. 3. Clan totals are not given, only the cumulative totals for each tribe (suggesting that the family-clan names have been added to the list—from Gen 46?).

Verse 4 presents a textual problem: v. 4c seems incongruous since *those who came out of Egypt* are precisely the ones *not* being counted. The large numbers reported present the same problems here as found in chap. 1. Two different criteria are put forth for deciding each tribe's apportionment of land; the size of the tribe (vv. 53-54), and the casting of lots (v. 55). Verse 56 tries to combine the two criteria.

Moses oversees the division of the land. His presence and role suggest that the allocations of tribal boundaries were based on the word of *the LORD* through Moses (v. 52). Other traditions trace the division of the land to a decision Joshua made by casting lots at Shiloh (cf. Josh 18:10).

As in the first census, a separate census is also made of the Levites (cf. 3:14–4:49). A similar total is given in both lists. The same three clan names are given in chap. 3 and v. 57, but in vv. 58-61 the list of sons is different. The Levites are not counted in the general census because they do not share in the apportionment of land. However, they do receive towns and pastureland (see 35:1-8).

The point of the second census is underscored in vv. 63-65. This census marks the end of the Exodus generation: *not one of those enrolled* in this census was old enough to be counted in the first census—*except Caleb . . . and Joshua*. A new Israel is ready.

Daughters of Zelophehad, 27:1-11

The allocation of ancestral land (anticipated by the census, chap. 26) is to be perpetual. The LAND is Yahweh's; his apportionment of it is a gracious gift. Land is not to be alienated from the family to whom it is given. Normally it is passed to the eldest son (Deut 21:15-17). When a man died leaving no sons, levirate marriage laws required the deceased's brother to take the widow as his wife and to have a son (Deut 25:5-10). If these provisions failed, the nearest kinsman was to "redeem" the land for the family (cf. Jer 32:6-15). Jubilee laws would have required sold or confiscated land to revert to the original family every fifty years (Lev 25, esp. v.23).

The daughters of Zelophehad introduce a case of a man survived only by daughters. *Zelophehad . . . of Manasseh* died in the desert. He did nothing that would cause his family to be excluded from the allotment of land. Yet his only heirs were daughters.

The daughters contend that refusing to give them *a possession* would be tantamount to taking away their father's *name* (v. 4), i.e., causing him never to have existed. Without a sense of life after death, Hebrews believed that the perpetuation of a person's character, reputation, and name were closely linked to the land.

Here we meet case law being developed to apply the general Mosaic principles to specific situations. The daughters are granted an allotment. And a line of inheritance contingencies is worked out (vv. 8-11).

The ruling suggests that Hebrew women were not shut out of the inheritance system. However, the passage is concerned primarily with keeping the land in the family. Other contingencies would arise, as chap. 36 illustrates.

Following Snaith (1966, 126-27) some have wondered if this passage is not an explanation of why Manasseh ended up with allotments on the west bank of the Jordan, too.

Joshua's Commissioning, 27:12-23

As events move towards the invasion of Canaan proper, God communicates to Moses a sense of his imminent death. Moses is to ascend a mountain in *the Abarim range* (v. 12). Nebo also was part of this range (cf. Deut 32:49). There he could view a panorama of the central highlands. There he would die. Moses' sin is again described in terms like those used in 20:12-13.

Moses asks that a successor be chosen and installed. In v. 16 Yahweh is addressed as *the God of the spirits of all flesh*, i.e., all humanity. Moses fears Israel's becoming leaderless, *without a shepherd*, especially as they wage war, *go out . . . come in* (v. 17).

The LORD designates *Joshua* as Israel's next leader (v. 18). Joshua has already appeared in the account, at Moses' side (11:28; cf. Exod 17:8-13; 24;13; 33:11). *The spirit* in Joshua has long marked him out. The term "spirit" suggests some extraordinary God-given abilities.

Joshua is *commissioned* in a ceremony as he stands before Eleazar, Aaron's successor. Moses lays *his hand upon* Joshua, an ancient symbol for imparting blessing. *Some of* Moses' *authority* (Heb. *hod*, "prestige," "honor," "vitality") passes to Joshua, but he is not a second Moses. God communicated with Moses directly and personally (12:6-8). Joshua must get his instruction from God via the priest, with whom the LORD will communicate his instruction by means of the sacred lots URIM AND THUMMIM, even in the conduct of war (v. 21). The precise way the priests manipulated the Urim and Thummim remains a mystery (see Exod 28:30-31; 1 Sam 14:41-42; 28:6; Ezra 2:63; Neh 7:65). The commissioning of Joshua provides a glimpse of a theocracy, with priests in control.

With the installation of Eleazar as priest (20:23-29) and Joshua as military leader, continuity is assured in Israel's government.

Laws Concerning Offerings and Festivals, 28:1–29:40

The modern reader may be tempted to spiritualize—or dismiss altogether—this detailed section of the Book of Numbers. A clear grasp of what the priestly writer is doing here is necessary to take the passage seriously. The writer draws together and systematizes various cultic regulations into a comprehensive CALENDAR of sacrifices and festivals. Materials found in Exod 29, Lev 23, and Ezek 45–56 provide a broader picture of the assumptions that undergird worship. A cultic calendar of sacrifices for the entire year is laid out: daily, at *morning* and *twilight* (28:1-8); *sabbath* (28:9-10); the new moon (28:11-15); *unleavened bread* and *passover* (28:16-25); *firstfruits* or *weeks* (28:26-31); the new year, i.e., *the first day of the seventh month* (29:1-6); the day of *atonement* (29:7-11); and tabernacles (29:12-38). Passover, although a family sacrifice rather than a community-wide sacrifice, is listed for completeness. Sabbath was not a festive day for families.

Individual and shared offerings are not denigrated (29:39), but attention is focused on those sacrifices that are solely Yahweh's, *offering by fire* (28:3, 6, 8, 13, 19, 24; 29:6, 13, 36), which is burned up completely. In the case of the festivals *a sin offering*, always *a male goat* (28:15, 22; 29:5, 11, 16, 19, 22, 25, 28, 31, 34, 38), is also required. Such offerings covered offenses that would make the community ritually unclean. Thus, they are referred to several times as an *atonement*. Animal, cereal, and drink sacrifices are all specified. Quantities are stipulated and are often generous, sometimes extravagant, e.g., see the first day of tabernacles (29:12-16). The concern seems to be that Israel insure that they are fit for worship and that they dedicate themselves to costly worship.

Israel's worship calendar varied through the years. Most scholars think that this calendar represents the latest development to be found in the Pentateuch. It reflects the community's practice after the Exile.

The *sabbath* (28:9-10) was a day of rest and did not become a day of worship until after the Exile. The new moon festival evidently was significant (28:11-15; see also 1 Sam 20:5; Amos 8:4). The reasons for its importance are not known.

After the exile, the sacred *seventh month* became important and was much elaborated (29:7-11). The day of atonement (*holy convocation*) mentioned in 29:7-11, is not found in preexilic Israel. Noth suggests as a better translation for *holy convocation*, "holy proclamation" (28:18, 25-26, 29:1, 7, 12 [Noth 1968, 220]).

Laws Concerning Women's Vows, 30:1-16

The law concerning vows was clear (Lev 5:4, Deut 23:21-23). The vows should be fulfilled exactly—*a man shall not break his word* (v. 2). Failure to make good on a vow exposed a person to God's judgment. The law assumed that the person making the vow had the autonomy and the means to do what he vowed; and the law assumed the person was male.

What then about women, who would lack the independence or the resources to carry out their vows? In Israel's patriarchal society, a woman was under the authority of her father or husband. Usually, she would be dependent on her father or husband for the means to fulfill her vow. If he refused to support her in her vow, she was exposed to the danger of nonfulfillment. So, the law made the father or husband equally liable, as soon as he heard of the vow.

Provision is made for vows by a young unmarried woman (vv. 3-5) or by a married woman. The provisions for a married woman are similar to those for an unmarried one, whether she took the vow before she married (vv. 6-8) or after (vv. 10-15). Only *a widow* and *a divorced woman* could assume a vow on her own (v. 9).

Since the father or husband becomes liable, he can, when he first learns of the vow, disallow it. The vow thence becomes void, no danger to anyone. *The LORD will forgive her* (vv. 5, 8, 12). However, if he fails to act when he first hears of the vow, it stands. He becomes responsible. He cannot dawdle, vacillate, or change his mind. Vows to the LORD are to be fulfilled.

The terms "vow" and "pledge" are inclusive (v. 3). The *vow* refers to a promise to give something to God, e.g., Hannah's vow to give her son (1 Sam 1:9-11) The *pledge* refers to an oath to abstain from something for the LORD's sake, e.g., the Nazirite vows Hannah promised her son would live by (1 Sam 1:11; cf. Num 6:1-21).

Holy War Against Midian, 31:1-54

This chapter describes the last military action of Moses, how Israel would behave during and after holy war (if they were obedient), and a foretaste of the battles and victories that lay ahead. The account is so exaggerated, idealized, and stylized that one may easily dismiss it. It is probably best, with Snaith (1967, 324), to read chap. 31 as a midrash, that is, a theological reflection on an event.

The identification of Moabites and Midianites in the account of the Peor affair (25:1-18) and the instruction to *harass the Midianites*, and *defeat them* (25:16), along with the information in Josh 13:21 about the defeat of Midianite kings, become the grist for the reflection. Holy war is declared on Midian *to execute the LORD's vengeance* and to *avenge the Israelites* (vv. 2-3).

A 1,000-fighter contingent is required from each tribe, large and small, vv. 4-5. Thus, the victory is to be equally everyone's. Out ahead of the ranks of the fighters are *Phinehas*, the zealous *priest* (see 25:7-13), *the vessels of the sanctuary*, and the trumpets, v. 6. This is Yahweh's fight, and these are the symbols of his leadership.

The absence of the most powerful symbol of the LORD's leadership in battle—the ark of the covenant—is not explained (cf. 10:35-36; 14:44; 1 Sam 4:4).

The destruction is massive. *Every male* Midianite is killed (v. 7), including the famous seer BALAAM. Vast numbers of women, children, animals and goods are taken *as booty* (v. 9). All the towns and villages are *burned* (v. 10). In accordance with the requirements of the "ban" of HOLY WAR, everything is "devoted" to Yahweh.

Still Moses is unsatisfied. The women who had seduced Israel into the Peor affair must not be spared. So, only females who were virgins are spared. The genocide is thorough. A strong Midianite presence in the Transjordan during the era of the judges (Judg 6–8) is curious in light of this passage.

Most of the narrative deals with the aftermath of the battle, especially with the division of the spoils taken. First, care is taken to fulfill the demands for ritual purification (vv. 7-24). All contamination caused by contact with corpses must be cleansed, including every tool and bit of clothing that may have touched a corpse (see chap. 19). This is the only OT instance of cleansing by *fire* (v. 23).

A full *inventory* is taken of the *booty captured* (vv. 25-26). The totals amaze: *sheep*—675,000; *oxen*—72,000; *donkeys*—61,000; and virgins—32,000. This inventory is made in order to share the goods with the priests and the Levites. Everything (including the virgins?) is divided into halves (cf. 1 Sam 30:24-25), half for *the warriors* and half for all *the congregation* (v. 27). The fighters are required to give one five-hundredth to the priests *as a tribute for the LORD* (v. 28). From the peoples' share, one-fiftieth goes *to the Levites* (v. 30). Once again, the fantastic totals are spelled out in detail (vv. 36-47).

The annihilation of Midian is accomplished without a single Israelite casualty, *not one of us is missing* (v. 49). Twelve thousand warriors wipe out a people from whom 32,000 virgins survive, 808,000 animals are taken alive—all without losing one warrior.

To express their gratitude and to cover any possible infractions of the law (*to make atonement for* themselves, v. 50) the commanders present to Moses *the LORD's offering* from the goods the warriors *found*. Various items of jewelry are mentioned (v. 50). The offering itself weighs *16,750 shekels* (v. 52; modern weight would be as much as 240 kg.). The offering becomes part of the treasure held in the shrine. It is placed in *the tent of meeting as a memorial for the Israelites before the LORD* (v. 54). Either the memorial reminds the LORD of Israel's faithfulness and generosity; or it reminds Israel of the great victory given them by the LORD.

Thus is drawn a portrait of Israel as it should be: totally intolerant of foreign influences, obedient to the Mosaic law in every detail, and generously providing for the priesthood, the Levites, and the sanctuary itself.

Settlements in Transjordan, 32:1-42

On a first reading, chap. 32 appears to be a fairly straightforward account of a final piece of business to be cared for before Israel's thrust west into Canaan proper, i.e., the allocation of the land east of the Jordan already taken. Careful analysts of the passage agree that several traditions are present; there the agreement ends. Any literary history is, therefore, tentative (Budd 1983, 337–42).

The tribes Gad and Reuben find the plateaus east of the Jordan attractive. The good pasturelands suit these cattle keepers (v. 1). They ask agreement that they settle there. They also seek to avoid the dangers ahead, *do not make us cross the Jordan* (v. 5).

Moses adds two and two and gets nine. Overcome by a sense of *deja vu*, he assumes the worst. On the threshold of the promised land of Canaan elements within Israel are again about to rip the heart out of the people, he fears. Moses lashes out at the Reubenites and Gadites. He compares what they are doing to what the faithless spies did at Kadesh. *You brood of sinners*, he calls them, threatening them with *the LORD's anger* (v. 13). Verses 8-13 summarize chaps. 13–14, giving a deuteronomistic interpretation of those awful days.

Gad and Reuben quickly qualify their intentions. They volunteer to build themselves fortified towns where their *little ones* (families) can stay and to lead Israel's army as they conquer Canaan. *We will not return to our homes until all the Israelites have obtained their inheritance*, they pledge (v. 18). Moses agrees and requires the two tribes to take a public oath to that effect (vv. 28-32).

Verses 33-42 outline the allocation of the Transjordan by Moses to Gad, Reuben, and three clans of *the half-tribe of Manasseh*. The other half of Manasseh will settle on the west bank (cf. Josh 13:15-31; Deut 3:12-17). The inclusion of *Manasseh* seems intrusive. They settle north of the Jabbok in Bashan.

This account establishes several things: an explanation of the fact that three tribes settled outside the promised land; that Canaan proper was conquered by all twelve tribes; and that the new generation did not fail the tests of faithfulness to the LORD's purpose.

An Exodus Itinerary, 33:1-49

As a conclusion to the long Exodus narrative, the priestly writer includes a list of camp sites, a recapitulation of Israel's movements from Rameses in *Egypt* (v. 3) to the *plains of Moab* (v. 49). The itinerary is interesting for several reasons. Most of the camp sites mentioned cannot be identified today. The lists may be grouped into five phases or journeys: *Rameses* to *Sinai* (vv. 3-15), *Sinai* to *Ezion-Geber* (vv. 16-35), *Ezion-Geber* to *Kadesh* (v. 36), *Kadesh* to *Edom* (v. 37), and *Edom* through the Transjordan (vv. 41-49).

The first part of the list (vv. 5-15) parallels the itinerary laid out in the final form of Exodus 12:32–19:2, with the addition of places not otherwise known, e.g., *Dophkah* and *Alush* (vv. 12-13). The *Sinai* to *Ezion-Geber* journey is mentioned only here (cf. 10:11-12; 11:3, 34-35; 12:16). Most of the site names are unique to this list.

Only the point of departure and the terminus are listed for the Ezion-Geber-Kadesh and the Kadesh-Edom journeys. Many of the names in the Transjordan trek are unusual, too. Several places, important to the Yahwist's account of the Exodus, are not mentioned, e.g., Shur, Massah and Meribah, Taberah and Hormah. Clearly, this is a composite list. Its sources and relations to other itinerary information in the Pentateuch can only be surmised (Davies 1979).

By including these itineraries the priestly writer adds another signal to his narrative that the forty-year Exodus is ending and the day of promise is at hand. The LORD has brought Israel safely down a long, rough road.

Ideal Boundaries of the Promised Land, 33:50–34:29

As part of the book's conclusion, and as an anticipation of the imminent occupation of Canaan, the priestly writer lays out absolutist goals for the conquest and repeats plans for the future division of Palestine among the tribes. The Mosaic origins of both are emphasized.

When they do *take possession of the land*, Israel is to receive it as a gift from Yahweh (v. 53). Note the repeated use of the word *inheritance*. The coming invasion is to be fought according to the rules of holy war: Israelites are to completely clear the country of its pagan population; particularly, they are to *destroy* every vestige of the indigenous, idolatrous cults—*their figured stones* (idols used in manipulating gods), *their cast images* (molten idols), and *all their high places* (notorious hilltop shrines devoted to the baals). Israel is gravely warned of the consequences should they be less than thorough: the Canaanites will *trouble you in the land*, they will remain as *barbs in your eyes and thorns in your side* (v. 55). The DEUTERONOMIST/DEUTERONOMISTIC HISTORIAN was sure that many of Israel's woes could be traced to failures at this point.

The anticipated apportionment of Palestine to the various tribes is spelled out in more detail than before. Verse 54 repeats the content of 26:52-56. Chapter 34 defines *boundaries* for the Israel of the future. Sites mentioned along the northern borders are the most difficult to identify. At no time, even under DAVID and SOLOMON, did Israel actually control all of the territory delimited. The boundaries describe an ideal Israel often evoked in the OT (see Ezek 47:15-18; 48:1-2; cf. Gen 15:18; Josh 15:1-4; Judg 20:1; 1 Kgs 8:65). The LORD's promise-gift to his people will include specific geography—and spacious at that.

Further, allocation of the land to the various tribes and subtribes is to be perpetual. Although *Eleazar*, the Aaronite high priest, and *Joshua*, the military leader, along with designated leaders of the tribes (cf. this list of tribal leaders with lists in 1:5-15 and 13:4-15), will supervise the process, authority for the apportionment is seated in the revelation to Moses (*The LORD spoke to Moses*, v. 16). The parceling-out ceremonies are described in Josh 13–17, with which the writer seems acquainted.

Levitical Cities and Cities of Refuge, 35:1-34

The recital of guidelines for apportioning the land to the twelve tribes (chap 34), suggests the need to provide designated cities for Levites (vv. 1-8); this in turn leads the priestly writer to describe the provision of six of these Levitical cities as *cities of refuge* (vv. 6, 9-15); and to put forward laws related to those who take refuge in them (vv. 9-34).

As guardians and servants of the sacred precincts, the Levites were not to share in the inheritance of the land (18:24). Rather, the other tribes were to provide for them (chap. 18). But where were Levites and their livestock to live? Some traditions remembered that they lived here and there in the towns (Deut 18:1, 6). The writer of Numbers gives a different, somewhat idealized answer: forty-eight towns with over 200 acres of adjoining pastureland (v. 7) each were to be set aside for Levites to *live in* (v. 2) but not own (cf. Josh 20–21; Ezekiel 48:13-22 envisioned their all living together in one central place). There is little to suggest that this provision for Levites was actually ever implemented.

The provisions for six *cities of refuge* (vv. 6, 11, 13), respond to two ancient convictions and, perhaps, an historical development. Many ancient taboos had to do with human blood. Shedding blood (killing a person) was an awesome defilement of the land, expiated only by the death of the killer. The ancient laws of blood revenge required the closest-of-kin (Heb. *go'el*) to carry out the sentence.

Early on *a slayer* (v. 24) could take refuge at a local shrine—if he could get there (Exod 21:12-14; Deut 19). Once in the sanctuary, he took hold of the horns of the altar, thus appealing to God. These provisions for cities of refuge may reflect needs that arose following Josiah's abolishment of local shrines.

But should not *intent* (vv. 11, 15) influence what is done? And who decides guilt and intent? Numbers addresses these legal and ethical issues. The ancient law of blood revenge is not questioned. *The avenger of blood (go'el) shall execute the sentence*. But the ways the sentence is carried out are ameliorated: A clear distinction is laid down between murder and accidental killing. Murder is defined by citing several examples (vv. 16-21). Several other examples of killing *without enmity* are listed; these are not punishable (vv. 22-23).

The avenger of blood shall do nothing until there is a trial by the congregation (vv. 12, 24) and not only the town elders. They shall judge motive and grant asylum. The priestly writer gives interpretations that parallel deuteronomic interpretations (Deut 19).

Once given refuge, the slayer must not leave the town—on pain of exposure again to blood guilt. Only the death of the high priest can make a general amnesty possible for everyone in the town.

The congregation shall require at least two witnesses in capital cases and must not, even for accidental killings, allow a money payment (*ransom*, v. 32). The principle stands: *blood pollutes the land, and no expiation* is possible *except by the blood of the one who shed it* (v. 33.) Once again the theological reason for such laws is given: *I the LORD dwell among the Israelites* (v. 34).

Protecting Tribal Property: Women as Heirs, 36:1-13

Allocations of land to tribes and clans were to be held sacrosanct—intrinsic to the LORD's gift of the land to Israel. The case of *the daughters of Zelophehad* (27:1-11) protected a family's inheritance in the land by providing that the land of a man who died without male heirs could pass to his daughters. Now an appendix is added to Numbers that deals with a derivative case, a daughter who marries outside the tribe. Would the land become part of another tribe's inheritance (any sons would be members of their father's clan), and, eventually, would not the entire system of tribal territories be compromised (v. 3)?

It is not at all clear how v. 4 relates to the question. The Jubilee seems only to have applied to property that was sold (see Lev 25:8-34). And if it applied to this case, the Jubilee would have dealt with the problem—requiring the land to revert to the original tribe, clan, or family.

The eventuality is dealt with by requiring the women to marry within their own tribe, which they agree to and do. Thus, no *inheritance* is *transferred from one tribe to another* (v. 9).

This is yet another case illustrating the fact that the tradition was flexible, and that adaptations of the Mosaic law to on-going developments were expected.

Verse 13 concludes the section of the book describing preparations to move across *the Jordan*. It also concludes the book (cf. Lev 27:34).

Works Cited

Ackerman, James. 1987. "The Book of Numbers," *The Literary Guide to the Bible*, ed. Alter and Kermode.
Budd, Philip J. 1979. *Numbers*. WBC.
Davies, G. I. 1979. *The Way of the Wilderness*.
Noth, M. 1968. *Numbers*. OTL.
Olson, Dennis T. 1985. *The Death of the Old and the Birth of the New*.
Thompson, J. A. 1970. "Numbers," in *NBC*.
Snaith, N. H. 1966. "The Daughters of Zelophehad," *VT* 16:124–27. 1967. *Leviticus & Numbers*. NCB.
de Vaux, Roland. 1961. *Ancient Israel: Its Life and Institutions*.

Deuteronomy
John H. Tullock

Introduction

Deuteronomy is the fifth book of the TORAH or Pentateuch. The Hebrew name, "the words" (הַדְּבָרִים *haddebarim*), follows a Hebrew tradition of naming a book after its opening words. The English title, Deuteronomy, probably is based on the phrase "this second [or "repeated"] law" (τὸ δευτερονόμιον τοῦτο *to deuteronomion touto*) found in the Septuagint, or LXX (Deut 17:18), the Greek translation of the Hebrew Bible. In this passage, the king is instructed to *have a copy of this law written for him in the presence of the levitical priests* (see Wright 1953, 311).

Nature of the Book

Deuteronomy is not primarily a royal book, however. Instead it is a book designed to proclaim the faith of the Israelite community. While it contains legal materials, principally in chaps. 12–26, it also is a book of exposition, structured as three sermons or addresses by MOSES (see outline).

Place of Deuteronomy in the Canon

Until the rise of modern biblical studies, Deuteronomy had traditionally been viewed as one of the five books of Moses (Genesis–Deuteronomy). As such, it does have certain affinities with the other four books, with its legal materials, its recapitulation of the Wilderness story, and its accounts of the choice of Joshua and of the death of Moses. It ends with a fitting tribute to Moses as leader of the people (Deut 34:10-12).

On the other hand, Deuteronomy also has affinities with several of the books that follow (Joshua, Judges, 1 and 2 Kings). It introduces Joshua as leader of the conquest of the land, but, more importantly, it introduces themes that are developed in the books that follow. Most notably among these are: 1) the theme of one central place for worship (see especially Deut 12:1-28), an idea brought to life in the reforms of King Josiah (640–609 B.C.E.; see 2 Kgs 22–23); 2) the theme of holy war that spoke of God's fighting for the people, the point of view from which the author of the Book of Joshua interprets the conquest of Canaan; 3) a view that Israel's history followed a pattern wherein the people would sin, judgment would come, the people would repent, and God would raise up a deliverer (see esp. Judg 2:6 to 3:6). Modern scholars refer to this interpretation of history as the "Deuteronomistic theme." This pattern is seen as recurring in the history of Israel by the writer(s) of Judges through 2 Kings, popularly known as the DEUTERONOMISTIC HISTORY.

Authorship and Date

Jewish tradition names Moses as the author of Deuteronomy, but modern scholarship has caused considerable doubt about this conclusion. For all but the most conservative interpreters, views range from those who still see a Mosaic core of materials in the book (Craigie 1976, 24–29) to those who do not give any credence to Mosaic authorship. Rather, the latter scholars see Moses only as the chief human character in a book, developed by scribes in what is called the "Deuteronomistic school." This school is credited not only with Deuteronomy but also the Deuteronomistic history (Joshua–2 Kings). Most recently, Deuteronomy has been described as a "kind of manual for future kings of Israel," similar to a type of literature found in Egyptian and Mesopotamian royal circles (Weinfeld 1991, 4; for a fuller discussion of authorship, see Christensen 1990, 211–12).

Regardless of one's view of the origins of the book, there is general agreement that at least the core of the book, chaps. 12–26, first appeared as a public document during the reign of King Josiah, serving as the basis of his reform in 622–621 B.C.E. (2 Kgs 22, 23).

Structure

Gerhard von Rad was the first scholar to propose that the book had been developed to be used in a ceremony for covenant making or covenant renewal. Later studies have tended to support his views, especially in the light of the discovery of Hittite and Assyrian treaty forms that were present in the Near East before Deuteronomy was written. Most of the elements of these treaty forms are present in Deuteronomy: an historical prologue, identifying the maker (the LORD) and specifying what he has done for the people (1-11); the stipulations as evidenced by the law code (12:1–26:15); provision for public reading (26:16-19); and a series of blessings for the proper keeping of the treaty and cursings for violations (chaps. 27–28). Until recently, the focus has been on the Hittite treaties as the model, but now the focus is on Assyrian vassal treaties as a more likely model (Weinfeld 1991, 9–13).

As an extended re-presentation of the demands of the covenant, the Book of Deuteronomy has the form of a long and complex speech of Moses to the Israelites, delivered on the plains of Moab shortly before Moses' death. The outline below seeks to preserve this feature of the book by using brief quotations from Deuteronomy to mark the divisions of the book.

For Further Study

In the *Mercer Dictionary of the Bible*: DEUTERONOMIST/DEUTERONOMISTIC HISTORIAN; DEUTERONOMY, BOOK OF.

In other sources: I. Cairns, "The Fifth Book of Moses, Called Deuteronomy," *Word and Presence*, ITC; P. C. Craigie, *Deuteronomy: Introduction*, NCIOT; A. D. H. Mayes, *Deuteronomy*, NCB; M. Weinfeld, *Deuteronomy 1–12*, AncB.

Commentary

An Outline

I. "These are the words"— On the Plains of Moab, 1:1-5

II. "The LORD our God spoke to us"— The First Sermon of Moses, 1:6–4:40
 A. "You have stayed long enough"— Departure from Sinai, 1:6-8
 B. "I am unable . . . to bear you"— Organizing for Leadership, 1:9-18
 C. "We set out from Horeb"—First Attempts at Conquest, 1:19-45
 D. "After you had stayed at Kadesh"— Travels in Transjordan, 1:46–3:29
 E. "So now, Israel, give heed"— Conclusion to the First Sermon of Moses and an Interlude, 4:1-43

III. "This is the law"—The Second Sermon of Moses, 4:44–26:19; 28:1-68
 A. "These are the decrees"—The Setting for the Sermon, 4:44-49
 B. "Moses convened all Israel"— The Giving of the Law at Sinai, 5:1–11:32
 C. "These are the statutes and ordinances"—12:1–25:19
 D. "When you have come into the land"— The Concluding Rituals and an Interlude, 26:1–27:26
 E. "If you will only obey the LORD your God"—The Conclusion of the Sermon, 28:1-68

IV. "These are the words of the covenant"—The Third Sermon of Moses, 29:1–30:20
 A. "The covenant . . . in Moab"— Renewing the Covenant, 29:1-29
 B. "When all these things happened to you"— Blessings and Choices, 30:1-20

V. "When Moses had finished speaking"— Moses' Final Days, 31:1-29
 A. "I am now one hundred twenty years old"—Moses' Final Charge to Joshua and the People, 31:1-8
 B. "Then Moses wrote down this law"—The Ceremony of Covenant Renewal, 31:9-13
 C. "The Lord said to Moses"—The Commissioning of Joshua, 31:14-23
 D. "When Moses finished writing"— The Continuation of the Covenant Ceremony, 31:24-29

VI. "Then Moses recited the word of this song"—The Song of Moses, 31:30–32:47

VII. "On that very day the LORD addressed Moses"—Moses Views the Land, 32:48-52

VIII. "This is the blessing"— The Blessing of Moses, 33:1-29

IX. "Then Moses went up"— The Death of Moses, 34:1-12

"These are the words"—On the Plains of Moab, 1:1-5

This prologue forms the setting for three sermons or addresses by Moses. The setting of this first address is twofold: geographical (vv. 1-2) and temporal (vv. 3-5). The third-person narration is typical of a later editor.

Moses speaks to the whole of the assembly (*all*) of Israel. The location is to the east and south of the Jordan and the Dead Sea, in the *land of Moab*. Most of the locations mentioned, except Moab, have not been identified at all, or if so, very tentatively. The time suggested would place this covenant-making scene just prior to the death of Moses. Indeed, Deuteronomy closes with the death and an evaluation of the ministry of Moses (chap. 34). Note, however, that the introduction is a third-person narrative reporting the events from an historical perspective.

"The LORD our God spoke to us"—
The First Sermon of Moses, 1:6–4:40

"You have stayed long enough"—Departure from Sinai, 1:6-8

Moses reminds Israel of the LORD'S commands to resume their journey and to begin the conquest of the land. The primary goal is the central hill country. From there they are to branch out into the surrounding areas. The ultimate boundaries are those contained in the promises to Abraham (Gen 15:18-19).

"I am unable . . . to bear you"—Organizing for Leadership, 1:9-18

This is an abbreviated version of an incident found in Exod 18. Here, however, there is no mention of Jethro, Moses's father-in-law, who according to that account suggested the plan of organization to Moses. The judges are charged with the responsibility to be fair and impartial. Only the hardest cases are to be brought to Moses. This basic pattern of organization is still to be found in judicial systems today. Note especially the phrase *the God of your ancestors* (see Gen 26:24), one of a number of old tribal names for God.

"We set out from Horeb"—First Attempts at Conquest, 1:19-45

These verses give another account of the events described in Num 13–14. When the journey from Horeb to Kadesh-barnea is completed (v. 19), Moses gives orders to prepare for the conquest (vv. 20-21). The countersuggestion by the people that spies be chosen to bring back a report on the territory to be conquered is accepted by Moses (vv. 22-25).

The spies give Moses a favorable report, but some of them report otherwise to the people; as a result, the people lose heart and are unwilling to proceed with the invasion. Their refusal brings a rebuke from Moses for their lack of faith. The gifts of the LORD God's leadership are contrasted with the people's ungratefulness and lack of faith (vv. 26-33). The LORD responds by sentencing the people to die in the

DEUTERONOMY

wilderness, allowing only Caleb and Joshua of that generation to enter the land (vv. 34-40). Then follows the abortive invasion that meets with defeat (vv. 41-45).

"After you had stayed at Kadesh"—Travels in Transjordan, 1:46–3:29

1:46–2:8a. Avoiding conflict with Edom. Israel journeys southward toward the Red Sea (Gulf of Aqaba), ostensibly to avoid conflict with the Edomites, traditional relatives to the Israelites through Esau, Jacob's twin (Gen 36:1). While this may reflect a tradition that some tribes encircled Edom on its eastern borders, the narrative says that they turned northward along the Arabah, the rift valley extending southward from the Dead Sea.

2:8b-25. Marching through Moab. Moab, tied to Israel by tradition through Lot, the nephew of Abraham (Gen 19:36-38), also is not to be conquered. The implication is that the LORD has given the Moabites their territory as a possession just as Canaan was given to Israel (v. 12). This is more clearly stated with regard to the Ammonites (v. 21). The doctrine of holy war, that is, that the LORD God fights for the people, is here extended to peoples other than Israel (cf. Amos 9:7). Such a blessing had not been extended to Sihon and Og, kings of the Amorites, however (vv. 24-25; 3:1-2). Deuteronomy interprets the defeat of Sihon as holy war: *The LORD our God gave him over to us* (v. 33; cf. Num 21:21-23).

2:26-37. Conflict with Sihon. Despite efforts to negotiate safe passage through the territory of Sihon, the holy war ensues with resulting devastation for the Amorites and Sihon.

3:1-11. Conflict with Bashan. A similar attitude on the part of Og, king of Bashan, brought a similar result. All that remained to mark Og's presence was his iron bed, preserved as a *museum piece* in Rabbah (NRSV note on v. 11).

3:12-22. Tribal allotments in Transjordan. Tribal territories for Reuben, Gad, and a half tribe of Manasseh were east of the Jordan River, often called Transjordan (see Num 32; Josh 13). The assurance that *it is the LORD your God who fights for you* (v. 22) is in keeping with the doctrine of holy war.

3:23-29. Moses forbidden to cross the Jordan. When Moses pleads to be allowed to cross the Jordan, he is forbidden to do so. As in Deuteronomy 1:37, the reason given is that he has to bear the brunt of the LORD's anger on behalf of the people (v. 26). This is in line with the ancient belief of corporate responsibility wherein the leader (the patriarch, or in Moses' case, a sort of surrogate patriarch for all of the people) is answerable for the sins of the people. But the reason given in Numbers 20:10-13 is that Moses' own lack of faith had caused him to lose the privilege of crossing the Jordan.

"So now, Israel, give heed"—
Conclusion to the First Sermon of Moses and an Interlude, 4:1-43

4:1-8. God demands obedience. To realize their dream for a homeland, Israel has to concern itself with obeying the LORD their God. To do otherwise will bring disaster (vv. 1-4). Diligent observance of the LORD's demands will bring admiration by the nations for Israel's *wisdom and discernment* (v. 6). No other nation has such an opportunity (v. 8).

4:9-40. Learning the lessons of the wilderness days. What follows is a plea to Israel to learn the lessons of its history. Among these are: (1) There is no physical image by which the LORD is to be worshiped. This is a reminder that nothing created is to be worshiped instead of the LORD, whether an idol carved by human hands, a bird or an animal, or the heavenly bodies—sun, moon, or stars. God controls all of these creatures just as the deity has controlled Israel (vv. 9-20). (2) While the LORD has chosen Israel as a possession of the deity, this does not mean that God could not or would not punish disobedience on their part. That Moses has been forbidden to cross the Jordan should serve as a reminder *that the LORD demands absolute obedience.* Surely God would not allow the breaking of the covenant to go unpunished, especially a violation so serious as the making of idols (vv. 21-24). (3) Israel's greatest danger is the temptation to become complacent (v. 25). This could lead to the making of idols, which in turn could bring destruction and exile (v. 26). Yet, being *utterly destroyed* did not mean annihilation, since the purpose would be to stir up a desire to return to the LORD, who, in turn, would respond to the repentant people in mercy. The LORD surely would be faithful to the covenant made with the ancestors (vv. 26-31). (4) Their experiences should have taught them that the LORD their God is the only God. The themes of creation, the Sinai experience, the exodus, the leading of the ancestors and the giving of the land are evoked against a background of reminders of the LORD's wondrous powers. These reminders serve to prove that the LORD not only loved their ancestors, but that God also chose Israel because of that same love (vv. 32-37). The obvious conclusion is that *the LORD is God in heaven above and on earth beneath; there is no other* (v. 39). This statement is closely akin to the theme of monotheism so boldly stated in Isa 40–48. It, plus the reminder that the land had been given them as a possession *as it is still today* (v. 38), supports the argument for a fairly late date for Deuteronomy since this latter quotation suggests that the conquest is a thing of the past.

4:41-43. An interlude: Moses chooses cities of refuge. Cities of refuge represent a step in the development of dealing with homicide, moving the act from the realm of family vengeance to state punishment. The punishment for a person's violent death in more primitive societies was a family matter; there was no state to act independently to determine the guilt or innocence of the one who caused the death. The three cities mentioned here probably were sites of important shrines. Shrines seemed to be neutral ground where the accused could stay while negotiations were carried out to determine guilt or innocence. Israel's oldest law code seems to envision such a role for the sanctuary (Exod 21:12-14; see also 1 Kgs 1:49-53 where Adonijah flees to the shrine until he can make a deal with Solomon). More extensive passages dealing with the cities of refuge are to be found in Deut 19:1-13; Josh 20:1-6; and Num 35:9-34.

"This is the law"—The Second Sermon of Moses, 4:44–26:19; 28:1-28

"These are the decrees"—The Setting for the Sermon, 4:44-49

The editorial introduction presents the subject matter of the sermon as *the decrees and the statutes and ordinances that Moses spoke to the Israelites* (v. 45); the site is *beyond the Jordan* (v. 46); the time is after the defeat of Kings Sihon and Og (vv. 47-49). The narrator seems be recounting events of the distant past.

"Moses convened all Israel"—The Giving of the Law at Sinai, 5:1–11:32

5:1-33. The giving of the law. What follows is a retelling of the giving of the TEN COMMANDMENTS from the perspective of the writer of Deuteronomy (v. 1a).

5:1b-5. Hear, O Israel. This call to worship introduces the sermon as a whole and the narrative about the Ten Commandments in particular. *The LORD our God made a covenant with us* (v. 2) connects *today* (v. 1b) and the past events at Horeb, emphasizing the covenant's continuing relevance. A further reminder is to be found in the assertion that *the LORD spoke with you face to face* (v. 4). These references may be taken from a ritual for a ceremony of COVENANT renewal.

5:6. I am the LORD your God. This statement identifies the LORD as covenant maker while *who brought you out of the land of Egypt* establishes the historical basis for his rights as covenant maker and giver of the commandments. Harrelson suggests the commandments are to be divided into four groups: 1–3, *God's absolute demands*; 4–5, *God's basic institutions*; 6–7, *God's fundamental personal demands*; 8–10, *God's fundamental social demands* (Harrelson 1990, 883–85).

5:7. You shall have no other gods before me. This demand for absolute loyalty on Israel's part, while not ruling out the belief in the existence of other gods, nonetheless gives Israel no choice as to where its obligations for worship lie. Such a standard eventually leads to a clear MONOTHEISM. That it was well on the way to fruition by the time Deuteronomy reached final form is strongly implied in Deuteronomy 4:39: *the LORD is God . . . there is no other* (see Ellis 1990, 581–82). Roman Catholic tradition connects this verse to 5:8-10 to form the first commandment; in Jewish usage, 5:7-10 comprise the second commandment, with 5:6, "I the LORD am your God, who brought you out of the land of Egypt," as the first commandment.

5:8-10. You shall not make for yourself an idol. The concept that the LORD could not be portrayed in any material form is a unique contribution that the religion of Israel makes to the history of religious thought (see IDOLATRY). It becomes the basis for the doctrines of God's omnipresence (the unlimited ability to be anywhere at all times) and God's omniscience (all-knowingness).

5:11. You shall not make wrongful use of the name of the LORD your God. This reflects the view that one's name summed up the essence of who one was. To misuse or abuse one's name is, in a real sense, to misuse or abuse the bearer of the name. To misuse the LORD's name would thus be abusive both to the divine power and person. Such a misuse would be involved in invoking the LORD's name to injure another person by means of a curse. That is the LORD's prerogative (see Smith 1990, 188–89).

5:12-15. Observe the sabbath day and keep it holy. This basic institution in Israelite religious life has no parallel in any other society. The emphasis in on rest, not activity (Harrelson 1990, 884). Deuteronomy sees this as the primary reason for the sabbath's existence—providing rest for self, family, servants, and animals after six days of labor. Exodus 20:11 ties it to the LORD's rest after six days of creation. Thus, both versions emphasize rest, Exodus from the divine standpoint, Deuteronomy from the human standpoint (Tullock 1990, 779–81).

5:16. Honor your father and your mother. The second basic institution of Israelite life is the FAMILY. This commandment may also be viewed as introducing a segment on societal relationships, beginning with the most basic unit, the family. That this commandment is taken seriously is evidenced by laws in the Covenant Code providing for the death penalty for the abuse of parents (Exod 21:15, 17). The positive emphasis is on care for parents. The reward for such conduct is that *it may go well with you*. Deuteronomy has a longer version of this promise than Exodus does.

5:17. You shall not murder. MURDER is the preferred translation here since the verb is used in the prophets to imply intentional killing (Hos 4:2; Isa 1:21, cf. Judg 20:4; 1 Kgs 21:19). Life belongs to the LORD, who gives it and who alone has the right to take it. For people to assume that right is to presume upon the privileges of the LORD. When human life loses its value, human society loses its stability.

5:18. Neither shall you commit adultery. ADULTERY is viewed in this time as a violation both of one's MARRIAGE rights and of one's property rights. Wives are seen as a part of the husband's property (cf. Exod 20:17). Because of this, adultery on the wife's part probably was viewed as a more serious offense than adultery by the husband. The teachings of Jesus helped overcome this disparity (Matt 5:27-32; John 8:1-11). Beyond that, any threat to the family unit is viewed in Israel as a threat to the peace and stability of the society as a whole. Weak families mean a weak society. And adultery by the husband also weakened the family unit, while damaging another family as well.

5:19. Neither shall you steal. This is another commandment that deals with destructive elements in society. The Israelite view of the close relationship of persons to their tangible property makes theft a serious offense (cf. the story of Achan and the destruction of his property along with him, Josh 7). One's property is a means for sustaining the owner's life. To deprive a person of his/her property by theft is, in a sense, a threat to that person's continued existence.

5:20. Neither shall you bear false witness against your neighbor. The spoken word has power (Isa 55:11). Great stress is placed on truth-telling in the courts (Exod 23:1; Deut 19:15-21; 1 Kgs 22:16; Hos 4:2), especially when the lawsuit involved a neighbor (see also the story of Susanna in the Apocrypha). The damage done by lying can also threaten life. A common phrase in Israelite court procedure is the admonition to avoid shedding *innocent blood* (19:10, 13; cf. Jer 26:15). To convict a person of a capital crime on the basis of false testimony can, of course, lead to the shedding of innocent blood.

5:21. Neither shall you covet. This commandment differs from Exodus 20:17 where the order is *house . . . wife . . . slave*, etc. The order reflects the same concern for human values that appears in the sabbath commandment (5:12). In Exodus the wife is part of the property. Here she is given priority over the property. This commandment addresses the motivation that leads to the violation of the commandments listed earlier. In that sense, it is a summary commandment. The NRSV translation of the tenth commandment reflects the Roman Catholic and Lutheran traditions of dividing it into two commandments, since those traditions combine commandments one and two to form their first commandment.

5:22-27. The LORD and the people. The commandments are the LORD's gift to Israel. That they were written on stone emphasizes their permanent nature. The personal revelation of the LORD to *all the heads of your tribes and your elders* (v. 23) symbolizes the personal nature of that revelation, as well as its awe-inspiring gravity. So overwhelming is the experience that it moves the people to request that any further revelation be mediated to them through Moses (v. 27).

5:28-33. The LORD and Moses. Moses is not only to hear the *commandments, the statutes and the ordinances*, but he is also to *teach them*, so that Israel may *do them in the land that I am giving them to possess* (v. 31). He is to be mediator and teacher, both receiver and proclaimer of the will of God to the people.

6:1-11:32. An exposition of the first commandment. What follows in the next six chapters is a long expository sermon based, it seems, on the first commandment. We should note that in the Jewish tradition the first commandment is *I am the LORD your God, who brought you out of the land of Egypt, out of the house of slavery* (v. 6; Exod 20:2). In Judaism the commandment against the making of carved images is considered to be part of the commandment to worship no other gods besides the LORD. It is perhaps best to say that Deut 6:1–11:32 is an exposition of all three of these: the self-identification of the LORD as Israel's savior, the prohibition of the worship of any other deity, and the prohibition of the making of carved images. While many subjects are treated in these chapters, the underlying theme is what it means for Israel to worship the LORD only. According to these chapters, it means that Israel is to demonstrate utter loyalty and fidelity to the God of the COVENANT, the REDEEMER of Israel, the LORD.

6:1-3. This is the commandment. This phrase seems to refer to the first commandment, the basis for all the others, as well as to *the statutes and the ordinances* (v. 1). To *hear . . . and observe* are the basic requirements for blessing in the land (v. 3; 5:1), just as the LORD promised Israel's ancestors (Gen 12:1-7). If there is to be blessing, there must be reverent obedience to all that the LORD commands.

6:4-9. The great commandment. *Hear [shema], O Israel: The LORD is our God, the LORD alone.* This call for Israel's undivided loyalty to the LORD is called the

SHEMA in Jewish tradition after its first word in Hebrew. This demand for undivided loyalty is the basic principle of Israelite religion. Out of that principle, all legal and religious themes and institutions flow. Israel's commitment is to be to the LORD alone. It is to be a commitment of the whole person: *with all your heart*, involving emotional as well as mental capacities; *with all your soul*, all those unique qualities that makes one a person, the essence of one's existence; *with all your might*, centering one's efforts and attention on living in total devotion to the one God who is LORD alone (vv. 4-5; cf. Mark 12:29-30). *Keep . . . recite . . . bind . . . write* all are action words suggesting practical means for maintaining the *shema* at the center of personal and family attention.

While Israelite religion is to be imageless as regards deity, it does not lack for symbols. This passage furnishes the inspiration for a number of those symbols that are found in later Judaism (vv. 6-9). The phrase *emblem on your forehead* becomes the basis for the phylactery, a small box containing verses of scripture and attached to a leather thong to tie around the arm and the head (Matt 23:5). The command *write them on the doorposts* (*mezuzot*) is the inspiration for the Mezuzah, a small box containing a bit of parchment and attached to the trim surrounding the door, showing that an observant Jewish family resides there.

6:10-19. The LORD your God you shall fear. When the people come into the land and become accustomed to its bounty, they will find it easy to become careless and become distracted, causing them to *forget the LORD* who has brought them there (vv. 10-12). For that reason, their dedicated love should be blended with profound reverence for the LORD. *Fear* here does not imply terror so much as it does a sense of awe and profound respect. Such reverence prevents idolatry (v. 13), promotes obedience and right conduct (vv. 17-18a) and will lead to Israel's inheritance of the promises God made to the ancestors (vv. 18b-19).

6:20-25. Teach the children. Jewish history has illustrated the wisdom of the principle enunciated in this passage. To preserve the family, one thing that is vital is the passing on of a sense of identity and history. That can be done most effectively as each generation assumes the responsibility to pass on the sense of family heritage and values to the next generation. This, indeed, is *for our lasting good, so as to keep us alive* (v. 24).

7:1-26. Holy land, holy people, and holy war. No teaching in Deuteronomy poses more of a moral dilemma for modern religious folk than the teaching concerning HOLY WAR. In practical terms, its objective is to allow Israel to "occupy and settle the land of God's promise with no risk of any residual heathen contamination" (Wilson 1990, 385–86). It involves carrying the exclusive worship of the LORD to its most extreme limits—by the elimination not only of other gods but also of those who worship other gods, lest their worship be a snare to lead Israel astray *to serve other gods* (v. 4). Israel is to be *a people holy to the LORD your God: the LORD your God has chosen you . . . to be his people* (v. 6). Holy war probably is best understood as part of the fabric of ancient cultures, interpreted by Israel in the light of its own understanding of God (see further, Wilson 1990, 385–86).

Ironically, in the midst of this harshest portrayal of the LORD's demands we are introduced to the most striking statement about God's choice of Israel as the people of the LORD: not because they were numerous but *because the LORD loved you and kept the oath he swore to your ancestors* (vv. 7-8). The evidence of covenant loyalty is an answering love that motivates the keeping of God's commandments, *to a thousand generations* (v. 9). If they faithfully follow God's will as revealed in the commandments and ordinances, they can confidently go forth to battle against their enemies, knowing that the LORD is going before them to give them success (vv. 12-26).

8:1-10. Obedience brings blessing. Deuteronomy alternates between the poles of positive promises and negative warnings. As the experience in the wilderness should have taught Israel, obedience brings blessing. The LORD's discipline is as the discipline of a parent (v. 5). Israel's responsibility is to "live according to his laws and have reverence for him" (v. 6b TEV).

8:11-20. Disobedience brings judgment. The plea for obedience is coupled with a warning not to forget all that the LORD has done for the people in the past (vv. 11-16). Failure to remember those lessons, coupled with disobedience, will bring judgment on Israel just as it has on other nations (vv. 17-20).

9:1-7. Why the LORD gives the land. *Hear, O Israel* (v. 1) introduces another rehearsal of the events in the wilderness. It is done so as to remind the people that neither their personal righteousness nor their past experience qualifies them to receive the gift of the land. They have no cause for self-righteousness. The land is theirs for two reasons: (1) *because of the wickedness of these nations;* and (2) so the LORD can *fulfill the promise . . . made on oath to your ancestors* (v. 5).

9:8-10:11. Recounting Israel's rebellion. What follows is Deuteronomy's most extended account of the giving of the law at Horeb: the giving of the first tablets to Moses (9:8-10); the golden calf incident, with a passing reference to Aaron's role (9:11-21, cf. Exod 32); coming to Kadesh-barnea and the failure to invade from the south (9:22-24; cf. Num 13–14); an account of Moses intervening for the people, appealing to the LORD's honor and reminding God that *they are the people of your very own possession* whom God has brought out by *great power and . . . outstretched arm* (9:29; cf. Exod 32:11-14, 31-34).

The account ends with the making of the second set of tablets. What is new here is that Moses is credited with building the ark to hold the tablets (10:1-5; cf. Exod 25:1-22). There follows an interlude with a travel narrative fragment, serving as a background for naming the Levites as bearers of the ark (10:6-9; cf. Num 33:30-38). After this, Moses once again intercedes and gets the LORD's approval to continue leading the people (10:10-11).

10:12-11:32. What does the LORD require of you? The final summation of the exposition of the first commandment begins with a restatement of the LORD's requirements: reverential awe (*fear*, see 6:13), proper conduct (*walk*), joyful devotion (*love*), humble submission (*serve . . . with . . . heart . . . and . . . soul*), and to live in keeping with God's revealed will by keeping the divine commandments. Israel is to do this for the sake of their *own well-being* (10:12-13). The LORD loved their ancestors and chose Israel to be God's own people (10:15). As the LORD who is *God of gods, and Lord of lords* (10:17), God is just and compassionate to all peoples. Israel is to exemplify that love even to aliens in the community. After all, they had been privileged to witness *great and awesome things* (10:21).

Keeping the covenant is not just a responsibility to be passed on to a future generation. Instead, this generation, on the basis of its own experiences, must live in the light of those experiences (11:1-7). Faithfulness to the covenant will be rewarded by blessing when they come into the land. Unfaithfulness, i.e., allowing themselves to be seduced into worshiping idols (11:16), will bring crop failure and famine (11:8-17). Therefore, full attention must be given to keeping and teaching the words and will of the LORD (11:18-21; see 6:5-9). Israel must be a holy people if they are to be successful in the holy war (11:22-25; chap. 7). The choice before Israel, then, is the choice between blessing that comes with obedience or the curse that will follow disobedience (11:26-28; Smith 1990, 188–89). On vv. 26-30, see comment on chap. 27.

"These are the statutes and ordinances," 12:1–25:19

The core of the second address is the Deuteronomistic Code, one of three such codes of Israelite law, the others being the Covenant Code and the Priestly Code (see Dahlberg 1990, esp. 503–07). While this particular code usually is regarded as the second oldest of the three, dating from the seventh century B.C.E., many of its laws reflect an earlier time. It is generally accepted that it was discovered during Josiah's reign and gave the theological basis for his reform (2 Kgs 22–23; Cochran 1990, 472). In general, it grows out of a settled society and advocates a more humane attitude toward less fortunate members of society, especially women and resident aliens.

12:1-28. One place to worship. A remedy that Deuteronomy proposes to combat the dangers of paganism is twofold: (1) to destroy pagan shrines (vv. 2-4); and (2) to have only one central place to worship (vv. 5-7). Both of these aims are fulfilled in JOSIAH's reform, following the finding of a document in the Temple (2 Kgs 22–23). In this single SHRINE, all SACRIFICE would be carried out (vv. 6, 11, 14). The Covenant Code provides for multiple shrines (Exod 20:24), as does an older part of the Priestly Code, known as the Holiness Code (Lev 17). As a result of the demand that all sacrifice be carried out at one central location, the code had to provide for nonpriestly slaughter of animals for food, while still maintaining the ban on eating blood (vv. 15-27, esp. vv. 23-24; Gen 9:3-4; Lev 17:10-11).

12:29–13:18. Avoiding idol worship and its advocates. A major concern of the Deuteronomistic Code was that Israel was continually being drawn to the worship of the gods of its neighbors. Coupled with the positive emphasis on total devotion to the LORD were warnings against being drawn into the worship of idols.

12:29-32. Do not worship other gods. The practices of others, whether they are social practices or religious practices, tempt Israel to *want to do the same* (12:30). The people, however, are to avoid such practices. Two examples of things to be avoided are cited: *every abhorrent thing* probably refers to cult prostitution (23:17-18), and the reference to burning *their sons and daughters* (v. 31) refers to the practice of human sacrifice, especially of children. Ample archaeological evidence of such practices has been found at ancient Carthage, a colony of the Phoenicians, where the children were sacrificed to the Phoenician god MOLECH (see Cornfeld 1976, 52; cf. Lev 18:21; 2 Kgs 23:10; Judg 11:29-40; Jer 32:35; also see Andrews 1990, 580–81 for a different interpretation of Molech).

13:1-5. The danger of false prophets. True prophets do not lead people into idolatry, no matter how spectacular their *omens or portents* (v. 1). False prophets serve only to test the sincerity of one's love for the LORD God (12:3-4). Israel is to take radical measures to rid itself of false prophets. To fail to do so would lead to idolatry (v. 5).

13:6-11. Unfaithful family members. Perhaps a more insidious threat to the health of one's religious life would be family members who try to lead others into the worship of false gods. The same radical measures are to be taken against them as against false prophets (vv. 9-11).

13:12-18. Idolatrous cities. Centers of idol worship are subject to the rules of holy war (vv. 12-16; see comments on chap. 7). Behind such radical measures as proposed by Deuteronomy are the twin convictions that: (1) the LORD God is holy, and (2) God demands an answering dedication to holy living by Israel. Anything less will not be sufficient (vv. 17-18).

14:1–15:23. Rules for holy living. In keeping with the LORD's demands, Deuteronomy sets forth specific rules for holy living. The rules cover a broad area of concern, from religious rites to be avoided to dietary taboos to humanitarian easing of religious demands.

14:1-2. Shun pagan customs. As acts of mourning, probably connected with seasonal worship, Israel's neighbors trimmed their forelocks and gashed their faces. Israel was forbidden to follow such practices (Lev 19:27-28; cf. Ezek 24:15-24; 1 Kgs 18:28).

14:3-21. Clean and unclean animals. Cleanness and uncleanness had both a physical and a religious significance. Here, an animal is clean that has *the hoof cleft in two, and chews the cud* (v. 6). A fish is clean if it *has fins and scales* (v. 9). All other fish and animals are unclean. While no clean birds are listed, unclean ones are; but no clear reason is given for the distinction, as is the case with the animals (vv. 11-20; see Eakin 1990, 159 and the commentary above on Lev 11). The ban against eating animals that die naturally did not arise out of sanitary considerations, but rather from the fact that they are not bled properly when they die. Eating flesh with blood still in it is expressly forbidden for *a people holy to the* LORD *your God* (v. 21). Boiling *a kid in its mother's milk* is a Canaanite religious practice and thus forbidden for Israel (v. 21).

14:22-29. The use of the tithe. Thanksgiving is an essential part of worship in early Israel. The tithe is part of that thanksgiving. It provides material support for the central sanctuary (Neh 10:35-39; Mal 3:8-10; Lev 27:30). Deuteronomy makes it clear, also, that those who bring the tithes eat a portion of them in the meals associated with the sacrifices (vv. 22-23). In light of its demand for a central sanctuary, Deuteronomy modifies the law of the tithe in two practical ways: (1) people who live too far away to bring animals or produce to the sanctuary may bring money to buy whatever is necessary for the sacrifices—*oxen, sheep, wine, strong drink, or whatever you desire* (v. 26); (2) instead of requiring the tithe to be brought annually, it can be brought *every third year* (v. 28).

15:1-18. The sabbatical year. The sabbath principle is applied to years as well as to weeks. For Deuteronomy it is, like the weekly sabbath, given for a humanitarian purpose. It is a time for the forgiveness of debts that one Israelite owes to another. Foreigners still have to pay, but the Israelite creditor has to *remit your claim on whatever any member of your community owes you* (v. 3). Lest anyone refuse to lend money as the sabbatical year approaches, there is the warning that failure to heed the cries of the needy neighbor will result in guilt being incurred. Instead, one is to *give liberally and be ungrudging,* for such liberality will bring the LORD's blessing (v. 10).

Closely related to the forgiveness of debt is the release of people who have been enslaved for debt. An Israelite can become a slave: (1) when one steals something, is caught, and cannot make the loss good (Exod 22:1 [21:37 MT]); (2)when one becomes so poor for some reason that slavery is the only option left for survival (Lev 25:39); or (3) when children are taken from their parents in lieu of payment of a debt (2 Kgs 4:1). Not only is the slave to be freed in the sabbatical year; he or she is to be *given some of the bounty with which the* LORD *your God has blessed you,* as an aid in starting a new life (v. 14). The Priestly Code has no such provisions (Lev 25:40-41). While earlier laws do not provide equal treatment for female slaves, Deuteronomy does (vv. 12, 17). These actions are to be taken without complaint, since *for six years they have given you service worth the wages of hired laborers.* In addition, ungrudging compliance will cause the LORD God to *bless you in all that you do* (v. 18).

15:19-23. The sacrifice of firstborn animals. Ancient people held that the firstborn of both humans and animals had a special significance. While some other peoples sacrificed firstborn children, Israelite law provides for the redemption of such (Num 18:15; Exod 34:20; cf. Gen 22:1-19). Firstborn animals are to be taken to the central sanctuary and sacrificed, provided they have no physical deformities. Such sacrifices are joyous occasions, since the person who is offering the sacrifice eats a portion of the animal after a portion is given to the priest (v. 20; Lev 1:3-13).

Defective animals are not sacrificed, but can be eaten, if they are killed in the proper way (vv. 21-23).

16:1-17. Holy days. This is Deuteronomy's version of laws for the festival days: Passover/Unleavened Bread, the Festival of Weeks, and the Festival of Booths. These regulations occupy a middle position between those found in Exodus (23:12-19 and 34:18-26), which are earlier, and those in Leviticus (chap. 23) and Numbers (chaps. 28–29), which are later.

16:1-8. Passover/Unleavened Bread. *Observe . . . by keeping the passover* (v. 1). Passover probably originated as a shepherd's festival, celebrated in the Spring (March–April), and designed to insure a successful lambing season. As a result of the exodus experience, Israel adapts it to commemorate the conviction that *the LORD your God brought you out of Egypt by night* (v. 1). The word "passover" is based on the Hebrew verb *pasach*, meaning *to pass or spring over*, and most likely has to do with the conviction of Israel that "they were *passed over* or spared by the *destroyer (death)* (Joines 1990, 648). *You shall offer . . . at the place that the LORD will choose* (v. 2) represents a change in two important aspects: (1) previously passover was to be eaten in one's own town and essentially was a family festival (Exod 12:21-28), but now it becomes one of three major festivals celebrated at the central shrine; (2) it is combined with the festival of unleavened bread, another older festival that originated as an agricultural festival, celebrating the harvest of grain. In the Covenant Code (Exod 23:14-15), this latter festival is the first major festival of the year. Deuteronomy retains it by combining it with passover to maintain the number of three major festivals. Thus, there is *the passover sacrifice . . . from the flock and the herd* (v. 2) followed by seven days when *you shall eat unleavened bread* [*matsot*] (v. 3). The ban on offering the passover sacrifice *within any of your towns* (v. 5) is in line with Deuteronomy's emphasis on the centralization of worship. The reform of King Josiah was based on these principles and included a national celebration of the passover, the likes of which had not been kept "since the days of the judges who judged Israel" (2 Kgs 23:22). This would seem to indicate that Josiah was reviving an ancient practice (cf. Josh 5:10-11; see Kraus 1966, 51).

16:9-12. The Festival of Weeks. *Seven weeks*, that is, fifty days after the month of Abib (March–April), brings one to May–June, the time for the grain harvest that this festival celebrates. Later, it is called Pentecost (Acts 2:1), based on the Greek word for the number fifty. This is a joyous festival requiring *a freewill offering in proportion to the blessing that you have received* (v. 10). A bountiful harvest is cause for joy for all: *you . . . sons . . . daughters . . . male and female slaves . . . the Levites . . . strangers . . . orphans . . . widows* (v. 11). In short, it means that God is showing favor to Israel and that there will be enough to eat in the days ahead (Hancock 1990a, 873; 1990b, 957–58).

16:13-15. Festival of Booths. This seven-day festival comes *when you have gathered in the produce from your threshing floor and your wine press* (v. 13). It originally celebrated the fruit harvest. In later practice, it came to commemorate the wilderness experience when Israel lived in tents. Thus, the name "festival of booths" or "tabernacles." It, too, calls for general rejoicing (v. 14) and becomes "the most joyous and universal" of the major festivals (1 Kgs 8:2,65; 2 Chr 7:8; Ezek 45:23-25; Hancock 1990a, 873). The reforms of Ezra gave it an especially prominent place (Neh 8).

16:16-17. Attendance at the festivals. *All your males* were expected to attend the major festivals. They are not to appear *empty-handed*, but are *to give as they are able* as the LORD God has blessed them. This requirement is an ideal that becomes increasingly difficult to achieve, especially after the Babylonian EXILE and the scattering of the Israelites, now called Jews, all over the Near East and the Mediterranean world. For many, to be able to journey to Jerusalem for the great festivals once in a lifetime was a major event.

16:18–17:20. Civil and religious laws. Here are found rules for the administration of justice and for the regulation of religion. The rules include the appointment of judges who will be concerned with *justice, and only justice* (16:20); how to deal with persons accused of idolatry; how to handle cases that are unusually difficult to adjudicate; and how kings are to be controlled.

16:18-20. Administration of justice. The hope for real justice always begins with the appointment of *judges and officials* . . . [who] *shall render just decisions for the people* (v. 18). Justice can be distorted in two ways: (1) by showing partiality and favoritism in its administration, and (2) by the giving and the taking of bribes, *for a bribe blinds the eyes of the wise and subverts the cause of those who are in the right* (v. 19). The preservation and promotion of justice in any society is essential for the continuing health and prosperity of the community (v. 20).

16:21-22. Avoid Canaanite customs. The *tree* or *sacred pole* could represent phallic symbols of Baal, but a more likely interpretation is that the pole was a carved representation of Asherah, "the wife/consort of the chief god of the Canaanite and Phoenician pantheons" (Vinson 1990, 68). Likewise, the tree would have the same symbolism. These, along with the *stone pillar*, are Canaanite cult objects, things that *the LORD your God hates* (v. 22).

17:1. An unworthy sacrifice. To offer an animal *that has a defect* is insulting to the LORD God because it is less than one's best and reveals an improper attitude (cf. Mal 1:7-8).

17:2-7. Penalties for pagan worship. Just as enticing one to worship idols calls for severe penalties, so also the presence of idol worship itself calls for strong measures to stamp it out in Israel (cf. 13:6-18). Imbedded in this section is a fundamental principle of Israelite jurisprudence: capital punishment cannot be carried out unless two or three persons witnessed the crime. The accused cannot be sentenced to death based on the testimony of one person alone (v. 6). Death is by stoning and the witnesses also are to lead in the execution (v. 7). This requirement, in itself, should be a deterrent to giving false testimony. See the commentary on the Book of Susanna for a later example of how this type of procedure was carried out.

17:8-13. Disposal of difficult cases. Cases too difficult for local courts to decide may be appealed to a higher court. In general, these cases are in three categories: (1) homicide cases, whether they were premeditated or unpremeditated (Exod 21:12-14; see further the comments on Deut 19:4-7); (2) civil matters, i.e., one kind of legal claim or another; or (3) physical assault (Exod 21:18-27). The higher court consists of *the levitical priests and the judge who is in office in those days* (v. 9). The priests would be those at the central sanctuary and the judge is probably a layperson (vv. 8-9; see 2 Chr 19:5-11). Their decision is to be carried out to the letter. Anyone who presumes to do otherwise is subject to the death penalty (vv. 10-13).

17:14-20. Rules for kingship. An antimonarchical bias continued to flourish in Israel long after the beginning of the monarchy. At Saul's inaugural, Samuel is said to have laid down rules for the kingship; he wrote the rules "in a book and laid it up before the LORD" (1 Sam 10:25). Such a bias undoubtedly contributed to the breakup of the kingdom at Solomon's death. Israel's kings are to be native-born: *you are not permitted to put a foreigner over you* (v. 15). *Many horses . . . many wives . . . silver and gold . . . in great quantity* all represent dangers for the king, leading to entanglements with foreign governments, too much physical pleasure, and pride, *exalting himself above the other members of the community* [or] *turning aside from the commandment* (vv. 16-20; cf. 2 Kgs 22:8).

18:1-22. Rules for proper worship. Two important categories of religious officials are the subjects of these rules—priests and prophets. Both offices have heavy responsibility. Singled out for special attention are the dangers of idolatry and of false prophecy.

18:1-8. Priests and their support. *The levitical priests, the whole tribe of Levi, shall have no allotment* refers to the fact that the Levites (LEVI/LEVITES) are, by tradition, a landless tribe, dependent upon the people for their support. At one time, they seem to have been a secular tribe who, because of their service to the LORD, were made PRIESTS (Exod 32:25-29). Yet, some passages cast doubt on this conclusion (Exod 4:14; Judg 17:7; Num 3:5-9). In later tradition, the Levites are usually spoken of more as a guild of religious workers. Tradition has it that they lost favor with the monarchy when ABIATHAR, a Levite, plotted against the elevation of Solomon to the throne and was replaced by the priest Zadok, whose descendants then became the dominant priestly family (see Bjornard 1990a, 510–11; 1990b, 710–11). Deuteronomy's laws seem to exalt the Levites more than other codes do. Deuteronomy follows a more traditional view of the origin and function of the Levites (v. 2). Their support comes from the animals that are sacrificed (*they shall give to the priest the shoulder, . . . jowls, and the stomach*), as well as *the first fruits . . .* [and] *the first of the fleece of your sheep* (vv. 3-4). Since ministry is the function of the priest, he deserves the support of all the people for his service (v. 5). It should be observed that such a ministry covered more functions than strictly religious duties. The priest was also teacher, a medical practitioner, and legal expert. A Levite in *any of your towns* denotes Levites who presided over local shrines before worship was centralized during Josiah's reign (2 Kgs 23:8). While Deuteronomy decrees that they are to be allowed to function as priests in Jerusalem (vv. 6-8), it seems that, in reality, they did not do so (2 Kgs 23:9).

18:9-14. Avoiding false worship. This is yet another warning against being drawn into the worship of pagan gods. Making *a son or daughter pass through fire* (v. 10) seems to be a rite associated with the worship of MOLECH, the Ammonite deity (see 2 Kgs 16:3 where Pekah of Israel is said to have burned his son; cf. 2 Kgs 21:6; Jer 7:31; 19:5; 32:35). Israel is warned to *remain completely loyal to the LORD your God* (v. 13).

18:15-18. Respect for the LORD's prophets. While the priest is perceived as a professional who is skilled in directing communication *toward* God, prophets are known as spokespersons *for* God. Their message is not their own; it is the LORD's message. The prophet is only the messenger. Moses is seen as the prophet *par excellence* (34:10-11), the one who is the model for all other prophets. Any true prophet must be *a prophet like* Moses (v. 15). A true prophet is one to whom the LORD speaks and who, in turn, is the LORD's spokesperson (v. 18; cf. Exod 7:1). How to separate the true prophet from the false always is a continuing problem, even in modern society. Such an influential and powerful function is a magnet for charlatans. The test of the true prophet is: *If* [one] *speaks in the name of the LORD but the thing does not take place or prove true, . . . the LORD has not spoken* (v. 22; cf. Jer 28). Other tests of true prophecy also appear: those who prophesy *smooth things* (Isa 30:10) are not trustworthy, while those who have stood in God's council (Jer 23:32) have received God's true word.

19:1-21. Rules for administering justice. Several legal procedures are the subject of this section. Chief among them is the provision for cities of refuge, designed to offer temporary protection to persons who have committed homicide.

19:1-13. Cities of refuge. Here Deuteronomy gives a further elaboration of a subject introduced in 4:41-43 (see comments there). *You shall set apart three cities* in addition to those named in 4:41-43. These are to be on the west side of the Jordan (19:1-3). *This is the case of a homicide* introduces a more precise delineation between intentional and unintentional killing. Here the emphasis is on an accidental killing, illustrated by an example: an axehead comes loose from the handle, striking a bystander and killing him (v. 5; cf. Num 35:13-28 where many examples are given; see also Exod 21:12-14). The briefest of these texts dealing with places of refuge (Exod 21:12-14) is from the oldest code (Covenant) while the more elaborate discussion in Numbers is from the Priestly Code. That our passage from Deuteronomy is more detailed than Exodus but less detailed than Numbers would seem to suggest it stands between these two passages chronologically as well. *The killer may flee to one of these cities and live* reveals the purpose of the cities of refuge—to provide a chance for a fair hearing for one who is not guilty of murder. Yet there is danger, for *if the distance is too great* the killer may not be able to escape the vengeful hand of the *avenger of blood* whose *hot anger* would certainly color his sense of fairness toward one who had killed his relative accidentally (v. 6). Deuteronomy envisions that Israel's territorial expansion may necessitate the addition of *three more cities*, for a total of nine (vv. 8-10; but see Num 35:13-15 and Josh 20:7-9 where the number is six). Judgment seems to be in the hands of the elders of the killer's home city. If the elders determine that a murder has been committed, then the murderer is to be taken from the city of refuge *and handed over to the avenger of blood to be put to death* (v. 12). Here we see the beginning of the practice of the state's playing a role by judging the person who has killed someone, while still allowing the nearest of kin of the deceased to carry out the execution. This manner of dealing with murder was in vogue in Israel at least until the time of Solomon (see Solomon's belated punishment of Joab for the murder of Abner, 1 Kgs 2:28-35).

19:14. Property markers. That *your neighbor's boundary marker* is an ancient law is attested by the fact that there is reference to the same law twice in the Book of Proverbs (22:28; 23:10).

19:15-21. Rules for witnesses. *A single witness shall not suffice* introduces an expansion of the principle first laid down in 17:6 (see comment on that verse). A charge can only be sustained on the testimony of two or more witnesses (v. 15). If a malicious person deliberately gives false testimony against an innocent person, the penalty is that the assembled spectators *shall do to the false witness just as the false witness had meant to do to the other* (v. 19). Thus, the lecherous old men who were rebuffed by the heroine in the apocryphal story of Susanna accuse her of adultery. When Daniel unmasks their plot, it is they, not Susanna, who are stoned.

This passage concludes with the law of retaliation (*lex talionis*); *life for life, eye for eye, tooth for tooth*, etc. (v. 21). *Lex talionis* was a progressive step in the development of law because it adjusted the punishment to the nature of the crime. Before this development, which probably arose as the state took a more active role in law enforcement, the older law of vengeance could lead to all sorts of excessive punishment, since the avenger was the one who would determine what punishment was sufficient to satisfy the desire for vengeance (cf. Gen 4:23-24).

20:1-20. Rules for holy war. This section is a further elaboration of the rules for holy war (see comments on 7:1-26, and Wilson 1990, 385–86). The institution of holy warfare probably was no more than a cherished memory by the time the Book of Deuteronomy was completed.

20:1-9. Preparation for holy war. When Israel faces *an army*, even one that is larger than their own, in holy war, the people are not to fear, for *the LORD your God is with you* (v. 1). The basic premise of holy war is that it is the LORD God who fights for the people. The use of the priests to provide inspiration and encouragement, including the offering of special sacrifices prior to the battle, lends further emphasis to this point (vv. 2-4; cf. 1 Sam 13:8-12 where Saul, in desperation, offers the sacrifice after Samuel is delayed). The rules also provide for certain persons to be exempt from going to battle: one who has *built a new house but not dedicated it* (v. 5); one who has *planted a vineyard but not yet enjoyed its fruit* (v. 6); one who is newly betrothed but not yet married (v. 7); or anyone who is *afraid or disheartened*, since his attitude may cause *the heart of his comrades to melt like his own* (v. 8; cf. Judg 7:2-3). The warriors must have no distractions as they go into battle.

20:10-20. Prosecution of the holy war. Whether those people being attacked are allowed to sue for peace depends upon where they are located. Those outside Israel's borders are allowed to make peace and serve *at forced labor* (v. 11; cf. Josh 9 and the story of the Gibeonites). If, however, there is resistance, the men are to be killed, but *the women, the children, livestock and everything else in the town* are spoils of war. They are to be taken and used since *the* LORD *your God* has given them to the people (v. 14). Within the land, a different rule applies. Here, Israel *must not let anything that breathes remain alive*, lest the survivors *teach you to do all the abhorrent things that they do for their gods*, causing Israel to sin against the LORD God (vv. 16-18; cf. Josh 7; 1 Sam 15:17-23). This is not to be scorched earth warfare, however. To destroy the trees, especially fruit trees, would be self-defeating, since the people can *take food from them* (v. 19). Only non-fruit-bearing trees can be cut for the purpose of building siegeworks. The rule against cutting fruit trees such as the olive is still observed in the modern state of Israel. An olive tree that dies must stand for three years before it is cut, thus making sure it actually is dead.

21:1–23:14. Miscellaneous laws. The laws found in this section cover a variety of subjects and situations. Included are several laws designed to maintain the holiness of the land and others regulating family life on the land.

21:1-9. Bloodguilt and an unsolved murder. Because of an ancient belief that any shedding of human blood causes a ritual defilement of the land, this law addresses incidents of such ritual defilement and how to overcome the defilement. The shedding of innocent blood is one of the strongest taboos in early Israel. When a person is killed by another and the killer is known, proper punishment can be inflicted upon the guilty person, thus removing the stigma of bloodguilt (Gen 9:6; see Jer 26:1: Jeremiah plays on this fear as part of his defense in a trial for his life). This passage deals with the guilt incurred when *it is not known who struck the person down* (v. 1). The first problem is to determine what town is nearest the scene. This is to be done by measuring *the distances to the towns that are near the body* (v. 2). Then, *the elders of the town nearest the body shall take a heifer* that has never been used as a draft animal (*has not pulled in the yoke*) to be used as a sacrifice of substitution (v. 3). The place of sacrifice is to be a valley (*wadi*) *with running water, which is neither plowed nor sown*. Here, the animal is to be killed by breaking its neck (v. 4). Nothing is said about cutting the animal's throat as is prescribed in other sacrifices, but the proclamation by the elders that *our hands did not shed this blood* (commit this murder) might seem to suggest that the animal's blood may also have been shed (v. 7; cf. Lev 1:5, 11). *The priests, the sons of Levi,* those from the central sanctuary (18:1) then *pronounce blessings in the name of the LORD*. Their decisions *in all cases of dispute and assault are final* (v. 5). At this point in the ceremony, *the elders of that town nearest the body shall wash their hands over the heifer* and declare their innocence, both as to having committed the crime and as to having witnessed its commission. All this is accompanied by a prayer to the LORD for absolution of the guilt (vv. 7-8). This done, the priests then pronounce them free from bloodguiltiness (vv. 8-9).

21:10-14. Treatment of female captives. This is a supplement to the rules of holy war. Should a beautiful non-Palestinian woman be captured some soldier may wish to take her as his wife (Num 31:18). This can be done if the prescribed rituals are observed (vv. 12-13) If the marriage does not prove satisfactory, she is to be set free, not sold to someone else as a slave. This law was undoubtedly for the purpose of cutting down on the incidence of rape in warfare, as well as emphasizing the importance of family in Israelite culture. It is in keeping with Deuteronomy's humanitarian attitude toward the less powerful members of society.

21:15-17. Status of firstborn sons. This law established the inheritance rights of firstborn sons of a man's primary wife, regardless of any change in feelings he might have toward her when he has acquired other wives (vv. 15-16). Favoritism toward a second wife and her children cannot deprive the firstborn son of the rights inherent with his position. He is to receive *a double portion* of his father's possessions: *since he is the first issue of his virility, the right of the firstborn is his* (v. 17; see Gen 25:29-34).

21:18-21. Treatment of rebellious children. This seemingly harsh law is designed to protect the sanctity and stability of the family. Not even a child of the family is allowed by disgraceful behavior to threaten the stability of the family. According to Deuteronomy, such disgraceful behavior must be dealt with by strong measures, since such behavior constitutes an evil that must be removed (vv. 18-21).

21:22-23. Burial of dead criminals. *You hang him on a tree* refers to the practice of impaling the body of an executed criminal on a sharpened upright stake. This practice was reserved for those whose crimes were especially heinous, or for one's enemies, especially pagan kings (Josh 8:29; 10:26-27; 1 Sam 31:8-10; 2 Sam 4:12). The body, moreover, is to be taken down and buried before nightfall, since the failure to do so will *defile the land that the LORD* is giving Israel. This is true because such a person is *under God's curse* (v. 23).

22:1-4. Care of lost and injured animals. Israelite law is concerned to promote mutual help among members of the community, as well as to emphasize the sacredness of property rights. *You shall not watch your neighbor's ox or sheep straying* (v. 1) introduces such a law. When a person owns only a few animals, they are an essential part of the person's livelihood. The loss of an ox, the chief means of breaking up the soil for agriculture, or of a sheep, the source of clothing as well as of meat, could be devastating for a small farmer or a shepherd whose holdings were minimal. To care for a neighbor's lost property as one would for one's own is essential for the well-being of the community. This is the practical expression of *love your neighbor as you love yourself* (Lev 19:18; cf. Mark 12:31). The same rule applies when one finds the *neighbor's donkey or ox fallen on the road . . . : you shall help to lift it up* (v. 4).

22:5. Proper dress. Since this prohibition against a woman's wearing of a man's clothing or *vice versa* is described as *abhorrent to the LORD your God* as are other Canaanite practices, this may also be a reference to transvestism or simulated sex changes practiced in Canaanite religion. It could, however, simply reflect a conservative bias against anything unusual or unnatural (see Wright 1953, 464).

22:6-7. Protection of bird life. *If you come on a bird's nest . . . you shall not take the mother* (v. 6). This is yet another instance in Israelite law of a practical ecological approach to life (cf. the prohibition of the unnecessary destruction of trees, esp. fruit trees, 20:19-20). Preservation of the female bird will insure the continued production of eggs and young, much the same as saving seed for field crops. From a practical standpoint, a continuing food supply is the best guarantee of the fulfillment of the promise that *you may live long* in the land given by the LORD (v. 7).

22:8. Proper roof construction. *When you build a new house . . . make a parapet.* This assumes a type of construction with a flat roof and an outside stairway where one can use the roof in the cool of the evening for rest and relaxation. The parapet, a wall around the four sides of the roof, protects both owner and guests—the guests from accidentally falling off the roof and the owner from bloodguilt, *if anyone should fall from it.*

22:9-11. Mixing of kinds. Prohibitions of sowing with *a second kind of seed* (v. 9), plowing *an ox and a donkey yoked together* (v. 10), or wearing clothes made of *wool and linen woven together* (v. 11) seem to arise from an Israelite belief that the LORD makes things distinctive for a purpose. To mix them is an attempt to defeat the LORD's purpose. Note the stress placed upon the different kinds of plants and animals in Gen 1:11-12, 21, 24-25.

22:12. Tassels on clothing. *You shall make tassels.* According to Num 15:39, tassels or fringes are used so that the people *will remember all the commandments of the LORD and do them.* In other words, they serve as visual reminders and thus are teaching devices. Such tassels are a prominent feature on the prayer shawls worn in synagogue services today.

22:13-30. Divorce and sexual relationships. This section is a series of case laws that pose a violation and then establish the punishment ("If this is done, the result will be this"). These laws are believed to have been taken by the writer(s) of Deuteronomy from an older source. They all deal with relations between the sexes.

Suppose a man marries a woman (22:13) introduces the case of a husband who tries to divorce his wife by falsely accusing her of not being a virgin at marriage. His real reason, however, is that after consummating the marriage (*going in to her*), he decides that *he dislikes her* (v. 13). The parents *submit the evidence of the young woman's virginity to the elders* (v. 15). This evidence is a bloody cloth, showing that when the husband first penetrated her, her hymen was ruptured and she bled on the cloth that she had under her body. The cloth is *spread out . . . before the elders of the town* (v. 17). Since they have the proof, the husband is to be fined *one hundred shekels of silver*, which is paid to the bride's father in compensation for the damage done to the bride's family. In addition, *she shall remain his wife* with no divorce allowed (v. 19). On the other hand, should the parents be unable to produce evidence of her virginity, she is to die by stoning *because she committed a disgraceful act . . . by prostituting herself in her father's house* (v. 21).

The death penalty is applied to both parties when a man is found *lying with the wife of another man* (v. 22). Regarding a virgin who is engaged and has intercourse with a man other than her intended husband, two possible situations are noted. In the first, if a man meets an engaged virgin *in the town and lies with her* and they are caught in the act, it is assumed that she had consented. The reasoning is that if she had cried for help inside a town, she would have been heard. Judgment is to be carried out in *the gate of that town* (vv. 23-24).

"In the gate" is the equivalent of our saying, in the courthouse or courtroom: the town gate, in reality, was more of a building, as a recent discovery at Tell Dan in Northern Israel has vividly illustrated. The penalty for both the man and the woman is death; she, because she consented, and he, because *he violated his neighbor's wife* (v. 24). That she is spoken of as *his neighbor's wife* shows the binding nature of betrothal or engagement in Israelite culture.

A different situation arises where a man engages in intercourse with an engaged woman in the open country. The assumption is that he raped her; therefore *only the man who lay with her shall die* (v. 25). Her innocence is assumed on the basis that *she may have cried for help but there was no one to rescue her* (v. 27).

Still another situation involves the rape of an unengaged virgin by a man who is *caught in the act* (v. 28). The rapist must pay the girl's parents *fifty shekels* (v. 29) as a bride price, a financial transaction that was part of all marriage arrangements. In a regular marriage, the amount could vary, depending upon the economic status of the families involved (see Gen 24:52-53 where Abraham's servant Eliezer pays Rebekah's family a huge sum for her). The young woman who is raped becomes the man's wife, with no divorce permitted (v. 29).

The prohibition against a man's marrying *his father's wife* (v. 30) reflects the polygamous nature of early Israelite society. The woman involved would be the man's stepmother. Such a relationship would be incestuous (27:20; Lev 18:8; 20:11).

<u>23:1-8. Bars to membership in the assembly.</u> *The assembly of the LORD* here refers to "a gathering of influential males" (Sutherland 1990, 70). This ban against a man whose sexual organs are mutilated probably arises from the fact that eunuchs (castrated men) were priests in pagan cults, particularly among the Canaanites (2 Kgs 9:32; Jer 34:19; but see Isa 56:4-5; Acts 8:27-38).

Since illicit sexual unions (v. 2) were so severely punished (see comments on 22:22-30), it is not surprising that a child born of such a union would be shunned. The banning of anyone who is *Ammonite or Moabite* (vv. 3-6) is justified by the fact that they are traditional enemies who *did not meet you with food and water on your journey out of Egypt* and hired BALAAM to curse Israel (see Num 22–24 on Balaam). On the other hand, the Edomites and the Egyptians are less noxious since the Edomites are kinsfolk and Egypt was Israel's home before the exodus. Egyptian influences seem to have figured strongly in the rule of Solomon, especially with regard to the wisdom tradition (Prov 22:17–24:22).

23:9-14. More rules for holy war. These rules deal with sanitary and ritual cleanness during the HOLY WAR. Early people were not aware of the dangers of a lack of proper sanitation, but would be concerned about exposed body wastes in living areas. *Any impropriety* (v. 9) is further defined in the verses that follow. *Nocturnal emission* refers to a discharge of semen, while the other references are to other normal bodily functions. For the camp to *be holy*, it must be clean, both ritually and otherwise.

23:15–25:19. Humanitarian and religious obligations. These laws highlight Deuteronomy's concern for the less fortunate members of Israelite society.

23:15-16. Treatment of escaped slaves. The phrase *slaves who have escaped to you . . . shall not be given back* seems to assume that the owner is a non-Israelite and that the slave has been mistreated, causing him to flee. The evidence that Israelite law protected an escaped slave is all the more striking in light of Law 16 in the Code of Hammurabi—a law demanding the death of anyone who harbors an escaped slave.

23:17-18. Temple prostitution. The terms for both male and female prostitutes are those that indicate that they were dedicated to a deity. Literally, they are called "holy ones," meaning "those dedicated to a special purpose." Such prostitution of both sexes was a prominent feature of fertility cults such as Baalism. The practice was strictly forbidden in Israel; in addition any financial gain from the practice was not to be given as an offering to God, for that would be *abhorrent to the LORD your God* (v. 18).

23:19-20. Loans to fellow Israelites. The matters covered here are essentially the same as those listed in 15:1-11. The kinds of interest named here (*on money, . . . on provisions, . . . on anything that is lent*) would seem to cover those things loaned to a fellow Israelite who was in need (v. 19). In other words, one does not charge interest on charitable loans. These are not business loans, but loans designed to meet a need (see Wright 1953, 472).

The permission to lend to foreigners (v. 20) provided the rationale during the Middle Ages for Christian states to permit Jews to be bankers, since Jews could make loans to Gentiles and charge interest. It also, unfortunately, became the real basis for much of the persecution of the Jews. When a ruler did not want to repay his loans, he started a pogrom or persecution, driving the Jews out of his country.

23:21-23. Vows to the LORD. The phrase *If you make a vow to the LORD* introduces a warning against foolish promises, especially dealing with acts of devotion to the LORD (v. 21). Vows are to be taken seriously, since words spoken in solemn situations were thought to carry unusual power. Thus one should speak such words carefully and carry out what is promised (v. 23; Lev 27; Acts 21:23-24).

23:24-25. Use of other's crops. To *go into your neighbor's vineyard* for the purpose of satisfying one's immediate hunger is acceptable (v. 24). Carrying off the *grapes* or *standing grain* is not (v. 25). Only the owner has the right to harvest the fruit or the grain.

24:1-5. Divorce and marriage rights. This law places the right to a divorce with the husband on the grounds that *he finds something objectionable* in the wife (v. 1). After the divorce, if the woman should become the wife of another and if he, likewise *writes her a bill of divorce* or dies, the first husband is not permitted to remarry her *after she has been defiled* (v. 4). Why this would defile her is not clear, but it is serious enough to be seen as bringing *guilt on the land* (v. 4; but see 2 Sam 3:14-15 where David insists that Michal be returned to his harem even though she is married to another). This case differs from the one treated in 22:13-19, which is designed to protect the woman from being divorced because of a false accusation (Snodgrass 1990, 218).

The holy war regulation allowing a newly married man exemption from military or related duty so that he may *be free at home one year*, is designed to assure the continuity of families. Great emphasis is placed on a man's having a son to bear his name. It is through one's sons that one continues to live, since there was no developed concept of life after death (v. 5; cf. Isa 53:8, 10; Jer 16:1-4; Job 3).

24:6. A forbidden pledge. To take away one's grinding stones, either *the mill or the upper millstone*, would deprive that person of bread, the basis of life. This would be the equivalent of *taking a life in pledge*.

24:7. A forbidden act. *Kidnaping another Israelite* in order to force that person into slavery or to sell that person to someone else as a slave is an offense that merits the death penalty.

24:8-9. Treatment of leprosy. *A leprous skin disease* may refer to various types of skin disorders, including Hansen's disease (which causes the loss of fingers and toes), as well as other skin rashes such as psoriasis (Geren 1990, 508–509). The instruction to *carefully observe whatever the levitical priests instruct you* (v. 8) seems to indicate that these levitical priests served both as religious and as medical practitioners.

24:10-15. Care for the needy. These rules dealing with the collection of debt are designed both to preserve the debtor's dignity and privacy and to minimize the person's suffering. In the first instance, when making a loan, the creditor is not allowed to invade *the house to take the pledge* or collateral. Instead, the creditor *shall wait outside*, and the debtor *brings the pledge* outside (vv. 10-11). In the second instance, while the words *the garment given you as* are not in the Hebrew text, NRSV assumes this is the meaning of the reference to sleeping *in . . . the pledge* and by the reference to the *cloak* in v. 13. Keeping a poor person's cloak overnight is seen as an act of cruelty, since the cloak is not only an article of clothing but also serves as a cover at night to keep the owner warm (cf. Amos 2:8, and King 1988, 24–25).

To *withhold wages of poor and needy laborers* (v. 14) would be a callous act. Wages are to be paid *daily before sunset*. Since the LORD is on the side of the poor and needy, one who withholds wages risks incurring guilt should the poor *cry to the LORD* about their mistreatment (24:15; cf. Matt 20:1-16).

24:16. Individual responsibility. This is Deuteronomy's modification of the ancient belief in corporate guilt or responsibility (Num 16:31-33; Josh 7:24-25; 2 Sam 21:1-9). What is stated here is more in line with Jer 31:29 and Ezek 18:1-24.

24:17-22. Care for the less fortunate. Three groups—resident aliens, orphans, and widows—are viewed as a community responsibility, since they share a common plight. Each has been deprived of family support groups. Their rights in court are not to be abridged, nor is one to *take a widow's garment in pledge* (v. 17). Since the LORD *your God redeemed* Israel from Egypt when they were still slaves, there is now a responsibility for the members of the community to share their blessings to help alleviate the sufferings of impoverished or destitute members of society. Care is extended by leaving grain in the field and fruit on the trees and vines for the needy to harvest (vv. 19-22; Lev 19:9-10; 23:22; cf. Ruth 2:1-7).

25:1-3. Corporal punishment. In the case of a judgment where *two persons have a dispute* and one is declared *to be in the wrong* (v. 1) and the wrongdoer *deserves to be flogged*, the maximum prescribed penalty is forty lashes, but may be less (vv. 2-3). In later times, the maximum number of lashes given is thirty-nine, so that if the number is miscounted, the law will not be violated by excessive punishment. Such excesses are illegal as well (2 Cor 2:6-7).

25:4. Humane treatment of animals. Proper treatment of work animals is a matter both of good business and of sound religion (cf. 22:6-7).

25:5-10. Rules for levirate marriage. *When brothers reside together. . . . Her husband's brother shall go in to her* (v. 5). The levirate marriage required a man's widow to marry his nearest male relative, here spoken of as his brother. *Brother* is to be interpreted in the context of the extended family, where the term "brother" covers a much wider range of relationships than is common in today's nuclear family. Even cousins and uncles could assume the obligations of a *brother* (Lev 25:47-49) who is called the *go'el*. Fulfilling the obligations of levirate marriage is one of three functions of the near kinsman. In addition to the obligations of levirate marriage, the *go'el* sees that his brother's murder is properly punished and that family property is redeemed so as not to be lost to the family if the present owner should need to dispose of it (see 19:6 where he is the *avenger of blood*, and Jer 32:1-15 where the redemption of property is involved). The law of the levirate marriage is designed to preserve a man's name in the event that he dies before he fathers a son to bear his name. The brother of the deceased is to marry the latter's widow. The firstborn son of that union is given the name of the dead husband (Gen 48:15-16; Ruth 4:17) While there is no punishment as such for one who refuses to assume the obligations of the levirate, there is a ceremony in the presence of the elders in which the culprit is held up to shame because *he does not build up his brother's house.* (vv. 7-10).

25:11-12. Sexual impropriety. This case law deals with a threat to a man's ability to father children (v. 11). Even though a woman would be defending her husband in this situation, seizing a man's genitals is a serious offense, calling for a severe penalty (v. 12).

25:13-16. Honest weights. This law deals with honesty in the marketplace, a universal problem. *Two kinds of weights* were used on balances to get more than an honest amount when selling or to pay less than the fair price when buying. One might also use false measures to give less than full measure when selling and to take more than honest measure when buying. The standard should be *a full and honest weight* and *a full and honest measure* (v. 15). Anything less is unacceptable (v. 16). That these practices were common in the marketplace is confirmed by archaeological discoveries from the time of the eighth-century prophets (Mic 6:10-11; Amos 8:5-6; see King 1988, 22–23).

25:17-19. Treatment of the Amalekites. Comments above on 23:1-8 provide a context for treating the issues surrounding the relationship between the Israelites and the Amalekites (also cf. Exod 17:8-15).

"When you have come into the land"—
The Concluding Rituals and an Interlude, 26:1–27:26

The purpose of this section and the concluding exhortation of Moses in chap. 28 is to impress upon the people that the possessions they have are the gift of the LORD. They also are urged to reflect on the blessings that accrue from that gift, and the responsibilities that go with those blessings.

26:1-11. Liturgy for the firstfruits. A central element in Israel's worship is thanksgiving—thanksgiving for the land the LORD God is *giving . . . as an inheritance to possess* (v. 1) and thanksgiving for the produce that is harvested from that land (v. 2). Here the reference is to the liturgy for firstfruits, performed at the central shrine during the festival of Weeks, which celebrated the wheat harvest (16:9-12). The worshiper is to take *some of the first of all the fruit of the ground,* that is, some of each type of produce, *put it in a basket,* and take it to the central shrine (v. 2). There the worshiper is to recite a confession of faith, recalling the historical circumstances that led to Israel's possession of the LORD God's gift of the land. These circumstances include the seminomadic wanderings of the ancestors that led to the sojourn in Egypt where numerically they prospered but then became slaves (vv. 7-9); the LORD's attentiveness to their cries of distress; and their deliverance with *a mighty hand and an outstretched arm, . . . and with signs and wonders,* climaxing with the giving of the land (vv. 5-10). The use of plural pronouns throughout the confession identifies the worshiper with the community of faith, past and present. It is widely agreed by scholars that this is an old confession.

Much has been made of the failure to mention the giving of the law at Sinai. This omission could arise from the nature of the act of worship in which the confession is used. The act is designed to *celebrate with all the bounty that the LORD your God has given to you and to your house* (v. 11). Since that is the prime emphasis, rather than the giving of the law, there was no need to mention Sinai. Others argue, however, that Sinai is not mentioned because the Sinai story is from a different set of traditions, perhaps originating among Israelites who entered the land with a different set of experiences than those from whom this confession originates (see von Rad 1962, 121–28). Whatever the origin of the Deuteronomy confession, its purpose is to celebrate God's gift of the land by annually (or perhaps every seventh year—see Deut 31:9-13) bringing the first and best of the harvest as an offering to the deity.

26:12-15. Liturgy of the tithe. A similar sense of celebration also accompanied the paying of the tithe, part of which is to be eaten *in the presence of the LORD your God, you and your household rejoicing together* (14:26). It is to be paid *in the third year (which is the year of the tithe)* and its function is to provide support for *the Levites, the aliens, the orphans, and the widows, so that they may eat their fill within your towns* (v. 12). The ceremony includes an oath by the tither in which he disavows any misuse of the tithe. Indeed, it is being given *in accordance with your entire commandment that you commanded me*, a vow to the LORD that would seem to address the question of attitude or motivation (v. 13). An assurance that the tithe is ritually clean is given with three negative examples: (1) the tithe has not been eaten during a period of mourning; (2) it has not been removed (from the remainder of the produce) while the worshiper was in a state of uncleanness; and (3) it has not been used in any pagan rites for the dead (v. 14). As with the offering of the firstfruits (vv. 1-11), the tithe is an expression of worship and gratitude to the LORD who has given the land as a fulfillment of the promises made to the ancestors (v. 15).

26:16-19. Exhortation to observe the statutes and ordinances. *This very day* suggests that a COVENANT ceremony is in progress, a ceremony of covenant renewal in which the covenant will be read, followed by a recommitment to its provisions on the part of the people. This exhortation contains echoes of the *shema* (6:4-5) with its call *to observe these statutes and ordinances . . . with all your heart and with all your soul* (v. 16). The emphasis on the agreement between the LORD and the people—the LORD to be their God and they *to be* [God's] *treasured people* who are to be set *above all nations, . . . in praise and in fame and in honor*—is the kind of vow one would expect to find in a ceremony of covenant making (vv. 17-19).

27:1-26. An Interlude: The Shechem ceremony. The shift to a third person narrative in this chapter interrupts the flow of the exhortation of Moses in chap. 26 that is taken up again in chap. 28. Since chap. 27 describes what obviously is an old ceremony of covenant making, it may have been inserted here because of the suggestions of a covenant ceremony at the end of the previous chapter.

27:1-8. Instructions for building an altar to the LORD. *Moses . . . charged all the people* marks a shift from the exhortation of the sermon to a narrative about instructions for building an altar in central Palestine at Shechem (v. 1). The people are instructed to *set up large stones and cover them with plaster*, the purpose being to provide a suitable surface for writing *all the words of this law* (vv. 2-3). The practice of writing important religious matters on plaster is attested by finds at Tell Deir 'Alla, not far from where the Jabbok empties into the Jordan River (Cornfeld 1976, 55–56). These stones are to be part of an altar to be built on Mt. Ebal. It is to be an *altar of stones on which you have not used an iron tool* (v. 5). This prohibition may reflect a reaction against Canaanite religious practices, but more likely it comes from the idea that some natural sacred aura about the stone might be lost when it was worked with iron tools (Galling 1962, 1:97). In the times of the monarchy, altars of hewn stone are found as well as bronze altars used for the burning of incense (Haak 1992, 1:162–67). The sacrifices are to be *sacrifices of well-being* (see Lev 3), accompanied by a communal meal and *rejoicing before the LORD your God*. The instruction to write *all the words . . . of this law* is in keeping with a covenant ceremony (vv. 7-8).

27:9-10. The purpose of the ceremony. The purpose of the ceremony is to affirm that *this very day* Israel has become *the people of the LORD your God* (v. 9). This sense of affirmation and immediacy kept alive in the religion of Israel and later in Judaism is the cohesive force that binds the people together with a sense of history and belonging.

27:11-26. The cursing ceremony. The tribal list in vv. 12-13 is very old, as is shown by the fact that Levi and Joseph are listed as tribes (v. 12; cf. Gen 49). Later lists divide the tribe of Joseph into Ephraim and Manasseh and drop both Joseph and Levi, while still maintaining the total of twelve tribes. *Mount Gerizim* and *Mount Ebal* (vv. 12, 13), where the ceremony takes place, are mountains that stand opposite each other. Between these two mountains is the site of ancient Shechem, probably the site of the first central shrine for the Israelites.

One would expect the twelve curses (vv. 15-26) to be accompanied by twelve blessings, since both were an essential part of a ceremony of covenant making. While there are blessings given in the next chapter (28:3-6), there are only six and they are given in a somewhat different context than that of the curses found here. The expression *Amen* that accompanies each curse can be translated "Let it be so," in effect saying, "Let this fate befall us if we should commit such a crime." The first two curses closely parallel the third and fifth of the Ten Commandments: the prohibition against the making of idols (v. 15; cf. Exod 20:4-6; Deut 5:8-10) and the curse on *anyone who dishonors father or mother* (v. 16; cf. 5:16 and Exod 20:12). The former curse is directed more specifically toward one *who makes an idol or casts an image, anything abhorrent to the LORD, the work of an artisan and sets it up in secret* (v. 15). Second Isaiah and Jeremiah elaborate on this theme in their prophecies (Isa 44:9-20; Jer 10:1-16). Curses three through five are against those who violate the rights of members of the community: moving *a neighbor's boundary marker* (v. 17); misleading *a blind person on the road* (v. 18); and depriving *the alien, the orphan, and the widow* of what is their due (v. 19), reaffirming again Deuteronomy's commitment to the well-being of the community, especially as to the property rights of its members and care for those within its bounds who were weak and defenseless.

Aberrant sexual behavior is the subject of four of the curses, three of them dealing with sexual relations between relatives (incest) and one with using an animal for sexual purposes, or bestiality (v. 21). The curse on *anyone who lies with his father's wife* seems to assume that the woman is another wife other than the mother of the guilty person, although sex with one's own mother certainly would be strictly forbidden (v. 20). Relationships are more clearly defined as regards sex with one's sister; the prohibition applies whether the woman is *the daughter of his father or the daughter of his mother*. It applies as well to *anyone who lies with his mother-in-law* (vv. 22-23). Turning attention again to the broader community, the tenth curse falls on *anyone who strikes down a neighbor in secret* (v. 24). It has been suggested that the phrase *in secret*, here and in 27:15, is the key to understanding the necessity of these curses, since the crimes mentioned may not be discovered and thus escape public punishment. The power of the curse is believed to be such that punishment is inevitable (Craigie 1976, 331). The eleventh curse is double-barreled since it condemns bribe-taking and shedding *innocent blood*, two offenses that are condemned numerous times in both legal and prophetic materials (v. 25; cf. Amos 5:12; Ps 26:10; Isa 33:15; Deut 19:13; 21:9; Jer 7:6; 26:15). The final curse upon *anyone who does not uphold the words of this law by observing them* is a summary curse, covering all that has gone before, in much the same manner that *you shall not covet* seems to function for the Ten Commandments (v. 26; see comment on 5:21). Taken together, the curses emphasize the serious nature of the covenant and the solemnity with which commitments were to be made. In Israelite history, covenants were a major force in binding the community together (Hayes 1990, 177-81).

If You Will Only Obey the LORD Your God— The Conclusion of the Sermon, 28:1-68

When one reads Deut 26:16-19 and then proceeds to read the opening verses of chap. 28, it is clear that there is continuity between the two chapters interrupted by the inclusion of chap. 27.

28:1-14. Six blessings and a commentary. The introductory call to *obey the LORD your God* (28:1) and the promise that obedience will result in Israel's being set on high *above all the nations* echoes 26:19 and introduces six blessings. Since blessings are a common element in covenant ceremonies, these blessings may originally have been associated with the twelve curses of chap. 27. The first two,

Blessed . . . in the city, and blessed . . . in the field, are comprehensive in their nature, saying, in effect, "Blessed shall you be, wherever you are." The second group of two blessings is more specific. They promise large families (*the fruit of your womb*), a necessity for the continuation of family, tribe, and people as a whole; abundant crops (*fruit of your ground*) and success in the breeding of their animals, both the larger animals (*your cattle*) and of sheep and goats (*your flocks*), all these being necessary for physical preservation and economic prosperity (v. 4). The blessing on the *basket* and the *kneading bowl* is a more intimate blessing, since these were common utensils used daily in providing for the sustenance of the family, the basket for gathering food and the kneading bowl for making bread (v. 5). As the series begins with a general blessing, so it ends with one that covers all the movements of life (*when you come in, and . . . when you go out* [v. 6]).

What then do these blessings mean? They mean the defeat of enemies, who will flee *seven ways* (in complete confusion) (v. 7). The soil will be blessed, as evidenced by the abundance of produce stored in the barns of Israelite farmers (v. 8). Most important of all, the LORD God will establish Israel *as his holy people* if they keep his commandments and *walk in his ways* (v. 9). They will thus be unique among the earth's peoples, causing the latter to be afraid of Israel when they see that Israel is *called by the name of the LORD* (v. 10). This reference reflects the ancient idea of the LORD as a god of war who leads the people to triumph over enemies in holy warfare. Prosperity in the form of numerous children, large flocks, and abundant crops, assured by plenty of rain and accompanied by blessings on *all your undertakings*, will make Israel a nation that can lend to others and not one that has to borrow (vv. 11-12). To be *at the top, and not at the bottom*, Israel must be diligent in its obedience to the LORD's commandments, not turning aside, *either to the right or to the left, following other gods to serve them* (vv. 13-14).

28:15-68. Six curses and a commentary. The six blessings are balanced by six curses as a judgment for not obeying *the LORD your God by diligently observing all his commandments and decrees* (v. 15). They are mirror images of the blessings, using precisely the same language, except that the opening words are *Cursed shall you be* (vv. 16-19). The disasters that follow the curses are to take many forms. There will be *disaster, panic, and frustration*, bringing destruction *on account of the evil of your deeds* (v. 20). This will be accompanied by a variety of maladies—pestilence ("disease after disease," TEV) afflicting the human population (vv. 21-22a) and crop failure brought on by drought and plant diseases (vv. 22b-24). They will suffer defeat at the hands of their enemies; moreover, the plagues that worked for their deliverance from Egypt will now be turned against them (vv. 25-29). None of the losses will be restored, and they will be powerless to stop the abuse (vv. 30-34). *The LORD will bring you . . . to a nation that neither you nor your ancestors have known* would seem to refer to the conquest by the Assyrians in 721 B.C.E. (v. 36). Added to these disasters will be crop failure due to a variety of causes: locusts and other insects (vv. 38, 42); worms (v. 39); failure of olives to mature, possibly from lack of proper pollination (v. 40). The most disastrous loss will be that of *sons and daughters* who will be taken *into captivity* (v. 41), erasing hope for the future. Added to this, resident aliens will come to rule over them (vv. 43-44). Such are the disasters that Israel can expect if it fails to observe *the commandments and the decrees* that the LORD God gave (vv. 45-46).

In a further commentary on the curses in 28:47-68, images are evoked that suggest the Babylonian attack on Jerusalem (*The LORD will bring a nation from far away. . . . It shall besiege . . . your high and fortified walls* (vv. 49, 52). The desperate conditions brought on by the siege will lead to cannibalism (vv. 53-57). Such a situation is described in horrifying detail by an eyewitness to the siege of Jerusalem in Lam 4:10 (cf. Lev 26:29). The commentary ends with the suggestion that the failure to live up to the requirements of the covenant will bring a reversal of the blessing of the Exodus. Israel once more will go into exile—*The Lord will bring you back . . . to Egypt*, which here undoubtedly is a reference to the Babylonian Exile. (vv. 58-68). Thus ends the second sermon of Moses, which began with covenant making and now ends with covenant making as well.

"These are the words of the covenant"— The Third Sermon of Moses 29:1–30:20

"The Covenant . . . in the land of Moab"—Renewing the Covenant, 29:1-29

29:1. Covenant renewal. The phrase *in the land of Moab, in addition to the covenant that . . .* indicates that a ceremony of covenant renewal follows (v. 1).

29:2-9. What the LORD has done for Israel. After the identification of the LORD God as the maker of the covenant, God's power and privileges as covenant maker are given historical foundation by recounting the deity's wondrous deeds on Israel's behalf. This reminder should inspire the people to be diligent in observing *the words of this covenant, in order that you may succeed in everything that you do* (v. 9).

29:10-29. The renewal of the covenant. *You stand assembled today . . . to enter into the covenant* (vv. 10, 12). Through covenant renewal, each generation of Israel stands once again at the foot of Sinai, experiencing the awesome presence of the LORD God, hearing the story of God's wondrous deeds, committing itself afresh to the principles of the covenant. It is a covenant made not only with those *who stand here with us today . . . but also with those who are not here with us today*, that is, all future generations (vv. 14-15). The danger of idolatry is always present. It can arise from any source, like a *root sprouting poisonous and bitter growth* (29:18). It especially flourishes in the midst of complacency, *bringing disaster on moist and dry alike* (good and bad people [v. 19]). Idolaters will face the LORD's judgment, for *all the curses written in this book will descend on them, and the LORD will blot out their names from under heaven* (v. 20). The resulting disaster will be like the *destruction of Sodom and Gomorrah, Admah and Zeboiim* (v. 23; cf. Gen 19 and Hos 11:9). There are *secret things*—"divine wisdom beyond the human ken"

(NOAB, note), over and beyond those things that God has revealed to Israel. This revelation is reserved only for those who *observe all the words of this law* (v. 29).

"When all these things have happened to you"—Blessings and Choices, 30:1-20

These words and what follows appear to be a reference to the Exile. The text makes clear that exile offers a fresh opportunity for the people of God to commit themselves to God's law—and live.

30:1-14. The conditions for blessings. Even the trauma of exile will not bring an end to the LORD's concern for Israel. Even there, if they will call to mind their past experiences of *the blessings and the curses that I have set before you* (v. 1), *return to the LORD your God, and . . . obey him with all your heart and . . . soul* (v. 2), the LORD's blessing will follow (v. 3).

The key words, then, are *remember, return,* and *obey. Return* is the equivalent of *repent*. It involves a radical change in direction, a turning away from one's former loyalty and giving allegiance to a new way of doing. It is evidenced by obedience. The result will be a return to the land of promise, even from the *ends of the world*. Also included is a promise that the returnees will be *more prosperous and numerous than your ancestors* (vv. 3-5).

Moreover, the LORD your God will circumcise your heart and the heart of your descendants (v. 6; cf. Jer 4:4). Circumcision originally was to be an outward sign borne by those who were set aside as the LORD's covenant people (see Gen 17:9-14). Now, the sign of the people of the LORD, borne by males and females alike, will be changed hearts—an all-encompassing love and obedience for the LORD their God (v. 6). Their enemies will be cursed (v. 7), and their obedience will cause them to be *abundantly prosperous* in the family, the flocks, and the fields (v. 9). Total commitment on their part to *observing his commandments and decrees* (v. 10) will be answered by God's delight in prospering them, *just as he delighted in prospering your ancestors* (v. 9).

Neither is this commandment *too hard . . . nor is it too far away* (v. 11). It is not impractical—something off *in heaven*, out of human reach; nor is it on the other side of the world (30:12-13). Instead, it is an intimate, personal matter of one's inner self, *in your mouth and in your heart for you to observe* (v. 14).

30:15-20. The choices. Covenant making involves the making of choices, the choices between *life and prosperity, death and adversity* (v. 15). In every re-enactment of the covenant ceremony, Israel is urged to *choose life so that you and your descendants may live* (v. 19; cf. Josh 24:14-15). And what is life? Is it not *loving the LORD your God, obeying him, and holding fast to him* (v. 20)? Compared to following idols, there is no other viable possibility.

"When Moses had finished speaking"—Moses' Final Days, 31:1-29

"I am now one hundred twenty years old"—
Moses' Final Charge to Joshua and the People, 31:1-8

You shall not cross over this Jordan (v. 2) refers to the incident at Meribah (Num 20:2-13; cf. Exod 17:1-7) where Moses was denied entry into the land for striking the rock (see 32:50-52). *The LORD your God himself will cross over before you. He will destroy these nations before you, and you shall dispossess them* (v. 3). These promises reflect the convictions of HOLY WAR: the LORD God fights for the covenant people. They, therefore, are to *be strong and bold; have no fear or dread* of the enemy, for the LORD God *will not fail you or forsake you* (v. 6). These words are especially appropriate for Joshua, the *one who will go with this people into the land* (v. 7). He, too, can expect the LORD God to lead him (vv. 8-9).

"Then Moses wrote down this law"—
The Ceremony of Covenant Renewal, 31:9-13

Moses wrote down this law (31:9) reflects the tradition that Moses is the author of Deuteronomy. Writing down the provisions of a covenant was a climactic event in a covenant-making ceremony, signifying the permanence of the covenant relationship and its terms.

He *gave it to the priests . . . and to all the elders of Israel* who had the responsibility of preserving, protecting, and propagating the principles of the covenant among the people (v. 9). *Every seventh year . . . during the festival of booths* (v. 10) there is to be a ceremony of covenant renewal, in which the provisions of the covenant are read to all Israel—*men, women, and children, as well as the aliens residing in your towns* (v. 12). That this was ever carried out during the history of Israel on such a systematic basis is questionable. The uproar caused by the finding of the law book in the Temple during the reign of JOSIAH which, in turn, instituted a covenant ceremony, suggests such a ceremony was *not* being observed on a systematic basis in the period shortly before the Babylonian Exile. Some interpreters believe this provision arose only as a consequence of Josiah's reforms, but it is more likely that it is an old regulation that periodically fell into disuse, only to be revived in times of national renewal (vv. 12-13; cf. 2 Kgs 22–23; Josh 24; Neh 8).

"The LORD said to Moses"—The Commissioning of Joshua, 31:14-23

31:14-15. Joshua commissioned. *Call Joshua and present yourselves in the tent of meeting* (v. 14b). This text points to the spiritual element in the choice of leadership that was regarded as ideal. Leaders, whether they were priests, prophets, or community or national leaders like Moses and Joshua, as well as the later kings, ideally were chosen and commissioned by the LORD God. Thus the early kings, Saul and David, were anointed by a prophet as the sign of the LORD's choice of them (1 Sam 10:1; 16:12-13). The king's court on earth was considered to be organized by analogy with the heavenly court (1 Kgs 22:19-23). Here, Joshua is brought to the tent of meeting so that the LORD can *commission him* (v. 14; cf. Num 27:12-23).

31:16-22. The people after Moses. Since Moses is soon to die, the people will forget the LORD, *breaking my covenant that I have made with them* (v. 16). Moses, therefore is to write a song and *teach it to the Israelites . . . in order that this song may be a witness* to the Israelites concerning the LORD's dealings with them (vv. 19-22; see chap. 32).

31:23. A final charge to Joshua. Joshua is admonished to *be strong and bold, for you shall bring the Israelites into the land that I promised them; I will be with you* (v. 23; see the discussion above on 31:14-15).

"When Moses finished writing"—
The Continuation of the Covenant Ceremony, 31:24-29

When Moses had finished writing down in a book the words of this law (v. 24), is a continuation of the covenant ceremony found in 31:9-13. *Put it beside the ark of the covenant*, that is, for preservation and keeping, so that it may *remain there as a witness against you* (v. 26). *Assemble to me all the elders . . . that I may recite these words . . . and call heaven and earth to witness against them* (v. 28). This probably takes the place of calling on the gods as witnesses, a common element in Near Eastern treaty making. In Israelite tradition the LORD God, maker of heaven and earth, swore by the divine nature that the Creator would uphold the covenant and would see that Israel upheld the covenant as well.

"Then Moses recited the words of this song"—
The Song of Moses, 31:30–32:47

The song of Moses is a psalm like those found in the Book of Psalms. It contains elements of the "covenant lawsuit," a favorite literary vehicle used by the prophets to put over their messages. While the characteristic term *rib*, usually translated "contention" or "controversy," is not present, the elements of indictment and judgment are present. All that is missing is the defense that the accused would offer to refute the charges and accusations. There is general agreement that the poem is relatively old, dating at least to the period of the early monarchy.

32:1-3. The summons. *Give ear, O heavens* (v. 1) is a call for other nations or facets of the natural world to be observers when the LORD hears his lawsuit against the people; such a summons is quite common (see Isa 1:2; Mic 6:1-2). *I will proclaim the name . . . ascribe greatness to our God* (v. 3). Usually, in the prophetic versions of the lawsuit, the LORD speaks; here the poet speaks in God's behalf.

32:4-6a. The indictment. The LORD, described as *the Rock*, symbol of strength, is known for faithfulness, honesty (*without deceit*), justice, and moral integrity—*upright is he* (v. 4). In sad contrast, *his degenerate children* have dealt dishonestly with God, for they are a *perverse and crooked generation, . . . [a] foolish and senseless people* (vv. 5-6a).

__32:6b-14. The evidence: The LORD's goodness.__ This summary statement of the problem is followed by an enlarged bill of particulars, first delineating the LORD's loving care and keeping of the people (vv. 6b-14), followed by Israel's ungracious response to what the LORD has done (32:15-18). It is the *father, who created* Israel, who, in the beginning (*the days of old*), *apportioned the nations*, i.e., assigned each people a territory of its own *according to the number of the gods* (32:6-8). The Hebrew text here reads "the Israelites" while one Qumran manuscript and the LXX read "the gods," a reference to the heavenly court (cf. Job 1). This seems to be what is meant. While the LORD has shown divine care for all peoples (cf. Exod 19:5 and Amos 9:7), only Israel (here called Jacob) became *the LORD's own portion*, God's personal and specific people (v. 9). Because of this, God has led them through the desert (*a howling wilderness waste*), protecting them with the kind of care that an eagle gives its young. The LORD has led them into the land, given them abundant crops and healthy flocks, so that *Jacob ate his fill; Jeshurun grew fat* (vv. 10-15a). *Jeshurun*, meaning "the upright one," is used ironically since here the people are anything but upright.

__32:15-18. The evidence: Israel's ingratitude.__ When a people is *fat, bloated, and gorged*, trouble is not long in coming. Israel *abandoned God who made him* and even went so far as to scoff *at the Rock of his salvation* (v. 15). Israel has gone after all sorts of strange gods, even sacrificing *to demons . . . to deities they had never known* (vv. 16-17). They have forgotten the God who gave them birth, forgetting who God is and whose they are (v. 18).

__32:19-27. The LORD's righteous anger.__ Israel's callous attitude toward the LORD's blessings provoked God to righteous indignation. They are *children in whom there is no faithfulness* who follow *what is no god*; as a result, the LORD *will make them jealous with what is no people* (vv. 20-21). They have spurned the LORD's grace, exchanged faithfulness for faithlessness, turned from the true God to worship an empty symbol, a "no-god," and now will be made fools of by a nation of fools. Such perverse people are deserving of what will surely follow—*burning consumption, bitter pestilence*, attacks by wild beasts, with death stalking the streets, striking young and old alike (vv. 22-25). The LORD has even been tempted to *blot out the memory of them from humankind*, but this would give their enemies the idea that it was their doing and not the LORD's (vv. 26-27).

__32:28-33. Israel is bad, but the nations are worse.__ Despite their advantages, Israel is *a nation void of sense*, unable to perceive the end result of their foolish ways (v. 28). Otherwise, how could they have been defeated by an enemy unless *the LORD had given them up* and allowed enemies who have no real God and who basically are fools to defeat Israel, the LORD's chosen people (vv. 30-31)? Israel has been defeated by a worthless people (vv. 32-33)!

__32:34-43. The triumph of the LORD and the vindication of God's people.__ The time is coming when the LORD will bring things back to a state of wholeness and well-being. When the LORD says, *Vengeance is mine*, what is being said is that the

LORD is the one who has the power to make things as they should be in a time when everything seems to be going wrong. Vengeance (Heb *naqam*) arises from customary law where justice was a family matter. When a family member was slain, there was no state to bring the killer to justice. The nearest of kin (*go'el*, see discussion on 25:5-10) was the avenger of blood. By executing the relative's killer, the avenger restored a balance between the two families involved. In v. 41, the term "vengeance" is used as a parallel term for "peace," or "wholeness" (*shalem*). To say that the LORD takes vengeance is a primitive way of saying that God sets things back in balance, restoring peace or wholeness.

One result of the LORD's activity against enemies will be that God *will vindicate his people*. God's compassion for them will overrule his wrath *when he sees that their power is gone, neither bond nor free remaining* (v. 36). God will then chide the enemy to call on their worthless gods to *rise up and help you, let them be your protection* (vv. 37-38)! Those false gods can do nothing, for the LORD declares that *there is no god beside me . . . and no one can deliver from my hand* (v. 39). God has taken an oath on his own honor utterly to defeat *the long-haired enemy* and *cleanse the land for his people*. For this, the LORD is due universal praise (vv. 40-43).

32:44-47. Moses sings his song. Moses recites this song to Joshua and all the people. It is to be a reminder to them that they are responsible for what they are hearing. They are diligently to observe *all the words of this law* (v. 46). That, God declares, is *no trifling matter for you, but rather your very life* (v. 47).

"On that very day the LORD addressed Moses"— Moses Views the Land, 32:48-52

This is a somewhat expanded version of an earlier passage found in Num 27:12-14. That account identifies the site as the Abarim range (Num 27:12). Here, Deuteronomy specifies that it is from Mount Nebo in that range that the vision is to take place. In this instance, Moses is told that he cannot go in because he failed *to maintain my holiness among the Israelites* at Meribath-kadesh (32:51; see Num 27:14).

"This is the blessing"—The Blessing of Moses, 33:1-29

33:1. The blessing with which Moses . . . blessed the Israelites before his death. Deathbed blessings are a prominent feature in Israelite tradition, one of the most notable being Jacob's blessing of his sons (Gen 49). The list of tribes here differs somewhat from that of Jacob's blessing. The most notable changes are that the tribe of Simeon is missing, perhaps reflecting the historical reality of its disappearance by the time the poem was composed; and the mention of Joseph as a tribe but then, in effect, recognizing its division by the naming of Ephraim and Manasseh, the two tribes that took its place.

Modern scholars have pointed out the fact that the Deuteronomistic history (see Wells 1990, 210–11) has a similar emphasis on covenant renewal with blessings and curses at certain significant occasions—when, for example, a prominent leader passes from the scene (Joshua, Josh 24; Samuel, 1 Sam 12; Solomon, 1 Kgs 8:14, 55; Josiah, 2 Kgs 22:11-13). As Urbrock (1992, 1:760) has observed: "The theology of blessing and curse clearly pervades the Deuteronomistic History."

33:2-5. The LORD came from Sinai. Here the image is of the LORD as a triumphant warrior deity, accompanied by *myriads of holy ones; at his right a host of his own* (v. 2). The tone of this poem is similar to Hab 3, with its mention of Mount Paran, a place that cannot be located with precision. Seir is another name for Edom. The reference to *favorite among peoples* seems to be to a leader, perhaps the king, since there is mention of a king in v. 5. That it is not Moses would seem to be implied by the fact that Moses is spoken of as a figure of the past (*Moses charged us with the law* [v. 4]). *There arose a king in Jeshurun* (v. 5) may refer to Israel's king and would seem to be in keeping with the proposal that Deuteronomy was seen in some measure as a book designed to instruct the kings of Israel. Secondly, it can be interpreted as referring to the LORD as king, a concept that is common in the Psalms (Pss 95–99). Those who see Deuteronomy as having Mosaic rootage translate v. 5: "Let there be a king in Jeshurun" (Craigie 1976, 392). On Jeshurun, see comment on 32:15a.

33:6. The blessing of Reuben. *May Reuben live* suggests that this tribe, one of those assigned territory in Transjordan (Josh 22:1), faced possible extinction, since its territory was frequently under attack from Israel's enemies.

33:7. The blessing of Judah. Judah, one of the two most prominent tribes (the other was Ephraim), while not facing the possibility of extinction as is Reuben, does, nevertheless, seems to be under attack, probably from the Philistines, since this a plea to the LORD to *strengthen his hands for him, and be a help against his adversaries*.

33:8-11. The blessing of Levi. The long and laudatory blessing of Levi may be a clue to the ultimate source of this psalm of blessing. *Your Thummim, and your Urim* (v. 8; see Exod 28:30) refers to the sacred lots, or "holy dice." Since God directed how the lots fell when thrown, they were used to find divine direction in matters that could be answered by "Yes" and "No," or the choice between two possibilities (see 1 Sam 14:41-42). This placed great power and responsibility in the hands of the Levites. The blessing commends them as worthy since they passed the test at Massah and Meribah (Exod 17:1-7; Num 20:2-13). Because of their important responsibilities, they turned their backs on families (see Exod 32:25-29) and *observed your word, and kept your covenant* (v. 9). They function as teachers (*teach Jacob your ordinances*); they officiate in the worship (*place incense . . . and whole burnt offerings on your altar*). Their zeal qualifies them for the LORD's blessing upon them and upon their substance (vv. 10-11).

33:12. The blessing of Benjamin. The phrase *the beloved of the LORD* is a play on the name of Benjamin which means, "son of the right hand" or "the favored one." The right hand was the place of blessing and favor. Thus *the beloved rests between his* [the LORD's] *shoulders*, the imagery of a small boy riding on the shoulders of his father.

33:13-17. The blessing of Joseph. The blessing of Joseph, which is even longer than the blessing of Levi, gives evidence that this poem originated in Northern Israel. Ephraim is Judah's chief rival throughout the history of the Israelite kingdom. Judah is given only one verse, while Joseph (whose chief representative is Ephraim) has the longest of all the blessings. Ephraim did, in fact, possess far better territory from a strategic and an economic standpoint than did Judah. By its very nature and location, it was more likely to have had the *choice gifts of heaven above . . . choice fruits of the sun . . . the finest produce . . . the choice gifts of the earth*, all tangible symbols of *the favor of the one who dwells on Sinai* (vv. 13-16). That Joseph is called *the prince among his brothers* (v. 16) is indicative of the strength of the Joseph tribes as compared to their rival Judah. Joseph is a majestic bull, driving his enemies *to the ends of the earth; such are the myriads of Ephraim, such the thousands of Manasseh* (v. 17).

33:18-19. The blessing of Zebulun and Issachar. *Zebulun, in your going out* suggests that this tribe, located on the seacoast in the northern part of Israel, gains wealth from the sea. *Issachar, in your tents*, is located inland, along the Sea of Galilee. While Issachar gained wealth from the waters of the Sea of Galilee, the mention of tents indicates that its members also followed a more traditional way of life. The two are mentioned together because *they suck the affluence of the seas* (v. 19).

33:20-21. The blessing of Gad. The tribe of Gad, described as living *like a lion* (v. 20), was assigned territory in Transjordan on the tableland just north of the Dead Sea. This land included parts of the "thickets of the Jordan" (Jer 12:5), where lions were to be found in early Israel. Gad is commended here because it left its territory to assist in the conquest of the western side of the Jordan. Thus, *he came at the head of the people, he executed the justice of the LORD* (v. 21). In a word, he did his share and more (see Num 32).

33:22. The blessing of Dan. Dan, one of the smaller and weaker tribes, had already moved from its original location west of Judah to the base of Mount Hermon, in the far north.

33:23. The blessing of Naphtali. Naphtali is another tribe that was located in the region of the Sea of Galilee, one of the prime agricultural areas of the country. Thus it is *sated with favor*.

33:24-25. The blessing of Asher. Asher was located just south of the Phoenicians on the Mediterranean coast. In view of the cordial relations that Phoenicia enjoyed with various Israelite kings, Asher stood to profit more than any other Israelite tribe, given their location. The references to *oil* and to *bars of iron and* *bronze* possibly refer to the trade in these items that would contribute to the blessing of *the sons of Asher*.

33:26-29. Concluding words of praise. This is a brief psalm of praise to God *who rides through the heavens to your help* (v. 26). It reminds one of the lines from the song of Deborah: "the stars fought from heaven, from their courses they fought against Sisera" (Judg 5:20). *He subdues the ancient gods* refers to the fact that the conquest of a people is viewed as the conquering of their gods as well, as the parallel statement *he drove out the enemy* indicates (v. 27). The people of Israel have every reason to be happy, since they live in safety *in a land of grain and wine, where the heavens drop down dew*; their enemies are so jealous at Israel's good fortune of being a *people saved by the* LORD that they come fawning to Israel, who will tread on their backs, that is, put them in subjection (33:28-29).

"Then Moses went up"—The Death of Moses, 34:1-12

The account of the death of Moses, along with numerous third person references to Moses in Deuteronomy, have been part of the standard arguments against the Mosaic authorship of Deuteronomy. Those who accept Moses as author would suggest that Joshua is responsible for this account, even though there is little said in tradition about Joshua as an author.

34:1a. Moses went up . . . to Mount Nebo, to the top of Pisgah. Present identifications of these mountains suggest that there is a double tradition here, since two separate mountains are named. *The* LORD *showed him the whole land* (v. 1). The story of Israel begins with the patriarch Abram's being told to look in all directions "for all the land that you see I will give to you and to your offspring forever." To establish his claim to it, Abram was told to "walk through the length and breadth of the land" (Gen 13:14-17). Moses' vision of the land from the mountaintop gives a kind of literary symmetry to the Pentateuch, an appropriate closure to this phase of Israel's story.

34:1b-3. Gilead . . . as far as Zoar. The sweep of Moses' vision moves first up the eastern side of the Jordan to what today is known as the Golan Heights to Mount Hermon (*Gilead as far as Dan*); then, Upper Galilee (*all Naphtali*); the central hill country from the Carmel range to just north of Jerusalem (*the land of Ephraim and Manasseh*); Judah, westward to the coastal plain and the Mediterranean Sea, and, finally, south and east to the Negev and the Jordan Rift valley and the Arabah, ending with Jericho and the Dead Sea.

34:4. The Lord said . . . This is the land. Abraham was told, This is the land "I will give to you" (Gen 13:15), and Moses is assured that *This is the land that I swore to Abraham . . . saying, "I will give it to your descendants."* While Moses cannot enjoy the land, he can die with the assurance that he has made possible the achievement of the promise made to the ancestors.

34:5-8. Then Moses, the servant of the LORD**, died.** The greatness of Moses is bound up in the title *servant of the* LORD (v. 5). Like most great figures in history and literature that are remembered for their contributions to human good, the qualities of servanthood, sacrifice, and selflessness are almost always present. Whether or not we ever uncover irrefutable evidence of Moses' existence and achievements, even as a literary figure he stands for what is best and highest in human history. He is not his own; he is the LORD's servant. That *no one knows his burial place* (v. 6) contributes to the sense of awe with which tradition associates him. Like Elijah, the symbol of prophecy for Israel, who is taken up in a chariot of fire, so Moses, the liberator of his people, has a private burial by the LORD whose servant he is. *One hundred twenty years*, or three times forty, is a round number symbolizing completion or full quota. Three times that would be in keeping with the common view that righteous living leads to a long life (cf. Job 1).

34:9. Joshua . . . was full of the spirit of wisdom. The mantle now passes to Joshua *because Moses had laid his hands on him*. The mark of a great leader is to be able to train those who are left behind to build on the work that has been done. Joshua's wisdom grew out of the fact that Moses had given him on-the-job experience so that he was not thrown into the fray unprepared (Exod 17:9). Because they had confidence in him, *the Israelites obeyed him, doing as the LORD had commanded Moses*.

34:10-12. Never since has there arisen . . . a prophet like Moses. This is Moses' epitaph. He becomes the symbol of what is great about the prophets of Israel, men and women of whom the LORD has said, *I will put my words in the mouth of the prophet* [NRSV gives an alternate reading, "mouths of the prophets"] *who shall speak to them everything that I command* (18:18). A later prophet was to say of Moses, "By a prophet the LORD brought Israel up from Egypt" (Hos 12:13). The prophet stood in the council of the LORD (*the LORD knew [him] face to face* (v. 10; cf. 1 Kgs 22:19-23; Amos 3:7). Of all those prophets who stood in the council of the LORD, none had the privilege and responsibilities that Moses had: to perform *signs and wonders . . . in the land of Egypt . . . and . . . mighty deeds and . . . terrifying displays of power . . . in the sight of all Israel* (vv. 11-12). Although the stories told about Moses may have magnified his personality and accomplishments, Deuteronomy's estimate of Moses carries credibility. Behind the Moses traditions is a towering figure—a magnificent personality, a preeminent prophet, and one *whom the LORD knew face to face* (v. 10).

Works Cited

Andrews, Stephen J. 1990. "Molech," MDB.
Bjornard, Reidar B. 1990a. "Levi/Levites," MDB. 1990b. "Priests," MDB.
Christensen, Duane L. 1990. "Deuteronomy, Book of," MDB.
Cochran, Bernard H. 1990. "Josiah," MDB.
Cornfeld, Gaalyah. 1976. *Archaeology of the Bible: Book by Book.*
Craigie, Peter C. 1976. *The Book of Deuteronomy.* NICOT.
Dahlberg, Bruce. 1990. "Law in the Old Testament," MDB.

Eakin, Frank. 1990. "Clean/Unclean," MDB.
Ellis, Judy. 1990. "Monotheism," MDB.
Galling, Kurt. 1962. "Altar," IDB.
Geren, William H. 1990. "Leprosy," MDB.
Haak, Robert A. 1992. "Altar," AncBD.
Hancock, Omer J. 1990a. "Tabernacles, Festival of," MDB. 1990b. "Weeks, Festival of," MDB.
Harrelson, Walter. 1990. "Ten Commandments," MDB.
Hayes, John H. 1990. "Covenant," MDB.
Joines, Karen R. 1990. "Passover," MDB.
King, Philip J. 1988. *Amos, Hosea, Micah—An Archaeological Commentary*.
Kraus, Hans-Joachim. 1966. *Worship in Ancient Israel. A Cultic History of the Old Testament*.
Rad, Gerhard von. 1962. *Old Testament Theology* 1.
Smith, David A. 1990. "Curse and Blessing," MDB.
Snodgrass, Klyne R. 1990. "Divorce," MDB.
Sutherland, Ray. 1990. "Assembly," MDB.
Tullock, John H. 1990. "Sabbath," MDB.
Urbrock, William J. 1992. "Blessings and Curses," AncBD.
Vinson, Richard B. 1990. "Asherah," MDB.
Weinfeld, Moshe. 1991. *Deuteronomy: 1–11*. AncB.
Weir, Jack. 1990. "Josiah," MDB.
Wells, Roy D., Jr. 1990. "Deuteronomist/Deuteronomistic Historian," MDB.
Wilson, Johnny L. 1990. "Holy War," MDB.
Wright, G. Ernest. 1953. "The Book of Deuteronomy. Introduction. Exegesis," IB.

Mercer Commentary on the Bible.
Volume 1. *Pentateuch/Torah.*

Mercer University Press, Macon, Georgia 31210-3960.
Isbn 0-86554-506-5. Catalog and warehouse pick number: MUP/P133.
Text, interior, and cover designs, composition,
    and layout by Edmon L. Rowell, Jr.
Cover illustration (*Coburg Pentateuch.* "A rabbi reading from the torah")
    by Simhah ben Samuel Halevi (see p. ii, above).
Camera-ready pages composed on a Gateway 2000
    via dos WordPerfect 5.1 and WordPerfect for Windows 5.1/5.2
        and printed on a LaserMaster 1000.
Text fonts: TimesNewRomanPS 10/12; ATECH Hebrew and Greek.
Display fonts: TimesNewRomanPS bf and bi,
    plus University Roman titles (covers and title page).
Printed and bound by McNaughton & Gunn Inc., Saline, Michigan 48176,
    via offset lithography on 50# Natural Offset and perfectbound into 10-pt.
        c1s stock, with 4-color-process illustration and lay-flat lamination.
                                                                   [March 1998]

---

www.ingramcontent.com/pod-product-compliance
Lightning Source LLC
Chambersburg PA
CBHW020746160426
43192CB00006B/264